FOOD OF LIFE

ANCIENT PERSIAN AND MODERN IRANIAN
COOKING AND CEREMONIES

NAJMIEH BATMANGLIJ

MAGE PUBLISHERS

Acknowledgements, Credits, and Permissions are on pages 622 and 623

MAGE PUBLISHERS INC.
WASHINGTON, DC
WWW.MAGE.COM

Library of Congress Cataloging-in-Publication Data

Batmanglij, Najmieh, author.
Food of life : ancient Persian and modern Iranian
cooking and ceremonies / Najmieh Batmanglij.
— Fourth edition.
p. cm.
Includes index.
ISBN 978-1-933823-47-8 (fourth hardcover edition : alk. paper)
1. Cooking, Iranian. 2. Food habits—Iran.
3. Persian literature. 4. Iran—Social life and customs. I. Title.
TX725.I7B3713 2011
641.5955—dc22
2010042123

ISBN 13: 978-1933823-47-8
ISBN 10: 1-933823-47-X

FOURTH EDITION
Printed in Korea

To the memories of my mother and father and my past in Iran
and to the future of my sons, Zal and Rostam

روزه داری و قناعت هوسَم بود ولی

چشمکی میزند آن مُرغ و فِسِنجان که مپُرس

To fast and lead a frugal life
Was all I ever wished.
But the Food of Life's temptation
Is too much—do not ask!

          —Bos'haq Ata'meh, circa 1400

ON USING THIS BOOK

Please browse. I am very excited about this new edition. After thirty years of cooking outside of Iran, and in response to the input of my readers and fellow cooks, I have refined the structure of the book in general and each recipe in particular. With this edition I have unified, streamlined, and turned some of the recipes that began as my mother's into my own. Most recipes now have a photograph of the finished dish facing them, and for some of the classics, such as saffron rice with golden crust, jeweled rice, fillet kabab or baklava, I have included step-by-step photos to guide you. I have also included vegetarian cooking variations for many of the recipes. Here and there are some of my food memories from my childhood in Iran. Colorful spreads with information about some classic Persian ingredients such as saffron, bitter orange *(narenj),* and the rose are scattered through the book. There are also some street food scenes from contemporary Iran. The first edition of *Food of Life* appeared when my sons, Zal and Rostam, were toddlers. Now, as grown men, they have inspired me to redesign the book and make it accessible for a new generation of readers and a broader audience.

None of the recipes requires cooking techniques that are unusual or difficult to learn. To help in planning, I've listed preparation and cooking times for each dish, indicated whether it can be made in advance, and noted how many people it will serve.

These days, almost all of the ingredients in the recipes are available at your local supermarket—not the case in the 1980s. Those that might not be or that require preliminary preparations are marked with an asterisk, which indicates that they are discussed in How To Make and Store Kitchen Ingredients on page 529 and also in A Glossary of Ingredients, Terms and Persian Cooking Techniques on page 599. Please do check—even read through—the glossary: The entries describe the history of each ingredient and its use in Iran, and explain how to shop for it and how to prepare it. I suggest you try to find the original ingredients since they are widely available in the U.S. The guide to Iranian Stores and Restaurants on page 616 offers a comprehensive list of shops around the country that sell specialized ingredients. Several of them have a good Internet presence and can ship you whatever you need, wherever you are.

I want you to use this book to get together, to cook, to laugh, to tell jokes and stories, and to recite poetry, just as Iranians do. *Nush-e Jan!* literally "food of life"—a traditional wish in Iran that a dish will be enjoyed.

CONTENTS

PREFACE

Food of Life is the result of thirty years of collecting and testing recipes and creating new techniques for cooking Persian food in the West. Its intended audience are those new to Persian food and culture, those who enjoy having creative fun in the kitchen, and gourmet cooks.

I have revised and added many new recipes to the original book. I have also added more color photographs to show how Persian dishes are as colorful as our most beautiful carpets and textiles. For us, feasting our eyes is the first pleasure of a good meal. My objective in writing this book was not just to compile a collection of recipes, however delicious they might be, but to share my view of the best of Persian culture. I believe that the same qualities that govern the Persian arts—a particular feeling for the "delicate touch," *letafat*—govern the art of Persian cuisine. I have tried to demonstrate this by including not only photographs of the dishes but also textiles, copper ware and pottery, miniatures, poetry, calligraphy, travelogues, and pieces from classical Persian literature, all related to food. I have tucked in among the recipes many pearls of Persian wisdom. I have explored the rich garden of Persian literature and art through the ages and have made a selection that ranges from a fourth-century Pahlavi language text describing a refined cuisine to the new, naturalistic poetry of Sohrab Sepehri.

I have described an Iranian wedding and some of our joyful holiday traditions—ancient ceremonies and rituals still maintained in various parts of Iran and now also continued by many Iranians living outside the country.

Persian food is a very important and integral part of Persian life and culture—so important that fruit and nuts are frequently used as metaphors for describing beauty. Farzaneh Milani tells us in her book *Veils and Words,* for example, "Moon-faced beauties have almond-shaped eyes, peachy complexions, pistachio-like mouths, jujube colored lips, hazelnut-like noses, red apple cheeks, and lemon- or pomegranate-like breasts—a mobile green grocery, if you will."

The cuisine of any country is a fundamental part of its heritage. The ingredients reflect its geography, while the savor and colors accent the aesthetic tastes of its inhabitants.

And food is associated with so many major social events—births, weddings, funerals—that culinary traditions are intertwined with a country's history and religion. This is especially true of Iran (called "Persia" by Westerners from ancient times).

Thousands of years ago, Zoroaster elaborated the ancient myth of the Twins. One became good and the other evil, one the follower of truth and the other of falsehood. This concept of duality is typically Persian, and it extends beyond moral issues. We often balance light and darkness, sweet and sour, hot and cold.

For us, food is also classified as "hot" *(garmi),* which "thickens" the blood and speeds the metabolism, and "cold" *(sardi),* which "dilutes" the blood and slows the metabolism. Dates, and grapes, for instance, are "hot" fruits; plums, peaches, and oranges are "cold."

It takes a certain skill to correctly select food for the family, since people too can have "hot" and "cold" natures. An extremely out-of-balance diet can lead to illness. For example, those with "hot" natures must eat "cold" foods to achieve a balance. My older son, like many other children, sometimes eats too many dates or chocolates. Because he has a "hot" nature—something I learned very early in his life—too much of this hot food does not agree with him at all. Drinking watermelon or grapefruit juice, or the nectar from other "cold" fruits, quickly helps restore his balance—and his smile. (I have included a list of my mother's classifications of "hot" and "cold" foods.)

Increasingly, science is discovering links between food and health. And while the ancient Persian system of balance does not eliminate the need for doctors, experience has proven that it is an excellent nutritional adjunct to good health.

When I am at home with the samovar steaming and the house fragrant with the smell of onions and garlic cooking, when the air is filled with the captivating aromas of mint and spices, what beautiful memories come back to me! I see the pantry behind the kitchen of my childhood home in Iran once again. The odors of savory, fenugreek, marjoram, and angelica burst through the white cloth sacks that hang from the ceiling. Perhaps this book was inspired most by those perfumed memories. Above all, Persian cuisine brings back to me the image of my parents and friends sitting cross-legged on a Persian carpet around the *sofreh,* a special cotton cloth embroidered with poems and prayers.

Iranians wake up early, with the sunrise. In our family, my father and grandmother engaged in an amusing little contest every morning. The first one up was the proud winner. As soon as he awoke, my father would usually go out into the garden and head straight for the jasmine we had growing in red clay pots. He would pick all the flowers that had bloomed overnight and lay them at my mother's place on the *sofreh*. But sometimes Grandmother would get to the garden first. I can still hear father speaking in that mock-angry tone of his as he discovered that the jasmine bushes had been stripped of their flowers. "That grandmother has been here already!" he would say out loud. When our grandmother nonchalantly joined the rest of the family at breakfast, she casually brought the flowers out from their hiding place under her shawl and dropped the fragrant bouquet near my father. He would pretend to ignore her, no doubt planning to take his sweet revenge the next morning.

I have fond memories of those breakfasts, or *sobhaneh*. The meal itself usually consists of sweet tea, feta cheese, and *nan-e barbari,* a crusty flat bread made fresh very early every morning. Breakfast sometimes includes other types of bread, jam and honey, fresh cream, butter, and hot milk. Fried or soft-boiled eggs, saffron brownies, or pudding *(halva or sholeh zard)* might also be served, or even, before a long mountain hike, a soup made of tripe *(sirab shir-dun)* and lamb head and feet *(kalleh pacheh). Sobhaneh* is a very important and pleasant moment in the life of an Iranian family, a time to share before everyone leaves for work.

When I think of a meal, I think of the family all together. I hope that my sons will have similar memories of the simple pleasures of life. I dedicate this collection to them and to all Iranian children living, by the course of political events, far from the country of their heritage.

First millennium BCE bas-relief of a kitchen scene showing (clockwise from top left): (a) wine jars being opened; (b) two women preparing food; (c) a baker at his oven; and (d) the butcher preparing a lamb.

A FEW TIPS BEFORE YOU START COOKING

Oil or Butter

I am giving you the option to use oil, butter, or clarified butter (ghee) throughout the book—please choose according to your taste. I use mostly oil these days; for salads and light sauté-ing, olive oil is great, but for rice and pastries, canola (a rapeseed oil low in saturated fats) is better because it has a higher smoke point and does not interfere with the flavor of the dish. Clarified unsalted butter has been traditionally used in Persian cooking. It gives rice a wonderful, nutty flavor. It is also used for cooking pastries. It is available in stores or you can make and store your own from my recipe in the How To Make and Store Kitchen Ingredients section on page 533.

Salt

I cook with a fine-grain sea salt. Keep in mind that coarse grains salt less because there are fewer of them in a given measure. Ordinary Morton Iodized Salt tends to salt more. More or less salt is up to you, but rice dishes in particular need the minimum recommended amount of salt for both taste and texture. For "finishing" the flavor upon serving, or for adding tex-ture (for kababs, for example), I recommend a delicate coarse-grain sea salt such as a *fleur de sel* or Maldon Sea Salt.

Skillet, Pot, and Heat

When sautéing, use a wide skillet so that the ingredients are not crowded. When simmering, which you will be doing often and for long periods when cooking *khoresh*es (braises), use a Dutch oven and be sure to adjust your temperature and to surveil the pot from time to time. For a successful, fluffy, saffron-flavored steamed rice and its golden crust, use a good, deep, wide pot (I use Anolon lidded pots) and good quality basmati rice. The key is the flame you set on your own stove for the various phases of the cooking. My recipe can serve as a guide, but practice and adjust settings according to your cooktop. Oven temperatures also vary, some ovens might be off by as much as 25°F (4°C), so be sure to check yours.

Taste before Serving

It is crucial to taste your dish before serving. Adjust the taste according to your fancy by adding a little sea salt or freshly ground black pepper, lime juice, or grape molasses (honey or sugar). Happy cooking and *Nush-e Jan!*

APPETIZERS & SIDE DISHES

مخلفات و نقل می

APPETIZERS & SIDE DISHES

YOGURT, CUCUMBER & ROSE DIP
mast-o khiar 24

YOGURT & SPINACH DIP
borani-e esfenaj 26

YOGURT & CELERY DIP
borani-e karafs 26

YOGURT & SHALLOT DIP
mast-o musir 28

YOGURT & CARDOON DIP
borani-e kangar 28

YOGURT & FAVA BEAN DIP
borani-e baqala 29

YOGURT & WHITE BEAN DIP
borani-e baqala sefid 29

YOGURT & COOKED BEET DIP
borani-e labu 30

YOGURT & EGGPLANT DIP
borani-e bademjan 32

KASHK & EGGPLANT DIP
kashk-o bademjan-e kubideh 32

CHEESE & WALNUT DIP
nan-o panir-o gerdu 34

CASPIAN OLIVE TAPENADE
zeytoun parvardeh 38

CASPIAN OLIVE SALAD
salad-e zeytoun o gerdu 38

RED KIDNEY BEAN DIP
mashallah musho 40

KASHK & EGGPLANT CASSEROLE
kashk-o bademjan 41

EGGPLANT CASSEROLE
yatimcheh-ye bademjan 42

EGGPLANT & POMEGRANATE SPREAD
nazkhatun 45

SPLIT PEA PATTIES
shami 46

TONGUE WITH TOMATO SAUCE
khorak-e zaban 48

SAVORY TURNOVER (SANBUSEH)
sanbuseh 50

SAUTÉED LAMB LIVER, KIDNEYS & HEART
khorak-e del-o jigar-o qolveh 56

LAMB SPREAD, ISFAHANI-STYLE
beriyani 54

BRAIN PATTIES
kotlet-e maghz 55

LENTIL SALAD
salad-e adas 56

LENTIL DIP
adasi 56

CUCUMBER &POMEGRANATE SALAD
salad-e khiar-o anar 58

CUCUMBER & MINT SALAD
serkeh khiar 58

TOMATO & CUCUMBER SALAD SHIRAZI-STYLE
salad-e gojeh khiar (Shirazi) 60

PERSIAN CHICKEN SALAD
salad-e olivieh 62

CAVIAR
khaviar 65

Traditionally, Iranian meals are served on the *sofreh*, a cotton cover embroidered with prayers and poems, which is spread over a Persian carpet or a table. The main dishes are accompanied by bread and a number of small bowls and relish dishes filled with appetizers and condiments. These are called *mokhalafat* or *mazzeh*, or *noghl-e mey* (literally "little tastes for wine"). The essential elements are:

Nan-o panir-o sabzi-khordan—no Persian table is complete without it. It is, quite simply, bread and goat cheese with fresh herbs and raw vegetables. Persian bread is called *nan*, and there are several kinds. The most popular are: *nan-e sangak*, *nan-e lavash*, and *nan-e barbari*. (Many of these are now available in the U.S. either at you local market or at Iranian markets, often made fresh daily.) *Panir* is a cheese similar to feta cheese. It can be made from either goat's, sheep's, or sometimes cow's milk. *Sabzi-khordan* refers to fresh herbs and raw vegetables, and includes radishes, spring onions, cilantro, watercress, tarragon, mint, and basil. The vegetables and herbs are arranged on a platter with a piece of cheese.

Various other condiments, side dishes, toasted nuts, and seasonal fruit can also be included on the *sofreh* or tray of *mokhalafat*:

Bowls of peeled and sliced cucumbers; seeded pomegranates with angelica powder *(gol-par)*; sweetened melon slices; grapes; shelled nuts and raisins; butter, confectioners' sugar and honey; peeled steamed beets; yogurt *boranis* such as yogurt with spinach, yogurt and Persian shallots *(musir)*, yogurt and celery, yogurt and cucumber, yogurt and beets, and yogurt and eggplant *(borani-e bademjan)*. Various spreads, dips, and salads can also be included—among them, eggplant and pomegranate spread *(nazkhatun)*; lentil dip; red kidney bean dip; cucumber salad with mint and vinegar; cucumber and tomato *(salad-e shirazi)*; and cucumber and pomegranate salad. Also included are various pickles and relishes *(torshi)*, as well as bottles of fresh lime juice, olive oil, and wine vinegar.

All those sitting around the *sofreh* are asked to help themselves according to their fancy, before, throughout, and after the meal.

CAT AND MOUSE

And seven elders of the mousey nation
Were chosen as a special deputation –
Each of them carried something rare and fine
To give the cat: one bore a glass of wine
And one a spit of lamb-kebab, another
Took currants in a salver, while his brother
Sported a tray of figs, one cheese he'd made,
And one a syrup of sweet lemonade,
One bore him yogurt, butter and fresh bread,
The last a tray of rice upon his head.

Obeyd-e Zakani, circa 1350

THE STORY OF YOGURT

The word yogurt comes from the Turkish *yoghurt*. In Arabia it is called *laban*; in India, *dahi*; in Armenia, *madzoon* or *matsun*; in Azerbaijan and Georgia, *matsuni*; and finally in Iran it is *mast*. Yogurt was introduced to Western Europe in the sixteenth century.

In 1920, the Armenian Colombosians family founded the first yogurt company in Massachusetts and called it Colombo. Although in America yogurt is considered a new product, it is one of the older foods known to mankind. Regional records of ancient civilizations from Egypt to Iran refer to the healthful properties of yogurt. Yogurt was probably discovered accidentally by a nomad long before people could write about it.

A well-known story goes like this: A desert nomad, possibly Persian, was carrying some milk in his goatskin canteen. During his journey, heat and the right bacteria (lactobacillus) transformed the milk into yogurt. The nomad took his chance and drank the mixture. Much to his astonishment he found a sour, creamy, and pleasant taste. When he did not get sick, he shared his discovery with others. In 500 BCE India, the Yogis called the mixture of yogurt and honey "the food of Gods."

Throughout this century a number of healthful characteristics have been attributed to yogurt. They range from prolonging life, increasing sexual potency, remedying baldness, and calming the nervous system to curing skin diseases and gastrointestinal ailments.

In Iran, yogurt is usually drained to make it thicker and richer (*mast-e khiki*), which is available in Iranian markets (or you can drain your own, see page 530). A good equivalent, available in supermarkets in the U. S., is known as Greek yogurt.

Yogurt, Cucumber and Rose Petal Dip

Makes 4 servings
Preparation time: 15 minutes
plus 10 minutes to 1 hours'
refrigeration

Mast-o khiar

NOTE

Drained yogurt, mast-e khiki, *is available in Persian stores, or Greek yogurt is available at your supermarket.*

4 Persian cucumbers, or 1 long seedless, peeled and diced
½ cup green raisins
3 cups plain whole-milk drained yogurt
¼ cup chopped spring onions
2 tablespoons chopped fresh mint
2 tablespoons chopped fresh dill weed
2 tablespoons chopped fresh oregano
1 tablespoon chopped fresh thyme
2 tablespoons chopped fresh tarragon
2 cloves garlic, peeled and grated
¼ cup shelled walnuts, chopped
1 teaspoon sea salt
½ teaspoon freshly ground pepper

GARNISH
½ teaspoon dried mint
2 tablespoons dried rose petals
1 tablespoon green raisins

1. In a serving bowl, combine cucumbers, raisins, yogurt, spring onions, mint, dill weed, oregano, thyme, tarragon, garlic, and walnuts. Stir thoroughly and season to taste with salt and pepper.

2. Cover and refrigerate for 10 minutes before serving.

3. Garnish with mint, rose petals, and raisins. Just before serving, stir gently, and serve as a side dish or as an appetizer with bread. *Nush-e Jan!*

VARIATIONS

Shirazi-Style Yogurt and Cucumber Dip *(Mast-o khiar-e Shirazi)*—Add the following to the garnish: 1 teaspoon toasted sesame, 1 teaspoon toasted nigella seeds, 1 teaspoon toasted coriander seeds, and 1 teaspoon toasted cumin seeds. Stir well just before serving.

Yogurt, Cucumber, and Rose Petal Soup *(Abdugh khiar ba gol-e sorkh)*—This dip can be transformed into a refreshing cold soup by adding 1 cup of cold water (or more to taste) and 2 or 3 ice cubes to the mixture. Add more salt and pepper to taste. Toast flat Persian bread or pita bread, cut into 1-inch squares, and add to the soup, just before serving, as croutons.

Yogurt and Spinach Dip

1 pound fresh spinach, washed and
  chopped, or frozen spinach, chopped
¼ cup chopped fresh cilantro
¼ cup chopped fresh mint
4 tablespoons oil
2 onions, peeled and thinly sliced
2 cloves garlic, peeled and thinly sliced

1½ cups plain drained yogurt
½ teaspoon sea salt
¼ teaspoon freshly ground
  black pepper
¼ teaspoon saffron dissolved in
  1 tablespoon hot water (optional)

Makes 4 servings
Preparation time: 10 minutes
  plus 10 minutes to 1 hour of
  refrigeration
Cooking time: 10 minutes

1. Place the spinach, mint, and cilantro in a steamer. Cover and cook over high heat until wilted (about 5 minutes).

2. Heat the oil in a wide skillet over medium heat, add the onion and garlic, and sauté until golden brown.

3. Add the spinach mixture, and cook for 2 minutes. Remove from heat and let cool.

4. In a serving bowl, mix yogurt and spinach mixture and season to taste with salt and pepper. Cover and refrigerate for 10 minutes to 1 hour before serving.

5. Garnish with saffron water. Serve as an appetizer with Persian bread, or as a side dish. *Nush-e Jan!*

Borani-e esfenaj

Yogurt and Celery Dip

4 or 5 celery stalks (the inner, more
  tender stalks)
2 spring onions, chopped
2 tablespoons fresh parsley
2 tablespoons chopped fresh cilantro
2 tablespoons chopped fresh mint

1½ cups drained plain yogurt
½ teaspoon sea salt
¼ teaspoon freshly ground
  black pepper
2 tablespoons fresh lime juice

Makes 2 servings
Preparation time: 10 minutes
  plus 1 hour of refrigeration

1. Chop the celery into ½-inch pieces.

2. In a small bowl, place celery, spring onions, parsley, cilantro, mint, yogurt, salt, pepper, and lime juice. Toss well. Cover and refrigerate for an hour.

3. Serve with bread as an appetizer or as an accompaniment. *Nush-e Jan!*

VARIATION

Yogurt and Cauliflower Dip (*Borani-e gol-e kalam*)—Replace the celery with half a head of cauliflower cut into small florets.

Borani-e karafs

Yogurt and Persian Shallot Dip

Makes 4 servings
Preparation time: 10 minutes plus
overnight soaking and chilling

Mast-o musir

1½ cups dried Persian shallots *(musir)*
  or ¼ pound fresh shallots
2 cups plain drained yogurt
1 teaspoon sea salt

¼ teaspoon freshly ground
  black pepper
1 tablespoon dried mint (optional)

1. If using fresh shallots, peel and soak in cold water overnight. Change the water several times. Drain, pat dry, and chop finely. If using dried shallots, place in a saucepan, cover with water, bring to a boil over high heat, reduce heat, and simmer for 15 to 20 minutes until tender. Drain, allow to cool, and chop finely.

2. Combine the shallots with the yogurt, salt, pepper, and mint. Chill in refrigerator for several hours before serving.

3. Serve as an appetizer (with *lavash* or pita bread) or to accompany kababs.

Nush-e Jan!

Yogurt and Cardoon Dip

Makes 2 servings
Preparation time: 20 minutes
plus 1 hours' refrigeration

Borani-e kangar

4 or 5 cardoon stalks
1½ teaspoon sea salt
1 tablespoon olive oil
2 cups drained plain yogurt

¼ teaspoon freshly ground
  black pepper
2 tablespoons chopped fresh mint

1. Carefully remove and discard the prickly parts of the cardoon stalks. After removing leafy heads, be sure to remove the strings by lifting them, using the tip of a knife, and peeling them off. Chop into 1-inch-long pieces. To prevent discoloring, soak in a bowl of water with a splash of vinegar until ready to use.

2. Drain the cardoon and transfer to a saucepan, cover with water and 1 teaspoon salt, and boil for 10 minutes over medium heat. Drain.

3. Sauté the cardoon with 1 tablespoon olive oil and 2 tablespoons yogurt for 5 minutes over medium heat. Allow to cool.

4. Place in a serving bowl and add the remaining yogurt, salt, pepper, and mint. Toss well. Refrigerate for an hour.

5. Serve with bread as an appetizer. *Nush-e Jan!*

Yogurt and Fava Bean Dip

Makes 4 servings
Preparation time: 10 minutes
Cooking time: 10 minutes
plus at least 15 minutes of
* refrigeration*

برانی باقلاسبز

Borani-e baqala

¼ cup oil
4 cloves garlic, peeled and grated
2 pounds fresh fava beans or 1 pound
  frozen fava beans, second skin
  removed, and rinsed

½ teaspoon sea salt
½ teaspoon fresh ground pepper
2 tablespoons lime juice
½ cup fresh dill weed, chopped
1½ cups drained yogurt

1. Heat the oil in a wide skillet until hot. Add the garlic, fava beans, salt, and pepper. Sauté for a few minutes.

2. Add ½ cup water, bring to a boil, reduce heat, and simmer for 5 to 10 minutes, or until fava beans are tender.

3. Add the lime juice and dill weed. Remove from heat and allow to cool.

4. In a serving bowl, mix the yogurt and fava mixture and season to taste. Refrigerate for at least 15 minutes before serving. *Nush-e Jan!*

White Broad Bean Yogurt Dip

Makes 6 servings
Preparation time: 10 minutes
Cooking time: 2 hours 55 minutes

برانی باقلا

Borani-e baqala sefid

2½ cups dried white uncooked broad
  beans, picked over and rinsed, or
  cooked white beans in a jar
6 cups water
2 teaspoons salt
½ cup oil

1 small red onion, diced
2 cloves garlic, crushed and chopped
¼ cup fresh lime juice
1 tablespoon grape molasses
1 cup chopped fresh dill weed
1½ cups plain drained yogurt

1. To cook the beans, in a medium saucepan, bring the beans, water, and salt to a boil. Reduce heat to medium, cover and cook for 2¼ hours until the beans are tender (add more warm water if necessary). Remove from heat, drain, and allow to cool (or use already cooked white beans, drained and rinsed with cold water).

2. Heat the oil in a skillet over medium heat. Add the onion and garlic, and sauté for 5 minutes until the onion is golden brown. Add the lime juice and grape molasses. Remove from heat and set aside.

3. In a large mixing bowl whisk the dill weed and the yogurt. Add the beans and onion mixture. Toss well. Adjust seasoning to taste. Serve with bread.

VARIATION

Potato and Yogurt Dip *(Borani-e sib zamini)*—Replace broad beans with 2 large russet potatoes that are covered with water and cooked for 20 minutes or until tender, peeled and diced into ½-inch cubes.

Yogurt and Cooked Beet Dip

2 large uncooked beets or 1 can
  (16 ounces) cooked beets, drained
2 tablespoons sugar
1 cup drained plain yogurt

GARNISH
1 tablespoon chopped fresh mint or
  1 teaspoon dried mint
½ teaspoon black sesame seeds

Makes 4 servings
Preparation time: 5 minutes
Cooking time: 1 hour 30 minutes
  if fresh beets are used

Borani-e labu

1. To cook the beets: place them in a medium-sized baking dish, add 3 cups of water and the sugar. Bake the beets in a 350°F (180°C) oven for about 1½ hours or until tender.

2. Peel and cut the beets (slices or cubes according to your fancy). If using canned beets, be sure to drain.

3. Place the yogurt in a serving bowl or platter and chill in the refrigerator.

4. Just before serving add the beets to the yogurt and garnish with mint and sesame seeds. Mix the beets gently with the yogurt as you serve (do not overmix or homogenize). *Nush-e Jan!*

NOTE

The beets can also be cooked on a stovetop. Place them in a saucepan, add 2 cups water, cover and cook over low heat for ¾-1 hour until tender (depends on the size of the beets).

Yogurt and Eggplant Dip

Makes 4 servings
Preparation time: 15 minutes
Cooking time: 1 hour

كُلانی بادمجان

Borani-e bademjan

2 or 3 large eggplants (2 pounds)
¼ cup olive oil
1 onion, peeled and thinly sliced
4 cloves garlic, peeled and chopped
1 teaspoon sea salt
¼ teaspoon freshly ground
   black pepper

1 cup plain drained yogurt

GARNISH
1 teaspoon dried mint
½ cup chopped walnuts (optional)
Lavash bread

1. Preheat oven to 350°F (180°C). Wash eggplants and prick in several places with a fork to prevent bursting. Place whole eggplants on oven rack and bake for 1 hour. Be sure to put a tray under the eggplants to catch drips.

2. Remove eggplants from oven, let cool, then peel and mash.

3. Heat the oil in a wide skillet over medium heat and sauté the onion and garlic until golden. Add the eggplant, salt, and pepper, and sauté for 5 minutes. Cover and cook for 5 minutes over low heat. Remove from heat and let cool.

4. Transfer to a serving dish, mix with yogurt, and garnish with mint, and walnuts. Place on a platter. Cut up the *lavash* bread and arrange around the dish on the platter. Serve as an appetizer. *Nush-e Jan!*

Eggplant and Kashk Dip

Makes 4 servings
Preparation time: 50 minutes
Cooking time: 30 minutes

كشك بادمجان كوبیده

Kashk-o bademjan-e kubideh

9 Chinese eggplants (2 pounds), or 2 to
   3 large eggplants
¼ cup olive oil
2 large onions, peeled and chopped
3 cloves garlic, peeled and crushed
½ teaspoon sea salt
¼ teaspoon freshly ground
   black pepper
½ teaspoon turmeric
½ cup liquid *kashk* (sun-dried yogurt)*

GARNISH
1 tablespoon oil
2 cloves garlic, thinly sliced
1 tablespoon dried mint
2 tablespoons liquid *kashk* (sun-dried
   yogurt)*
¼ teaspoon ground saffron,
   dissolved in 1 tablespoon hot water
   (optional)

1. Peel eggplants and cut into 2x2-inch squares. (If not using Chinese eggplants, bitterness must be removed by placing eggplants in a colander and sprinkling with water and 2 teaspoons salt. Let stand in the sink for 20 minutes, then rinse with cold water and *blot dry*. Eggplants should be thoroughly dry.)

2. Heat ¼ cup oil in a wide skillet over medium heat. Add the eggplants, onion, and garlic and sauté for 15 minutes. Add the salt, pepper, turmeric, and 1 cup water, cover, and cook over medium heat for 15 to 20 minutes, or until tender. Transfer to a food processor, add the *kashk*, and pulse until you have a thick puree. Transfer to a serving dish.

3. Just before serving, brown garlic in 1 tablespoon oil. Remove skillet from heat, add dried mint, and mix well. Garnish with a dollop of *kashk*, the garlic and mint mixture, and a few drops of saffron water. Serve with bread and fresh herbs. *Nush-e Jan!*

Cheese and Walnut Dip

Makes 2 servings
Preparation time: 30 minutes

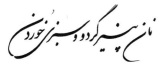

Nan-o panir-o gerdu

¼ pound white cheese, rinsed and drained
2 cups shelled walnuts
2 fresh spring onions, chopped
½ cup fresh basil
½ cup fresh tarragon
½ cup chopped fresh mint
1 clove garlic, peeled and crushed
½ teaspoon sea salt

¼ teaspoon freshly ground black pepper
Juice of one lime
¼ cup olive oil

GARNISH
Lavash bread
Persian cucumbers, peeled and sliced lengthwise

1. In a food processor, place all the ingredients and pulse until coarsely grainy.

2. Transfer the mixture to a serving bowl and place it on a round platter.

3. Cut bread in small 4-inch slices, place in a baking sheet, and toast under the broiler. Arrange the bread and cucumber slices around the bowl on a platter.

Nush-e Jan!

VARIATION

Cheese and Walnut Roll *(logmeh-ye nun-o panir)*—Place a piece of 9x9-inch aluminum foil on the counter, place an equal sized Cellophane wrap on top of it, and spread a 7x7-inch *lavash* bread over it. Spread a layer of the cheese and walnut dip over the *lavash* bread. Arrange a few slices of cucumber and some fresh aromatic herbs such as mint, basil and tarragon on top, roll up the bread tightly, and wrap the aluminum and Cellophane around it. Seal the ends and store in the refrigerator for 30 minutes and up to 24 hours. Just before serving, unwrap the aluminum and Cellophane, place the roll on the counter, and slice it diagonally with a sharp knife. Arrange on a plate for serving.

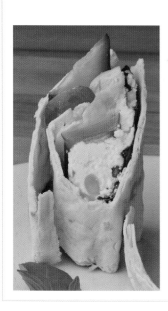

My father has died beyond the ages.
When my father died the sky was blue …
When my father died, the police were all poets.
The grocer asked me, "How many pounds of melons
　　do you want?"
I asked him, "How much an ounce for a happy heart?"

Sohrab Sepehri

پدرم پشت زمان ها مرده است .

پدرم وقتی مُرد، آسمان آبی بود ،

پدرم وقتی مُرد، پاسبان ها همه شاعر بودند .

مرد بقال از من پرسید : چند من خربزه می خواهی ؟

من از او پرسیدم : دل خوش سیری چند ؟

It is He Who sends down
Rain from the skies:
With it We produce
Vegetation of all kinds:
Out of which
We produce grain,
Heaped up at harvest;
Out of the date-palm
And its sheaths
Come clusters of dates
Hanging low and near:
And then there are gardens
Of grapes and olives,
And pomegranates,
Each similar in kind
Yet different in variety:
When they begin to bear fruit,
Feast your eye with the fruit,
And the ripeness thereof.
Behold! In these things
There are Signs for people
Who believe.

Koran, Sura VI, The Cattle, Verse 99

Caspian Olive Tapenade

Makes 4 servings
Preparation time: 30 minutes

زیتون پرورده

Zeytoun parvardeh

To toast the walnuts, place them in a baking sheet and bake in a preheated 350°F (180°C) oven for 10 minutes. (Beware, walnuts burn easily).

WALNUT AND OLIVE MIXTURE
1 cup walnuts, toasted
5 cloves garlic, peeled
1 cup fresh mint or 1 tablespoon dried mint
1 cup chopped fresh cilantro or parsley
1 tablespoon chopped fresh oregano, or ⅛ teaspoon dried oregano
1 tablespoon angelica powder (*gol-par*)
½ teaspoon sea salt
¼ teaspoon freshly ground pepper

½ jalapeño pepper, seeded and diced (optional)
1 teaspoon ground cumin (optional)
1 teaspoon grape molasses or honey
¼ cup olive oil
½ cup fresh pomegranate juice
1 pound green pitted olives

GARNISH
1 tablespoon walnuts, toasted and chopped
¼ cup pomegranate arils
½ cup pitted green olives
3 sprigs cilantro

1. In a food processor, place all the ingredients for the walnut and olive mixture and pulse until you have a grainy paste. Adjust seasoning to taste. Cover and refrigerate for 15 minutes and up to 3 days.

2. Just before serving garnish with walnuts, fresh pomegranate arils, whole olives, and cilantro. Serve as a dip with toasted bread cut into 4-inch pieces. *Nush-e Jan!*

Caspian Olive Salad

Makes 4 servings
Preparation time: 30 minutes
Cooking time: none

سالاد زیتون و گردو

Salad-e zeytoun-o gerdu

DRESSING
½ teaspoon grape molasses
½ teaspoon pomegranate molasses
2 tablespoons lime juice
2 tablespoons pomegranate juice
½ teaspoon red pepper flakes
½ teaspoon paprika
1 teaspoon angelica powder (*gol-par*)
½ teaspoon sea salt
½ teaspoon fresh ground pepper
2 tablespoons pistachio oil
2 tablespoons olive oil

SALAD
1 cup walnuts, toasted and chopped
1 cup green pitted olives, chopped
1 cup pomegranate arils (about 1 large pomegranate)
2 pickling cucumbers, peeled and diced
2 spring onions, green and white parts cleaned and chopped
2 tablespoons chopped fresh parsley or basil
2 tablespoons chopped fresh mint

The combination of walnuts, olives, and pomegranates go back in the Caspian region to at least the first millennium BCE.

1. In a salad bowl, prepare the dressing by whisking all the ingredients for dressing and set aside.

2. Just before serving add the salad ingredients to the sauce and toss well. *Nush-e Jan!*

Red Kidney Bean Dip

Makes 4 servings
Preparation time: 10 minutes
Cooking time: 2 hours

1 cup dried kidney beans, soaked in
  water for at least 4 hours and drained,
  or one 12-ounce can cooked beans
2 teaspoons sea salt
¼ cup olive oil
2 large onions, peeled and thinly sliced
2 tablespoons tomato paste
¼ teaspoon freshly ground
  black pepper
½ teaspoon ground cumin
½ teaspoon smoked paprika

¼ teaspoon red pepper flakes
2 teaspoons angelica powder *(gol-par)*
Juice of 2 bitter oranges (or a mixture of
  the juice of 1 lime and 1 orange)
1 teaspoon grape molasses or brown sugar
¼ cup chopped fresh dill

لوبیای پخته و یا ماش موشو

Lubia pokhteh
(mashallah musho)

NOTE

If using canned beans, drain,
rinse, and begin with step 2.

1. Place the beans in a medium saucepan, add 4 cups water and 1 teaspoon salt, and bring to a boil over high heat. Reduce the heat to medium-low, cover, and simmer for about 1½ hours or more until tender.

2. Meanwhile, heat the oil in a wide skillet over medium heat and sauté the onions until golden brown. Add tomato paste, 1 teaspoon salt, pepper, cumin, paprika, red pepper flakes, and angelica powder, and sauté for 2 minutes and add to the beans.

3. Add grape molasses and bitter orange juice. Use a handled mixer to partially puree the beans. Cook over medium heat for another 10 minutes. Adjust seasoning to taste and keep warm until ready to serve.

4. Just before serving, add the dill, mix, and transfer to a serving bowl. Serve with *lavash* bread. *Nush-e Jan!*

Eggplant and Kashk Casserole

Makes 4 servings
Preparation time: 25 minutes
Cooking time: 1 hour

کشک بادمجان

Kashk-o bademjan

8 Chinese or Japanese eggplants
1 cup oil
3 large onions, peeled and thinly sliced
6 cloves garlic, peeled and thinly sliced
1 teaspoon sea salt
1 teaspoon freshly ground black pepper
½ teaspoon turmeric
3 tablespoons dried mint flakes
½ teaspoon grape molasses or sugar
½ cup liquid *kashk* (sun-dried yogurt)*
  diluted with ½ cup water
¼ teaspoon ground saffron threads
  diluted in 1 tablespoon hot water

GARNISH
¼ cup toasted walnuts*, chopped
¼ cup chopped dates,
¼ cup fresh mint leaves

1. Rinse the eggplant and pat dry. Peel and cut into 4x2-inch lengths and place on paper towels on the counter. Blot dry (there should be no water on the eggplants).

2. Heat ¼ cup oil in a wide skillet over medium heat until very hot. Sauté the eggplants in batches on all sides until golden brown. Add more oil if necessary. Remove the eggplants using a slotted spoon and set aside on towels (to absorb the oil).

3. Add the remaining oil to the skillet and reheat over medium heat until very hot. Sauté the onion and garlic until golden brown. Add the salt, pepper, turmeric, mint flakes, and grape molasses, and sauté for 20 seconds. Gently return the eggplants to the skillet and add ½ cup water. Cover and cook over low heat for about 15 minutes until the eggplants are tender.

4. Meanwhile, preheat the oven to 350°F (180°C). Gently transfer the eggplant mixture from the skillet to a medium-sized baking dish. Drizzle the diluted *kashk* and the saffron water over the top, and bake uncovered for 15 minutes.

5. Keep the eggplant mixture warm until ready to serve. Just before serving garnish with walnuts, dates, and fresh mint leaves. *Nush-e Jan!*

VARIATION

Beet and Kashk Casserole—Replace the eggplants with 8 small beets (peeled and sliced). Proceed with step 2.

Eggplant and Zucchini Casserole

Makes 6 servings
Preparation time: 20 minutes
Cooking time: 1 hour

9 slim eggplants, chopped in 2-inch cubes
2 zucchini, chopped in cubes
1 large green or yellow pepper, chopped
2 large onions, peeled and chopped
2 stalks celery, chopped
4 large tomatoes, peeled and chopped
1 whole garlic bulb, peeled and sliced

½ cup olive oil
1 teaspoon grape molasses
3 teaspoons sea salt
1 teaspoon freshly ground black pepper
3 bay leaves
3 sprigs of thyme

Yatimcheh bademjan

1. Preheat oven to 500°F (260°C).

2. Place all the vegetables in a large baking dish.

3. In a bowl, combine olive oil, grape molasses, salt, pepper, bay leaves, and thyme. Pour this mixture over the vegetables, mixing gently but thoroughly.

4. Bake uncovered on middle rack of oven for 30 minutes. Open the oven, pull out the rack, and mix the vegetables gently. Push back the rack and continue baking for another 30 minutes.

5. Serve hot or cold. *Nush-e Jan!*

THE EGGPLANT STORY

They brought an eggplant dish to Sultan Mahmud when he was very hungry. It pleased him greatly and he said, "Eggplant is a tasty dish." A court favorite who was present gave a lecture in praise of the eggplant. When the sultan was full, he declared, "Eggplant is a very harmful thing." Then the same courtier made an exaggerated speech on the harmfulness of the eggplant. The sultan asked in amazement, "You wretch! How come you are not praising it anymore?" The man said, "I am your courtier, not the eggplant's. What I say has to please you, not the eggplant."

Obeyd-e Zakani, circa 1350

Eggplant with Pomegranate Spread

Makes 4 servings
Preparation time: 5 minutes
Cooking time: 1 hour 20 minutes

ناز خاتون

Nazkhatun

3 medium eggplants (2 pounds)
½ cup olive oil
2 medium onions, peeled and finely chopped
2 cloves garlic, crushed, peeled and chopped
1 medium tomato, peeled and diced
1 tablespoon pomegranate molasses or ½ cup verjuice (*ab-ghureh*, unripe grape juice)*
2 teaspoons sea salt
½ teaspoon freshly ground

black pepper
1 teaspoon angelica powder (*gol-par*)
1 teaspoon grape molasses or brown sugar
½ cup chopped fresh mint or 2 teaspoons dried mint

GARNISH
sprigs of mint
lavash or pita bread
fresh basil

1. Preheat oven to 500°F (260°C). Prick eggplants with a fork to prevent bursting and place on oven rack. Bake for 40 minutes. Be sure to put a tray under the eggplants to catch drips.

2. Place the eggplants on a cutting board and let stand until cool enough to handle. Peel, seed, and chop finely.

3. In a wide skillet, heat the oil and sauté the onion and garlic until golden. Add the eggplants, tomato, pomegranate molasses, salt, pepper, angelica powder, grape molasses, and mint. Cover and simmer over low heat for 30 minutes, stirring occasionally. Adjust seasoning to taste.

4. Transfer to a deep serving dish, garnish with sprigs of mint and place the serving dish in a platter. Surround with toasted flat breads, such as *lavash* or pita, and fresh herbs. This recipe can be made 24 hours in advance and served warm or at room temperature. *Nush-e Jan!*

First millennium BCE bas-relief of men carrying offerings of pomegranates and wheat.

Split Pea Patties

Servings: 4
Preparation time: 1 hour
* 30 minutes plus 2 hours of*
* refrigeration*
Cooking time: 20 minutes

Shami-e lapeh

VEGETARIAN VARIATION
Eliminate the meat. Replace it
in step 1 with 1 chopped
jalapeño pepper and ½ cup
fresh chopped cilantro.

VARIATION
Sweet and Sour Sauce—These
patties are traditionally served
with a sweet and sour sauce. In
a wide skillet, fry 1 chopped
onion in 3 tablespoons oil. Add 1
teaspoon turmeric, 1 teaspoon
dry mint, stir-fry for 20 seconds,
add ½ cup water, ½ cup vinegar,
and ½ cup sugar. Bring to a boil.
Just before serving, gently
arrange the patties in the sauce
and let simmer for 3 minutes.
Serve hot.

1 pound boned leg of lamb (beef, veal, or
  turkey) cut into 2-inch pieces
1 medium onion, peeled and chopped
2 teaspoons sea salt
1 teaspoon freshly ground black pepper
1 teaspoon turmeric
1 pound split peas, picked over and rinsed
1 teaspoon baking soda
½ teaspoon ground saffron dissolved in
  2 tablespoons hot water

3 eggs
2 cups canola oil (or more), for frying

GARNISH
Greenleaf lettuce, washed and
  patted dry
Fresh basil, mint, cilantro, tarragon,
  spring onions and *lavash* bread Quince
  paste (¼ pound, store bought, or use
  recipe on page 365)

1. In a medium saucepan combine the meat, onion, 1½ teaspoons salt, pepper, turmeric and 2 cups water; cover and cook over medium heat for 45 minutes or until
tender. Remove from the heat and drain (reserve the juice to use later on if the meat
is too dry). Puree the meat in the food processor and transfer to a large mixing bowl.

2. Meanwhile, in another medium-sized saucepan, combine the split peas with
4 cups water and ½ teaspoon salt. Bring to a boil, reduce heat to medium, cover, and
cook for 30 minutes or until tender. Drain and reserve the juice. In the same food
processor puree the split peas and transfer to the mixing bowl with the meat.

3. When the meat mixture is cool, add the baking soda, saffron, and the eggs one by
one, and knead for a few minutes until a soft paste is created. If it is too dry, add some
of the reserved juices. Cover and refrigerate for 2 to 24 hours.

4. Place a bowl of warm water next to your cooking pan. Scoop the meat paste (use
ice cream scoop) into lumps the size of walnuts. Moisten your hands and flatten
each lump between your damp palms into a round shape and press a hole in the
center with your finger; this helps to cook the inside of the patties.

5. In a wide skillet, heat ¼ cup of oil over medium-low heat until hot (but not smoking). Fry the patties on each side for about 5 minutes until golden brown, adding
more oil if necessary. There should be enough oil so that the patties are half
immersed in oil. Remove the patties gently with a slotted spatula and place in a wide
container lined with parchment paper. Continue for remaining patties, separating
each layer with parchment paper. Allow to cool. If not used immediately, cover and
keep in the refrigerator for later use (up to 3 days).

6. Serve wrapped in greenleaf lettuce together with fresh herbs and a slice of quince
paste, or replace the quince paste with a traditional sweet and sour sauce (see side
note for this variation.) *Nush-e jan!*

VARIATION

Chickpea Patties *(Shami-e nokhodchi)*—This variation makes patties from chickpea
  flour and ground meat. Combine 1 pound ground lamb, 1 large grated onion, ½ cup
  chickpea flour, 2 tablespoons warm water, 1 teaspoon salt, ½ teaspoon pepper, ½
  teaspoon ground saffron dissolved in 4 tablespoons rose water, ½ teaspoon baking
  soda, and 1 teaspoon *advieh*. Knead to create a soft paste, cover, and allow to rest for
  at least 1 hour and up to 24. Proceed with the recipe above from step 4.

Tongue with Tomato Sauce

Makes 4 servings
Preparation time: 20 minutes
Cooking time: 4 hours

خوراک زبان

Khorak-e zaban

TONGUES
6 lamb tongues, or 2 calf, or 1 large beef
1 large onion, peeled and sliced
3 cloves garlic, peeled and crushed
2 bay leaves
4 whole cloves
½ teaspoon freshly ground pepper
½ teaspoon turmeric
3 tablespoons tomato paste

BROTH
3 tablespoons butter or oil
1 large onion, peeled and thinly sliced

1 clove garlic, peeled and sliced
½ pound mushrooms, sliced
1 tablespoon tomato paste
1 tablespoon flour
2 tomatoes, peeled and sliced
2 tablespoons sour cream
Juice of 1 lime
1 teaspoon sea salt
¼ teaspoon fresh ground pepper

GARNISH
2 tablespoons chopped fresh parsley

I have particularly fond memories of tongue sandwiches during my school years in Iran.

1. Wash and rinse the tongues and place in a large pot. Cover with water and bring to a boil. Skim the froth as it rises until it stops foaming. Add the onion, garlic, bay leaves, cloves, pepper, turmeric, and tomato paste (do not add salt because it changes the color of the tongue). Cover and simmer over low heat for 3 to 3½ hours until the tongues are tender.

2. Remove the bay leaves and tongues from the broth and allow to cool. Reserve the broth. Remove the skin and excess fat from the tongues using a sharp knife and cut the tongues into thin slices.

3. In a wide skillet, melt the butter over medium heat. Sauté the onion and garlic. Add the mushrooms and Sauté for 2 minutes. Add the tomato paste and the flour, and stir-fry for 1 minute longer. Add the tomatoes and 1½ cups of the reserved tongue broth and simmer for 5 minutes.

4. Add the sour cream, lime juice, salt, and pepper. Stir well and simmer for 10 minutes over low heat. Adjust seasoning to taste.

5. When ready to serve, arrange sliced tongue on a serving platter and pour the sauce over it. Sprinkle with chopped parsley. Serve hot with plenty of Persian pickles (*torshi*), platter of fresh herbs and vegetables (*sabzi khordan*), and warm bread. *Nush-e Jan!*

Savory Turnover (Sanbuseh)

Makes 15 pieces
Preparation time: 1 hour plus
*   3 hours for dough to rise*
Cooking time: 20 minutes

سنبوسه گوشت و کلم

Sanbuseh

HOMEMADE DOUGH
2 egg yolks, beaten
1 cup plain yogurt or sour cream
1 cup oil or butter
¼ cup milk
3 cups all-purpose, unbleached flour
   sifted with 1 teaspoon baking powder

GROUND LAMB AND CABBAGE FILLING
½ cup oil, butter, or ghee*
1 onion, peeled and finely chopped
2 cloves garlic, peeled and grated
1 pound ground lamb (chicken, or fish)
6 cups shredded napa cabbage,
   sprinkled with 2 teaspoons sea salt; let
   stand for 15 minutes; squeeze out
   liquid through a cheese cloth
1 egg, lightly beaten
½ teaspoon sugar
2 teaspoons cinnamon
¼ teaspoon ground cloves
¼-inch ginger, peeled and grated
1 teaspoon ground cumin
2 cups chopped fresh cilantro or parsley
½ teaspoon cayenne
1 teaspoon sea salt
2 teaspoons freshly ground pepper
½ teaspoon turmeric

MUSHROOM FILLING
½ cup oil, butter, or ghee*
1 small onion, peeled and thinly sliced
1 clove garlic, peeled and crushed
½ pound ground lamb (chicken, or fish)
½ pound mushrooms, cleaned with a
   towel and thinly sliced
2 teaspoons sea salt
1 teaspoon fresh ground pepper
1 tablespoon dried mint or ¼ cup
   chopped fresh parsley
1 teaspoon cayenne

VEGETARIAN POTATO FILLING
4 russet potatoes, cooked,
   peeled and grated.
½ cup oil, butter, or ghee*
1 large onion, peeled and sliced
1 large carrot, peeled and grated
1 cup fresh or frozen green peas
½ teaspoon turmeric
½ teaspoon cayenne
1 teaspoon hot curry powder
2 teaspoons sea salt
½ teaspoon freshly ground black pepper
½ cup chopped fresh cilantro or dill

GLAZE
1 egg, lightly beaten with
   2 teaspoons milk

VARIATIONS
You can make your own dough or use 1 pack ready made frozen puff pastry thawed for 1 hour before use. (For steam frying, use 1 package, ready-made, large-sized egg roll skins. In a wide skillet, combine 2 tablespoons oil and 4 tablespoons water, and arrange the *sanbusehs* leaving spaces between them. Cover and steam over low heat for 15 minutes.)

In Ahwaz in southern Iran, they use lavash bread cut into three-inch strips, stuffed with the filling and folded into a triangle. These are fried on both sides. Sanbuseh is traditionally fried, but it can also be baked.

1. For the dough, beat the egg yolks until creamy. Add yogurt, oil, and milk. Mix well. Gradually blend in 3 cups of the flour mixture. Knead well to produce a dough that does not stick to your hands (add more flour if necessary). Place the dough in a zip-locked plastic bag, seal, and refrigerate for 3 hours.

2. Meanwhile, prepare the filling of your choice by heating ½ cup of the oil in a large skillet over medium heat. Add the onion and stir-fry for 10 minutes. Add the rest of the ingredients for the filling and sauté for another 10 to 15 minutes until the filling is completely dry. Adjust seasoning to taste. Remove from heat and allow to cool.

3. Heat the oven to 350°F (180°C). Line a baking sheet with parchment paper.

4. On a cool, floured surface, roll the dough out very thin with a rolling pin. Cut the dough into 3-inch circles, using a cookie cutter dipped in flour or the open end of a glass. Fill each circle with 2 teaspoons of the filling. Fold each circle to a crescent shape and seal using your fingers. Use a fork to press down the edges to double seal and decorate. Carefully transfer to the baking sheet. Do not crowd. Paint the *sanbusehs* with the glaze.

5. Bake until golden brown, about 20 to 25 minutes. Serve *sanbusehs* simply, dipped in rice vinegar or serve with a fruit chutney or pickles (torshi) of your choice. Nush-e Jan!

جینج و آرد برنج پندالو و آرد برنج تیل رایی آرد چارولی
آرد نخود و چارولی منک و آرد بادام خرما و آرد برنج تمر
هندی و شکر تری و برنج پویی و آرد برنج سو نف

و آرد برنج

کشنین

قرنفل

مشک

پترج

A POETIC RECIPE FOR A SAVORY TURNOVER
(SANBUSEH OR MANTU)

If thou wouldst know what food gives most delight
Best let me tell, for none hath subtler sight:
Take first the finest meat, red, soft to touch,
And mince it with the fat, not overmuch;
Then add an onion, cut in circles clean,
A cabbage, very fresh, exceeding green,
And season well with cinnamon and rue;
Of coriander add a handful, too,
And after that of cloves the very least,
Of finest ginger, and of pepper best,
A hand of cumin, murri just to taste,
Two handfuls of Palmyra salt; but haste,
Good master, haste to grind them small and strong.
Then lay and light a blazing fire along;
Put all in the pot, water pour
Upon it from above, and cover o'er.
But, when the water vanished is from sight
And when the burning flames have dried it quite,
Then, as thou wilt, in pastry wrap it round,
And fasten well the edges, firm and sound;
Or, if it please thee better, take some dough,
Conveniently soft, and rubbed just so,
Then with the rolling pin let it spread
And with the nails its edges docketed.
Pour in the frying pan the choicest oil
And in that liquor let it finely broil.
Last, ladle out into a thin tureen
Where appetizing mustard smeared hath been,
And eat with pleasure, mustarded about,
This tastiest food for hurried diner-out.

Ishaq Ibn Ibrahim, tenth century

Sautéed Lamb Liver, Kidneys, and Heart

Makes 4 servings
Preparation time: 15 minutes
Cooking time: 15 minutes

*Khorak-e del-o
jigar-o qolveh*

1 lamb liver
2 lamb hearts
8 lamb kidneys
2 tablespoons oil
2 large onions, chopped
4 cloves garlic
2 tablespoons tomato paste
1 tablespoon flour
2 tablespoons lime juice

1½ teaspoons sea salt
½ teaspoon freshly ground
  black pepper
½ cup water
2 teaspoons red wine vinegar
2 teaspoons grape molasses
½ cup sliced cucumber pickles
  for garnish
1 tablespoon chopped fresh parsley

1. Slice liver and hearts lengthwise into strips ½-inch thick. Cut kidneys into 1-inch cubes. Wash and pat dry.

2. In a large skillet, heat the oil over medium-high heat and add the liver, hearts and kidneys. Sauté for 2 minutes. Add the onions and garlic and sauté for 3 to 5 minutes until brown. Add tomato paste, flour, lime juice, salt, and pepper and stir-fry for 1 minute. Add the water, cover, and simmer over medium heat for about 5 minutes. Add the vinegar and grape molasses. Adjust seasoning to taste and remove from heat.

3. Arrange on a serving platter and garnish with cucumber pickles and parsley. Serve immediately. *Nush-e Jan!*

Lamb Spread, Isfahani-Style

Makes 4 servings
Preparation time: 15 minutes
Cooking time: 1 hour 45 minutes

Beriyani

NOTE

You can also add a sheep's lung in step 3. Be sure the lung is fresh. Pound it with a mallet to release any air. Use a knife to remove any bronchi or cartilaginous parts. Cover with water and cook until tender. Grind before adding it to step 3. (Necks and lungs can be found at your halal butchers)

3 pounds leg of lamb with bone
6 cups water or broth
2 large onions, peeled and thinly sliced
2 teaspoons sea salt
1 teaspoon freshly ground pepper
1 teaspoon turmeric
3 tablespoons butter or oil

2 teaspoons *advieh* (Persian spice mix)*
1 teaspoon cinnamon
1 sangak bread cut into 6-inch squares,
  or 4 whole wheat pitas

GARNISH
fresh basil, tarragon, mint, and radishes

1. In a medium-sized pot, place the lamb and add the water. Bring to a boil. Remove any froth as it rises. Add the onion, salt, pepper, and turmeric. Reduce heat to medium, cover, and cook for 1 hour 45 minutes or until the meat separates from the bone. Remove the lamb from the pot, discard the bones, but save juice for later use. Grind the meat in a food processor.

2. Heat 3 tablespoons butter in a wide skillet over medium heat, add the ground lamb, advieh, and 1 cup of the saved broth. Sauté for 10 minutes or until all the juice has been absorbed. Adjust seasoning to taste.

3. Toast the bread and moisten it with some of the broth, sprinkle with a pinch of cinnamon, spread a spatula of the ground meat, and some fresh herbs on top. *Nush-e jan!*

VARIATION

You can replace the leg of lamb with two necks of lamb and increase the cooking time to 3 hours. Separate the meat and discard the bones. Proceed with step 3.

In one hand Mulla Nasruddin was carrying home some liver he had just bought. In the other hand he had a recipe for liver pie that a friend had given him. Suddenly a crow swooped down and carried off the liver.

"You fool!" shouted Mulla. "The meat is all very well—but I still have the recipe."

Brain Patties

Makes 4 servings
Preparation time: 15 minutes
Cooking time: 10 minutes

BRAINS
6 lamb brains
1 tablespoon vinegar
1 small onion, peeled
2 bay leaves
½ teaspoon salt
½ teaspoon fresh ground pepper

BATTER
2 eggs
1 teaspoon sea salt
1 teaspoon ground lemon pepper

2 cloves of garlic, peeled and chopped
3 tablespoons milk

DUSTING
¼ cup flour
1 cup dry bread crumbs

1 cup oil for frying

GARNISH
2 tablespoons chopped parsley
2 tablespoons balsamic vinegar or
    freshly squeezed lime juice

Kotlet-e maghz

1. If the brain membrane is already removed, skip this step. Place brains in a colander under running water. Remove the outer membrane and veins by pulling on them with a sharp knife.

2. In a saucepan, place the vinegar, onion, bay leaves, salt, pepper, and 2 cups water. Bring to a boil add the brains and bring back to a boil. Drain immediately (do not overcook). Allow to cool and then cut each brain in half horizontally.

3. In a bowl, beat the eggs with the salt, lemon pepper, garlic, and milk. Set aside.

4. Dust the brains with 2 tablespoons flour. Dip into the egg mixture and let excess drip off. Coat the brains with a mixture of 1 cup bread crumbs and 2 table-spoons flour.

5. Heat the oil in a wide skillet over medium heat until hot (but not smoking). Fry the brains on all sides until golden brown.

6. Place the fried brains on a serving dish and sprinkle with parsley and vinegar. Serve immediately with bread, fresh herbs, and pickled cucumbers. This also makes a great *lavash* roll or crispy baguette sandwich. *Nush-e Jan!*

Lentil Salad

Makes 4 servings
Preparation time: 10 minutes
Cooking time: 30 minutes

1 cup brown lentils, rinsed
1 teaspoon sea salt

DRESSING
1 cup chopped fresh spring onions
¼ cup olive oil
¼ cup rice vinegar or lime juice
½ teaspoon salt
½ teaspoon freshly ground pepper
1 tablespoon angelica powder
  (gol-par)

1 teaspoon ground cumin

SALAD
2 tablespoons chopped fresh parsley
2 tablespoons chopped fresh mint
1 large carrot, peeled and diced
2 pickling cucumbers, peeled and diced
1 celery stalk, diced
½ yellow bell pepper, seeded and
  diced (optional)
½ red onion, peeled and diced

Salad-e adas

1. Place lentils in a medium-heavy saucepan. Pour in 4 cups water and 1 teaspoon salt and cook, uncovered, over medium heat for 30 to 45 minutes until tender (depending on the type of lentils used). Drain and set aside.

2. In a salad bowl, combine the spring onions, oil, rice vinegar, salt, pepper, angelica powder, and cumin. Mix well.

3. Add lentils and the rest of the ingredients to the mixture, toss thoroughly, and serve with greenleaf lettuce and toasted flat bread. *Nush-e Jan!*

Lentil Dip

Makes 6 servings
Cooking time: 2 hours 15 minutes

2 cups brown lentils, cleaned and
  washed
1½ teaspoons sea salt
¼ cup oil
2 large onions, peeled and thinly sliced
4 cloves garlic, peeled and crushed
½ teaspoon freshly ground
  black pepper

¼ teaspoon red pepper flakes
1 teaspoon turmeric
1 teaspoon ground cumin
2 tablespoons angelica powder
  (gol-par)
½ cup bitter orange juice
1 teaspoon grape molasses or sugar
1 cup fresh chopped mint

Adasi

1. Place lentils in a medium-sized, heavy-bottomed saucepan and add 8 cups water and 1½ teaspoons salt. Bring to a boil. Cover and simmer over low heat for about 1½ hours, stirring occasionally.

2. In a wide skillet, heat 3 tablespoons oil over medium heat until hot. Sauté the onion and garlic until golden brown. Add it to the lentils, season with pepper, red pepper, turmeric, cumin, and angelica powder, and let simmer over low heat for another 45 minutes.

3. Add the bitter orange juice, grape molasses, and mint. Stir well and adjust seasoning to taste. Serve warm with *lavash* bread as an appetizer. *Nush-e Jan!*

Cucumber and Pomegranate Salad

Makes 4 servings
Preparation time: 25 minutes

½ cup chopped spring onions
½ cup chopped fresh mint or
  1 tablespoon dried mint
1 teaspoon sea salt
½ teaspoon freshly ground pepper
½ teaspoon angelica powder
  (gol-par)
1 long seedless cucumber, peeled and
  diced
Seeds of 2 pomegranates
Juice of 1 lime

سالاد انار و خیار

Salad-e khiar-o anar

1. In a serving bowl, combine all the ingredients and toss lightly.

2. Season to taste with salt and lime juice. *Nush-e Jan!*

Cucumber and Mint Salad

Makes 4 servings
Preparation time: 15 minutes

1 seedless, long English cucumber, or 6
  baby (Persian) cucumbers
1 onion, peeled and thinly sliced
1 tablespoon chopped fresh mint, or 1
  teaspoon dried mint
2 tablespoons vinegar
½ teaspoon sea salt
¼ teaspoon freshly ground
  black pepper

سالاد سرکه خیار

Serkeh khiar

1. Peel cucumber (optional) and slice thinly using a mandolin slicer.

2. Combine all ingredients in a bowl and toss well. Serve as an appetizer or accompanied with Persian bread. *Nush-e Jan!*

Tomato and Cucumber Salad Shirazi-Style

Makes 4 servings
Preparation time: 15 minutes

2 firm ripe tomatoes
1 long seedless cucumber or 6 Persian cucumbers
2 spring onions, chopped
3 radishes, sliced
2 tablespoons chopped fresh parsley
2 tablespoons chopped fresh mint
2 tablespoons chopped fresh cilantro

DRESSING
3 tablespoons olive oil
Juice of 1 lime
1 clove garlic, peeled and grated
½ teaspoon sea salt
¼ teaspoon freshly ground black pepper

Salad-e gojeh khiar (Shirazi)

1. Cut out the tomato stems and score a crosshair at the bottom. Drop tomatoes into scalding hot water for about 1 minute or until the skins lift up. Remove with tongs or a slotted spoon, place in bowl of ice or cold water, peel, and cut into quarters. Peel and cut cucumber into 1-inch cubes.

2. Whisk together the olive oil, lime juice, garlic, salt, and pepper. Add tomatoes, cucumber, remaining vegetables and herbs, and toss. Serve immediately.

Nush-e Jan!

THE MOST SPLENDID OF ALL THINGS

ز یبا ترین اشیا، فاخرترین اعیان ۔ از هرچه هست پیدا و از هرچه هست نهان

از مرغها هزار است، از روقتها سحرگه ۔ از فصلها بهار است، از نوعها است انسان

از عهد شباب است، از آبها شراب است ۔ از نجم آفتاب است، از ماهها است نیسان

از سنگها دل دوست، از غمها غم اوست ۔ از تیغها است ابرو، از دشنه ها است مژگان

از زیبها است افسر، از طیبها است عنبر ۔ از عضوها است دیده، از خلقها است احسان

What's the most splendid of all things, most beautiful,
Of all that is invisible and visible?

Of times it is the dawn, of birds sweet nightingales,
Of seasons it is spring, of creatures man prevails;

Of ages youth, of liquids wine's the loveliest one,
Of months it's April, and of stars it is the sun;

Of stones a friend's heart, and of grief' a lover's sighs,
Swords, it's her eyebrows; daggers, the lashes of her eyes;

Of splendor it's a crown, it's ambergris of scents,
Of senses sight, of virtues it's benevolence.

Neshat

Persian Chicken Salad

Makes 12 servings
Preparation time: 1 hour
45 minutes plus 2 hours of
chilling time in refrigerator

1 chicken, about 2 or 3 pounds, with skin removed
1 large onion, peeled and finely chopped
1 teaspoon sea salt
5 large russet potatoes
4 carrots, peeled and chopped
2 cups fresh or frozen green peas
3 hard-boiled eggs, peeled and chopped
1 cup toasted walnuts, chopped (optional)*
2 spring onions, chopped
2 celery stalks, chopped
3 medium cucumber pickles, finely chopped
½ cup chopped fresh parsley
⅔ cup olives, pitted and chopped

DRESSING
1 cup chicken broth (from cooking chicken in step 1)
3 cups mayonnaise
2 tablespoons Dijon mustard
¼ cup olive oil
¼ cup vinegar
¼ cup lime juice
1½ teaspoons sea salt
1 teaspoon freshly ground black pepper

Salad-e olivieh

VEGETARIAN VARIATION

Eliminate the chicken from the ingredients and from step 1 altogether. For the dressing, replace the chicken broth with 2 tablespoons plain yogurt. Increase the number of hard-boiled eggs from 3 to 6.

NOTE

To toast walnuts: Place oven rack in the center and preheat oven to 350°F (180°C). Spread the walnuts in a rimmed baking sheet and bake for 10 minutes. Beware, walnuts burn easily.

1. Place the chicken in a pot. Add the onion and salt. Cover and cook for 1½ hours over low heat (no water is added because chicken makes its own juice). When done, allow to cool, debone the chicken, and chop finely. Set aside the chicken broth for later use.

2. In large saucepan, bring 8 cups of water to a boil. Score around the center of each potato and drop in the boiling water. Cook for 15 to 20 minutes until tender. Remove the potatoes using a slotted spoon and place in a large bowl of ice water until cool enough to handle. Use your hands to remove the skins by pulling them off. Chop the potatoes.

3. Steam the carrots and peas for 5 minutes and set aside. (If using frozen peas, follow package directions.)

4. In a large bowl, whisk together chicken broth, mayonnaise, mustard, olive oil, vinegar, lime juice, salt, and pepper.

5. Combine chicken, prepared vegetables, eggs, and walnuts with the rest of the ingredients. Pour the dressing over it and toss well. Adjust seasoning to taste.

6. Transfer salad to a flat plate and decorate with hearts of romaine lettuce. Chill for at least 2 hours. Serve with *lavash* bread, hot pita bread, or French bread. *Nush-e Jan!*

VARIATION

Instead of combining all the prepared ingredients in step 5, you may arrange the ingredients separately on a serving platter and put the dressing in a small bowl on the side.

Caviar

Makes 4 servings

خاویار

Khaviar

4 ounces Caspian Sea caviar
Thin toast

Butter
2 fresh limes, cut in half

Caviar is the unfertilized, processed roe of the sturgeon fish. The name for caviar comes from the Persian, *mahi-e khayeh dar,* literally meaning "fish bearing eggs." The best caviar comes from the Caspian Sea. There are three main types of caviar, each from a different species of sturgeon. The largest eggs, known by the Russian name beluga, come from the *fil-mahi,* literally "elephant fish." The average-sized roe, osetra, comes from *tas-mahi,* or the "bald fish"; and the smallest eggs, sevruga, are those from the *uzunbrun,* or the "long-nosed fish." Besides the size, each type has its own particular flavor, and you have to try each one to see which you prefer.

The most important step in the production of caviar is the salting. The different brands available vary in quality. As long as it comes from the Caspian Sea it is the real thing, and then it is up to you to decide which type you prefer.

I have often been asked, "How does one know if the caviar is fresh or not?" The best answer I can give is that it should smell of the sea but never fishy.

Caviar has never been widely appreciated by Iranians except by the local inhabitants of the provinces, Gilan and Mazandaran, around the Caspian. This has been mainly because of the difficulty of refrigerated transport and the religious dictum that fish without scales or their parts should not be eaten. Nowadays, of course, the roughly 200 tons of yearly production are exported to the West.

Around the Caspian there are various recipes that include the roe of the sturgeon—one is with garlic chives in an omelet. The Russians also like to garnish their caviar with onions and egg whites, but I believe good-quality caviar should be eaten simply. Place a good-sized dollop on a thin piece of lightly buttered toast (*sangak* bread is my favorite) and squeeze a little fresh lime over it.

SOUPS
OSHES &
PORRIDGES

SOUPS, OSHES & PORRIDGES

*S*oup plays a vital role in Iranian tradition. Many different kinds of soup are served to mark special occasions, and sharing a bowl of soup is believed to forge the bonds of friendship. Sometimes, in an act symbolizing great intimacy, friends or lovers sip from the same spoon to seal their devotion.

Most soups in Persian cooking are substantial enough to serve as a main course. They fall into three categories. One group consist of meat-based, salted broths such as lamb shank soup *(abgusht)*, which were called *shurba* in the past in Iran (*shurba* still remains the general term for soup in many Middle Eastern countries); hearty soups called *osh* (rhymes with squash), which are wonderfully flavorful thick soups; and finally, a type of thick elastic soup, more like a porridge, called *halim* (an example of *halim* is lamb and wheat porridge, *halim-e gandom)*.

*Osh*es are further divided into three categories: those that are cereal-based, as in barley soup *(osh-e jow);* bean-based, as in beggar's soup *(osh-e sholeh qalamkar);* and a pasta-based, as in noodle soup *(osh-e reshteh)*. The usual souring agent for most *osh*es is sun-dried yogurt *(kashk)*. But in some regions it is replaced with vinegar, pomegranate, lime, bitter orange, tamarind, and sumac. Most *osh*es are garnished with *na'na daq,* which usually is sautéd garlic, mint, and turmeric.

Just as "supper" comes from "soup" in English, in Persian the cook is called *osh-paz,* the "soup preparer," and the kitchen is called *osh-paz khaneh,* "the place where the soup is prepared." For best results, make *osh*es a day in advance to give the flavors a chance to meld, and reheat them just before serving. Add the garnish at the last minute, after pouring the soup into the tureen or individual servings. Iranians like to decorate soups with various garnishes, creating patterns that are pleasing to the eye. Just before serving, stir in the garnish. Serve with warm crusty Persian bread such as *sangak* or *lavash*.

Photo left: Onion Soup, *Eshkeneh*, recipe on page 81

DUCK SOUP

A relative came to see Mulla Nasruddin from the country and brought a duck. Mulla was grateful and had the bird cooked and shared it with his guest. Presently another visitor arrived. He was a friend, as he said, "of the man who gave you the duck." Mulla fed him as well. This happened several times. Mulla's home had become like a restaurant for out-of-town visitors. Everyone was a more and more distant friend removed from the original donor of the duck. Finally Mulla was exasperated.

One day there was a knock at the door and a stranger appeared. "I am the friend of the friend of the friend of the man who brought you the duck from the country," he said.

"Come in," said Mulla. They seated themselves at the table, and Nasruddin asked his wife to bring the soup. When the guest tasted it, it seemed to be nothing more than warm water. "What sort of soup is this?" he asked Mulla.

"That," said Mulla, "is the soup of the soup of the soup of the duck."

هر جنسی تیل انداخته بپزند بعده
آس کرده
بیامیزند
درمیان
آرد که بو

هر جنسی پس آبشنه خوب شود دو یا یدایست
خاله بیفکند پوست سیب پوست نارنگی کلاب

Homemade Broth

Makes 6 cups
Preparation time: 20 minutes
Cooking time: 2 hours

1 teaspoon peppercorns
2 bay leaves
1 bunch dill (stalk and roots)
3 sprigs parsley
1 sprig coriander (stalk and roots)
4 or 5 pounds chicken parts (skinless drumsticks, breast bones, wings, backs, or scraps), or raw beef or veal bones

1 large onion, peeled and thinly sliced
2 cloves garlic, whole
2 carrots, chopped
2 celery stalks, chopped
2 leeks, chopped
1 parsnip, chopped
1 teaspoon salt

گوشتابه

Gushtabeh

1. Bundle the peppercorns, bay leaves, dill, parsley, and coriander together in a piece of cheesecloth and tie shut.

2. Place all the ingredients in a large pot. Cover with 8 cups water and bring to a boil. Skim off the froth as it rises.

3. Reduce heat, add the salt, cover, and simmer for about 2 hours over low heat, adding more warm water if necessary.

4. Strain broth through a sieve and discard the solids. Allow broth to cool.

5. Pour broth into a gravy strainer (a container with a spout from the base that allows one to pour the liquid while the fat stays on top). Remove excess fat from the top, cover, and refrigerate. Use as needed. *Nush-e Jan!*

Lamb Shank Soup with Yellow Split Peas and Meat Paste

Makes 6 servings
Preparation time: 10 minutes
Cooking time: 2 hours
*   15 minutes*

آبگوشت لپه و گوشت کوبیده

Abgusht-e lapeh-o gusht kubideh

2 pounds lamb shanks and 1 pound
    breast of lamb
2 large onions, peeled and quartered
8 cups water
1 cup yellow split peas
1 teaspoon turmeric
2 teaspoons sea salt
½ teaspoon freshly ground
    black pepper
3 large russet potatoes, peeled and cut
    into halves
4 tomatoes, peeled and sliced

1 tablespoon tomato paste
1 teaspoon ground cinnamon
4 whole dried *limu-omani* (dried
    Persian limes)*, pierced, or
    ¼ cup lime juice
½ teaspoon ground saffron dissolved
    in 2 tablespoons hot water
1 teaspoon *advieh* (Persian spice mix)*

GARNISH
1 teaspoon ground cinnamon
1 large onion, peeled and sliced

1. Place the meat, onions, and water in a large, heavy pot. Bring to a boil, skimming the froth as it forms. Add split peas, turmeric, salt, and pepper. Cover and let simmer for 1½ hours over low heat.

2. Add the potatoes, tomatoes, tomato paste, cinnamon, pierced Persian limes, saffron water, and *advieh*. Cover and continue to simmer 45 minutes over low heat. Test with a knife tip to see if the meat and potatoes are tender. Adjust seasoning.

3. Using a slotted spoon, remove all of the ingredients. Debone the meat and reserve the bones. Mash the meat and vegetables together to make the paste called *gusht kubideh*. It should have the consistency of lumpy mashed potatoes. Iranian cooks would use a mortar and pestle to pound the *gusht kubideh* to just the right consistency. A food processor may be used instead, by pulsing, but take care not to let the paste get too smooth. Season to taste with salt and pepper and arrange on a serving platter. Pour 3 tablespoons hot soup over the paste. Sprinkle with cinnamon and garnish with fresh slices of raw onion.

4. Reheat the broth and scoop out the marrow from the bones. Mix the marrow with the broth and serve in a bowl as soup. Serve the *gusht kubideh* separately with Persian pickles (*torshi*), a platter of spring onions, radishes, fresh tarragon, basil, mint (*sabzi-khordan*), and *sangak* or pita bread. *Nush-e Jan!*

VARIATION

This soup may be made with beef, veal, or turkey. Also, ½ cup chickpeas and ½ cup red kidney beans (soaked in water for 4 hours and drained) may be substituted for the split peas.

VARIATIONS

Lamb Shank Soup with Eggplant and Meat Paste *(Abgusht-e bademjan)*—In step 2 with the potatoes, you can add 3 medium-sized eggplants, peeled and halved, soaked in salt water, rinsed and blotted, and sautéed on all sides in 3 tablespoons oil until golden brown.

Lamb Shank Soup with Quince and Meat Paste *(Abgusht-e beh)*—Substitute the eggplants with 2 peeled and diced quinces and 2 cups pitted prunes.

Lamb's Head and Feet Soup

Makes 4 servings
Preparation time: 30 minutes
Cooking time: 4 hours

Kalleh pacheh

This is a favorite street food, often eaten in the early morning or before going hiking.

Traditionally it is made with the head (including the tongue) and the feet of a sheep or lamb. Shanks may be substituted for the feet, which are not available everywhere. The head, feet, and tripe can be ordered from butcher shops with halal *or Middle Eastern clientele.*

1 sheep or lamb's head with tongue
4 sheep or lamb's feet
6 lamb tongues
6 cups water
2 large onions, peeled and quartered
4 cloves garlic, peeled and crushed
2 bay leaves

1 teaspoon turmeric
2 tablespoons white vinegar
2 teaspoons sea salt
1 teaspoon freshly ground pepper
1 teaspoon ground cinnamon
Croutons of toasted *sangak* bread

1. Sear sheep head and between the feet (cloven hoofs) over an open flame to burn off hairs. Make a slit between the hoofs and remove a hairy gland that is there. Scrape and wash thoroughly. Remove the nose completely. Split the head in half vertically, with the tongue in one half, unless the butcher has already done so. Rinse with cold water.

2. Bring 6 cups water to a boil and add the head, tongues, and feet. Skim froth as it forms; as soon as it stops forming add the onion, garlic, bay leaves, turmeric, and vinegar (to prevent discoloring, do not add salt until cooking is complete). Reduce heat to low, cover, and simmer for 3 to 4 hours until the meat separates easily from the bone. Add more warm water if necessary to keep the water level at a minimum of 3 cups. Remove bay leaves. Add salt, pepper, and cinnamon.

3. Remove the head from the soup, then peel the tongues and the skin off the bones. Separate the meat and brains from the skull. Return meat to broth and season to taste.

4. Pour soup into a tureen. Place croutons in each soup bowl before ladling out the soup. Serve with lots of Persian pickles (*torshi*), fresh herb platter (*sabzi-khordan*), and *sangak* bread. *Nush-e Jan!*

Tripe Soup

Makes 4 servings
Preparation time: 20 minutes
Cooking time: 4 hours

Sirab shir-dun

1 pound calf or lamb tripe, soaked, cleaned, rinsed, drained, and cut up
6 cups water
2 large onions, peeled and quartered
2 cloves garlic, peeled and crushed

2 whole bay leaves
1 teaspoon turmeric
2 tablespoons white vinegar
1 teaspoon sea salt
½ teaspoon freshly ground pepper

1. Place tripe in a heavy-bottomed pot with 6 cups water and bring to a boil. Skim froth as it forms; as soon as it stops forming add the onion, garlic, bay leaves, turmeric, and vinegar (do not add salt because it changes the color of the tripe). Cover and simmer over low heat for 3 to 4 hours or until tender. Skim broth occasionally while cooking. Add more warm water if necessary to keep level of water covering the tripe at a minimum of 3 cups.

2. Remove bay leaves. Add salt and pepper. Pour into a tureen and serve with Persian eggplant pickles (*torshi*), a platter of raw vegetables, fresh herbs, and *sangak* bread. *Nush-e Jan!*

Lamb Shank Soup with Green Herbs

Makes 4 servings
Preparation time: 10 minutes
Cooking time: 2 hours
15 minutes

Abgusht-e bozbash

2 pounds lamb shanks and 1 pound
  lamb breast
8 cups water
2 onions, peeled and quartered
1 cup dried kidney beans
2 teaspoons sea salt
½ teaspoon freshly ground
  black pepper
1 teaspoon turmeric
3 cups chopped fresh parsley
  or ¾ cup dried parsley

3 cups chopped spring onions
1 tablespoon dried or 4 tablespoons
  chopped fresh fenugreek leaves
3 tablespoons oil
4 whole dried *limu-omani* (dried
  Persian limes)*, pierced, or ¼ cup
  lime juice
5 large russet potatoes, peeled and cut
  in chunks
1 onion, peeled and sliced,
  for garnish

1. Place the lamb and 8 cups water in a large, heavy pot. Bring to boil, skimming the froth as it forms. Add the onions, beans, salt, pepper, and turmeric. Cover and simmer for 1½ hours over low heat.

2. In a wide skillet, sauté parsley, spring onions, and fenugreek in 3 tablespoons oil over medium heat for 3 minutes. Add them to the large pot.

3. Add *limu-omani* and potatoes, cover, and simmer over low heat for another 45 minutes or until the lamb and beans are tender. Add more warm water if necessary. Adjust seasoning to taste by adding more salt or lime juice.

4. Remove all of the ingredients, using a slotted spoon. Separate the meat from the bones, and mash the meat and the vegetables together to make the paste called *gusht kubideh*. Iranian cooks would use a mortar and pestle, but a food processor may be used instead. Pulse a few times, but beware not to make the paste too smooth (you want the consistency of lumpy mashed potatoes). Season to taste with salt and pepper and pile it up on a platter. Drizzle 3 tablespoons of broth over it. Garnish with onion slices.

5. Reheat the broth, adjust seasoning to taste, and serve in a bowl as soup. Serve the *gusht kubideh* with Persian pickles (*torshi*), a fresh herb platter of spring onions, radishes, fresh tarragon, basil, mint (*sabzi-khordan),* and *lavash* or pita bread. *Nush-e Jan!*

VARIATION

This dish may also be made with veal, beef, or turkey with the bone.

NOTE

If using dried herbs, place a sieve in a bowl of lukewarm water and soak the dried herbs for 20 minutes. Remove the sieve from the bowl and use the herbs.

Sun-Dried Yogurt Soup

Makes 4 servings
Preparation time: 20 minutes
Cooking time: 20 minutes

Kalleh jush

¼ cup oil
3 large onions, peeled and thinly sliced
10 cloves garlic, peeled and thinly sliced
½ teaspoon sea salt
½ teaspoon freshly ground
  black pepper
1 teaspoon turmeric
¼ cup raw ground walnuts

3 tablespoons dried mint flakes
2 cups liquid *kashk* (sun-dried yogurt)*
  diluted in 2 cups water

GARNISH
1 tablespoon chopped walnuts
1 tablespoon dried mint flakes
2 cups croutons

1. Heat the oil in a large, heavy pot over medium heat and brown the onions and garlic. Sprinkle with salt, pepper, turmeric, walnut, and mint flakes, and sauté for 20 seconds. Add 2 cups of water and bring to a boil. Reduce heat to medium, cover, and simmer for 5 minutes.

2. Slowly stir in the *kashk* with a wooden spoon, stirring constantly, and cook over low heat for 10 minutes. Do not allow the soup to come to a boil. Adjust seasoning to taste.

3. Remove from heat and pour into a tureen. Garnish soup with chopped walnuts and mint flakes. Serve with croutons. *Nush-e Jan!*

VARIATION

The walnuts may be replaced with raw hazelnuts, pistachios, or almonds.

Onion Soup

Makes 6 servings
Preparation time: 20 minutes
Cooking time: 1 hour 30 minutes

Eshkeneh

Photo on page 71

½ cup oil
4 onions, peeled and thinly sliced
1 teaspoon sea salt
½ teaspoon freshly ground
  black pepper
1 teaspoon turmeric
2 tablespoons flour
2 tablespoons dried fenugreek leaves
8 cups water

1 cup dried pitted tart cherries or 2
  tablespoons pomegranate molasses
  or ¼ cup lime juice
3 russet potatoes, peeled and cut
  in halves
1 tablespoon grape molasses or sugar
3 eggs

drained yogurt and *lavash* bread

1. In a large pot, heat the oil over medium heat until hot and sauté the onions until golden brown. Add salt, pepper, turmeric, flour, and fenugreek. Sauté for 1 minute. Add water, cherries, and potatoes. Bring to a boil, reduce heat, cover, and simmer over medium heat for 55 minutes or until the potatoes are tender. Adjust seasoning to taste.

2. Add the eggs and stir for a few minutes to combine them with the soup. (An alternate method is to add the eggs one by one and allow them to poach in the soup.)

3. Pour soup into a tureen and serve with drained yogurt and bread. *Nush-e Jan!*

Pistachio Soup

Makes 4 servings
Preparation time: 25 minutes
Cooking time: 1 hour

GARNISH
1 tablespoon oil
⅓ cup barberries, picked over and
  rinsed thoroughly with cold water
1 teaspoon grape molasses or sugar
2 tablespoons raw shelled pistachios,
  picked over and any shell bits removed

SOUP
1 cup raw shelled pistachios
2 tablespoons oil or butter
1 shallot, peeled and thinly chopped
1 leek (white and green parts), washed
  thoroughly and finely chopped

1 clove garlic, peeled and thinly sliced
½-inch fresh ginger, peeled and grated
1 tablespoon ground cumin
1 teaspoon ground coriander
½ teaspoon cayenne
1 tablespoon rice flour
8 cups homemade chicken broth
  (recipe on page 74)
1 teaspoon sea salt
¼ teaspoon pepper
1 teaspoon grape molasses or sugar
½ cup bitter orange juice or
  mixture of 2 tablespoons fresh lime
  juice and ¼ cup orange juice

سوپ پسته

Sup-e pesteh

VEGETARIAN VARIATION
Replace the chicken broth with
vegetable stock and proceed
with the recipe.

NOTE
For the garnish, replace the
barberries and pistachios with
⅓ cup fresh pomegranate arils
when in season. Pomegranate
and pistachio make a
wonderful combination.

The word "pistachio" comes from the Persian word pesteh. *One ancient nickname for the Persian people was "pistachio-eaters." According to a Greek chronicler, when King Astyages of the Medes gazed from his throne over his army, which had been defeated by Cyrus the Great, he exclaimed, "Woe, how brave are these pistachio-eating Persians!"*

1. To make the garnish: Heat 1 tablespoon oil in a medium-sized skillet over low heat. Add the barberries and grape molasses, and sauté for 1 minute (be careful, barberries burn easily). Add the pistachios and sauté for 20 seconds. Remove from heat and set aside.

2. To make the soup: Pick over the shelled pistachios to be sure there are no broken shells or other particles in them. Grind the pistachios in a food processor or grinder until very smooth. Set aside.

3. In a heavy, medium-sized pot, heat the oil over medium heat. Add the shallots, leeks, garlic, ginger, cumin, coriander, and cayenne. Sauté for 3 minutes. Add the rice flour and sauté for 1 minute. Add the broth, stirring constantly until it comes to a boil.

4. Reduce heat. Add pistachios, salt, pepper, and grape molasses. Stir well. Cover and simmer over low heat, stirring occasionally, for 55 minutes.

5. Add bitter orange juice. Adjust seasoning to taste.

6. Pour the soup into a tureen and garnish. Serve with hot flat bread. *Nush-e Jan!*

VARIATION

Pistachios can be substituted with either almonds or hazelnuts.

Cream of Barley

Makes 6 servings
Preparation time: 20 minutes
Cooking time: 3 hours (if using
*   homemade broth)*

سوپ جو

Sup-e jow

VEGETARIAN VARIATION

Eliminate step 1 and replace
the meat broth with
vegetable stock. Increase
the barley to 1 cup, and in
step 4, increase the sour
cream to 1 cup.

BEEF OR CHICKEN BROTH (HOMEMADE)
2 pounds beef or chicken bones
10 cups water
1 onion, peeled and chopped
1 teaspoon sea salt
¼ teaspoon freshly ground
  black pepper

SOUP
3 tablespoons oil
2 onions, peeled and thinly sliced
2 cloves garlic, peeled and sliced
1 carrot, peeled and sliced
3 leeks, white and green, washed
  thoroughly and finely chopped
½ cup barley

1 teaspoon sea salt
½ teaspoon freshly ground
  black pepper
8 cups broth (homemade instructions
  below, or use ready-made broth)
½ cup sour cream
Juice of 1 lime
1 teaspoon grape molasses or sugar

GARNISH
⅓ fresh chopped cilantro
⅓ cup fresh chopped tarragon
⅓ cup fresh chopped dill
⅓ cup chopped fresh parsley
Zest of ½ lime (optional)

1. To make homemade broth, place the bones in a large, heavy pot. Cover with 10 cups water. Bring to a boil, skimming the froth as it forms. Add the onion, salt, and pepper. Cover and simmer for 1 hour over medium-low heat. Drain in a fine-mesh colander and reserve the broth to use later (you can make this broth the day before).

2. In the same pot, heat the oil over medium heat and sauté the onions, garlic, carrot, and leeks for 5 minutes. Add the barley, salt, pepper, and the broth, and bring to a boil. Reduce heat to low, cover, and simmer for 1½ hours.

3. Use a handheld mixer to partially puree the soup. If the soup is too thick, add some warm water.

4. To temper the sour cream, in a small bowl stir together a few spoonfuls of soup and the sour cream. Add it to the soup. Add the lime juice and grape molasses. Cover and continue to simmer over low heat for 20 minutes. Keep warm until ready to serve.

5. Just before serving, add the herbs and the lime zest for the garnish and stir well. Correct seasoning to taste, adding more salt, pepper, or lime juice.

6. Pour soup into a tureen and serve with flat bread. *Nush-e Jan!*

Borscht

Makes 4 servings
Preparation time: 15 minutes
Cooking time: 2 hours
 35 minutes

1½ pounds fresh beef brisket, cut up
 and rinsed with cold water
8 cups water
2 medium onions, peeled and
 thinly sliced
2 cloves garlic, peeled and sliced
1 bay leaf
2 teaspoons sea salt
1 teaspoon freshly ground pepper
1 teaspoon smoked paprika
2 teaspoons ground cumin
3 large fresh beets (about 1½ pounds),
 peeled and diced into 1-inch cubes
 (leaves can also be washed, chopped,
 and included)
1 head cabbage (white, green, or red),
 shredded

1 carrot, peeled and diced into
 1-inch cubes
2 stalks of celery, diced into 1-inch cubes
2 large russet potatoes, peeled and
 diced into ½-inch cubes
1 large tomato, peeled and diced into
 1-inch cubes
1 teaspoon grape molasses or brown
 sugar
1 tablespoon wine vinegar

GARNISH
1 cup sour cream (or drained yogurt)
1 clove garlic, peeled and grated
1 cup chopped fresh dill
½ teaspoon ground cumin (optional)

Borsh

VEGETARIAN VARIATION
Eliminate the meat from the
ingredients and eliminate step
1. Begin with step 2. Use 8 cups
vegetable stock with all the
ingredients in step 2. Bring to a
boil and simmer for 15 minutes
over medium heat. In step 4
increase the number of
potatoes from 2 to 4 and add ½
teaspoon cayenne. Proceed
with the recipe.

This is a popular soup among the Armenians of Iran.

1. In a large, heavy-bottomed pot place the meat with 8 cups water. Bring to a boil over medium heat and skim any froth that forms.

2. Add onion, garlic, bay leaf, salt, pepper, paprika, and cumin. Cover and simmer for abut 1½ hours over medium heat.

3. Remove the bay leaf from the broth. Add beets, cover, and simmer for 30 minutes.

4. Add the rest of the ingredients. Cover and simmer over medium heat for 40 minutes longer.

5. Check to see if the meat and vegetables are tender. Adjust seasoning to taste, adding salt or vinegar if necessary. This soup should be reddish and slightly tart. Cover and keep warm until ready to serve.

6. To prepare the garnish: combine the sour cream, grated garlic, and fresh dill in a small serving bowl to accompany the soup. Pour soup into a tureen. Garnish individual serving bowls with a dollop of the sour cream mixture (and dust with ground cumin if you desire). *Nush-e Jan!*

VARIATION

You may use 8 cups beef or chicken broth instead of the meat, in which case begin with step 2.

HOT SOUP IN THE WINTER

When he was an old man the mulla thought of marrying again. One of his friends said contemptuously, "An old man like you, what kind of a time is this for you to think of getting married?"

The mulla said, "You poor fool, a man needs good hot soup in the winter much more than during the other seasons."

THE SMELL OF A THOUGHT

Mulla Nasruddin was penniless and sat huddled in a blanket while the wind howled outside. At least, he thought, the people next door will not smell cooking from my kitchen, so they can't send round to cadge some food.

At that, the thought of hot, aromatic soup came to his mind, and he savored it mentally for several minutes. Then there came a knocking on the door.

"Mother sent me," said the little girl, "to ask whether you had any soup to spare, hot seasoned soup."

"Heaven help us," said Mulla, "the neighbors even smell my thoughts."

Sweet and Sour Soup

Makes 6 servings
Preparation time: 30 minutes
Cooking time: 2 hours 10
  minutes

Osh-e miveh

VEGETARIAN VARIATION
Eliminate the meat from the
ingredients and replace it
with 1 pound firm tofu,
water squeezed out,
combined with 1½ cups
ground walnuts, 2 eggs, 1 cup
bread crumbs, and ½
teaspoon red pepper flakes.
Add to the rest of the
ingredients in step 3 to make
tofu balls. Add tofu balls in
step 5 and simmer for 10
minutes uncovered.

NOTE
If using dried herbs, place a
sieve in a bowl of lukewarm
water and soak the dried
herbs for 20 minutes. Remove
the sieve from the bowl and
use the herbs.

BROTH
¼ cup oil
2 onions, peeled and thinly sliced
1 teaspoon sea salt
½ teaspoon freshly black ground pepper
½ teaspoon turmeric
½ cup yellow split peas
10 cups water
1 cup chopped fresh parsley
½ cup chopped spring onions
½ cup chopped fresh beet leaves
¼ cup fresh chopped mint
  or 1 tablespoon dried
1 cup chopped fresh cilantro
1 cup dried pitted prunes
1 cup dried apricots
½ cup rice
¼ cup chopped walnuts

¼ cup grape molasses* or sugar
¼ cup red wine vinegar

MEATBALLS
1 onion, peeled and grated
1 pound ground lamb or chicken
1 teaspoon sea salt
½ teaspoon freshly ground pepper
½ teaspoon turmeric
½ teaspoon cinnamon
2 tablespoons chopped fresh parsley

GARNISH *(NA'NA DAGH)*
2 tablespoons oil
1 large onion, peeled and finely sliced
5 cloves garlic, peeled and thinly sliced
½ teaspoon turmeric
2 tablespoons dried mint flakes,
  crushed

1. To make the broth: Heat the oil in a large heavy-bottomed pot over medium heat until hot. Add the onion and sauté until golden brown. Add the salt, pepper, and turmeric. Add the split peas and sauté for 2 minutes. Pour in the water. Bring to a boil, reduce heat to medium, cover and simmer for 25, stirring occasionally.

2. Add the parsley, spring onions, beet leaves, mint, and cilantro to the pot. Cover and simmer for 25 minutes longer.

3. To make the meatballs: In a mixing bowl, combine the grated onion, ground lamb, salt, pepper, turmeric, cinnamon, and parsley. Knead lightly (do not overmix) and with moist hands shape into meatballs the size of walnuts, and add them to the simmering broth. Bring back to a boil, add the prunes, and apricots to the pot. Partially cover and simmer over low heat, for 25 minutes longer.

4. Add the rice and walnuts. Cover and simmer for 45 minutes longer.

5. Mix the grape molasses and vinegar together and stir into the soup. Simmer uncovered for 10 minutes longer. Season to taste and add more molasses or vinegar if needed. Keep warm until ready to serve.

6. To prepare the garnish: Heat 2 tablespoons oil in a medium-sized skillet over medium heat. Add the onion and garlic and sauté until golden brown. Add the turmeric, give it a stir, and remove from heat. Crumble the dried mint flakes in the palm of your hand and add it to the skillet. Stir well and set aside.

7. Pour the soup into a tureen and garnish. Stir the garnish in just before ladling soup into individual bowls. Serve with Persian flat bread. *Nush-e Jan!*

Mung Bean and Turnip Soup

Makes 6 servings
Preparation time: 20 minutes
Cooking time: 2 hours

Osh-e maash

⅓ cup oil
3 large onions, peeled and thinly sliced
5 cloves garlic, peeled and crushed
1 teaspoon sea salt
1 teaspoon freshly ground black pepper
1 teaspoon turmeric
1 cup dried mung beans
10 cups broth or water
½ cup rice
2 cups peeled and diced turnip
1 pound butter squash or kohlrabi
   (German turnip), peeled and diced
1 cup chopped fresh cilantro or ¼ cup
   dried cilantro
½ cup fresh chopped tarragon
2 cups chopped fresh parsley
   or ½ cup dried

½ cup chopped fresh dill
   or 2 tablespoons dried
1 cup chopped chives or
   ¼ cup dried chives
2 cups pearl onions, blanched and
   peeled (see note below)
1 teaspoon grape molasses or sugar
1 cup liquid *kashk* (sun-dried yogurt)*

GARNISH *(NA'NA DAGH)*
2 tablespoons oil
1 large onion, peeled and finely sliced
5 cloves garlic, peeled and thinly sliced
1 teaspoon turmeric
1 tablespoon dried mint flakes

VEGETARIAN VARIATION
Replace the broth with vegetable stock, and then proceed with the recipe.

NOTES
To blanch the pearl onions, drop them into scalding hot water for about 1 minute. Remove with a slotted spoon, place in bowl of ice water, and peel by placing in a towel and rubbing.

If using dried herbs, place a sieve in a bowl of lukewarm water and soak the dried herbs for 20 minutes. Remove the sieve from the bowl and use the herbs.

1. In a large heavy pot, heat the oil over medium heat and brown the onions and garlic. Add salt, pepper, and turmeric. Add the mung beans and sauté for 2 minutes. Pour in the broth. Bring to a boil. Reduce heat to medium-low, cover, and simmer for 20 minutes, stirring from time to time.

2. Add the rice, turnip, squash, cilantro, tarragon, parsley, dill, chives, pearl onions, and grape molasses. Cover and simmer over low heat for another 1½ hours, stirring occasionally.

3. Check to see if beans and vegetables are done. Use a hand-held mixer to partially puree the soup. Add the *kashk* and stir well for 5 minutes. Adjust seasoning to taste. Keep warm until read to serve.

4. To prepare the garnish: Heat 2 tablespoons oil in a medium-sized skillet over medium heat. Add the onion and garlic and sauté until golden brown. Add the turmeric, give it a stir, and remove from heat. Crumble the dried mint flakes in the palm of your hand and add it to the skillet. Stir well and set aside.

5. Pour soup into a tureen. Decorate the surface of the soup with the garnish. Stir the garnish in just before ladling soup into individual bowls. *Nush-e Jan!*

VARIATIONS

Qeymeh (page XXX) prepared without the potatoes may be used for garnish.

You can add 3 eggplants—peeled, sliced, and fried on both sides—in step 3.

You can add 1 cup ground walnuts in step 2.

Beggar's Soup

Makes 8 servings
Preparation time: 20 minutes
Cooking time: 3 hours

Osh-e sholeh qalamkar

4 tablespoons oil
3 onions, peeled and thinly sliced
5 cloves garlic, peeled and sliced
1 pound stew beef (lamb, or veal)
2 teaspoons sea salt
½ teaspoon freshly ground
　black pepper
1 teaspoon turmeric
⅓ cup dried red kidney beans
½ cup dried lentils
¼ cup dried chickpeas
¼ cup dried mung beans
12 cups water or broth
2 cups chopped fresh parsley
　or ½ cup dried

1 cup chopped fresh cilantro or
　¼ cup dried
¼ cup chopped fresh dill
　or 1 tablespoon dried
1 pound fresh spinach, washed and
　chopped, or ½ pound frozen
　spinach, chopped
1 cup chopped chives or spring onions
　or ¼ cup dried chives
½ cup rice

GARNISH *(NA'NA DAGH)*
2 tablespoons oil
1 onion, peeled and thinly sliced
3 cloves garlic, peeled and thinly sliced
¼ teaspoon turmeric
2 tablespoons dried mint

In the past, people used to leave a kettle by the side of the road to make a wish come true. Passersby would throw in a few coins to be used to buy the ingredients for the soup. The more people pitched in, the better the chances of the wish coming true. Thus was born beggar's soup. Today, although kettles are no longer left at the roadside (perhaps for fear they would disappear!), the custom lives on in a new form. Friends are told in advance on what day a wish is going to be made. That morning, each one arrives bringing a few ingredients for the soup. They prepare it together and sit down to share it at the midday meal. This way everyone can join in making a loved one's wish come true.

1. In a large, heavy pot heat the oil over medium heat, add the onion and garlic, and cook until golden. Push to one side and brown the meat. Add the salt, pepper, turmeric, kidney beans, lentils, chickpeas, and mung beans. Sauté for 2 minutes. Pour in the water and bring to a boil. Reduce heat to medium-low, cover, and simmer for 1 hour.

2. Add parsley, cilantro, dill, spinach, and chives. Simmer for 40 minutes longer, stirring occasionally to avoid sticking.

3. Add the rice. Cover and simmer for 55 minutes longer over low heat.

4. Check to be sure the meat is tender and beans are done. If you desire, use a handheld mixer to partially puree the soup (this gives the soup a rich thickness). Adjust seasoning to taste. Cover and keep warm until ready to serve.

5. To prepare the garnish: Heat 2 tablespoons oil in a medium-sized skillet over medium heat. Add the onion and garlic and sauté until golden brown. Add the turmeric, give it a stir, and remove from heat. Crumble the dried mint flakes in the palm of your hand and add them to the skillet. Stir well and set aside.

6. Pour soup into a tureen. Decorate the surface of the soup with the garnish. Stir the garnish in just before ladling soup into individual bowls. *Nush-e Jan!*

VEGETARIAN VARIATION
Osh-e Ommaj, eliminate the meat, chick peas and kidney beans from the ingredients, and replace them with pasta balls. To make the pasta balls (ommaj), place 2 cups of flour in a colander, sprinkle with a little water, and allow to rest for 20 seconds. Shake the colander over a baking sheet so balls of dough will fall into the baking sheet. Spread them around in the sheet and bake in a 350°F (180°C) oven for 10 minutes. Add them to the soup at the end of step 4 and cook for 5 more minutes.

Pomegranate Soup

Makes 6 servings
Preparation time: 20 minutes
Cooking time: 2 hours

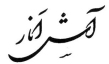

Osh-e anar

Eliminate the meat from the ingredients and replace it with 1 pound firm tofu, water squeezed out, combined with 1½ cups ground walnuts, 2 eggs, 1 cup bread crumbs, and ½ teaspoon red pepper flakes. Add to the rest of the ingredients in step 2 to make tofu balls. Add them in step 4.

NOTE

If using dried herbs, place a sieve in a bowl of lukewarm water and soak the dried herbs for 20 minutes. Remove the sieve from the bowl and use the herbs.

For best results, make the osh a day in advance to give the flavors a chance to meld. Reheat it just before serving.

You can replace the pomegranate molasses dissolved in water with 2 cups fresh pomegranate juice.

BROTH
3 tablespoons oil
3 onions, peeled and thinly sliced
3 cloves garlic, peeled and sliced
½ cup yellow split peas
1 teaspoon sea salt
½ teaspoon freshly ground pepper
1 teaspoon turmeric
½ teaspoon cinnamon
10–12 cups water
2 cups chopped fresh parsley,
2 cups chopped fresh cilantro
    or ½ cup dried
1 cup chopped fresh mint, or ¼ cup dried
1 beet, peeled and chopped
2 cups chopped fresh spring onions
1 cup rice
⅔ cup pomegranate molasses diluted
    in 2 cups water
⅓ cup grape molasses or sugar
2 tablespoons angelica powder *(gol-par)*

MEATBALLS
1 onion, peeled and grated
1 pound ground lamb
    (or beef, or chicken)
1 teaspoon salt
½ teaspoon freshly ground pepper
½ teaspoon turmeric
½ teaspoon cinnamon
2 tablespoons chopped fresh parsley
2 tablespoons chopped fresh mint

GARNISH *(NA'NA DAGH)*
2 tablespoons oil
5 cloves garlic, peeled and sliced
½ teaspoon turmeric
2 tablespoons dried mint flakes
1 cup pomegranate arils*

1. To make the broth: Heat 3 tablespoons oil in a large, heavy pot over medium heat and brown the 3 sliced onions and garlic. Add split peas, salt, pepper, turmeric, cinnamon, and sauté for 1 minute. Add 12 cups water and bring to a boil. Reduce heat to low, cover and simmer for 20 minutes. Add the parsley, cilantro, mint, beet, and spring onions. Cover and simmer for 20 minutes longer, stirring occasionally to prevent sticking.

2. To make the meatballs: Grease a baking sheet and place it next to you on the counter. In a mixing bowl, combine the grated onion, lamb, salt, pepper, turmeric, parsley, and mint. Knead lightly (do not overmix) and with moist hands shape into chestnut-sized meatballs and place them gently on the baking sheet as you make them.

3. Gently add the meatballs to the pot and bring back to boil. Add rice, reduce heat to low, cover and simmer for 55 minutes longer.

4. Stir in pomegranate molasses, grape molasses, and angelica powder, and simmer uncovered over low heat for 10 minutes longer.

5. Check a meatball to see if it is cooked. Add warm water if the soup is too thick to your taste. Adjust seasoning to taste (it should be sweet and sour). Cover and keep warm until ready to serve.

6. To prepare the garnish: Heat 2 tablespoons oil in a medium-sized skillet over medium heat. Add the onion and garlic and sauté until golden brown. Add the turmeric, give it a stir, and remove from heat. Crumble the dried mint flakes in the palm of your hand and add it to the skillet. Stir well and set aside.

7. Pour soup into a tureen. Decorate with the garnish and pomegranate arils. Stir the garnish in just before ladling soup into individual bowls. *Nush-e Jan!*

Spinach Soup

Makes 6 servings
Preparation time: 20 minutes
Cooking time: 1 hour
* 40 minutes*

BROTH
3 tablespoons oil
2 medium onions, peeled and sliced
2 cloves garlic, peeled and sliced
1 teaspoon sea salt
½ teaspoon freshly ground
  black pepper
1 teaspoon turmeric
8 cups water or broth
1 pound spinach, washed and chopped,
  or frozen spinach
½ cup rice flour diluted in 1 cup water

3 eggs, lightly beaten
½ cup verjuice (*ab-ghureh*, unripe
  grape juice),* or bitter orange juice or
  mixture ¼ cup lime juice and ¼ cup
  orange juice

MEATBALLS
1 onion, peeled and grated
1 pound ground lamb (beef or chicken)
1 teaspoon salt
½ teaspoon freshly ground black pepper
½ teaspoon turmeric
2 tablespoons dried mint

Osh-e saak

VEGETARIAN VARIATION
Eliminate the meat from the
ingredients and replace it with
1 pound firm tofu, water
squeezed out, combined with
1½ cups ground almonds, 2
eggs, 1 cup bread crumbs, and
½ teaspoon red pepper flakes.
Add to the rest of the
ingredients in step 2 to make
tofu balls. Gently add the tofu
balls to the soup in step 4 after
the verjuice.

1. To make the broth: Heat the oil in a large, heavy pot over medium heat. Brown the onions and the garlic. Add salt, pepper, and turmeric, and sauté for 20 seconds. Add the water and spinach, cover, and simmer for 20 minutes over medium heat.

2. To make the meatballs: In a mixing bowl, combine the grated onion, ground lamb, salt, pepper, turmeric, and dried mint. Knead lightly and, with moist hands, shape into chestnut-sized meatballs and gently add to the pot. Cover, and simmer for 40 minutes over low heat.

3. Gradually stir in the diluted rice flour and keep stirring gently for 3 minutes. Gently stir in the eggs and keep stirring for 3 minutes longer. Cover and simmer for 10 minutes.

4. Add verjuice and adjust seasoning to taste. Simmer uncovered over low heat for 10 minutes longer. Pour soup into a tureen and serve with hot bread. *Nush-e Jan!*

Golden Plum Soup

Makes 6 servings
Preparation time: 40 minutes
Cooking time: 2½ hours

آش آلو

Osh-e alu

VEGETARIAN VARIATION

Eliminate the meat from the ingredients and from step 1. Increase the chickpeas to ½ cup and proceed with the recipe.

NOTE

If using dried herbs, place a sieve in a bowl of lukewarm water and soak the dried herbs for 20 minutes. Remove the sieve from the bowl and use the herbs.

The flavors will meld for a richer result if you make your soup the night before. Just before serving, warm up the soup and add the garnish mixture of browned onion, garlic, and mint to the soup.

1 whole chicken (about 2 pounds), thoroughly washed inside and out
2 medium onions, peeled and thinly sliced
2 teaspoons sea salt
½ teaspoon freshly ground black pepper
1 teaspoon turmeric
¼ cup dried chickpeas, rinsed and soaked for at least 2 hours, drained
8 cups water
2 cups chopped fresh parsley leaves or ½ cup dried
1 cup chopped fresh chives or ¼ cup dried chives
1 cup chopped fresh mint or ¼ cup dried
2 cups chopped fresh cilantro or ½ cup dried
4 cups small fresh baby green plums or 2 cups dried golden Persian plums (*alu*)
1 cup rice

GARNISH (*NA'NA DAGH*)
2 tablespoons oil
1 large onion, peeled and thinly sliced
5 cloves garlic, peeled and thinly sliced
¼ teaspoon turmeric
3 teaspoons dried mint flakes

This soup is an excellent remedy for cold symptoms. My mother would make it whenever someone in the family had a cold.

1. In a large pot, place the chicken and onions. Sprinkle with the salt, pepper, and turmeric and add the chickpeas. Add the water and bring to boil. Reduce heat to medium, cover, and simmer for 45 minutes, stirring occasionally.

2. Add parsley, chives, mint, and cilantro. Cover and simmer over medium-low heat for 25 minutes longer.

3. Add plums, cover, and simmer for 25 minutes longer.

4. Add rice, cover, and simmer over low heat for 45 minutes longer. Check to see if the chickpeas are cooked.

5. Add more warm water if *osh* is too thick. Adjust seasoning to taste.

6. To prepare the garnish: Heat 2 tablespoons oil in a medium-sized skillet over medium heat. Add the onion and garlic and sauté until golden brown. Add the turmeric, give it a stir, and remove from heat. Crumble the dried mint flakes in the palm of your hand and add it to the skillet. Stir well and set aside.

7. Pour soup into a tureen. Decorate the surface of the soup with the garnish. Stir the garnish in just before ladling soup into individual bowls. Serve with Persian flat bread (*sangak* or *lavash*). *Nush-e Jan!*

VARIATION

Instead of a whole chicken, you may use 1 pound ground lamb or chicken to make meatballs. Combine ground meat with 1 grated onion, ½ teaspoon salt, and ¼ teaspoon pepper. Mix well and shape into meatballs the size of hazelnuts. Add to the soup in step 3.

MEMORIES OF MAKING NOODLES FOR OSH-E RESHTEH

Some of my happiest childhood memories are linked to my mother's noodle-making days for the *shab-e chardah* (fourteenth day of the month) festivities at our house in downtown Tehran. On those days, if I arrived home early in the afternoon, I would hear distant echoes of a setar and my mother singing verses by the thirteenth-century poet Rumi, a great favorite of hers:

Oh listen to the flute as it complains

بشنو از نی چون حکایت میکند   ازجدائیها شکایت میکند

The sweet, sad tones drew me to the brightest room in our house, where, sitting on the Persian carpet striped with light and color from the sunshine that seeped through bamboo shades, I found my mother and four or five old ladies, all distant relatives. From the crisply ironed white cotton cloths being spread over the carpet and the captivating aroma of fresh dough, I knew it was noodle-making day. "Come on in," said the old ladies, tearing off a piece of dough for me to play with.

They were kneading dough and rolling it into rectangles on large wooden boards. When they had rolled it thin, they folded each sheet twice; then, with one hand as a guide and working with fast, confident strokes, they used sharp knives to cut their dough sheets into quarter-inch strips. The room would fall silent as they concentrated on the task, joyfully competing to see who could cut the most even strips in the shortest time.

Every so often, as if reminded by something, my mother would stop cutting, put down her knife, and continue to sing her poem from where she had left off:

In anguished tales of separation's pains;
Since they have torn me from the reedbed I
Make men and women heartsick with my sigh . . .

از نفیــم مردوزن نالیــده اند   کزنیــتان تا مرابریــده اند

Everyone would stop working, some still kneading the dough, some with finished strips in hand. All would lean back from their work and join in the refrain:

Oh listen to the flute as it complains

Just as quickly as it had started, the singing would stop. Tea would appear and there would be some gossip, a few new jokes, and lots of laughing. Then, as if on cue, everyone would go back to work. One of the old ladies would give me some strands of the fresh noodles to arrange, carefully separated for drying, on the floured cotton sheets.

I found myself as delighted by the cheerful ceremony of preparation as by the reward for the work. The next day, convivial crowds of relatives would come to our house for a glorious Friday lunch of noodle soup garnished with fried garlic, onion, mint, and *kashk* (sun-dried yogurt).

See recipe and photo on the next two pages.

Noodle Soup

Makes 8 servings
Preparation time: 20 minutes
Cooking time: 3 hours

Osh-e reshteh

¼ cup oil
3 large onions, peeled and thinly sliced
5 cloves garlic, peeled and sliced
2 teaspoons sea salt
1 teaspoon freshly ground black pepper
1 teaspoon turmeric
¼ cup dried red kidney beans, washed and soaked in cold water for at least 4 hours, and then drained
¼ cup dried navy beans, rinsed and soaked for at least 4 hours, then drained
¼ cup dried chickpeas, rinsed, soaked for at least 4 hours, then drained
12–14 cups broth or water
1 cup lentils
½ pound Persian noodles *(reshteh)* or whole-wheat linguine noodles, broken in half
1 cup coarsely chopped fresh chives or spring onions

1 cup chopped fresh dill weed
2 cups coarsely chopped fresh parsley
3 pounds fresh spinach, washed and coarsely chopped, or 2 pounds chopped frozen spinach
1 fresh beet, peeled and diced in ½-inch pieces (optional)
1½ cups liquid *kashk* (sun-dried yogurt)*
½ cup verjuice *(ab-ghureh,* unripe grape juice)*

QEYMEH
A diced lamb garnish (optional, page 342)

GARNISH (NA'NA DAGH)
2 tablespoons oil
1 onion, peeled and finely sliced
10 cloves garlic, peeled and sliced
1 teaspoon turmeric
¼ cup dried mint flakes, crushed

1. Heat ¼ cup oil in a large, heavy pot over medium heat until hot. Add the onions and garlic and cook until golden brown. Add salt, pepper, turmeric, kidney beans, navy beans, and chickpeas, and sauté for 2 minutes. Pour in 12 cups broth and bring to a boil. Reduce heat, cover, and simmer for 45 minutes over medium heat.

2. Add the lentils, cover, and cook for 55 minutes longer. Check to be sure the beans are tender. Use a handheld mixer to partially puree the soup.

3. Add noodles and cook about 10 minutes, stirring occasionally.

4. Add all the herbs and the beet. Cover and cook, stirring from time to time for 10 minutes. Check to be sure the beans are tender.

5. Stir in the *kashk,* saving a dollop for the garnish. Add the verjuice and stir well with a wooden spoons for 5 minutes until the *kashk* is thoroughly incorporated. Add more warm water if the *osh* is too thick. Adjust seasoning to taste. Cover and keep warm until ready to serve.

6. Prepare the *qeymeh* without the potatoes by following the recipe on page 342.

7. To prepare the garnish: Heat 2 tablespoons oil in a medium-sized skillet over medium heat. Add the onion and garlic and sauté until golden brown. Add the turmeric, give it a stir, and remove from heat. Crumble the dried mint flakes in the palm of your hand and add it to the skillet. Stir well and set aside.

8. Pour the soup into a tureen. Garnish with the *na'na dagh, qeymeh,* and a dollop of *kashk.* Just before serving, use a long-handled ladle to stir the garnish, incorporating it into the soup. *Nush-e Jan!*

Kashk Soup Sanandaj-Style

Makes: 6 servings
Preparation time: 30 minutes
Cooking time: 1 hour 45 minutes

آش کشک

Osh-e kashk-e Sanandaj

BROTH
2 tablespoons oil or butter
2 onion, peeled and sliced
1 teaspoon sea salt
½ teaspoon fresh ground pepper
1 teaspoon turmeric
1 teaspoon *advieh* (Persian spice mix)*
3 tablespoons dried mint
1 cup chickpeas, soaked in water for at
  least 4 hours, then drained
8 cups chicken broth, or water

MEATBALLS
1 pound ground lamb or beef
1 onion, peeled and grated
½ teaspoon sea salt
½ teaspoon fresh ground pepper
1 teaspoon *advieh* (Persian spice mix)*
2 teaspoons ground rose petals
2 teaspoons angelica powder
1 teaspoon dried thyme
½ cup rice
½ cup fresh chopped dill
½ cup fresh chopped tarragon
1 cup liquid *kashk* (sun-dried yogurt)*

1. To make the broth: In a large pot, heat the oil over medium heat until hot. Add the sliced onions and sauté until golden. Add salt, pepper, turmeric, *advieh*, mint, and the chickpeas. Stir-fry for 20 seconds. Add the broth and bring to a boil. Reduce heat to medium-low, cover, and simmer for 55 minutes.

2. To make the meatballs: In a mixing bowl, combine the lamb, grated onion, salt, pepper, *advieh*, rose petals, angelica powder, and thyme. Knead lightly and shape into hazelnut-sized meatballs, and gently add them to the simmering pot.

3. Add the rice and bring to a boil. Reduce heat to low, cover, and simmer for another 45 minutes until chickpeas are tender. When ready to serve, add the dill, tarragon, and *kashk*, stirring for 5 minutes. Adjust seasoning to taste. *Nush-e Jan!*

Oat Soup

Makes: 6 servings
Preparation time: 20 minutes
Cooking time: 1 hour

سوپ جو دوسر

Sup-e jow-e do sar

¼ cup oil
2 onions, peeled and thinly sliced
1 pound potatoes, peeled and diced
1 large turnip, peeled and diced
1 zucchini, diced
2 stalks celery, diced
2 carrots, peeled and diced
¼ pound white cabbage, shredded

1 teaspoon sea salt
1 teaspoon fresh ground pepper
8 cups chicken broth
½ cup oats
2 tablespoons fresh lime juice

GARNISH
½ cup chopped fresh dill

1. Heat oil in a pot and add all the vegetables, salt, and pepper, and stir-fry for 2 minutes. Add the chicken broth and bring to a boil. Add the oats, cover, and simmer over medium heat for 55 minutes. Check to be sure all the vegetables are tender. Use a hand mixer to partially puree the soup. Add the lime juice and stir well. Adjust seasoning to taste. Keep warm until ready to serve.

2. Just before serving, add the dill, stir well, pour into a tureen, and serve with hot flat bread. *Nush-e Jan!*

Azerbaijani-Style Dumpling Soup

Makes: 6 servings
Preparation time: 20 minutes
Cooking time: 1 hour

دوش بَرَه

Dush bareh

VEGETARIAN VARIATION

Eliminate the meat from the ingredients and from step 4. Replace it with ¾ cup lentils, 1¼ cups bulgur, and ½ teaspoon red pepper flakes, cooked in 3 cups water for 30 minutes, and then drain. Combine with the rest of the ingredients in step 4 to make a lentil and bulgur filling. Proceed with the recipe.

NOTE

You can use ready-made dumpling wraps instead of making your own.

DOUGH
2 cups unbleached all-purpose flour
½ teaspoon baking powder
½ teaspoon salt
2 eggs
1 tablespoon oil
½ cup water

BROTH
6 cups chicken broth
4 large fresh tomatoes, peeled and finely chopped
1 teaspoon salt
½ teaspoon freshly ground pepper
½ teaspoon red pepper flakes
¼ teaspoon smoked paprika

FILLING
3 tablespoons oil or butter
½ pound ground lamb
1 onion, peeled and grated
½ teaspoon salt
½ teaspoon freshly ground black pepper
½ teaspoon turmeric
1 teaspoon dried oregano

GARNISH
½ cup chopped cilantro or parsley
1 tablespoon rice vinegar
1 cup drained yogurt (optional)

1. To make the dough: In a wide mixing bowl, whisk together flour, baking powder, and salt. Make a well in the center, and add the egg, oil, and water. Use your index and middle fingers to swirl together, starting at the center in a circular motion and bringing the flour into the well. Continue until you have a stiff dough.

2. On a floured board, knead the dough until soft and pliable. Cover with plastic wrap and allow to rest.

3. To make the tomato broth: in a medium saucepan, combine the broth, tomato, salt, pepper, pepper flakes, and paprika. Bring to a boil. Reduce heat and allow to simmer over low heat for 30 minutes.

4. To make the filling: In a wide skillet, heat the oil, and add the meat, onion, salt, pepper, turmeric, and oregano, and sauté until golden brown and all the juices have been absorbed. Set aside and allow to cool.

5. To assemble the dumplings: Place a baking sheet next to you and dust with flour. On a cool, floured board, knead the dough and use a rolling pin to roll it out very thin. Cut the dough into 3-inch-diameter circles, using a cookie cutter (or with the open end of a glass) dipped in flour. Fill each circle with 2 teaspoons of the filling. Fold each circle into a crescent shape, seal the edges with your fingers, and, using a fork, press the dough around the filling to double seal it. Gently place them, side by side, on the flour-dusted baking sheet.

6. Carefully transfer the dumplings into the simmering broth. Cook over low heat for 45 to 50 minutes, stirring gently once or twice to avoid any dumplings sticking to the bottom of the pan.

7. Just before serving, add cilantro and rice vinegar. Adjust seasoning to taste by adding salt, red pepper flakes, or rice vinegar. Serve with yogurt *Nush-e Jan!*

Lasagna Soup

½ cup oil
2 large onions, peeled and thinly sliced
4 cloves garlic, peeled and sliced
1 teaspoon sea salt
1 teaspoon freshly ground
   black pepper
1 teaspoon turmeric
2 tablespoons dried mint flakes

6 cups water or broth
¼ pound wide flat lasagna noodles cut
   into 2-inch lengths
1 pound chopped fresh spinach
2 cups liquid *kashk* (sun-dried yogurt)*
Garnish: 1 tablespoon dried mint flakes
   and 2 tablespoons chopped walnuts

Makes 6 servings
Preparation time: 20 minutes
Cooking time: 1 hour 15 minutes

1. In a large, heavy pot, heat the oil over medium heat until hot. Add the onions and garlic and sauté until golden brown. Add salt, pepper, turmeric, and mint flakes, and sauté for 20 seconds.

2. Add the water and bring to a boil. Reduce heat and simmer for 10 minutes. Add the noodles and bring back to a boil. Reduce heat to low and allow to simmer uncovered for 20 minutes. Add the spinach and simmer for another 10 minutes.

3. Reduce heat to very low and slowly stir in the *kashk*, stirring constantly for 5 minutes. Adjust seasoning to taste.

4. Remove from heat and pour into a tureen. Garnish with mint flakes and chopped walnuts. *Nush-e Jan!*

Osh-e lakhshak

Nomad Yogurt Soup

½ cup oil
2 large onions, peeled and thinly sliced
2 cloves garlic, peeled and crushed
2 teaspoons salt
2 teaspoons freshly ground
   black pepper
1 teaspoon turmeric
2 tablespoons dried mint flakes

4 *tarkhineh* patties soaked in 8 cups
   warm water for 20 minutes*
2 cups mung beans
1 cup fresh chopped parsley
1 cup fresh chopped cilantro
1 cup fresh chopped dill
1 cup fresh chopped spinach

Makes 6 servings
Preparation time: 20 minutes
Cooking time: 1¼ hours

1. Heat oil in a medium-sized pot over medium heat and brown onions and garlic. Add the salt, pepper, turmeric, and mint flakes, and sauté for 20 seconds.

2. Add the *tarkhineh* with its water and bring to a boil. Reduce heat to medium, cover, and cook for 20 minutes, stirring occasionally. Add the mung beans, bring back to a boil, cover, and cook over medium heat for 30 minutes.

3. Add the herbs and continue to cook for another 15 minutes. Adjust seasoning to taste. Remove from heat and pour into a tureen. *Nush-e Jan!*

Osh-e tarkhineh

NOTE

Tarkhineh is a yogurt and bulgur preparation dried into patties and popular in Kurdistan. Ready-made tarkhineh *patties can be found at some Persian grocers. You can also make your own (page 533). The walnuts may be replaced with hazelnuts, pistachios, or almonds.*

Sumac Soup

Makes 6 servings
Preparation time: 20 minutes
* plus 2 hours of soaking time*
Cooking time: 2 hours
* 40 minutes*

آش سماق

Osh-e somaq

VEGETARIAN VARIATION

Eliminate the meat from the
ingredients and from step 4.
Replace with 1 pound firm
tofu, water squeezed out,
combined with 1½ cups
ground raw, shelled pistachios
(or almonds), 2 eggs, 1 cup
bread crumbs, ½ teaspoon
red pepper flakes, and the rest
of the ingredients for
meatballs. Form the tofu balls
and gently add them to the
soup in step 5.

BROTH
3 cups sumac powder
3 tablespoons oil
1 large onion, peeled and thinly sliced
1 teaspoon sea salt
½ teaspoon freshly ground
  black pepper
1 teaspoon turmeric
2 cups rice
8 cups broth or water
2 cups chopped fresh parsley or ¾ cup
  dried
2 cups chopped fresh cilantro or
  ½ cup dried
1 cup chopped fresh mint
  or ¼ cup dried
1 cup chopped fresh tarragon
  or ¼ cup dried

1 cup chopped fresh summer savory, or
  ¼ cup dried

MEATBALLS
1 large onion, peeled and grated
1 pound ground lamb, beef, or chicken
  thighs
1 teaspoon sea salt
½ teaspoon freshly ground
  black pepper
½ teaspoon turmeric
2 tablespoons parsley
2 tablespoons sumac powder
1 tablespoon grape molasses or sugar

GARNISH (NA'NA DAGH)
2 tablespoons oil
5 cloves garlic, peeled and sliced
1 teaspoon dried mint flakes
½ teaspoon turmeric

1. To make the broth: Place 3 cups sumac and 6 cups water in a large, heavy pot and bring to a boil. Reduce heat to medium and simmer for 35 minutes. Drain through a fine-mesh sieve set over a bowl, reserving the sumac water and discarding the sumac.

2. Heat the oil in the same large, heavy pot over medium heat and brown the sliced onion. Add salt, pepper, turmeric, and rice. Sauté for 1 minute. Add the broth and bring to a boil.

3. Add herbs and sumac water, cover, and simmer for 45 minutes longer.

4. Meanwhile, to make the meatballs: Combine the grated onion, lamb, salt, pepper, turmeric, parsley, and sumac powder. Knead lightly (do not overmix) and shape into chestnut-sized meatballs. Gently add to the pot and bring back to a boil. Add grape molasses, reduce heat to low, partially cover, and simmer for 1 hour.

5. Taste soup for seasoning—it should be both sweet and sour—add more grape molasses or sumac if necessary. Simmer uncovered for 10 minutes longer.

6. Just before serving, prepare the garnish. Heat 2 tablespoons oil in a skillet and brown the garlic. Remove from heat. Crumble the dried mint flakes in the palm of your hand and add to the garlic. Add the turmeric and mix well.

7. Pour the soup into a tureen and garnish. *Nush-e Jan!*

THE CHICKPEA STORY

بنگر اندر نخودی در دیگ چون *** می جهد بالا چو شد ز آتش زبون

هر زمان نخو براید وقت جوش *** بر سر دیگ و برآرد صد خروش

که چرا آتش بمن در می زنی *** چون خریدی من چنین کوثم می کنی

می زند کفگیر که نه خوش بجوش *** خوش بجوش و در مجه ز آتش گریز

زآن بجوشانم ترا که مکرو منجی *** بلکه تا گیری تو ذوق و صاحبی

یا غذای گردی و ساموزی بجانه *** بهر خواری نیست این آتش نه

In a dialog between the chickpea in the noodle soup *osh-e reshteh* and the cook, the chickpea cries, "Why are you setting the fire on me? Since you bought me and approved of me, why are you turning me upside down?"

The cook replies, "I am not boiling you because I hate you but rather to make you tastier and more savory, so that you may become nutriment and mingle with the vital spirit. You, when green and fresh, were drinking water in the garden: that water-drinking was for the sake of this fire."

Jalal al-Din Rumi

Yogurt Soup

Makes 6 servings
Preparation time: 10 minutes
Cooking time: 2 hours
* 50 minutes*

آش ماست

Osh-e mast

VEGETARIAN VARIATION

Eliminate the meat. Replace it
with ¾ cup lentils, and 1¼
cups bulgur. Cook in
4 cups water over medium
heat for 30 minutes and
drain. Combine with 2 eggs,
½ teaspoon red pepper
flakes, and the rest of the
ingredients in step 2 to make
lentil and bulgur balls.
Proceed with the recipe. Add
the bulgur balls in step 7,
simmer uncovered for 5
minutes, and then prepare
the garnish.

VARIATION

You may substitute the meat
balls with ½ pound giblets. In
this case, brown the sliced
onions and giblets together
in step 1.

BROTH
¼ cup oil
2 large onions, peeled and thinly sliced
1 teaspoon sea salt
¼ teaspoon freshly ground
  black pepper
½ teaspoon turmeric
½ cup dried chickpeas, soaked in water
  for at least 4 hour, then drained
½ cup lentils
10 cups water
1 cup rice
1 cup chopped fresh parsley or
  ¼ cup dried
2 cups chopped fresh cilantro
  or ½ cup dried
½ cup chopped fresh spring onions
¾ cup fresh chopped tarragon
1 cup chopped fresh dill weed or
  ¼ cup dried
2 tablespoons dried fenugreek

1 pound fresh spinach, washed and
  chopped, or frozen
3 turnips, peeled and diced
3 cups yogurt, beaten for 5 minutes

MEATBALLS
1 onion, peeled and grated
1 pound ground chicken thighs
  (or ground beef)
1 teaspoon sea salt
¼ teaspoon freshly ground
  black pepper
½ teaspoon turmeric
2 tablespoons chopped fresh parsley

GARNISH *(NA'NA DAGH)*
2 tablespoons oil
1 onion, peeled and thinly sliced
10 cloves garlic, peeled and sliced
½ teaspoon turmeric
3 teaspoons dried mint flakes

1. To make the broth: Heat the oil in a large pot over medium heat until hot. Brown the onions, salt, pepper, and turmeric. Add the chickpeas and lentils and sauté for 1 minute. Pour in the water. Bring to a boil, reduce heat to low, cover, and simmer for 35 minutes.

2. To make the meatballs: In a mixing bowl, combine the grated onion, ground chicken, salt, pepper, turmeric, and parsley. Knead lightly and, with moist hands, shape into chestnut-sized meatballs. Gently add to the soup and bring back to a boil.

3. Add rice, reduce heat to low, cover, and simmer 25 minutes longer.

4. Add chopped parsley, cilantro, spring onions, tarragon, dill, fenugreek, spinach, and turnips, and simmer for another 1½ hours, stirring occasionally.

5. Check to see if chickpeas are tender. Add more warm water if necessary and bring back to a boil. Adjust seasoning to taste.

6. Place the yogurt in a small bowl and stir in a few spoonfuls of hot soup (to temper the yogurt). Add it to the pot, gently stirring constantly for 1 minute to prevent curdling. Do not allow the yogurt to come to a boil.

7. Just before serving, prepare the garnish by browning onion and garlic in 2 tablespoons oil in a wide skillet. Add the turmeric, give it a stir, and remove from heat. Crush mint flakes in the palm of your hand and add to the skillet. Stir well.

8. Pour hot soup into a tureen. Garnish on top. Serve with flat bread, *sangak*, *lavash*, or pita. *Nush-e Jan!*

Barley Soup

Makes 6 servings
Preparation time: 20 minutes
Cooking time: 3 hours

Osh-e jow

VEGETARIAN VARIATION

Eliminate the meat from the ingredients and from step 1. Increase the chickpeas to ½ a cup, 2 cups more water, and proceed with the recipe.

NOTE

If using dried herbs, place a sieve in a bowl of lukewarm water and soak the dried herbs for 20 minutes. Remove the sieve from the bowl and use the herbs.

For best results, cook your soup a day in advance so that the flavors meld. Reheat the soup the next day just before serving. Add kashk *and the garnish at the last minute.*

¼ cup oil
2 onions, peeled and thinly sliced
½ pound stew meat (lamb or beef), or boneless skinless chicken thighs, cut into ½-inch cubes
2 teaspoons sea salt
½ teaspoon freshly ground black pepper
1 teaspoon turmeric
¼ cup dried red kidney beans, soaked in water for at least 4 hours, and then drained
¼ cup dried chickpeas, soaked in water for 4 hours, and then drained
¼ cup brown lentils
12 cups water or broth
1 cup barley

2 cups chopped fresh parsley or ½ cup dried
1 cup chopped fresh cilantro or ¼ cup dried
½ cup chopped fresh dill or 2 tablespoons dried
1 pound fresh spinach, washed and chopped, or frozen
¼ cup rice
1 cup liquid *kashk* (sun-dried yogurt)* or sour cream

GARNISH *(NA'NA DAGH)*
2 tablespoons oil
1 onion, peeled and thinly sliced
5 cloves garlic, peeled and sliced
½ teaspoon turmeric
2 tablespoons dried mint leaves

1. In a large, heavy pot, heat the oil over medium heat until hot. Brown the onions and meat. Sprinkle with salt, pepper, and turmeric. Add the kidney beans, chickpeas, and lentils, and sauté for 2 minutes. Pour in the water and bring to a boil. Reduce heat to medium, cover, and simmer for 50 minutes, stirring occasionally.

2. Add barley. Cover and simmer for 50 minutes longer over low heat, stirring occasionally.

3. Add parsley, cilantro, dill, spinach, and rice. Cover and simmer for 50 minutes longer.

4. Check to see that the meat is tender and beans are done.

5. Stir in the *kashk* and continue stirring for 5 minutes with a wooden spoon to prevent curdling. Adjust seasoning to taste. Cover and keep warm.

6. Just before serving, prepare the garnish. Heat 2 tablespoons oil in a wide skillet over medium heat and brown the onion and garlic. Add turmeric, give it a stir, and remove from heat. Crush dried mint flakes in the palm of your hands and add to the skillet. Stir well.

7. Pour the simmering soup into a tureen. Garnish with mint-and-garlic mixture. *Nush-e Jan!*

Sweet Wheat and Lamb Porridge

Makes 6 servings
Preparation time: 15 minutes plus
*   24 hours of soaking time*
Cooking time: 2 hours 30 minutes

BROTH
2 pounds shoulder of lamb (or turkey
   on the bone)
8 cups water
2 onions, peeled and thinly sliced
1½ teaspoons sea salt
½ teaspoon freshly ground
   black pepper
½ teaspoon turmeric

WHEAT
1 pound whole wheat grain (2 cups),
   soaked in 4 cups water for 24 hours,
   and then drained
½ cup chickpeas, soaked in 4 cups
   water for 24 hours, and then drained

GARNISH
¼ cup butter, melted
1 teaspoon cinnamon
2 tablespoons confectioners' sugar

حلیم گندم

Halim-e gandom

Halims *fall somewhere between a porridge and a puree. They have a very old tradition in Persian cooking, and this one is particularly popular as a working man's early breakfast, served in and around bazaars.* Halims *are cooked all night to be ready in the early morning. A popular pastime among young, affluent Iranians living in the foothills of Tehran in the 1970s was to seek out these downtown cookshops after all-night parties because they were already serving* halims *for breakfast before sunup. More recently, I had an excellent* halim *with fried eggs and* shahtut *in Darband, at the foothills of Tochal, before a trek up the mountain.*

1. Place the meat in a large, heavy-bottomed pot, add the water, bring to a boil, skim the froth as it forms until it stops forming. Add onions, salt, pepper and turmeric. Bring back to a boil. Reduce heat, cover, and simmer over low heat for 2 hours or until the meat is tender and falling off the bone. Add more warm water if needed. Stir occasionally to prevent sticking to the bottom of the pot.

2. Meanwhile, in a medium-sized saucepan, place the drained wheat, chickpeas, and 4 cups water. Bring to a boil, reduce heat, cover and simmer over low heat for 2 hours or until the wheat is tender. Add more warm water if necessary.

3. To assemble the porridge: Drain the meat through a fine-mesh sieve. Pour back the strained stock into pot. Separate the meat from the bones and return it to the pot. Discard the bones and anything else left in the sieve. Add the cooked wheat and chickpeas to the pot. Place the pot over medium-low heat, and use a handheld mixer to puree the meat, wheat, and chickpeas in the pot, and mix for 10 to 15 minutes until you have a homogenized, slightly elastic puree and the meat and wheat have thoroughly blended together. Adjust seasoning to taste.

4. Spoon the porridge into individual serving bowls. Garnish to taste with a little melted butter, cinnamon, and confectioners' sugar on the top. *Nush-e Jan!*

EATING STEAM

A poor man walked by a stall where food was being cooked. The smell coming from the bubbling halim pot made him almost faint from hunger and pleasure; he took a piece of stale bread from his bag and waved it in the steam, then ate it. The cook asked him to pay for what he'd eaten.

"But I didn't eat anything of yours to pay for."

The mulla happened to be passing and he called to the cook to get his attention; then he took a few coins from his pocket, jingled them loudly in his hand so that the cook could hear them and said, "Here you are then, he ate the steam from your food, and I'm paying for it with the sound of my money."

Eggplant Porridge

Makes 6 servings
Preparation time: 20 minutes
Cooking time: 2 hours 30 minutes
to 3 hours

½ cup oil
2 pounds lamb shoulder with bone
2 onions, peeled and thinly sliced
6 cups water
2 teaspoons sea salt
1 teaspoon freshly ground
   black pepper
1 teaspoon turmeric
2 cups brown lentils or 1 cup chickpeas
6 small, or 2 medium, eggplants
2 cups liquid *kashk* (sun-dried yogurt)*

GARNISH
2 tablespoons oil
2 onions, peeled and thinly sliced
4 cloves garlic, peeled and crushed
½ teaspoon turmeric
4 tablespoons dried mint, crushed
½ cup walnuts, chopped
½ teaspoon ground saffron dissolved in
   2 tablespoons hot water or rose water
Sprigs of fresh mint

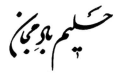

Halim-e bademjan

1. Heat 3 tablespoons oil in a large pot over medium heat and brown the meat and onions. Add 6 cups water and bring to a boil, skimming froth as it forms. Add salt, pepper, and turmeric. Cover and simmer over medium heat for 45 minutes, stirring occasionally.

2. Add the lentils and cook for another 55 minutes until the meat falls off the bone. Discard the bone.

3. To remove bitterness, peel and thinly slice the eggplants. Soak in a large container of water and 1 tablespoon salt. Let stand for 20 minutes, drain, rinse, and *blot dry*.

4. Heat 3 tablespoons oil in a wide skillet and brown both sides of the eggplant slices. Add to the meat, cover, and simmer for 20 minutes or until the meat, lentils, and eggplant slices have cooked and are tender.

5. In a small saucepan dilute the *kashk* in 1 cup water, bring to a simmer, and keep warm.

6. Add half of the warm *kashk* to the *halim* and mash to a thick paste. Adjust seasoning to taste. Cover and keep warm.

7. To make the garnish, heat 2 tablespoons oil in a skillet until hot, add the onion and garlic, and sauté until golden brown. Add the turmeric, mix well, remove from heat. Add the crushed mint flakes, stir well, and set aside.

8. Just before serving, transfer the *halim* to a serving platter. Decorate with the prepared garnish, walnut, the remaining *kashk,* saffron water, and the fresh mint. Serve with bread and fresh herbs. *Nush-e Jan!*

DOLMEHS & VEGETABLES

DOLMEHS & VEGETABLES

Rarely do Iranians eat vegetables as separate side dishes. Instead, vegetables are usually combined with dried beans, grains, and fruits or stuffed with fruits, rice, and meats.

Stuffed vegetables, called *dolmeh,* however, are popular. Some favorite *dolmehs* are grape and cabbage leaves, eggplant, zucchini, and tomatoes. Fruits such as quinces and apples are also excellent for stuffing. A basic *dolmeh* stuffing is made of onion, ground lamb, rice, split peas, tarragon, and summer savory. The flavors vary depending on the regions. For example, by the Caspian, citrus or pomegranate juice, olive oil, and saffron give the sauce its distinctive northern flavor. In central Iran, they use vinegar, grape molasses, and tail fat. In southern Iran, tamarind, cilantro, red pepper, and ghee flavor the sauce. Generally speaking, *dolmehs* may be served cold as an appetizer or hot as a main dish accompanied with bread and yogurt.

The good cook always chooses vegetables in season, when they are at their height of flavor and nutritional value. Herbs may vary in intensity even from season to season. For example, the perfume of dill in spring is strongest and therefore most desirable for cooking. Fresh fruits, vegetables, and herbs should be used in season whenever possible. They give superior results in every way.

Grape Leaves with Sweet and Sour Stuffing

Makes 6–8 servings
Preparation time: 1 hour
Cooking time: 2 hours

دلمه برگ مو

Dolmeh-ye barg-e mo

VEGETARIAN VARIATION

Grape Leaves with Pine Nut and Raisin Stuffing—Replace the meat with ½ cup toasted pine nuts and ½ cup raisins.

NOTES

If using dried herbs, place a sieve in a bowl of lukewarm water and soak the dried herbs for 20 minutes. Remove the sieve from the bowl and use the herbs.

Canned grape leaves are available in specialty food shops and sometimes supermarkets. If grape leaves are too thin, use two, one on top of the other.

You can replace the vinegar with pomegranate molasses for the souring agent.

50 fresh grape leaves (in season) or canned leaves

FILLING
⅔ cup rice
¼ cup yellow split peas
1 teaspoon sea salt
½ cup olive oil
1 onion, peeled and thinly sliced
2 cloves garlic, peeled and sliced
½ pound ground lamb (or beef, chicken thighs, or fish fillets)
1 cup chopped spring onions
¼ cup fresh summer savory or 1 tablespoon dried
½ cup chopped fresh dill, or 2 tablespoons dried
¼ cup chopped fresh tarragon, or 1 tablespoon dried
¼ cup chopped fresh mint or 1 tablespoon dried
3½ cups chopped fresh parsley or 1 cup dried
½ teaspoon ground black pepper
½ teaspoon red pepper flakes
1 teaspoon ground cinnamon
2 tablespoons lime juice

BROTH
1 cup broth (recipe on page 74)

SYRUP
⅔ cup grape molasses or brown sugar
⅓ cup wine vinegar
½ teaspoon sea salt
⅓ cup fresh lime juice

1. Preheat oven to 350°F (180°C).

2. If using fresh grape leaves, pick small and tender ones, tie them together in batches and blanch them in boiling water for 2 minutes, then drain in a colander, and rinse with cold water. For canned grape leaves, drain in a colander and rinse under cold running water.

3. In a saucepan, cook rice and split peas for 20 minutes over medium heat in 3 cups water and ½ teaspoon salt. Drain in a colander.

4. In a wide skillet, heat 3 tablespoons oil over medium heat and brown onion, garlic, and meat. Add the rice, split peas, and the remaining ingredients for the filling. Mix thoroughly, using hands or a wooden spoon.

5. Place three layers of grape leaves on the bottom of a well-oiled ovenproof dish.

6. Place a grape leaf on top of a wooden board with the vein side up and nip off the little stem. Top with 1 tablespoon filling. Roll up the leaf, folding in the ends to prevent the filling from leaking out while cooking. Place in the dish. Repeat, filling all the leaves and placing them in the dish side by side.

7. Pour broth and the remaining oil into the dish. Set a small ovenproof plate on top of the stuffed grape leaves. Cover and bake in the oven for 1 hour.

8. In a bowl, thoroughly mix all the ingredients for the syrup. Remove the baking dish from oven, uncover, and baste with this syrup. Cover and return to oven. Bake for another hour or until the leaves are tender. Taste sauce and adjust seasoning. The sauce should be quite reduced. Serve in the same baking dish or on a platter, while hot or warm, with bread and yogurt, or use cool as an appetizer. *Nush-e Jan!*

Quinces with Lamb and Rice Stuffing

Makes 6 servings
Preparation time: 45 minutes
Cooking time: 2 hours

FILLING
1 onion, peeled and thinly sliced
½ pound ground meat (lamb, beef, chicken thighs, or fish fillets)
½ cup butter or oil
¼ cup rice, cleaned and washed
1 teaspoon sea salt
¼ teaspoon freshly ground pepper
¼ teaspoon turmeric
¼ teaspoon cayenne
2 teaspoons *advieh* (Persian spice mix)*
½ cup water

QUINCE
6 medium-sized quinces
6 tablespoons brown sugar

BROTH
1 cup broth or water

SYRUP
¼ cup fresh lime juice
½ cup grape molasses or brown sugar
¼ cup balsamic vinegar
¼ teaspoon saffron dissolved in 1 tablespoon hot water

Dolmeh-ye beh

VEGETARIAN VARIATION
Quinces with Rice and Split Pea Stuffing—In step 1 replace the meat with ½ cup yellow split peas, increase the water to 3 cups, bring to a boil, reduce heat to medium, cover and cook for 30 minutes (instead of 15 minutes) or until all the water has been absorbed.

1. To make the filling, brown onion and meat in a skillet with 4 tablespoons butter. Add rice, salt, pepper, turmeric, cayenne, and ½ cup water. Mix thoroughly. Cover and simmer for 15 minutes over low heat.

2. Wash and rub quinces. Cut off tops and set aside. Hollow out quinces, using the tip of a knife or a melon baller to scoop out the seeds and some of the pulp, leaving a shell about ½ inch thick. Reserve the pulp to use later.

3. Sprinkle 1 tablespoon sugar inside each quince and then stuff with the filling. Replace tops and place in a deep pan wide enough for the 6 quinces to fit into. Pour broth and the pulp around the fruit. Add a dab of butter on top of each quince. Wrap the lid of the pan with a dish towel and cover tightly. Allow to steep over low heat for 1 hour.

4. In a bowl, combine all the ingredients for the syrup and mix thoroughly. Uncover the pan and pour the syrup over the fruit in the pan. Cover and simmer 45 minutes to 1 hour longer until the fruit is tender, basting occasionally with pan juices.

5. Adjust seasonings to taste with sugar or lime juice. Serve in same baking dish or on a platter. Serve with bread, yogurt, and fresh herbs. *Nush-e jan!*

VARIATION

Apples with Lamb and Rice Stuffing *(Dolmeh-ye sib)*—You may replace the quinces with apples (peeled or unpeeled according to your fancy). Prepare apples as in steps 1 and 2 above, then in step 3 cover and bake for 30 minutes. In step 4 bake uncovered for another 10 to 20 minutes, until apples are tender.

Oranges with Lamb and Rice Stuffing *(Dolmeh-ye Narenj)*—Replace the quinces with oranges. Boil 6 whole oranges in salted water for 10 minutes. Drain and rinse with cold water. Cut off the tops and gently remove the pulp, and then proceed with step 3.

Cabbage Leaves with Rice and Split Peas Stuffing

Makes 6 servings
Preparation time: 1 hour
Cooking time: 2 hours

2 large heads of green or savory cabbage

FILLING
¼ cup rice
¼ cup yellow split peas
1 teaspoon sea salt
½ cup oil
1 onion, peeled and thinly sliced
1 pound ground meat (lamb, beef, chicken thighs, or fish fillets)
2 tablespoons tomato paste
¼ cup chopped fresh parsley
2 tablespoon chopped fresh mint
2 tablespoons chopped fresh dill
1 tablespoon chopped fresh tarragon

½ teaspoon freshly ground black pepper
1 teaspoon ground cumin
½ teaspoon red pepper flakes
½ teaspoon smoked paprika
½ teaspoon ground cinnamon

SAUCE
1½ cups fresh tomato puree
¼ cup oil, butter, or ghee*

SYRUP
½ cup grape molasses or brown sugar
½ teaspoon sea salt
⅓ cup wine vinegar or fresh lime juice

Dolmeh-ye kalam

1. Preheat the oven to 350°F (180°C). Core cabbage and remove individual leaves. Plunge them into boiling salted water. Cover and boil for 5 minutes, drain in colander, and rinse under cold water.

2. To make the filling: In a saucepan, cook rice and split peas in 3 cups water and ½ teaspoon salt over medium heat for 30 minutes. Drain and set aside.

3. In a wide skillet, brown onion and meat in ½ cup oil. Add tomato paste and stir-fry for 1 minute. Remove from heat. Add the rest of the ingredients for the filling. Mix thoroughly with a wooden spoon.

4. Place two layers of cabbage leaves in a well-greased ovenproof dish.

5. To stuff the cabbage leaves, place one leaf on the counter and top with 1 tablespoon of filling. Roll tightly, folding in the sides of the leaf to prevent the filling from leaking out while cooking. Arrange stuffed cabbage leaves side by side in the dish.

6. Add the tomato puree and drizzle with a little oil on top of each stuffed cabbage. Cover with a layer of parchment paper and a layer of aluminum foil, and seal tightly. Bake for 1½ hours.

7. In a bowl, combine molasses, salt, and vinegar. Uncover the dish and pour this mixture over the cabbages. Re-cover and return to oven, and bake for another 30 minutes, basting once with the pan juices.

8. When the stuffed cabbage leaves are done, taste sauce and adjust seasoning by adding more vinegar or sugar. Serve hot or warm in same baking dish with bread and yogurt on the side, or cool as an appetizer. *Nush-e Jan!*

VEGETARIAN VARIATION
Cabbage Leaves with Tofu and Split Pea Stuffing *(dolmeh-ye kalam ba tofu)*—Replace the meat with 1 pound firm tofu, water squeezed out and finely chopped, combined with ½ teaspoon cayenne and rest of the ingredients for the filling. Add it to step 3 and proceed with the recipe.

Stuffed Green Peppers, Eggplants, and Tomatoes

Makes 4–6 servings
Preparation time: 45 minutes
Cooking time: 2 hours
* 30 minutes*

Dolmeh-ye felfel sabz-o bademjan-o gojeh farangi

2 eggplants or pattypan squash
2 green bell peppers
4 large tomatoes

FILLING
¼ cup rice
¼ cup yellow split peas
½ cup oil or butter
1 onion, peeled and thinly sliced
1 pound ground lamb (or chicken)
2 tablespoons tomato paste
1 cup chopped fresh parsley
½ cup chopped spring onions
1 cup chopped fresh mint or
  1 tablespoon dried
1 cup chopped fresh tarragon

1 teaspoons sea salt
½ teaspoon freshly ground
  black pepper
½ teaspoon cayenne
1 teaspoon *advieh* (Persian spice mix)*

SAUCE
1 cup tomato puree

SWEET AND SOUR SAUCE
¼ cup oil or butter
⅓ cup lime juice or vinegar
⅓ cup grape molasses or sugar
1 teaspoon ground cinnamon
1 teaspoon sea salt
¼ teaspoon saffron dissolved in
  2 tablespoons hot water

VEGETARIAN VARIATION
Eliminate the meat. In step 4 increase the rice and split peas to ½ cup each. Cook for 30 minutes in 4 cups water and ½ teaspoon salt. Drain and proceed with recipe from step 5.

VARIATION
Stuffed Yellow Onions —Whole peeled, cored onions are also excellent for stuffing. Core and use a melon baller to dig circular sections out of the onion to form a shell. Blanch in boiling water for 1 minute and drain before stuffing. Bake about 1½ hours at 375°F (190°C) in a baking pan along with the sauce as directed for other stuffing.

1. Preheat oven to 350°F (180°C). Slice off the tops of the eggplants squash and set aside. Slice off the bottoms so the eggplants can stand on their own. Hollow them out, using the point of a knife or a melon baller, leave a ¾–inch-thick shell, and save the flesh for later. Sprinkle the shells with 1 tablespoon salt and place in a colander to drain in the sink for 20 minutes.

2. Cut off the tops of the green peppers ½ inch from the stem and set them aside. Blanch peppers for 5 minutes in boiling water. Rinse in cold water and drain.

3. Remove stems from tomatoes. Cut a slice off the tops and set aside. Scoop out tomato pulp using a melon baller and reserve.

4. Cook rice and split peas for 30 minutes in 2 cups water and ¼ teaspoon salt. Drain.

5. Rinse eggplants and **blot dry.** In a wide skillet, heat ¼ cup oil over medium heat and brown the eggplants on all sides. Remove from skillet and set aside. In the same skillet, heat 2 tablespoons oil and sauté the onion and lamb until brown. Add the tomato paste and stir-fry for 1 minute. Remove from heat, and add the rest of the ingredients for the filling. Mix thoroughly. Stuff the eggplants, tomatoes, and green peppers with the filling. Replace their tops.

6. Place the stuffed eggplants and peppers side by side in an oiled ovenproof, deep dish, leaving room for the tomatoes, which do not need to cook as long. Pour tomato puree around the vegetables. Cover tightly and bake for 1½ hours.

7. To make the sweet and sour sauce, in a saucepan combine the reserved tomato pulp, oil, lime juice, molasses, cinnamon, salt, and saffron water. Mix well and bring to a boil. Remove the dish from the oven, uncover, and add the stuffed tomatoes. Pour the sauce over the stuffed vegetables, cover, and return to oven. Bake for 45 to 60 minutes longer until tender. When the vegetables are done, correct seasoning to taste. Add more lime juice, sugar, or salt. Serve with bread and yogurt. *Nush-e Jan!*

IF A POT CAN MULTIPLY

One day Mulla lent his cooking pots to a neighbor, who was giving a feast. The neighbor returned them, together with an extra one—a very tiny pot.

"What is this?" asked Mulla.

"According to law, I have given you the offspring of your property which was born when the pots were in my care," said the joker.

Shortly afterwards Mulla borrowed his neighbor's pots, but did not return them.

The man came round to get them back.

"Alas!" said Mulla Nasruddin, "They are dead. We have established, have we not, that pots are mortal?"

Eggplants with Lamb and Onion Stuffing

6 Italian eggplants, peeled
  (leave the stems intact)*

FILLING
1 cup oil, butter, or ghee*
2 large onions, peeled and thinly sliced
6 cloves garlic, peeled and sliced
1 pound ground lamb
2 teaspoons sea salt

½ teaspoon pepper
½ teaspoon red pepper flakes
1 teaspoon turmeric
2 teaspoons ground cumin
1 teaspoon sugar
2 large tomatoes, peeled and sliced
1 cup fresh chopped mint
¼ cup broth or water

Makes: 6 servings
Preparation time: 30 minutes
Cooking time: 2 hours

بادمجان شکم پر

Bademjan-e shekam por

VEGETARIAN VARIATION
Eliminate ground lamb in step 5 and replace it with 1 cup finely chopped walnuts, 1 tablespoon pomegranate molasses, and 1 cup fresh, chopped cilantro.

1. Make a slit, lengthwise, in each eggplant without opening the ends. Soak the eggplants in a container of cold water with 1 tablespoon salt for 20 minutes. Drain, rinse, *blot dry,* and set aside.

2. Preheat the oven to 350°F (180°C).

3. In a large skillet, heat ½ cup oil over medium heat and cook the eggplants until golden brown on all sides.

4. Arrange the eggplants side by side on an oiled baking dish.

5. In the same skillet, heat 2 tablespoons oil over medium heat and add the onions, garlic, and lamb. Sauté for 5 minutes. Add the remaining ingredients for the filling and sauté for 1 minute longer. Remove from heat.

6. Open up the slits in the eggplants with your hands and stuff each eggplant with the filling. Drizzle the remaining oil and pour ¼ cup broth around the eggplants. Cover with parchment paper and aluminum foil on top, and seal the baking sheet thoroughly so that no steam can escape. Bake for 1 hour, uncover, and continue to bake for another hour.

7. Serve hot or at room temperature with *lavash* bread and yogurt. *Nush-e Jan!*

Potatoes Stuffed with Lamb and Fresh Herbs

Makes 4 servings
Preparation time: 30 minutes
Cooking time: 1 hour 20 minutes

5–6 large russet potatoes of uniform size, peeled
¼ cup oil, butter or ghee*

FILLING
¼ cup oil, butter, or ghee*
2 large onions, peeled and thinly sliced
½ pound ground lamb
  (or beef, chicken or fish)
2 tablespoons tomato paste
1 teaspoon sea salt
½ teaspoon freshly ground
  black pepper
¼ teaspoon cayenne
1 teaspoon *advieh* (Persian spice mix)*

1 teaspoon grape molasses or brown
  sugar
2 tablespoons fresh lime juice
1 cup chopped fresh parsley
1 cup chopped fresh spring onions
2 eggs, hard-boiled and chopped
2 tablespoons barberries, rinsed
  thoroughly

SAUCE
1 cup broth (recipe on page 74)
1 large tomato, finely chopped
½ teaspoon turmeric
½ teaspoon sea salt

Dolmeh-ye sibzamini

VEGETARIAN VARIATION
Potatoes Stuffed with Eggs and Barberries—Eliminate the meat and increase the number of eggs to 5 chopped hard-boiled eggs. In step 5 replace the broth with water.

1. Preheat the oven to 400°F (200°C). Wash and peel potatoes. Cut off potato tops and place on a kitchen towel on the counter. Slice off the bottoms so potatoes can stand up straight. Hollow out with a potato peeler or a baller, leaving a ½-inch-thick shell. Save potato pulp to use later.

2. Heat ¼ cup oil in a wide skillet over medium heat, and brown potatoes on all sides (make sure the potatoes are fried on all sides and are golden brown). Remove from the skillet and place in an oiled baking dish that is large enough for the potatoes to sit side by side.

3. To make the filling, in the same skillet heat ¼ cup oil over medium heat, and brown the onions and meat. Add the tomato paste, salt, pepper, cayenne, *advieh*, molasses, and lime juice, and stir-fry for 1 minute. Add the remaining ingredients for the filling and mix thoroughly. Set aside

4. Stuff the potatoes with the filling, replace tops, and rearrange in the baking dish.

5. To make the sauce, in a mixing bowl combine broth, tomato, turmeric, and salt. Pour this mixture over and around potatoes. Add the reserved potato pulp to the dish. Cover (if the dish does not have a lid, use a layer of parchment paper and place a layer of aluminum foil on top). Seal all sides so steam cannot escape. Bake in the oven for 1 hour. Baste once with pan juices.

6. Check to see if potatoes are tender. Adjust seasoning. Serve in the same baking dish or arrange on a platter. Serve with bread, fresh herbs, and yogurt. *Nush-e Jan!*

KUKUS &
EGG DISHES

کوکوها
و تخم مرغ ها

KUKUS & EGG DISHES

*E*ggs and egg dishes are popular throughout the Middle East. Iranians are especially fond of *kuku,* a type of open-faced omelet similar to the Italian frittata and the Arab *eggah.* Filled with vegetables and herbs, a good *kuku* should be thick and rather fluffy.

Although nowadays this dish can be cooked in the oven, traditionally it was cooked in a large covered skillet that was set on hot coals. Coals were placed on the cover as well. Frittata pans consisting of two interlinking pans that fit one on top of the other are available and are perfect for *kukus.* They make flipping a stovetop-cooked *kuku* easy.

Kukus are served as appetizers or as side dishes or as main dishes with yogurt, salad, fresh herb platter, and bread. They may be eaten hot or cold and they keep well in the refrigerator for two or three days.

Most Iranian households keep *kukus* on hand for snacks or to serve unexpected guests. They are ideal for picnics as well.

Apple, Raisin and Date Omelet

Makes 4 servings
Preparation time: 10 minutes
Cooking time: 15 minutes

BATTER
4 eggs
2 tablespoons milk
½ teaspoon sea salt
⅛ teaspoon saffron dissolved in
  1 tablespoon rose water

APPLE, RAISIN AND DATE MIXTURE
2 tablespoons oil, butter, or ghee*
3 medium-sized apples, cored, peeled,
  and thinly sliced

2 tablespoons seedless raisins
6 dates, pitted and sliced
1 tablespoon fresh lime juice
¼ teaspoon cinnamon
⅛ teaspoon cayenne (optional)

2 tablespoons oil, butter, or ghee*
Flat bread
Fresh basil (optional)

Khagineh-ye sib

Khagineh comes from the old Persian word for eggs, khayeh, *used in the* Shahnameh *of Ferdowsi around 1000* CE. *The word caviar also comes from* khayeh.

1. For the batter: Break the eggs in a mixing bowl. Add the milk, salt, and saffron rose water, and whisk for 20 seconds (about 20 strokes).

2. For the apples: Heat a wide skillet over medium heat until very hot, add the oil and apple slices, and cook for 3 to 5 minutes until the apple is golden brown. Add the raisins, dates, lime juice, cinnamon, cayenne. Stir-fry for 20 seconds. Spread the apple mixture evenly in the skillet, reduce heat, drizzle 2 tablespoons oil on top, add the batter, and cook for 3 to 5 minutes until the egg has set. Transfer to a serving platter. Serve immediately with flat bread and fresh basil. *Nush-e Jan!*

VARIATION

A Simple Omelet—Replace the apples, raisins, and dates with 2 tablespoons confectioners' sugar sprinkled over the omelet before plating.

Individual Omelets—Heat an 8-inch non-stick omelet pan over medium heat until very hot, add 1 teaspoon oil and a thin layer of the batter (about 3 tablespoons) into the pan, and lift and tilt the pan to evenly coat it with the batter. Once it has set, spread some cooked apple, raisin, and date mixture from step 2 on top. Tilt the pan, fold over, and roll the omelet out onto a plate. Continue until you have made 4 omelets. Serve hot with flat bread and fresh basil.

Azerbaijan-Style Pancake

Makes 6 pancakes
Preparation time: 20 minutes
Cooking time: 30 minutes

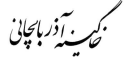

Khagineh-ye Azerbaijani

SYRUP
½ cup sugar
¼ cup water
¼ teaspoon saffron dissolved in
  2 tablespoons rose water

BATTER
1 egg
1 cup plain yogurt
1 teaspoon baking soda
½ teaspoon ground cardamom
½ cup unbleached all-purpose flour

¼ cup oil, butter, or ghee*

GARNISH
1 teaspoon dried rose petals, crushed
½ cup ground raw pistachios

1. To make the syrup: In a saucepan combine the sugar, water, and saffron-rose water and bring to a boil. Reduce heat to low and simmer for 5 minutes. Remove from heat.

2. To make the batter: In a mixing bowl whisk together the eggs, yogurt, baking soda, and cardamom. Gradually add the flour and whisk until you have a thick batter (do not overmix). Allow to rest for 5 minutes.

3. To cook the pancakes: Heat 2 tablespoons oil in a wide skillet over medium heat. Scoop ladlefuls (about ¼ cup) of batter and pour into the skillet. Cook for 4 to 5 minutes. Flip over each pancake and cook the other sides until golden. Add more oil and cook the pancakes in batches. Transfer to a serving dish, drizzle some syrup on top, and sprinkle with rose petals and ground pistachios. *Nush-e Jan!*

VARIATION
This recipe can also be made more traditionally as a single pancake. Heat the oil in a 12-inch skillet and cook the pancake in 1 batch.

Sunny-Side-Up Eggs with Yogurt

Makes 4 servings
Preparation time: 10 minutes
Cooking time: 5 minutes

Nimru ba mast

YOGURT SAUCE
2 cups drained yogurt
4 cloves garlic, peeled and grated

EGGS
4 tablespoons oil, butter, or ghee*
8 eggs

1 teaspoon sea salt
1 teaspoon freshly ground
   black pepper

2 loaves *lavash* bread
1 cup fresh basil leaves

1. In a saucepan, beat the yogurt and garlic for 5 minutes. Heat over low heat and keep warm.

2. In a large skillet, heat the oil over medium low heat. Break each egg into the skillet. Sprinkle with salt and pepper. Cook for about 1 minute until whites begin to set. Cover and cook over medium-low heat for about 2 to 4 minutes until you have gentle whites and creamy yolks.

3. Serve over *lavash* bread with the yogurt sauce and basil on the side. *Nush-e Jan!*

Eggplant Omelet

Makes 4 servings
Preparation time: 1 hour
Cooking time: 30 minutes

Mirza ghasemi

EGGPLANT
2 large eggplants (2 pounds)
5 tablespoons olive oil
3 cloves garlic, peeled and thinly sliced
1 teaspoon sea salt
1 teaspoon freshly ground
   black pepper
1 teaspoon turmeric

EGG
2 cloves garlic, peeled and grated
4 eggs, beaten lightly with
   ½ teaspoon sea salt

GARNISH
toasted flat bread
1 cup fresh basil leaves or dill weed
½ cup drained yogurt

1. Preheat oven to 350°F (180°C).

2. Prick eggplants with a fork to prevent bursting and place on oven rack. Bake for 60 minutes. Be sure to place a baking sheet under the eggplants to catch drips.

3. Remove eggplants from oven and place on the baking sheet. Remove the skin and seeds. Place eggplant on a cutting board and chop finely.

4. Heat 4 tablespoons oil in a 10-inch skillet and sauté half the garlic over medium heat. Add the salt, pepper, turmeric, and eggplants, and sauté over medium heat for 5 to 10 minutes, until all the juice has been absorbed.

5. Spread out the eggplant mixture evenly in the skillet. Make 4 openings. Pour ½ teaspoon oil and ¼ teaspoon grated garlic in each hole. Pour an equal amount of the egg mixture into each opening and cook over low heat for 10 to 15 minutes until eggs are firm. Stir gently with a wooden spoon.

6. Transfer to a serving platter. Serve with bread, fresh basil, and yogurt. *Nush-e Jan!*

Green Bean Kuku

Makes 6 servings
Preparation time: 20 minutes
Cooking time: 1 hour

½ cup oil, butter, or ghee*
2 medium onions, peeled and
  thinly sliced
2 cloves garlic, peeled and sliced
1 pound fresh or frozen green beans,
  stems removed and chopped into
  ¼-inch lengths
1 teaspoon sea salt
½ teaspoon freshly ground
  black pepper

½ teaspoon turmeric
Zest of 1 lime
¼ teaspoon cayenne
4 eggs
1 tablespoon flour
1 teaspoon baking powder
1 tablespoon lime juice

Kuku-ye lubia sabz

1. In a wide skillet heat 2 tablespoons oil over medium heat and sauté the onions and garlic for 5 minutes. Add green beans and sauté for another 5 minutes. Add the salt, pepper, turmeric, zest of lime, and cayenne, and sauté for 1 minute. Remove from heat and allow to cool.

2. Preheat oven to 350°F (180°C).

3. Break eggs in a bowl. Add flour, baking powder, and lime juice. Beat lightly with a fork.

4. Add the green-bean mixture to beaten eggs and gently fold.

5. Pour 6 tablespoons oil into an 8-inch ovenproof baking dish and place it in the oven for 5 minutes until hot. Pour in the egg mixture and bake uncovered for 35 to 40 minutes until lightly golden brown on top and a tester comes out clean.

6. Remove from the oven, place on a wet towel, and cover with a serving platter. Allow to rest for 10 minutes (this helps to unmold the *kuku* more easily). Loosen the edges with a knife and invert onto the serving platter (or serve it directly from the baking dish).

7. Serve with yogurt and bread. *Nush-e Jan!*

VARIATIONS

Stovetop-Style Kuku—*Kuku* can also be cooked on top of the stove. Heat 6 tablespoons oil in a 10-inch skillet (or frittata pan) over medium-low heat, pour in the mixture, and cook, covered, until it has set (about 15 to 20 minutes). If you have a frittata pan, simply flip over and cook for another 10 to 15 minutes until golden. If you do not have a frittata pan, cook the top under a hot broiler for 2 minutes until lightly golden.

Green Pea Kuku—Eliminate the green beans from step 1. Add 1 pound green peas and add ¼ cup chopped fresh dill to the mixture in step 4.

Fresh Herb Kuku

Makes 4 servings
Preparation time: 25 minutes
Cooking time: 1 hour

GARNISH
1 tablespoon oil, butter, or ghee*
⅓ cup barberries, picked over and thoroughly rinsed*
1 teaspoon grape molasses or sugar

BATTER
½ cup oil, butter, or ghee*
1 large or 2 medium yellow onions, peeled and finely chopped
6 eggs
1 teaspoon baking powder
2 teaspoons *advieh* (Persian spice mix)*
1 teaspoon sea salt
1 teaspoon freshly ground black pepper
½ teaspoon turmeric
2 cloves garlic, peeled and finely chopped
½ cup Romaine lettuce, finely chopped
½ cup finely chopped fresh spring onions
1 cup finely chopped fresh parsley
1 cup finely chopped fresh cilantro
1 cup finely chopped fresh dill
1 tablespoon dried fenugreek or 1 cup chopped fresh
½ cup coarsely chopped walnuts
1 tablespoon all-purpose flour

کوکوی سبزی

Kuku-ye sabzi

STOVETOP COOKING VARIATION
This *kuku* can also be cooked on top of the stove. Heat 6 tablespoons oil in a 10-inch skillet (or frittata pan) over medium-low heat, pour in the mixture, and cook, covered, until it has set (about 15 to 20 minutes). If you have a frittata pan, simply flip over and cook for another 10 to 15 minutes until golden. If not, cook the top under a hot broiler for 2 minutes until lightly golden.

Herb kuku is a traditional New Year's dish in Iran. The green of the herbs symbolizes rebirth. Eggs represent fertility for the year to come.

1. Preheat oven to 350°F (180°C).

2. To make the garnish, in a wide skillet heat 1 tablespoon oil over low heat. Add the barberries and grape molasses, and stir-fry for 1 minute (beware, barberries burn easily). Transfer the barberries to a serving bowl and set aside.

3. Heat 2 tablespoons oil in the skillet over medium heat and sauté the onions until lightly golden. Remove the onions and allow to cool.

4. Break eggs into a large mixing bowl. Add baking powder, *advieh,* salt, pepper, and turmeric. Beat lightly with a fork. Add the garlic, lettuce, herbs, walnuts, flour, and sautéed onions. Fold gently using a rubber spatula (do not overmix).

5. Heat 6 tablespoons oil in an 8-inch ovenproof baking dish in the preheated oven for 5 minutes. Pour in the egg mixture and bake uncovered for 40 to 45 minutes until lightly golden on top and a tester comes out clean.

6. Remove from the oven and cover with a serving platter. Allow to rest for 5 minutes (this helps to unmold the *kuku* more easily). Loosen the edges with a knife and invert onto the serving platter (or serve it directly from the baking dish). Garnish with some of the barberries (place the rest on the table to use according to your fancy).

7. Cut the *kuku* into small pieces and serve hot or cold with *lavash* bread and yogurt. *Nush-e Jan!*

Cauliflower Kuku

Makes 4 servings
Preparation time: 25 minutes
Cooking time: 1 hour

½ cup oil, butter, or ghee*
1 medium onion, peeled and thinly sliced
2 cloves garlic, peeled and sliced
1 small head cauliflower, half a large head, or 1 pound frozen florets, coarsely chopped
4 eggs
1½ teaspoons sea salt

¼ teaspoon freshly ground black pepper
½ teaspoon turmeric
¼ teaspoon smoked paprika
¼ teaspoon cayenne
½ teaspoon ground cumin
½ teaspoon baking powder
1 tablespoon flour
¼ cup chopped fresh parsley

Kuku-ye gol-e kalam

1. Preheat oven to 350°F (180°C).

2. Heat 2 tablespoons oil in a wide skillet over medium heat. Brown onion, garlic, and cauliflower. Remove from heat and allow to cool.

3. Break eggs into a mixing bowl. Add salt, pepper, turmeric, paprika, cayenne, cumin, baking powder, flour, and parsley. Beat lightly with a fork.

4. Add the onion, garlic, and cauliflower. Gently fold with a rubber spatula.

5. Heat 6 tablespoons oil in an 8-inch ovenproof baking dish in the preheated oven for 5 minutes. Pour in the egg mixture and bake uncovered for 50 to 55 minutes until lightly golden on top and a tester comes out clean.

6. Remove from the oven and cover with a serving platter. Allow to rest for 5 minutes (this helps to unmold the *kuku* more easily). Loosen the edges with a knife and invert onto the serving platter (or serve it directly from the baking dish).

7. Cut the *kuku* into small pieces and serve hot or cold with *lavash* bread and yogurt. *Nush-e Jan!*

VARIATION

Stovetop-Style Kuku—This *kuku* can also be cooked on top of the stove. Heat 6 tablespoons oil in a 10-inch skillet (or frittata pan) over medium-low heat, pour in the mixture, and cook, covered, until it has set (about 15 to 20 minutes). If you have a frittata pan, simply flip over and cook for another 10 to 15 minutes until golden. If not, cook the top under a hot broiler for 2 minutes until lightly golden.

Eggplant Kuku

2 pounds regular eggplants or slim,
  purple Chinese or Japanese eggplants
¾ cup oil, butter, or ghee*
2 large onions, peeled and thinly sliced
4 cloves garlic, peeled and thinly sliced
4 eggs
½ cup chopped parsley or mint
¼ teaspoon ground saffron dissolved
  in 1 tablespoon hot water
1 tablespoon fresh lime juice
½ teaspoon baking powder

1 tablespoon all-purpose flour
1 tablespoon plain bread crumbs
1½ teaspoons sea salt
½ teaspoon freshly ground
  black pepper

GARNISH
1 cup plain yogurt
1 cup fresh basil
flat bread

*Makes 4 servings
Preparation time: 35 minutes
Cooking time: 1 hour*

کوکو بادمجان

Kuku-ye bademjan

1. To remove bitterness from the eggplants, peel and thinly slice (a mandolin slicer is a useful tool for this). Soak in a large container of water with 1 tablespoon salt. Let stand for 20 minutes, drain, rinse with cold water, and **blot dry** or use a salad spinner to dry the eggplants (must be completely dry prior to cooking). If using Chinese eggplant, there is no need to soak or peel.

2. Preheat oven to 400°F (200°C).

3. In a wide skillet heat ¼ cup oil over medium heat and sauté all the eggplants at once on all sides for 15 minutes, stirring occasionally. Transfer to a container and allow to cool.

4. In the same skillet, heat 2 tablespoons oil over medium heat. Lightly brown onion and garlic, and add it to the eggplants. Set aside and allow to cool.

5. Break eggs into a mixing bowl. Add parsley, saffron water, lime juice, baking powder, flour, bread crumbs, salt, and pepper. Beat lightly with a fork. Add the eggplant mixture and fold gently using a rubber spatula (do not overmix).

6. Heat 6 tablespoons oil in an 8-inch ovenproof baking dish in the preheated oven for 5 minutes. Pour in the egg mixture and bake uncovered for 55 to 60 minutes, until lightly golden on top and a tester comes out clean.

7. Remove from the oven, place on a wet towel, and cover with a serving platter. Allow to rest for 10 minutes (this helps to unmold the *kuku* more easily). Loosen the edges with a knife and invert onto the serving platter (tap the bottom of the dish and allow to sit a moment before removing) or serve it directly from the baking dish. Serve with flat bread, fresh herbs, and yogurt. *Nush-e Jan!*

STOVETOP COOKING VARIATION

This *kuku* can also be cooked on top of the stove. Heat 6 tablespoons oil in a 10-inch skillet (or frittata pan) over medium-low heat until hot but not smoking. Pour in the mixture and cook, covered, until it has set (about 20 to 25 minutes). If you have a frittata pan, simply flip over and cook for another 10 to 15 minutes until golden. If you don't have a frittata pan, instead of flipping, you can cook the top under a hot broiler for 3 minutes until lightly golden.

VARIATION

Zucchini Kuku—In a skillet, sauté 1½ pounds zucchini (thinly sliced), onions, and garlic in the oil. Set aside to cool. In step 5, replace the saffron and lime juice with ½ teaspoon turmeric and ½ teaspoon red pepper flakes. Continue with the recipe.

Fava Bean Kuku

3 pounds fresh fava beans in the pod, or
  1 pound frozen, shelled
½ cup oil, butter, or ghee*
2 medium onions, peeled and sliced
4 cloves garlic, peeled and sliced
4 eggs
1 teaspoon sea salt

1 teaspoon freshly ground black pepper
1 teaspoon turmeric
½ teaspoon red pepper flakes
1 tablespoon flour
½ teaspoon baking powder
1 tablespoon yogurt
1 ½ cup chopped fresh dill

Makes 4 servings
Preparation time: 35 minutes
Cooking time: 1 hour

کوکوی شوید و باقلا

Kuku-ye shevid-o baqala

1. Preheat oven to 350°F (180°C).

2. If using fresh fava beans, remove from the pod and remove the second skin. If using frozen fava beans, soak in warm water for 5 minutes and drain, and remove the second skin.

3. In a wide skillet, heat 2 tablespoons oil over medium heat and sauté the onions and garlic. Add beans and stir-fry for 2 minutes until beans are almost tender. Remove from heat and set aside to cool.

4. Break eggs into a bowl. Add the salt, pepper, turmeric, pepper flakes, flour, baking powder, and yogurt. Beat lightly with a fork.

5. Add the fava bean mixture and the dill to the eggs and fold gently with a rubber spatula.

6. Heat 6 tablespoons oil in an 8-inch ovenproof baking dish in the preheated oven for 5 minutes. Pour in the fava bean mixture and bake uncovered for 45 to 50 minutes until lightly golden on top and a tester comes out clean.

7. Remove from the oven, place on a wet towel and cover with a serving platter. Allow to rest for 10 minutes (this helps to unmold the *kuku* more easily). Loosen the edges with a knife and invert onto the serving platter (or serve it directly from the baking dish). *Nush-e Jan!*

STOVETOP COOKING VARIATION

Kuku can also be cooked on top of the stove. Heat 6 tablespoons oil in a 10-inch skillet (or frittata pan) over medium-low heat until hot but not smoking. Pour in the mixture and cook, covered, until it has set (about 20 to 25 minutes). If you have a frittata pan, simply flip over and cook for another 10 to 15 minutes until golden. If you don't have a frittata pan, instead of flipping, you can cook the top under a hot broiler for 3 minutes until lightly golden.

VARIATIONS

Rice Kuku—Replace the fava beans and turmeric with 2 cups cooked rice, ½ teaspoon ground saffron, and 1 teaspoon ground cumin.

Cheese Kuku—Replace the fava beans and dill with ¼ pound crumbled goat cheese and 1 teaspoon ground coriander.

Quince or Apple Kuku—Replace the fava beans and dill with 2 quinces or 6 apples, cored and coarsely grated, ½ teaspoon ground nutmeg, ½ teaspoon cinnamon, ½ ground saffron, and 2 tablespoons sugar.

Walnut Kuku—Replace the fava beans and dill with 1½ cups ground walnuts (or other nuts according to your fancy), 1 cup chopped fresh parsley, 1 cup chopped fresh mint, and ½ teaspoon ground saffron.

Legume Kuku—Replace the fava beans with 2 cups cooked and drained mung beans, lentils, chickpeas, broad beans, or red beans.

Yogurt Kuku

Makes 4 servings
Preparation time: 15 minutes
Cooking time: 35 minutes

كوكوى ماست

Kuku-ye mast

4 eggs
1 teaspoon flour
¼ teaspoon ground saffron dissolved
  in 1 tablespoon rose water
½ teaspoon sea salt
¼ teaspoon freshly ground
  black pepper
½ cup chopped fresh spring onions
  (use green and white parts)
1 large carrot, grated
½ cup 2% fat yogurt, drained
1 tablespoon coarsely
  chopped almonds
6 tablespoons oil, butter, or ghee*

GARNISH
1 cup fresh herbs
flat bread

1. Preheat oven to 350°F (180°C).

2. Break eggs into a bowl. Add flour, saffron-rose water, salt, pepper, spring onions, and carrots. Beat lightly with a fork.

3. Add yogurt and almonds to the egg mixture and gently fold with a rubber spatula.

4. Heat 6 tablespoons oil in an 8-inch ovenproof baking dish in the preheated oven for 5 minutes. Pour in the mixture and bake, uncovered, for 25 to 30 minutes until lightly golden on top and a tester comes out clean.

5. Remove from the oven and cover with a serving platter. Allow to rest for 5 minutes (this helps to unmold the *kuku* more easily). Loosen the edges with a knife and invert onto the serving platter (or serve it directly from the baking dish). Serve with fresh herbs and flat bread. *Nush-e Jan!*

VARIATION

Stovetop-Style Kuku—*Kuku* can also be cooked on top of the stove. Heat 6 tablespoons oil in a 10-inch skillet (or frittata pan) over medium low heat until hot but not smoking. Pour in the mixture and cook, covered until it has set (about 15 to 20 minutes). If you have a frittata pan, simply flip over and cook for another 10 to 15 minutes until golden. If you do not have a frittata pan (instead of flipping) you can cook the top under a hot broiler for 1 minute until lightly golden.

Caspian Green Garlic Kuku

Makes 4 servings
Preparation time: 15 minutes
Cooking time: 45 minutes

سیر سبز و یا کوکوی تره و سیر

Kuku-ye sir bij

½ cup oil or butter
1 pound fresh green baby garlic, whites and greens, finely chopped
1 teaspoon turmeric

4 eggs
1 teaspoon sea salt
¼ teaspoon freshly ground black pepper
¼ teaspoon baking powder

1. In a wide skillet, heat 3 tablespoons oil over medium heat, add the garlic, and stir-fry for 5 minutes. Add turmeric and sauté for 1 minute. Remove from heat and allow to cool.

2. Break the eggs into a mixing bowl, add the salt, pepper, and baking powder. Add the garlic mixture and gently fold.

3. Heat 5 tablespoons oil in a 10-inch skillet (or frittata pan) over medium low heat until hot but not smoking. Pour in the mixture and cook, covered, until it has set (about 20 to 25 minutes). If you have a frittata pan, simply flip over and cook for another 10 to 15 minutes, until golden. If you don't have a frittata pan, instead of flipping, you can cook the top under a hot broiler for 1 or 2 minutes until lightly golden.

4. Serve with drained yogurt and *kateh. Nush-e Jan!*

Caspian Fava Bean Omelet

Makes 4 servings
Preparation time: 25 minutes
Cooking time: 25 minutes

با قلا قاتق

Baqala qataq

3 pounds fresh, or 1 pound frozen, fava beans (second skin removed)
6 tablespoons olive oil or butter
5 cloves garlic, peeled and thinly sliced
2 cups chopped fresh dill, or ¼ cup dried

2 teaspoons sea salt
1 teaspoon pepper
1 teaspoon turmeric
½ teaspoon sugar
5 cloves garlic, peeled and grated
4 large eggs

1. If you use fresh fava beans, first break the green pods (the outer shells) and then skin the beans. If you use frozen beans, soak in warm water for 5 minutes before skinning the beans (frozen fava beans with second skin removed is available in some Iranian markets— in which case just rinse and drain).

2. Heat 3 tablespoons oil in a wide skillet over medium heat until very hot. Add half the garlic and sauté for 1 minute. Add the fava beans, dill, salt, pepper, turmeric, and sugar, and sauté for 1 more minute. Add ¾ cups water. Reduce heat, cover, and simmer over low heat for 10 to 15 minutes or until the beans are tender and all the water has been absorbed. Adjust seasoning to taste and keep warm.

3. Just before serving, spread the beans evenly in the pan, make 4 holes in the beans, and drop ½ teaspoon oil and ¼ teaspoon garlic in each hole. Break one egg gently in each hole, cover, and allow to simmer for 5 to 8 minutes over medium heat until the eggs are set.

4. Serve immediately with drained yogurt over plain rice or bread. *Nush-e Jan!*

Lamb Kuku

Makes 4 servings
Preparation time: 20 minutes
Cooking time: 1 hour

½ cup oil, butter or ghee*
1 pound ground lamb (or beef or
   skinless, boneless chicken thighs)
2 onions, peeled and thinly sliced
½ bell pepper, seeded and diced finely
1 cup chopped fresh parsley
½ cup chopped fresh chives
   or spring onions
1¼ teaspoons sea salt

½ teaspoon freshly ground pepper
½ teaspoon red pepper flakes
1 teaspoon ground cumin
1 tablespoon lime juice
5 eggs
¼ teaspoon ground cinnamon
1 teaspoon curry powder
⅓ cup bread crumbs

Kuku-ye gusht

1. In a wide skillet heat 2 tablespoons oil over medium heat until hot. Brown the meat, onions, and bell pepper. Add the parsley, chives, salt, pepper, red pepper flakes, cumin, and lime juice. Stir-fry for 20 seconds. Remove from heat and allow to cool.

2. Preheat oven to 350°F (180°C).

3. Break eggs into a bowl. Add cinnamon, curry powder, and baking powder. Beat lightly with a fork.

4. Add lamb mixture and bread crumbs and mix with a fork (do not overmix).

5. Heat 6 tablespoons oil in an 8-inch ovenproof baking dish in the preheated oven for 5 minutes. Pour in the mixture and bake uncovered for 45 to 50 minutes until lightly golden on top and a tester comes out clean.

6. Remove from the oven and cover with a serving platter. Allow to rest for 5 minutes (this helps to unmold the *kuku* more easily). Loosen the edges with a knife and invert onto the serving platter (or serve it directly from the baking dish). Serve with fresh herbs and flat bread. *Nush-e Jan!*

STOVETOP COOKING VARIATION

This *kuku* can also be cooked on top of the stove. Heat 6 tablespoons oil in a 10-inch skillet (or frittata pan) over medium-low heat, until hot but not smoking. Pour in the mixture and cook, covered, until it has set (about 20 to 25 minutes). If you have a frittata pan, simply flip over and cook for another 10 to 15 minutes until golden. If you don't have a frittata pan, instead of flipping, you can cook the top under a hot broiler for 3 minutes until lightly golden.

VARIATIONS

Fish Kuku—You may replace the lamb with 1 pound boneless, chopped filleted white-flesh fish, such as catfish or halibut.

Leftover Chicken or Turkey Kuku—In step 4, use 1 pound chopped pieces of leftover chicken or turkey.

Potato Kuku

Makes 4 servings
Preparation time: 35 minutes
Cooking time: 1 hour 20 minutes

2 large potatoes or 3 medium russet
  (1 pound)
2 eggs
1 teaspoon sea salt
½ teaspoon freshly ground
  black pepper
½ teaspoon baking powder
½ teaspoon saffron dissolved in 2
  tablespoons rose water
1 medium onion, peeled and grated
½ cup oil, butter, or ghee

GARNISH
3 tablespoons confectioners' sugar
  (optional)
1 tablespoon ground rose petals

Kuku-ye sibzamini

NOTE
The egg-and-potato mixture can also be cooked as 3-inch patties by scooping a ladleful of the batter (about ¼ cup) at a time and pouring it in the hot oil in the skillet. Cook over **medium** *heat on both sides until golden brown.*

1. In a medium saucepan bring 4 cups water to a boil. Use a knife to score around the middle of the potatoes (this helps the skins come off easily after cooking). Add potatoes to the boiling water and cook for 15 to 20 minutes until potatoes are almost tender. Drain, allow to cool, peel, and grate coarsely.

2. Break eggs into a mixing bowl. Add salt, pepper, baking powder, saffron-rose water, potatoes and onion. Beat lightly with a fork.

3. Heat 6 tablespoons oil in a 10-inch skillet (or frittata pan) over medium low heat until hot but not smoking. Pour in the mixture and cook, covered, until it has set (about 20 to 25 minutes). If you have a frittata pan, simply flip over and cook for another 10 to 15 minutes until golden. If you do not have a frittata pan, instead of flipping, you can cook the top under a hot broiler for 2 to 3 minutes until lightly golden.

4. Garnish with confectioners' sugar and rose petals. This *kuku* makes an excellent breakfast. *Nush-e Jan!*

VARIATIONS

Butternut Squash Kuku—Replace the potato with 1 pound butternut squash, peeled, cut into cubes, and cooked covered in 2 cups water for 20 minutes. Drain and mash. Allow to cool and add to egg mixture with ½ teaspoon smoked paprika in step 2.

Sweet Potato and Apple Kuku—Cook 1 pound sweet potatoes, peel, and grate. Add a grated apple and mix. Add to the recipe in step 2.

Curry Potato Kuku—Replace the onions with 2 cloves garlic, peeled and grated. Replace saffron-rose water with 1 tablespoon curry powder.

Spinach Narcissus

Makes 4 servings
Preparation time: 20 minutes
Cooking time: 30 minutes

نرگسی اسفناج

Nargesi-ye esfenaj

1 pound fresh spinach, washed and coarsely chopped, or 1 pound frozen spinach, chopped
4 tablespoons oil, butter, or ghee*
2 large onions, peeled and finely chopped
2 cloves garlic, peeled and thinly sliced
½ cup fresh chopped mint
½ cup fresh chopped parsley

1 teaspoon sea salt
¼ teaspoon freshly ground black pepper
¼ teaspoon red pepper flakes (optional)
4 eggs
¼ cup or your favorite cheese, grated (optional)

1. Place the spinach in a steamer with 4 cups water. Cover and steam over high heat for 10 minutes until the spinach has wilted.

2. In a 10-inch skillet, heat 3 tablespoons oil over medium heat until hot. Brown onions and garlic. Add the spinach and herbs. Season with salt, pepper, and pepper flakes, and sauté for 5 minutes over medium heat.

3. Spread out the spinach mixture evenly in the skillet. Reduce heat to low. Use the handle of a wooden spoon to make 4 openings in the spinach mixture. Drop ½ teaspoon oil in each opening and break 1 egg gently into each opening. Sprinkle a pinch of salt and pepper on top. Cover and cook over low heat for 6 to 8 minutes or until the eggs have set.

4. Sprinkle with cheese and serve immediately with bread or plain steamed rice. *Nush-e Jan!*

VARIATION

Green Leaves Narcissus—1 pound of any kind of cleaned, washed, and chopped green leaves (stalks discarded), such as mustard greens, collard greens, kale, swiss chard, escarole, romaine lettuce, and bok choy—chopped broccoli rabe or asparagus may be substituted for the spinach.

Carrot and Pomegranate Narcissus—Replace the spinach with peeled and grated carrots. Replace red pepper flakes with 1 teaspoon *advieh* (Persian spice mix) and ¼ teaspoon ground saffron. Replace the cheese with 1 tablespoon pomegranate molasses and ¼ cup pomegranate arils.

NOTE
You can also make individual servings as shown in the photo.

دوش دیدم که ملائک در میخانه زدند
گل آدم بسرشتند و به پیمانه زدند

ساکنان حرم ستر و عفاف ملکوت
با من راه نشین باده مستانه زدند

Last night I saw the angels tapping at the wine shop's door,
And kneading Adam's dust, and plunging it in cups of wine;
And, where I sat beside the road, these denizens of heaven
Gave me their wine to drink, so that their drunkenness was mine.

Hafez

Pistachio Kuku

¼ cup brown sugar
½ cup shelled raw pistachios
4 eggs
2 tablespoons milk
1 teaspoon flour
½ teaspoon baking powder
¼ teaspoon ground saffron dissolved
  in 1 tablespoon hot water or
  rose water

½ teaspoon sea salt
¼ teaspoon freshly ground
  black pepper
6 tablespoons oil or butter
1 tablespoon whole raw
  shelled pistachios
1 tablespoon confectioners' sugar

Makes 4 servings
Preparation time: 10 minutes
Cooking time: 50 minutes

کوکوی پسته

Kuku-ye pesteh

1. Preheat oven to 350°F (180°C).

2. In a food processor, finely grind sugar and pistachios.

3. Break eggs into a bowl. Add milk, flour, baking powder, saffron water, salt, and pepper. Beat lightly with a fork.

4. Add the pistachio and sugar mixture to the egg mixture, and fold using a rubber spatula.

5. Heat 6 tablespoons oil in an 8-inch ovenproof baking dish in the preheated oven for 5 minutes. Pour in the mixture and bake uncovered for 45 to 50 minutes until lightly golden on top and a tester comes out clean.

6. Remove from the oven and cover with a serving platter. Allow to rest for 5 minutes (this helps to unmold the *kuku* more easily). Loosen the edges with a knife and invert onto the serving platter. Tap the bottom of the baking dish, let sit for a minute, then gently unmold. You may also serve it directly from the baking dish.

NOTES

Almonds or hazelnuts can be substituted for pistachios.

Photo left: Cluster of fresh pistachios on the tree.

VARIATION

Stovetop-Style Kuku—*Kuku* can also be cooked on top of the stove. Heat
  6 tablespoons oil in a 10-inch skillet (or frittata pan) over medium low heat until hot
  but not smoking. Pour in the mixture and cook, covered, until it has set (about 20 to
  25 minutes). If you have a frittata pan, simply flip over and cook for another
  10 to 15 minutes until golden. If you do not have a frittata pan, instead of flipping,
  you can cook the top under a hot broiler for 1 minute until lightly golden.

MEAT
CHICKEN &
FISH

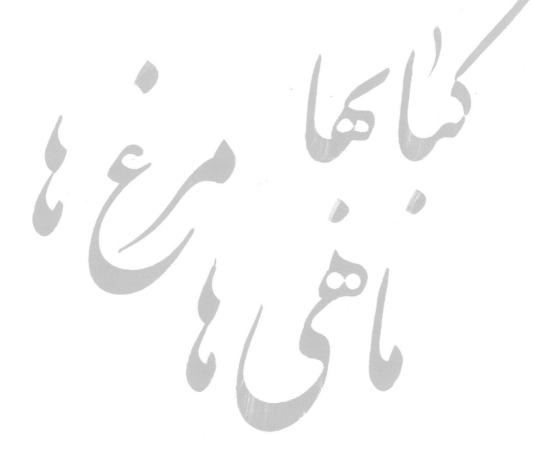

MEAT, CHICKEN, & FISH

PERSIAN GRILLING – KABABS

Since the discovery of fire, cooks have known that meats are imbued with a wonderful flavor when grilled over an open flame. The Persian word for grilled meat, kabab (I prefer this spelling and pronunciation; its common English variants are kebob and kabob), has entered the West's culinary vocabulary.

Kababs, convenient and virtually foolproof, are very popular. The meat is marinated in herbs, onion, garlic, and vinegar or lime juice or yogurt. Then, when it is nearly time to eat, the meat is threaded onto skewers (a small piece of lamb-tail fat can be placed between every two pieces of meat) and cooked over glowing charcoals for a subtly perfumed, flavor. Iranians prefer the very tender meat from the loin, but leg of lamb or even a beef sirloin can also be used. These are all best when marinated for at least 24 hours and up to 3 days before grilling.

The method for preparing and cooking kababs differs from traditional American barbecuing. Instead of wooden skewers, long, flat metal (preferably stainless steel) skewers are employed. Different widths serve for different types of kababs. For best results, ground meat kababs should not be cooked on a grill surface, rather they should straddle the coals and be supported at either end by the grill edges or bricks. The skewers should be turned frequently and the meat brushed with the baste mixture just before removing from the grill. The kabab is cooked just long enough to be seared on the outside, pink and juicy within. Keep in mind that the secret to a good kabab is a very hot fire. The following is a listing of the most popular kabab dishes:

Skewered Ground Lamb Kabab—
Kabab-e kubideh

Fillet Kabab—*Kabab-e barg*

Lamb Nugget Kabab—*Chenjeh kabab*

Veal Fillet Kabab—*Shahnameh kabab*

Lamb Rib Chops—*Shishlik-e Shandiz*

Shish Kabab—*Shish kabab*

Shirazi-Style Pan-cooked lamb kabab—
Kabab digy-e Shirazi

Lamb Fries Kabab—*Kabab-e donbalan*

Chicken Kabab—*Jujeh kabab*

Liver, Heart, and Kidney Kabab—
Kabab-e jigar-o del-o qolveh

Quail Kabab—*Kabab-e belderchin*

Sturgeon Kabab—*Kabab-e uzunbrun*

KABABS, AND MUSIC, AND WINE

در مجلس احرار چیست از فزونیه

و آن هر سه شرابست و ربابست و کباب

نه نقل به ما را از دفتر و فسانه

وین هر سه برین مجلس ما در نه صواب

دفتر به دبستان به و نقل به بازار

وین نو بجائی که خرابست خراب

ما کو شرابیم و ربابیم و کبابیم

خوشا که شرابست و ربابست و کبک

When those who know what's what
  Get together to dine,
We want three things, no more:
  Kababs, and music, and wine;
But snacks? Or books of poems?
  Or backgammon? These we decline:
Backgammon's strictly for hovels,
  Books in schoolrooms are fine,
And snacks belong in bazaars.
  No, we find we confine
Our requirements to three:
  Kababs, and music, and wine.

                    Manuchehri-e Damghani

Chelow Kabab (Rice with Meat Kabab)

Chelow kabab

Chelow kabab is Iran's national dish, the equivalent of steak and potatoes in the United States. It is served everywhere, from palaces to roadside stalls, but the best chelow kababs are probably those sold in the bazaars, where the rice is served with a tin cloche covering the plate to keep it warm, and the kababs are brought to the table by the waiter, who holds 5 or 10 skewers in his left hand and a piece of bread in his right hand. He places a skewer of meat directly on the rice and, holding it down with the bread, dramatically pulls out the skewer, leaving the sizzling kababs behind.

Chelow kabab consists of *chelow* (steamed rice) and kabab, skewers of lamb, veal, or beef cubes or ground meat marinated in saffron, onions, yogurt, and lime juice. Grilled tomatoes and raw onions are also an integral part of chelow kabab. The traditional way to serve *chelow kabab* is as follows:

Heap a pyramid of *chelow* on each plate. Add a dab of butter and sprinkle with a teaspoon of powdered sumac. Mix well.

Place the kababs (*kabab-e kubideh, kabab-e barg,* or a combination of both, called *sultani,* which literally means "kingly") and grilled tomatoes on the rice.

Serve hot with trimmings such as a fresh herb platter *(sabzi-khordan),* yogurt and cucumber *(mast-o khiar),* yogurt and shallots *(mast-o musir),* and Persian pickles *(torshi).* Chelow kabab is often washed down with *dugh,* a yogurt drink with mint, but a Pepsi with chelow kabab on Fridays for lunch was the treat of our childhood.

The prudent cook should always keep some meat marinating in the refrigerator at home to serve to unexpected guests and hungry members of the family. Then while the chelow is cooking, the fire can be started and the kababs prepared. This is truly convenience cooking—simple, yet nutritious and delicious. Children too love chelow kabab.

PHOTO ON THE FACING PAGE

A typical chelow kabab including, from left to right, skewered ground lamb kabab (kabab-e kubideh), *grilled tomatoes, a second skewer of ground lamb kabab, and a skewer of fillet kabab* (kabab-e barg). *On the plate there is steamed rice with a raw egg, butter, sumac, onion, basil, and radishes. On the side there is a plate of mixed vegetable pickle* (torshi-e makhlut). *The traditional drink with chelow kabab is made with yogurt and wild herbs* (dugh).

Fillet Kabab

Makes 4 servings
Preparation time: 20 minutes
 plus 2 hours of marinating
Cooking time: 2–3 minutes

Kabab-e barg

NOTES

Lamb fillet is hard to find and small, but some Whole Foods and most Halal meat butchers have it, or can get it for you (I get mine from Agha Reza at his Rockville Gourmet Halal Meat—he butchers his own lambs from Pennsylvania). Beef and veal tenderloin fillets are more readily available and make excellent kababs, but are not as tasty as a lamb kabab.

For a distinctively pomegranate-flavored kabab, replace the lime juice in the marinade with 2 tablespoons Sadaf pomegranate molasses, and replace the lime juice in the baste with 1 tablespoon pomegranate molasses.

2½ pounds lean lamb loin (fillet), or
  beef (tenderloin) or veal (veal tender)

MARINADE
Juice of 2 large yellow onions, peeled,
  grated, and juice squeezed out
  through a fine-mesh sieve
Zest of 1 fresh lime and its juice
½ cup olive oil
½ teaspoon sea salt
½ teaspoon freshly ground
  black pepper

8 cherry tomatoes or 4 large tomatoes,
  cut in quarters

BASTE
½ cup butter
1 tablespoon fresh lime juice
¼ teaspoon sea salt
½ teaspoon fresh ground black pepper
¼ teaspoon ground saffron dissolved
  in 1 tablespoon rose water (optional)

COOKING AND GARNISH
4 flat, thin ½-inch-wide skewers
1 package (12-ounce) *lavash* bread
2 tablespoons sumac powder
  (optional)

1. Have your butcher remove the backbone from the lamb loins, and trim all gristle from the main muscle.

2. Cut the whole fillet lengthwise into 2½-inch pieces (3 fingers wide). Each of these pieces then need to be cut into 2 horizontal slices. On a moist cutting board press down firmly one of the lamb pieces with your hand to flatten it slightly, and use a sharp knife to slice through it horizontally while holding down the meat. Repeat for the rest of the meat.

3. Thread each piece of meat onto the thinly flat, sword-like skewer, leaving a few inches free on both ends. Using another skewer, beat the edges of the meat, bringing them in to create a straight line. Arrange the skewers side by side on a large pan sheet.

4. Spear tomatoes on separate skewers.

5. In a mixing bowl, combine the onion juice, zest of lime and lime juice, olive oil, salt, and pepper, and pour over the skewered kababs. Cover with another pan sheet (inverted) and allow to marinate for 2 hours at room temperature. Turn the skewers in the marinade once during this period.

6. Start a bed of charcoal at least 30 minutes before you want to cook and let it burn until the coals glow. The secret to a good kabab is a very hot fire.

7. For basting, melt the butter, lime juice, salt, pepper, and saffron in a small sauce-pan. Keep warm.

8. When coals are ready, brush the tomatoes lightly with the baste. Place tomatoes on the grill first, and then arrange the skewered meat on the grill. Cook for 1 minute on one side, baste, and turn. Cook for another minute. The meat should be seared on the outside and pink and juicy on the inside.

9. Spread *lavash* bread on a serving platter. Place the kabab and grilled tomato skewers on the bread and brush them with the baste (keep them on the skewers until ready to serve). Sprinkle the kababs with sumac powder. Cover with *lavash* bread to keep warm.

10. Serve immediately with *chelow* (Saffron-flavored steamed), *lavash* bread, *torshi* (Persian pickles), and a dish of fresh herbs, especially spring onions and basil. Remove the meat from each skewer by placing a piece of *lavash* bread over several pieces of meat. Use a piece of bread to hold down the meat while you pull it off the skewer. *Nush-e Jan!*

1. PREPARING ONION MARINADE

2. CUTTING LOIN (WHOLE FILLET) INTO 2½-INCH LENGTHS

3. SLICING THE LOINS HORIZONTALLY

4. THREADING THE TENDERLOINS

5. BEATING EDGES WITH A SKEWER TO STRAIGHTEN

6. MARINATING LOINS

Skewered Ground Lamb Kabab

Makes 6 servings
Preparation time: 30 minutes
plus 30 minutes resting
Cooking time: 10 minutes

Kabab-e kubideh

NOTE

Keep the kabab paste cool at all times—before, during, and after skewering. If cooking outside be sure to keep the paste in a cooler.

The quantity of onion to meat is an essential factor in preventing the meat from falling off the skewer while cooking. For upscaling, use 4 medium yellow onions for 5 pounds of meat and 8 medium yellow onions for 10 pounds of meat.

LAMB KABAB
2 pounds twice-ground lamb shoulder, or 2 pounds twice-ground beef (85%)
2 teaspoons sea salt
2 teaspoons fresh ground black pepper
½ teaspoon ground saffron dissolved in 2 tablespoons rose water
¼ teaspoon turmeric
2 tablespoons sumac powder
½ teaspoon baking soda
2 medium yellow onions, finely grated
2 cloves garlic, peeled and grated

BASTE
½ cup salted butter
1 teaspoon fresh lime juice

COOKING AND GARNISH
14 flat ¾-inch skewers
1 package (12 ounces) *lavash* bread
½ cup sumac powder
2 limes, cut in half

1. To make the meat paste, in a warm, wide skillet, combine all the kabab ingredients. Knead with your hands for about 5 minutes. Cover the paste and let stand for at least 30 minutes and up to 24 hours in the refrigerator.

2. Start charcoal at least 30 minutes before you want to cook and let it burn until the coals are glowing evenly. For this kabab, you want the coals to be as high as possible, close to the meat, and at their hottest. Do not spread the charcoal thin. If you are using an indoor grill make sure it is preheated.

3. Using damp hands, divide the meat paste into equal lumps about the size of small oranges. Shape each into a 5-inch-long sausage and mold it firmly around a flat, sword-like skewer. Arrange on a baking sheet, separated from each other. Cover and keep in a cool place.

4. For the baste, melt the butter in a small saucepan and add the lime juice. Keep warm. Spread *lavash* bread on a serving platter.

5. Arrange the skewers on the fire 3 inches above the coals (bricks on either side make good platforms; keep in mind that the ground meat should not touch the grill). *After a few seconds, turn the meat gently to help it attach to the skewers and to prevent it from falling off* (these first few seconds are important for cooking skewered ground kabab).

6. Grill the meat for 3 to 5 minutes turning frequently. Baste just before removing from the fire. Avoid overcooking. The meat should be seared on the outside, juicy and tender on the inside.

7. Place all the kabab skewers on the *lavash* bread platter. Keep on skewers until ready to serve and cover with *lavash* bread to keep warm. Loosen the meat from each skewer and slide the meat off using a piece of bread. Sprinkle with sumac and lime juice to taste. Serve with fresh herbs and yogurt and cucumber dip. *Nush-e Jan!*

VARIATION

Ground Chicken Kabab—In a food processor, place 2 pounds chicken thighs, 1 small onion (peeled and chopped), 3 cloves garlic (peeled), zest of 2 limes, 2 teaspoons fine-grind sea salt, 1 teaspoon freshly ground black pepper, ¼ teaspoon ground saffron dissolved in 1 tablespoon rose water, and 1 tablespoon olive oil. Pulse for a few minutes until you have a thick paste. Do not overmix. Transfer to a glass container. Cover and allow to rest in the refrigerator for 30 minutes. Continue with step 2.

HOW IRANIANS BECAME MEAT EATERS

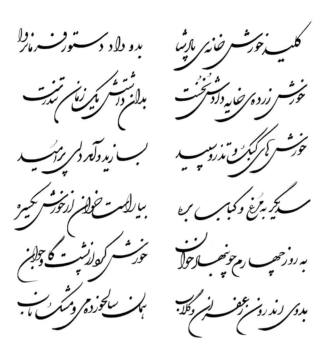

Iblis, the devil, presents himself to King Zahhak disguised as a charming young gourmet cook. The king gives him the key to the kitchen *(khoresh khaneh).* Up to that time people had been vegetarians and killing for food was unknown. The cook prepares a series of dishes *(khoreshes)* to ensnare the royal epicure. The feasts begin simply but increase in delicacy day by day.

The first night he cooks egg-yolk dishes to give the king vigorous health in a short time. The king thanks the cook for the delicacy of this food.

The second night the cook prepares a meal with partridge, gray pheasant, and quail.

The third night he serves a dish with chicken and lamb kabab mixed together.

The fourth night he sets a glamorous table and serves fillet of veal cooked in saffron, rose water, old wine, and pure musk.

By this time the king is literally eating out of the devil's hands and asks how he might express his gratitude. The reply seems innocent, even flattering; the cook wanted only to lay his face and eyes upon the king's shoulder. Zahhak grants the request. Iblis kisses him and vanishes. Suddenly, two ravenous black snakes sprout from Zahhak's shoulders.

From the *Shahnameh* of Ferdowsi (inspiration for kabab recipes on page 174)

Shahnameh Veal Kabab

Servings: 4
Preparation time: 20 minutes
 plus 2 hours of marinating
Cooking time: 2–3 minutes

کباب شاهنامه

Kabab-e Shahnameh

NOTES

The way the meat is cut and skewered for fillet kabab is important: Cut the veal fillet, against the grain, into 2½-inch strips. Cut each of these strips, along the grain, into 2 or 3 thin strips. Skewer these strips against the grain.

Kababs are delicate pieces of meat and are best eaten hot off the grill—they suffer if kept warm after they are ready. Make sure everything else is ready before serving the kababs. Serve with chelow (saffron-flavored steamed rice) or lavash bread, torshi (grape and garlic pickles), and a dish of fresh herbs, especially spring onions and basil. Loosen the first piece of meat on the skewer, hold all the meat down with the bread, and pull out the skewer.

2 pounds lean loin of veal
 (lamb or beef)

MARINADE
2 tablespoons olive oil
½ teaspoon sea salt
½ teaspoon freshly ground
 black pepper
Juice of 1 onion, peeled, pureed,
 and strained
½ teaspoon ground saffron dissolved in
 2 tablespoons rose water
2 cups Shiraz wine

BASTING
½ cup butter

COOKING AND GARNISH
4 flat, thin ½-inch-wide skewers
1 package (12 ounces) *lavash* bread
Coarse sea salt
Dried rose petals, crushed
Pickles
Basil
Spring onions

1. Cut the whole fillet lengthwise into 2½-inch pieces (3 fingers wide). Each of these pieces then need to be cut into 2 horizontal slices. On a moist cutting board press down firmly on one of the veal pieces with your hand to flatten it slightly, and use a sharp knife to slice through it horizontally while holding down the meat. Repeat for the rest of the meat.

2. Thread each piece of meat (against the grain) onto the flat, sword-like skewer, leaving a few inches free on both ends. Using another skewer, pound the meat gently with the edge to tenderize it. Place the skewers side by side on a large pan sheet.

3. In a mixing bowl, combine olive oil, salt, pepper, onion juice, saffron-rose water, and wine. Pour over the skewered kababs. Cover with another pan sheet (inverted). Allow to marinate for 2 hours at room temperature. Turn the skewers in the marinade once during this period.

4. Meanwhile, thread the meat onto the flat, sword-like metal skewer, leaving a few inches free on both ends. Using the edge of a skewer or the back of a large knife, beat the edges of the meat to straighten and to tenderize it (see photos on page 169).

5. Start a bed of charcoal at least 30 minutes before you want to cook and let it burn until the coals glow. Or, switch on the grill until very hot.

6. For basting, melt the butter in a small saucepan and keep warm. Spread *lavash* bread on a serving platter and set aside.

7. When coals are ready (the key to cooking any kabab is a very hot grill). Arrange the skewers on the grill. Cook for 1 minute on one side, baste and turn, cook for another minute, and baste again. The meat should be seared on the outside, pink and juicy on the inside.

8. When the meat is cooked, place the skewers of kababs on the bread. Sprinkle with salt and rose petals. Cover with *lavash* bread to keep warm. Serve with pickles, basil, and spring onions.

Lamb Nuggets Kabab

Makes 4 servings
Preparation time: 20 minutes
* plus 4 hours of marinating*
Cooking time: 6 minutes

2 pounds lean lamb tenderloin or
  leg of lamb
1 large onion, peeled and grated
4 tablespoons olive oil
2 tablespoons plain yogurt
½ teaspoon sea salt
½ teaspoon freshly ground
  black pepper
2 tablespoons fresh lime juice

COOKING AND GARNISH
¼ pound lamb tail-fat, cut into cubes
4 large tomatoes, cut in half
1 package (12 ounces) of *lavash* bread
6 flat, ½-inch-wide sword-like skewers

BASTE
½ cup melted butter or ghee*
2 tablespoons fresh lime juice or
  pomegranate molasses
¼ teaspoon ground saffron dissolved
  in 1 tablespoon hot water
½ teaspoon sea salt
¼ teaspoon freshly ground pepper

Chenjeh kabab

NOTE
You can find tail-fat from halal butchers.

1. Have your butcher remove back bones from the lamb loins, then the fillets from the loins, and then trim the gristle from the main muscles.

2. Cut meat into 2-inch cubes. If using leg of lamb, pound each piece lightly with a heavy-bladed knife to make shallow incisions along the meat. Cut tail-fat into 1-inch cubes. Place meat and tail-fat in a large bowl.

3. Add onion, olive oil, yogurt, salt, pepper, and lime juice. Toss well. Cover the meat and marinate for at least 4 hours in the refrigerator (if using leg of lamb, marinate for 2 days).

4. Start a bed of charcoal 30 minutes before you want to cook and let it burn until the coals glow (the secret of a good kabab is a very hot grill).

5. During this time, thread 5 or 6 pieces of meat onto each skewer and thread 1 piece of tail-fat between every two pieces of meat, leaving a few inches free on both ends. Using the edge of a skewer or the back of a large knife, pound the meat gently to tenderize it. Spear tomatoes onto separate skewers.

6. In a small saucepan, melt butter. Add the lime juice, saffron water, salt, and pepper to your taste. Keep warm. Baste the tomatoes with a little of this mixture.

7. When the coals are glowing, first place tomatoes on grill. After 1 minute, arrange the skewered on the grill. Cook for 1 minute, turning frequently and basting occasionally. The meat should be seared on the outside, pink and juicy on the inside.

8. Spread *lavash* bread on a serving platter. When the meat is cooked, place the skewers of meat on the bread and brush them with the baste. Garnish with grilled tomatoes. Try a piece to taste (cook's privilege). Cover with *lavash* bread to keep warm.

9. Serve immediately with Persian pickles (*torshi*) and a dish of fresh herbs, especially spring onions and basil. Remove the meat from each skewer by taking a piece of *lavash* bread, placing it over several pieces of meat, and using the bread to slide the meat off the skewer. *Nush-e Jan!*

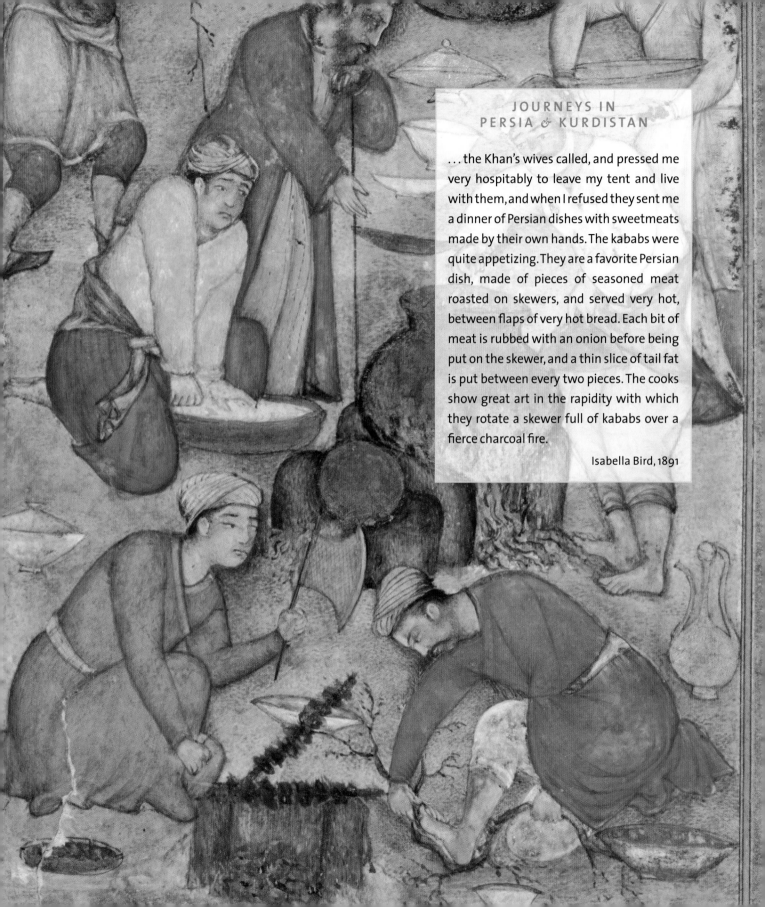

JOURNEYS IN PERSIA & KURDISTAN

...the Khan's wives called, and pressed me very hospitably to leave my tent and live with them, and when I refused they sent me a dinner of Persian dishes with sweetmeats made by their own hands. The kababs were quite appetizing. They are a favorite Persian dish, made of pieces of seasoned meat roasted on skewers, and served very hot, between flaps of very hot bread. Each bit of meat is rubbed with an onion before being put on the skewer, and a thin slice of tail fat is put between every two pieces. The cooks show great art in the rapidity with which they rotate a skewer full of kababs over a fierce charcoal fire.

Isabella Bird, 1891

Lamb Rib Chops

Makes 4 servings
Preparation time: 20 minutes
 plus 2 days of marinating
Cooking time: 6 minutes

شیشلیک

Shishlik-e Shandiz

24 small single lamb rib chops
  (French cut)

MARINADE
1 large onion, thinly sliced
1 bulb garlic (10–12 cloves), peeled and
  crushed
2 tablespoons orange zest
1 cup fresh lime juice
2 teaspoons sea salt
2 teaspoons freshly ground black pepper
¼ cup olive oil
1 cup plain yogurt
½ teaspoon ground saffron threads
  dissolved in 2 tablespoons rose water
1 teaspoon grape molasses or honey

BASTING
2 tablespoons melted butter
Juice of 2 limes
½ teaspoon sea salt
½ teaspoon freshly ground black pepper

COOKING & GARNISH
6 thin metal skewers, or bamboo skewers
  soaked in water for 2 hours
1 package (12 ounces) *lavash* bread
1 bunch spring onions
1 bunch rosemary

1. Rinse the lamb rib chops in a colander with cool water and pat dry thoroughly with paper towels.

2. Prepare the marinade by mixing all of its ingredients in a large, deep, nonreactive container. Rub the rib chops thoroughly on both sides, one at a time, with marinade. Cover and marinate for 2 days (for best results) in the refrigerator. Turn the chops once during this time.

3. Start a bed of charcoal at least 30 minutes before you want to cook and let it burn until the coals glow, or turn on the oven grill or broiler until *very hot*. The secret to good kababs is a very hot fire.

4. Meanwhile, thread the chops flat side up onto flat skewers; the skewers will go through the bone, which is soft.

5. For basting, combine the butter, lime juice, salt, and pepper in a small saucepan. Keep warm over very low heat.

6. When the coals are glowing, place the skewers on the grill. Grill for 4 to 6 minutes on each side, turning occasionally. The chops should be seared on the outside and juicy on the inside. Baste the chops just before removing from the flame.

NOTE

Kababs are delicate and are best eaten hot off the grill—they suffer if kept warm after they are ready. Make sure everything else is ready before serving the kababs. Spread lavash *bread on a serving platter. When the chops are done baste both sides again. Then hold the skewers over the platter, steady the meat with some* lavash *bread, and pull the skewers, leaving the chops on the platter. Sprinkle with a little coarse salt. Garnish with spring onions and rosemary, and cover with* lavash *bread to keep warm. Serve immediately.*

Shish Kabab

Makes 6 servings
Preparation time: 30 minutes
 plus 8–24 hours of marinating
Cooking time: 10 minutes.

MARINADE
1 large onion, chopped
4 cloves garlic, sliced
½ cup apple cider vinegar
Juice of 1 lime
½ cup olive oil
2 teaspoons fresh ground black pepper
2 teaspoons sea salt
1 cup chopped fresh dill
1 teaspoon dried thyme
Zest of 1 lime
2 cups plain whole yogurt

KABABS
2 pounds lamb, veal (or beef, from the
  boned loin or sirloin, or boneless
  chicken thighs, cut into 2-inch cubes)
4 green peppers, seeds and ribs
  removed, cut into 1-inch squares

6 large tomatoes, quartered
10 cloves garlic, peeled
10 pearl onions or 3 large ones, peeled
  and cut into 2-inch cubes
10 white button mushrooms
10 bay leaves

6 bamboo skewers

BASTE
½ cup butter
Juice of 1 lime

GARNISH
1 package (12 ounces) *lavash* bread
2 cups plain drained yogurt
Bunch of fresh spring onions
Bunch of fresh basil

Shish kabab

1. In a long, shallow glass or Pyrex dish combine all the marinade ingredients and set aside.

2. Thread each piece of meat onto the bamboo skewers, alternating them with pieces of pepper, tomatoes, garlic, onions, mushrooms, and bay leaves. Place the skewers in the marinade.

3. Agitate the dish so that the marinade coats all sides of the kababs. Cover and marinate for at least 8 hours and up to 3 days in the refrigerator. Turn the kababs at least twice, so that each side is equally marinated.

4. Start a bed of charcoal at least 30 minutes before you want to cook and let it burn until the coals glow. You can use a hair dryer to accelerate this process.

5. When the coals are glowing, arrange the skewers on the grill. Cook for 6 to 10 minutes, turning frequently.

6. In a saucepan, melt ½ cup butter and add the juice of 1 lime. Just before removing kababs from the fire, baste both sides with the butter and lime mixture.

7. Arrange the skewers on a serving platter and serve immediately with *lavash* bread, yogurt, fresh spring onions, and fresh basil. *Nush-e jan!*

NOTE
Shish *is the Turkish word for "skewer." The Persian word is* sikh.

Shirazi-Style Pan-Cooked Lamb Kabab

Makes 4 servings
Preparation time: 30 minutes
Cooking time: 2 hours 30 minutes

کباب دیگی

Kabab digy-e Shirazi

NOTE
You can replace the saffron with 1 teaspoon turmeric.

2 pounds boned leg of lamb, cut into 2-inch cubes
5–6 fig branch skewers or wooden skewers
½ cup oil or butter
2 large onions
2 teaspoons sea salt
1 teaspoon freshly ground pepper
½ teaspoon ground saffron dissolved in 2 tablespoons rose water or hot water
Zest of 2 limes

2 large tomatoes, peeled and sliced into rings

GARNISH
5 fig leaves, washed thoroughly (optional)
Juice of 1 lime
1 cup plain drained yogurt
1 package (12-ounce) *lavash* bread
Bunch of fresh spring onions
Bunch of fresh basil

1. Rinse the lamb thoroughly and drain.

2. Thread each fig branch with 5 pieces of lamb and set aside.

3. Grease a wide, shallow pot with ¼ cup oil.

4. Peel and cut the onion into thin rings and arrange a layer to fit the bottom of the pot.

5. Sprinkle with a pinch of salt and pepper, a few drops of saffron-rose water, and zest of 1 lime.

6. Place the kabab skewers side by side on top of the onion rings and sprinkle with a pinch of salt and pepper, the rest of the saffron-rose water, and zest of 1 lime.

7. Arrange the tomato slices on top, sprinkle with the rest of the salt and pepper, and drizzle with the rest of the oil

8. Cover tightly and cook over low heat for 2 to 2½ hours or until the lamb is tender. Adjust seasoning to taste by adding more salt or pepper. Keep warm until ready to serve.

9. Line a serving platter with fig leaves or lavash bread and arrange the kababs skewers on top. Pour the pan juices over the kababs. Drizzled with fresh lime juice and serve with drained yogurt, bread, or plain steamed rice, and fresh herbs. *Nush-e jan!*

Lamb and Fruit Casserole

Makes 6 servings
Preparation time: 15 minutes
Cooking time: 2 hours 30 minutes

4 tablespoons oil or butter
4 large onions, peeled and sliced
2 pounds leg of lamb, boned and thinly
　sliced (or choose chicken or beef)
2 cloves garlic, peeled and crushed
2 quinces, or 2 apples, cored and sliced
1 small eggplant, peeled and sliced
2 carrots, peeled and sliced
3 tomatoes, peeled and sliced
2 large potatoes, peeled and sliced
1 cup pitted prunes
2 cups dried apricots
2 teaspoons *advieh* (Persian spice mix)*

½ teaspoon turmeric
2 teaspoons sea salt
½ teaspoon freshly ground
　black pepper
1 cup tomato juice
½ teaspoon ground saffron dissolved
　in 1 tablespoon hot water
1 tablespoon *gard-e ghureh* (unripe
　grape powder)*
1 tablespoon *limu-omani*
　(Persian lime powder)*

Tas kabab

1. Preheat oven to 350°F (180°C). Pour 2 tablespoons oil into a large ovenproof casserole. Layer the ingredients in the following order: onions, meat, garlic, quinces or apples, eggplant, carrots, tomatoes, and potatoes. Top with a layer of prunes and apricots. Pour in the remaining oil. Sprinkle *advieh*, turmeric, salt, and pepper on top. Mix together the tomato juice, saffron water, grape powder, and *limu-omani* powder, and pour over the meat and vegetables. Cover tightly with a layer of parchment paper and a layer of aluminum foil, and cook in the oven for 2 to 2½ hours or until it is done. Season to taste.

2. Serve in the same dish with bread, yogurt, salad, and fresh herbs. *Nush-e Jan!*

NOTE

This casserole may also be cooked on the stove in a heavy Dutch oven over low heat for 2 hours, or until the lamb and potatoes are tender.

Ground Lamb Skillet Kabab

Makes 4 servings
Preparation time: 15 minutes
Cooking time: 35 minutes

Kabab-e kubideh-ye maitabehi

LAMB
1 pound ground lamb (beef or chicken)
1 medium onion, finely chopped
2 cloves garlic, peeled and finely chopped
1 teaspoon sea salt
½ teaspoon fresh ground pepper
1 teaspoon turmeric
1 tablespoon sumac
½ teaspoon red pepper flakes
1 teaspoon *advieh* (Persian spice mix)*
1 teaspoon grape molasses or sugar
2 tablespoons oil

TOPPING
1 large tomato, peeled and sliced
½ teaspoon sea salt
½ teaspoon fresh ground pepper
1 tablespoon oil

1. In a mixing bowl, combine all the ingredients for the lamb, except the oil. Knead lightly, using your hands, to create a soft paste (do not overmix).

2. Oil a heavy-based 8-inch skillet. Moisten your hands and shape the paste into a large meatball and place it in the skillet. Press down so the meat covers the base of the entire skillet. Raise the meat around the diameter of the skillet by 1 inch to form a well.

3. Cook over medium heat for 15 minutes. Cut the meat into pie wedges. Arrange the tomato slices on top and sprinkle salt, pepper, and oil. Cover and cook for 15 minutes over low heat until cooked through. Remove the cover and brown the top under a broiler for 1 or 2 minutes. Serve the wedges with some of the pan juices drizzled on top, bread, and fresh herbs. *Nush-e Jan!*

Meat Patties

Makes 10 patties
Preparation time: 45 minutes
Cooking time: 45 minutes

Kotlet-e gusht

VEGETARIAN VARIATION
Cook 2 cups dried lentils with 4 cups water and ½ teaspoon salt for 30 minutes or until lentils are tender. Drain thoroughly, allow to cool, and use in place of the lamb in step 1.

1 pound ground lamb (chicken, or beef)
1 medium onion, peeled and grated
2 eggs
2 large potatoes, boiled for 15 minutes, peeled, and coarsely grated
2 teaspoons sea salt
1 teaspoon freshly ground black pepper
1 teaspoon turmeric
2 teaspoons *advieh* (Persian spice mix)*
¼ teaspoon ground saffron dissolved in 1 tablespoon hot water
¾ cup oil (for frying)
¾ cup dry bread crumbs

GARNISH
2 tablespoons oil
4 ripe tomatoes, peeled and sliced
½ teaspoon sea salt
½ teaspoon pepper

1. In a mixing bowl combine lamb, onion, eggs, potatoes, salt, pepper, turmeric, *advieh*, and saffron water. Knead for 5 minutes to form a smooth paste.

2. Heat ½ cup oil in a wide skillet over medium heat. Dip your hands in a bowl of water to moisten them. Shape the lamb mixture into lumps the size of eggs. Flatten them into oval patties and roll in the bread crumbs. Brown the patties on both sides in the skillet. Add more oil if necessary.

3. To make a tomato sauce: Heat 2 tablespoons oil in a wide skillet and stir-fry the tomatoes. Add ½ teaspoon salt and ½ teaspoon pepper. Cover and cook over low heat for 15 minutes. Arrange the patties on a serving platter. Pour the tomato sauce on top. Serve with french fries, bread, salad, fresh herbs, and *torshi* (Persian pickles). *Nush-e Jan!*

Lamb Liver, Heart, and Kidney Kabab

Makes 4 servings
Preparation time: 20 minutes
Cooking time: 6 minutes

*Kabab-e jigar-o
del-o qolveh*

1 lamb liver
4 lamb kidneys
4 lamb hearts

½ teaspoon sea salt
1 teaspoon freshly ground pepper
Juice of 3 limes

1. Clean liver and cut into strips 1 inch thick. Cut kidneys into 1-inch cubes and slice hearts lengthwise into strips 1½ inches thick.

2. Light a bed of charcoal and let it burn until the coals glow evenly or preheat the broiler in your oven.

3. Skewer strips of liver, cubes of kidney, and slices of heart onto separate ⅛-inch-wide skewers (cooking times are different for each).

4. Grill over hot coals for approximately 6 minutes for hearts, 5 minutes for kidneys, and 4 minutes for the liver. Turn skewers frequently while grilling.

5. After cooking, sprinkle with salt, pepper, and lime juice.

6. Serve immediately with bread, spring onions, and Persian pickles (*torshi*) or serve as an appetizer with drinks. *Nush-e Jan!*

NOTE

A marvelous way to cook these meats is to grill them while you are sitting around the fireplace. Devise an ingenious cooking grill for inside your fireplace.

Lamb Fries Kabab

Makes 4 servings
Preparation time: 10 minutes
Cooking time: 6 minutes

Kabab-e donbalan

4 lamb fries
2 tablespoons melted butter

sea salt
freshly ground black pepper

1. Place the lamb fries in a large bowl of cool water. Wash and drain them and cut each one in half.

2. Remove the thin outer membrane from the fries.

3. Light a bed of charcoal and let it burn until the coals glow evenly or preheat the broiler in your oven.

4. Thread the fries onto the skewers. Paint them with melted butter and grill them over hot coals for about 4 to 6 minutes, turning them over often and quickly.

5. Serve very hot and season to taste with salt and pepper. *Nush-e Jan!*

NOTE

Wherever lamb is raised for meat, the fries, or testicles, are considered a great delicacy. They are usually referred to by terms such as Rocky Mountain or prairie oysters, or swinging steak in the United States, or caprices de femme (lady's whims) in France. Whatever you call them, they are excellent as an appetizer served with drinks.

Chicken Kabab

Makes 6–8 servings
Preparation time: 20 minutes
plus 24 hours of marinating
Cooking time: 15 minutes

Jujeh kabab

VARIATIONS

Goose or Duck—Meat must be cooked in a brine mixture prior to marination. Cook for 1 hour with 2 onions, 1 tablespoon parsley, 2 tablespoons vinegar, 2 tablespoons salt, and 4 cups water. Drain, cut up, and marinate as in step 1.

Quail and Partridge—Cut into pieces and marinate for 2 hours in milk. Drain and substitute for chicken.

NOTE

You may broil the chicken pieces in a broiler pan for 10 minutes on each side. During the cooking the door of the broiler should be shut. In this way the broiled chicken will be tender. Use wooden skewers soaked in water for 1 hour.

MARINADE
¼ teaspoon ground saffron dissolved in 2 tablespoons rose water
Zest of 2 limes
¼ cup fresh lime juice
¼ cup apple cider vinegar
¾ cup olive oil
2 large onions, peeled and thinly sliced
2 cloves garlic, peeled and crushed
½ cup whole plain yogurt
2 teaspoons sea salt
2½ teaspoons freshly ground black pepper

CHICKEN
6 Cornish hens, about 4 pounds, each cut into 10 pieces, or 6 pounds of chicken drumettes, or 4 pounds boneless chicken thighs cut into 2-inch pieces
5 medium tomatoes, halved, or 16 cherry

BASTE
½ cup butter
Juice of ½ lime

GARNISH
1 package (12 ounces) *lavash* bread
2 limes, cut in half
3 bunches fresh basil leaves
Sumac powder (optional)
12 flat ½-inch sword-like metal skewers or 16 wooden skewers

1. In a 4-quart nonreactive container with cover, combine all the ingredients for the marination. Beat well with a fork. Add the chicken and toss well. Cover and marinate for at least 24 hours and up to 3 days in the refrigerator. Turn the chicken twice during this period (best results are with 3 days of marination).

2. Start a bed of charcoal 30 minutes before you want to cook and let it burn until the coals glow evenly, or preheat the oven broiler. Keep in mind that the success of a good kabab depends on a very hot grill.

3. Meanwhile, skewer the tomatoes. Spear wings, breasts, and legs onto different skewers (they require different cooking times). Place on a baking sheet next to you.

4. In a small saucepan, heat the butter and lime juice over low heat. Keep warm.

5. Paint the tomato with the basting mixture. Grill the chicken and tomatoes 8 to 15 minutes, turning frequently until done. The chicken is done when the juice that runs out is yellow rather than pink.

6. Meanwhile, spread a whole *lavash* bread on a flat serving platter. Remove the chicken and tomato from the grill and place on the *lavash* bread. Paint the chicken with the basting mixture. Keep chicken on the skewers until just before serving— this helps to keep it warm. To remove the chicken from skewers steady them on the platter with a piece of bread and pull out the skewers. Garnish with limes and sprigs of basil. Cover the kababs with more bread.

7. Serve immediately with basil, yogurt, cucumber, and rose petal dip *(mast-o khiar)*, and, if desired, pinches of sumac. *Nush-e Jan!*

Quail Kabab with Verjuice and Saffron

Make 6 servings
Preparation time: 20
  minutes plus 8 – 24 hours
  of marinating
Cooking time: 10 minutes

QUAIL
12 semi-boned quails (leg and wing intact)

MARINADE
6 cloves garlic, peeled and sliced
1-inch fresh ginger, peeled and grated
1 cup olive oil
½ teaspoon ground saffron dissolved in 2 tablespoons rose water
½ cup grape molasses (*shireh-ye angur*)*
⅓ cup verjuice (*ab-ghureh*, unripe grape juice)*
2 tablespoons lime juice
2 teaspoons sea salt

2 teaspoons freshly ground black pepper

GLAZE
1 tablespoon butter
1 tablespoon fresh lime juice
1 tablespoon grape molasses

ROSE PETAL SALT
Mix together:
¼ teaspoon coarse salt
½ teaspoon freshly ground pepper
2 tablespoons ground dried rose petals
½ teaspoon ground cumin

1 package (12 ounces) *lavash* bread

كباب بلدرچين

Kabab-e belderchin

1. Rinse the quails and pat dry.

2. For the marinade: In a nonreactive container, combine the garlic, ginger, olive oil, saffron-rose water, grape molasses, verjuice, lime juice, salt, and pepper. Rub the inside and outside of the quails thoroughly with the marinade mixture.

3. Make an incision through the thigh of one leg of each quail and slide the end of the other leg through it to keep the legs together.

4. Place the quails in the container with the marinade, cover, and marinate in the refrigerator for 8 hours and up to 24 hours. Turn the quails in the marinade once during this period.

5. To make the kabab: Start a bed of charcoal at least 30 minutes before you want to cook and let it burn until the coals are glowing, or turn on the grill until very hot.

6. Spread a flat bread on a serving platter and set aside.

7. Remove the birds from the marinade and skewer on metal skewers.

8. Cook each side 7 to 10 minutes, turning frequently. The quails are cooked when they are crisp and golden on the outside and the juices that run out are yellow and not pink.

9. Meanwhile, to make the glaze, melt the butter in a saucepan and add the rest of the ingredients. Stir well. Brush the quail with the glaze just before removing from the grill.

10. Transfer the skewered quails onto *lavash* bread and cover with more bread. When ready to eat, place your hand on the bread, press down, and pull out the skewers. Sprinkle with rose petal salt. *Nush-e Jan!*

VARIATION

Pan-Roasted Quails—In a baking pan, heat 2 tablespoons butter and 1 tablespoon oil over medium-high heat and brown all sides of the quails. Remove from heat, cover, and set aside. Just before serving preheat oven to 500°F (260°C), uncover the quails, and bake in the same pan for 3 to 5 minutes until done. Meanwhile, make the glaze in a small saucepan and brush the quails.

Sturgeon Kabab

Makes 4 servings
Preparation time: 20 minutes
  plus 8 hours of marinating
Cooking time: 10 minutes

كباب ازون برون

Kabab-e uzunbrun

2 pounds sturgeon skin removed and
  cut into 2-inch cubes

MARINADE
1 large onion, peeled and grated
zest of 2 fresh limes and their juice
1 teaspoon sea salt
½ teaspoon freshly ground
  black pepper
½ teaspoon red pepper flakes (optional)

BASTE
6 flat, ½-inch-wide sword-like skewers
juice of one lime
⅓ cup butter or olive oil
1 cup tomato juice or 1 tablespoon
  tomato paste
1 teaspoon grape molasses
1 package (12 ounces) *lavash* bread

GARNISH
⅓ cup fresh chopped parsley

1. Wash the fish and pat dry. Cut into cubes and place in a mixing bowl with all the ingredients for the marinade. Toss well, cover, and refrigerate for 2 hours.

2. Start charcoal 30 minutes before you want to cook and let it burn until the coals are glowing evenly. Meanwhile, thread the cubes of fish onto the skewers.

3. In a saucepan, combine all the ingredients for the baste and keep warm.

4. Once the coals are evenly lit, grill the fish for 1 to 2 minutes, baste, turn, and grill for another 1 to 2 minutes. Avoid overcooking. The fish should be seared on the outside, juicy and tender on the inside.

5. Spread *lavash* bread on a serving platter. Arrange the fish on the bread and garnish with parsley. Serve immediately. *Nush-e Jan!*

Fish Kabab with Bitter Orange

Makes 4 servings
Preparation time: 10 minutes
  plus 2 hours of marinating
Cooking time: 5–7 minutes

كباب ماهی با نارنج

Kabab-e mahi ba narenj

4 thick fillets of swordfish or salmon,
  skin removed and cut into 2-inch cubes

MARINADE
2 onions, peeled and grated
5 cloves garlic, peeled and crushed
½ cup oil or butter

1 cup bitter orange juice or
  pomegranate juice or verjuice
1 teaspoon grape molasses or honey
1 teaspoon sea salt
½ teaspoon freshly ground
  black pepper
1 teaspoon angelica powder

1. Rinse the fish and pat dry. Place them in a nonreactive container and add all the ingredients for the marinade. Toss well, cover, and marinate for a minimum of 2 hours and up to 8 hours in the refrigerator.

2. Preheat the grill or broiler and spear fish cubes onto skewers.

3. Grill the fish for 1 to 2 minutes on each side.

4. Serve with smothered rice (*kateh*) and fresh herbs. *Nush-e Jan!*

Pomegranate-Infused Braised Leg of Lamb

Makes 6 servings
Preparation time: 45 minutes
Cooking time: 3 hours 30 minutes

بره بریان

Barreh-ye beriyan

NOTE

I like to serve this lamb with Rice with Fresh Dill and Fava Beans (Baghali Polow).

You can also make this recipe by searing the lamb, adding the rest of the ingredients to the baking pan (as I am doing in the photo), covering, and baking per step 6.

For a southern Iranian flavor, replace the pomegranate juice and molasses with 4 cups water and 1 cup tamarind paste.

1 leg of lamb (6–7 pounds)
10 cloves garlic, peeled

DUSTING
Mixture of 1 teaspoon sea salt,
    1 teaspoon pepper, 1 teaspoon
    turmeric, and 1 tablespoon flour

SAUCE
3 tablespoons oil, butter, or ghee*
2 large yellow onions, peeled and
    finely diced
1 cup walnuts, finely ground

3 cups pomegranate juice
¼ cup pomegranate molasses
2 tablespoons honey
2 teaspoons sea salt
2 teaspoons red pepper flakes
1 teaspoon fresh ground pepper
1 tablespoon ground cardamom
1 teaspoon saffron threads ground and
    dissolved in 2 tablespoons rose water
¼ cup lime juice

1. Preheat the oven to 350°F (180°C). Rinse and thoroughly pat dry the leg of lamb.

2. Use the point of a knife to make 10 slits all over the leg of lamb. Insert the cloves of garlic in the slits. Dust the lamb with dusting mixture.

3. In a large, deep baking dish heat 3 tablespoons oil over medium heat until very hot and sear the lamb on both sides. Remove from the pan.

4. Add the onions in the same baking dish and fry until golden brown. Transfer the onions to a food processor and add the remaining ingredients—but only 1 cup of pomegranate juice. Grind finely until you have a smooth sauce (not grainy).

5. Return the lamb to the pan and add the sauce and remaining pomegranate juice.

6. Cover the lamb with a piece of parchment paper and then with aluminum foil. Bake in a 350°F (180°C) preheated oven for 2½. Uncover and turn the lamb in its sauce. Continue to bake uncovered for 45 minutes or until the lamb falls off the bone easily. Remove the lamb from the baking dish, cover, and set aside. Reduce the sauce in the baking dish by cooking it over high heat for 4 to 5 minutes (you should have about 1½ cups sauce). Adjust seasoning of the sauce by adding more salt, pepper, or grape molasses. Return the lamb to the baking dish and keep warm in the oven until ready to serve.

7. Serve slices of the lamb with some sauce on top. *Nush-e Jan!*

VARIATIONS

Pomegranate-Infused Butterfly Turkey Braise—Replace the leg of lamb with a 9-10-pound butterflied turkey (backbone removed and turkey flattened—butchers will do this if you ask for it).

Kashk-Infused Braised Leg of Lamb—Replace the pomegranate juice and molasses with 2 cups water. Just before serving, add 4 cups hot liquid *kashk* and 4 tablespoons dried mint flakes, cover and allow to rest for 20 minutes.

Pistachio-Stuffed Leg of Lamb

Makes 12 servings
Preparation time: 1 hour 30 minutes
Cooking time: 5 to 6 hours

1 baby lamb, 14 to 18 pounds
Juice of 2 onions
1 tablespoon sea salt
¼ cup fresh lime juice
10 cloves garlic, peeled

STUFFING
2 cups long-grain basmati rice
½ cup oil, butter, or ghee*
4 large onions, peeled and thinly sliced
2 cups chopped raw pistachios
1 cup chopped fresh parsley
1 cup chopped fresh cilantro
1 cup raisins
2 cups dried apricots, chopped

1 cup dried barberries *(zereshk)*, cleaned, washed and drained
2 teaspoons sea salt
2 teaspoons freshly ground black pepper
1 teaspoon turmeric
2 tablespoons *advieh* (Persian spice mix)*

BASTE
1 cup melted butter, ghee,* or oil
2 teaspoons ground saffron dissolved in ¼ cup rose water
¼ cup lime juice or pomegranate juice or tamarind paste

Barreh-ye tu por ba pesteh

NOTE

This spectacular dish is served on festive occasions. It is often the centerpiece of a lavish wedding. Several lambs would be prepared to serve all the guests.

As an alternative, you may use a 5-pound boned leg of lamb. Place it in an ovenproof baking dish, stuff it by making a slit in the back and sewing it after it has been stuffed, or by butterflying it. Reduce the stuffing ingredients to ⅓ and bake for 3 or 4 hours.

1. Order your lamb ahead of time. Ask your butcher to prepare the lamb for stuffing and to bone the legs.

2. Rinse the lamb inside and out, and wipe dry with a towel. Place the lamb in a greased roasting pan. Rub inside and out with mixture of onion juice, salt, and lime juice.

3. Using the point of a small knife, make 10 slits in the lamb and insert a clove of garlic in each. Set aside while preparing the stuffing.

4. To make the stuffing: in a saucepan, cook rice for 20 minutes in 4 cups water and 1 teaspoon salt. Drain and set aside.

5. Preheat the oven to 350°F (180°C). In a large skillet, sauté the onions and garlic in the oil. Add the nuts, herbs, fruit, and spices. Sauté for 5 minutes. Set aside.

6. In a large mixing bowl, combine the rice with the rest of the stuffing. Stuff the lamb tightly with this mixture and sew up the belly. Use a large trussing needle and strong kitchen thread.

7. To make the baste: In a saucepan, combine the melted butter, saffron-rose water, and lime juice. Brush the entire lamb with this mixture. Cover with a layer of parchment paper and seal with aluminium foil. Bake in the oven for 4 hours basting occasionally. Uncover and bake for 30 to 45 minutes or until meat separates easily from the bone.

8. Lay the lamb on a mound of *chelow* (saffron-flavored steamed rice) on a platter, and serve with *torshi* (Persian pickles) and *sabzi-khordan* (fresh herbs and vegetables). *Nush-e Jan!*

Chickpea Flour Meatballs (Gondi)

Makes 6 servings
Preparation time: 20 minutes
Cooking time: 1 hour

MEATBALLS
2 tablespoons oil, butter, or ghee*
1 large onion, peeled and thinly sliced
1 pound ground lamb
  (chicken or turkey)
1 teaspoon sea salt
½ teaspoon freshly ground pepper
1 teaspoon ground cardamom
½ teaspoon ground saffron dissolved
  in 2 tablespoons rose water
½ cup chickpea flour

BROTH
2 tablespoons oil, butter, or ghee*
1 large onion, peeled and thinly sliced

1 teaspoon sea salt
¼ teaspoon freshly ground pepper
½ teaspoon turmeric
4½ cups water
1 tablespoon vinegar or ¼ cup verjuice
  (*ab-ghureh*, unripe grape juice)*

1 teaspoon grape molasses or sugar

GARNISH
2 tablespoons fresh chopped parsley
2 tablespoons fresh chopped cilantro
2 tablespoons fresh chopped basil
2 tablespoons fresh chopped mint

Gondi

1. To make the meatballs: Heat 2 tablespoons oil in a frying pan and sauté the onion. Remove from the heat and allow to cool. Line a baking sheet with parchment paper and set aside.

2. In a mixing bowl, add the lamb, sautéed onion, salt, pepper, cardamom, and saffron-rose water. Mix lightly using two forks. Add the chickpea flour, a little at a time, and 2 tablespoons water and continue to mix (do not overmix). Shape the mixture into walnut-sized meatballs and arrange on the baking sheet. Set aside.

3. To make the broth: Heat 2 tablespoons oil in a medium-sized pot and sauté the onions until golden brown. Add the salt, pepper, and turmeric, , and stir-fry for 1 minute. Add 4½ cups water and bring to a boil. Add the meatballs and bring back to a boil. Reduce heat, cover, and simmer over medium heat for 20 minutes.

4. Add the vinegar and grape molasses. Cook for another 10 minutes uncovered. Just before serving, adjust seasoning to taste and garnish with all the herbs. *Nush-e Jan!*

VARIATION

Sauté the meatballs before adding them to the broth. Heat 3 tablespoons oil in a wide skillet over medium heat and gently add the meatballs. Shake the pan back and forth until the meatballs are brown on all sides. Add them to the simmering broth in step 3.

Rice Meatballs

Makes 8 meatballs
Preparation time: 45 minutes
Cooking time: 1 hour

کوفته برنجی

Kufteh berenji

MEATBALLS
½ cup yellow split peas
1 cup rice, washed and drained
2 teaspoons sea salt
1 teaspoon freshly ground pepper
½ teaspoon turmeric
½ teaspoon red pepper flakes
2 eggs
2 teaspoons *advieh* (Persian spice mix)*
1 large onion, peeled and grated
1 pound ground meat (lamb, veal, beef,
  or chicken thighs)
2 cups chopped fresh parsley
1 cup chopped fresh dill
2 tablespoon dried summer savory
¼ cup chopped fresh tarragon

2 cups chopped fresh spring onions
2 cloves garlic, peeled and chopped

BROTH
½ cup oil
2 onions, peeled and thinly sliced
1 teaspoon sea salt
½ teaspoon freshly ground pepper
1 teaspoon turmeric
1 tablespoon tomato paste
2 tomatoes, peeled and chopped
6 cups beef or chicken broth
1 cup baby green plums *(gojeh sabz)* or
  ¼ cup fresh lime juice
¼ teaspoon ground saffron dissolved
  in 1 tablespoon hot water

1. To make the meatballs: In a saucepan place the split peas and rice in 4 cups water with ½ teaspoon salt. Cover and cook for 30 minutes over medium heat. Drain.

2. In a mixing bowl combine all the ingredients for the meatballs, and the cooled split peas and rice mixture. Knead lightly with your hands for about 3 minutes until it reaches the consistency of a smooth paste (do not overmix, which makes the meatballs dense).

3. Line a baking sheet with parchment paper. Shape meat paste into balls the size of oranges. Gently arrange them on the baking sheet.

4. For the broth: In a large, heavy-based pot, heat the oil over medium heat and brown the onions. Add the salt, pepper, turmeric, and tomato paste, and sauté for 1 minute. Add the tomato, broth, plums, and saffron water. Bring to a boil.

5. Use a large skimmer to lift the meatballs, one at a time, and gently slip them into the boiling broth. Bring back to a boil, reduce heat to low, and simmer uncovered for 15 minutes. Cover and simmer for 45 minutes longer. Adjust the broth seasoning to taste. Gently place the meatballs in a serving bowl and pour the broth on top. Serve hot with yogurt and bread. *Nush-e Jan!*

VARIATIONS

Fava Bean Meatballs—Eliminate the split peas from the ingredients and replace all the herbs with 4 cups chopped fresh dill. Add 1 pound shelled fava beans (second skin removed). In step 1 cook the fava beans with the rice.

Curried Meatballs— To make the meatballs, in step 2, add 2 tablespoons curry powder and 1 teaspoon red pepper flakes. Roll the meatballs in bread crumbs and brown on all sides in ¼ cup oil; add to the broth in step 5. Just before serving, beat 2 cups yogurt and ½ teaspoon salt for 5 minutes (to prevent curdling) and place dollops on the meatballs. Serve hot with bread.

VEGETARIAN VARIATION

For the meatballs, replace the meat with 2 cups of your favorite raw nuts, coarsely ground, and 1 cup bulgur soaked in 3 cups warm water for 20 minutes, drained and water squeezed out. Use a vegetarian stock or water for the broth. Proceed with the recipe.

OVEN BAKED VARIATION

Place the meatballs in a baking dish large enough for them to fit side by side. Gently pour the hot broth over them. Cover tightly and bake in a preheated 350° F (180° F) oven for 1 hour.

Pistachio and Pomegranate Meatballs

Makes: 24-30 meatballs
Preparation time: 30 minutes
 plus 30 minutes refrigeration
Cooking time: 15 minutes

كوفته پسته

Kufteh-ye pesteh-o anar

NOTE

Sadaf's California-made pomegranate molasses has an excellent balance of sweet and sour.

MEATBALLS
1 small onion, peeled and cut into 4
1½ cups pistachios or hazelnuts, shelled
½ cup bread crumbs
1½ cups chopped fresh parsley
½ cup chopped fresh tarragon
1 tablespoon fresh lime juice
1 teaspoon red pepper flakes
1 teaspoon freshly ground black pepper
1 tablespoon ground cumin
2 teaspoons sea salt
2 pounds ground lamb (or chicken thighs or fish fillets), boned and skinned
1 egg

COOKING
½ cup oil, butter, or ghee*
GLAZE
¾ cup pomegranate molasses
¼ cup honey or grape molasses
1 teaspoon salt
½ teaspoon freshly ground black pepper
½ teaspoon red pepper flakes

GARNISH
springs of basil, sprouts, mint
½ cup fresh pomegranate arils

1. To make the meatballs: Pulse all the ingredients, except the meat and egg, in a food processor until you have a grainy paste. Transfer to a large mixing bowl and add the meat and egg. Lightly knead with your hands for a few minutes (do not overmix). Cover and place in the refrigerator for 30 minutes and up to 24 hours.

2. Preheat the oven to 500°F. Generously oil a wide, nonreactive baking dish and set aside.

3. Remove the paste from the refrigerator and shape into bite-sized balls (about 1½ tablespoons each). Place the meatballs in the baking dish and brush well with oil. Bake in the oven for 10 minutes.

4. Meanwhile, in a mixing bowl combine all the ingredients for the glaze. It is important that you taste the glaze and be sure that it has a good balance between sweet and sour—add more honey if the pomegranate molasses you have used is too sour.

5. Reduce the oven to 400°F. Glaze the meatballs and bake for another 5 minutes to infuse them with the flavor of the pomegranate. Adjust seasoning to taste. If too sour add more honey; if too sweet add more pomegranate molasses. Keep warm in the oven until ready to serve.

6. Place the meatballs with its sauce in deep serving dish and garnish. *Nush-e jan!*

Tabriz-Style Meatballs

Makes 6 servings
Preparation time: 40 minutes
  plus 30 minutes resting
Cooking time: 2 hours

Kufteh tabrizi

VEGETARIAN VARIATION

Cook 2 cups dried lentils with 4 cups water and ½ teaspoon salt for 30 minutes or until soft. Drain thoroughly, allow to cool, and use it in place of the meat in step 3.

STOVETOP VARIATION

Prepare the broth in a large pot (wide enough for all 6 meatballs with space between them) and use a large skimmer to lift the meatballs and gently slip them into the boiling water. Cover and simmer over low heat for 2 hours.

NOTE

Meatballs can be individually wrapped and tied in cheesecloth to prevent them from coming apart.

FILLING
6 eggs
2 tablespoons barberries, rinsed
6 pitted prunes
6 walnut pieces
6 apricot halves

MEATBALLS
2 cups yellow split peas
1 cup rice
2 teaspoons sea salt
1 large onion, peeled and grated
1 teaspoon freshly ground black pepper
½ teaspoon turmeric
1 teaspoon ground saffron dissolved in 2 tablespoons hot water
½ cup rice flour
1 pound ground lamb (or beef, or chicken thighs)
2 cups chopped fresh summer savory, or 2 tablespoons dried
2 cups chopped spring onions
1 cup chopped fresh tarragon
1 cup chopped fresh mint, or 2 tablespoons dried
2 eggs

BROTH
2 tablespoons oil, butter, or ghee*
3 large onions, peeled and thinly sliced
1 teaspoon sea salt
1 teaspoon freshly ground pepper
1 teaspoon turmeric
2 tablespoons tomato paste
2 tablespoons fresh lime juice
2 tomatoes, peeled and chopped
8 cups broth

1. For the filling: Cook the eggs (hard-boiled), shell, and set aside.

2. For the meatballs: Cook split peas and rice for 20 minutes in 4 cups water and ½ teaspoon salt. Drain, mash, and set aside.

3. In a wide mixing bowl, combine onion, split peas and rice, salt, pepper, turmeric, saffron water, rice flour, ground lamb, summer savory, spring onions, tarragon, and mint, and knead by hand for 1 minute. Add the eggs, one by one, as they are absorbed, and continue to knead for about 1 minute until the mixture has reached the consistency of a smooth paste. Cover and allow to rest in the refrigerator for at least 30 minutes and up to 24 hours.

4. For the broth: In a large pot, heat the oil and brown the onions. Add the rest of the ingredients for the broth and bring to a boil. Reduce heat to low and allow to simmer.

5. Preheat the oven to 350°F (180°C). Oil a wide, ovenproof baking dish wide enough to fit 6 large meatballs with space between them.

6. Divide the meat into 6 equal pieces. Using damp hands, shape each piece into a large ball. Using your thumb, make a deep, wide indentation in the center of each ball. Press 1 hard-boiled egg, 1 teaspoon barberries, 1 prune, 1 piece of walnut, and 1 apricot half into each indentation. Press the meat securely over these to close it up. Shape each meatball into a large, smooth ball. Arrange gently in the baking dish. Ensure there is space between the meatballs.

7. Gently pour the hot broth around the meatballs. Cover with a layer of parchment paper and a layer of aluminum foil and seal tight. Bake for 1 hour. Uncover and bake for another 15 to 20 minutes. Baste once with pan juices to prevent drying out. Adjust the broth seasoning to taste. Serve with bread and yogurt. *Nush-e jan!*

Meatloaf

Makes 1 loaf
Preparation time: 25 minutes
Cooking time: 55 minutes

MEATLOAF
4 tablespoons oil, butter, or ghee*
2 large onions, peeled and thinly sliced
2 cloves garlic, peeled and chopped
2½ pounds ground beef (or chicken, turkey, or fillets of fish)
1 large Fuji apple, coarsely grated
¼ cup ketchup
3 tablespoons Worcestershire sauce
½ cup chopped fresh tarragon
2 teaspoons cumin powder
1 teaspoon cayenne
1½ teaspoons sea salt

1 teaspoon fresh ground pepper
½ teaspoon baking soda
2 eggs, lightly beaten
½ cup plain bread crumbs

FILLING
1 cup chopped fresh parsley
1 large carrot, peeled and grated
½ cup barberries, rinsed thoroughly
3 hard-boiled eggs (optional)

GLAZE
½ cup ketchup
3 tablespoons grape molasses or brown sugar

Dast peech-e gusht

CHEESECLOTH VARIATION

Oil a baking sheet and spread two layers of cheesecloth (wide enough for overlapping) over the baking sheet. Spread half of the meat mixture over the cheesecloth. Sprinkle a layer of parsley, carrots, and barberries on top. Arrange the eggs over the barberries, press down, and cover with the remaining meat mixture. Use your hands to shape it into a loaf. Glaze the top and wrap the loaf with the cheesecloth. Bake as above. To serve, transfer with the cheesecloth to a serving platter and gently remove cheesecloth.

1. Preheat the oven to 400°F (200°C) with a baking sheet in the middle rack.

2. To make the meatloaf: Heat 4 tablespoons oil in a skillet and sauté the onions and garlic until golden. Remove from heat and allow to cool.

3. In a large bowl, combine the cool, sautéed onions and the rest of the ingredients for the meatloaf. Use 2 forks to mix the ingredients until you have light paste (do not overmix).

4. Generously oil all sides of a 9x6-inch baking loaf pan and dust it on all sides with an even layer of bread crumbs.

5. Spread half of the meat mixture in the baking pan and pack it down with your hands. Sprinkle even layers of parsley, carrots, and barberries on top. Arrange the hardboiled eggs length-wise on top of the layer of barberries (pressing down slightly) centered along the length of the pan.

6. Place the remaining meat mixture on top and pack down to achieve a smooth even top.

7. Make the glaze by mixing ½ cup ketchup and 3 tablespoons grape molasses. Spread glaze over the top of the ground meat evenly and smooth out.

8. Place the pan on the baking sheet (for catching any drips) in the oven. Bake for 55 minutes or until the meatloaf separates from the pan and a tester comes out clean.

9. Remove the pan from the oven, cover, and allow to cool for 10 minutes (this helps to loosen the loaf from the pan). Use a spatula or knife to loosen the sides.

10. Place a flat serving plate over the pan and turn it over quickly and in one piece. Slice and serve with french fries and green beans.

Sweet and Sour Stuffed Chicken

Makes 4 servings
Preparation time: 30 minutes
Cooking time: 1 hour 45 minutes

CHICKEN
4 Cornish game hens or 2 small
  frying chickens
1 ½ teaspoons sea salt
1 teaspoon freshly ground pepper
½ teaspoon turmeric

FILLING
¼ cup oil, butter, or ghee*
1 large onion, peeled and thinly sliced
2 cloves garlic, peeled and crushed
1 cup pitted prunes, finely chopped
1 apple, cored and chopped
1 cup dried apricots, finely chopped
½ cup raisins

1 teaspoon sea salt
1 teaspoon freshly ground
  black pepper
2 teaspoons *advieh* (Persian spice mix)*
1 teaspoon grape molasses or sugar
½ cup melted butter or oil

BASTING
½ cup butter, ghee* or oil
¼ fresh lime juice
¼ teaspoon ground saffron

*Morgh-e tu por-e
torsh-o shirin*

1. Clean and rinse the birds in cold water, then pat dry. Mix the salt, pepper, and turmeric, and rub the birds inside and out with this mixture.

2. To make the filling: Heat the oil in a wide skillet and brown onion and garlic. Add prunes, apple, apricots, and raisins, and stir-fry for 1 minute. Add the rest of the ingredients and stir-fry for 20 seconds. Remove from heat and set aside.

3. Preheat oven to 425°F (220°C). Stuff the hens with the fruit mixture and pin or sew the cavities shut. Place the birds in an oiled ovenproof dish.

4. In a saucepan, combine the ingredients for the baste and paint the birds with this mixture. Cover with a layer of parchment paper and a layer of aluminum foil on top and seal tight. Place in the oven and bake for 1 hour. Uncover and bake for 30 to 45 minutes, basting occasionally, until the meat separates easily from the bone.

5. Serve in the ovenproof dish or arrange them on a serving platter. Serve with plain rice (*chelow*) or bread, salad, and fresh herbs. *Nush-e Jan!*

VARIATIONS

Chicken Stuffed with Rice and Cherries—In step 2, after browning the onion and garlic, replace the prunes, apple, and apricots with ½ cup rice, 2 cups chicken broth, ½ cup almonds, and ½ cup dried tart cherries. Cook for 20 minutes, remove from heat, and proceed with step 3 above.

Sumac and Walnut Stuffing—In step 2, replace the prunes, apple, and apricots with 1 cup coarsely chopped walnuts, 1 cup sumac powder, 1 teaspoon chili flakes, and 1 tablespoon pomegranate molasses. Proceed with step 3 above.

Sweet and Sour Stuffed Duck—In step 2, replace the prunes, apple, and apricots with 1 cup barberries (thoroughly cleaned and rinsed), ½ cup chopped fresh cilantro, ½ cup pomegranate molasses, and 3 tablespoons sugar. Proceed with step 3. Increase uncovered cooking time to 2 hours (total cooking time will be around 3 hours).

Sweet and Sour Stuffed Turkey

Makes 4 servings
Preparation time: 30 minutes
Cooking time: 3 hours
(20 minutes per pound of turkey)

بقلمون تو پر ترش و شیرین

Buqalamu-ye tu por-e torsh-o shirin

VARIATION

Sweet and Sour Lamb Stuffing (Barreh-ye tu por-e torsh-o shirin)
Cook ½ cup rice in 2 cups water with ½ teaspoon salt and drain. In a large skillet, fry ½ pound ground lamb and two large peeled and chopped onions. Add salt, pepper, 1 teaspoon turmeric, ½ cup ground walnuts, ½ cup dried chopped apricots, ½ cup dried barberries, ½ cup raisins, and the rice.

1 turkey, about 8 to 9 pounds

RUB
2 tablespoons sea salt
Juice of 1 lime
1 cup butter
1 bulb garlic, peeled and grated

FILLING
½ cup oil
3 large onions, peeled and thinly sliced
5 cloves garlic, peeled and crushed
1 cup rice
1 cup carrots, peeled and julienned
1 cup dried barberries, cleaned, or cranberries
¼ cup orange zest (6 oranges)

½ cup raisins
2 teaspoons sea salt
1 teaspoon freshly ground black pepper
1 tablespoon *advieh* (Persian spice mix)*
1 teaspoon ground saffron dissolved in 2 tablespoons hot water
½ cup sugar
1 cup raw almonds
1 cup raw pistachios
3 cups chicken broth

GRAVY
2 tablespoons butter
2 tablespoons flour
1 cup broth

1. Clean and rinse the turkey in cold water, then pat dry. Place, breast side down, on a greased rack in a roasting pan. Preheat the oven to 350°F (180°C).

2. In a small saucepan, combine the salt, lime juice, butter, and garlic. Rub the turkey thoroughly inside and out, lifting up the skin and placing some butter under the skin.

3. To make the filling: Heat ½ cup oil in a large, deep skillet over medium heat, and brown the onions and garlic. Add rice and sauté for a few minutes. Add the carrots, barberries, orange zest, raisins, salt, pepper, *advieh*, saffron water, sugar, almonds, and pistachios. Stir-fry for 5 minutes. Add chicken broth, cover, and simmer for 35 minutes over low heat. Remove from heat and allow to cool.

4. Stuff the turkey with the filling and pin or sew the cavity shut.

5. Cover tightly and roast for 2 hours. Baste with the pan juices and continue to cook, uncovered, for 2 hours, basting occasionally, until the meat separates easily from the bone. The turkey is ready when a meat thermometer reads 165°F (75°C).

6. Transfer the turkey to a serving platter. Cover with a layer parchment paper and a layer of aluminum foil and allow to sit for 20 minutes at room temperature.

7. To make the gravy: In a small saucepan, combine the butter and flour and stir-fry for a few minutes until golden brown. Transfer all the pan drippings to the saucepan and add the broth. Stir constantly over medium heat until the mixture thickens. Adjust seasoning to taste. *Nush-e Jan!*

NOTE

You may use wild rice in place of white rice. Follow directions on the package.

IF I SHOULD EVER SEE YOU, FACE TO FACE AND EYE TO EYE

گر بتو افتدم نظر چهره به چهره رو به رو   شرح دهم غمِ تو را نکته به نکته مو به مو

از پی دیدن رخت همچو صبا فتاده‌ام   کوچه به کوچه، در به در، خانه به خانه کو به کو

دورِ دهان تنگِ تو، عارضِ عنبرین خطت   غنچه غنچه، گل به گل، لاله به لاله، بو به بو

می‌رود از فراقِ تو خونِ دل از دو دیده‌ام   دجله به دجله، یم به یم، چشمه به چشمه، جو به جو

مهرِ تو را دلِ حزین بافته بر قماشِ جان   رشته به رشته، نخ به نخ، تار به تار، پو به پو

If I should ever see you, face to face and eye to eye,
I'd tell you of my sorrow, point by point sigh by sigh.
But like the wind I seek you, searching where we might meet,
Searching from door to door, from house to house, from street to street.
Searching for that small mouth, the scent that cheek bestows,
Searching from bud to bud, from flower to flower, from rose to rose.
My heart's blood spills as tears that fall unceasingly,
Flowing from creek to creek, from stream to stream, from sea to sea.
My life is woven through with love; the broken heart you left,
Is yours now—thread by thread, and warp by warp, and weft by weft.

Tahereh Ghoratolein, circa 1850

Caspian-Style Fish with Walnut and Pomegranate

Makes 4 servings
Preparation time: 15 minutes
Cooking time: 50 minutes

ها هی تو پر با انار

Mahi-ye tu por ba anar

1 whole rockfish, scaled and scored on top, or 2 pounds firm-fleshed white fish fillets, about ½ inch thick

RUB
1 teaspoon sea salt
¼ teaspoon freshly ground black pepper
½ teaspoon turmeric
1 teaspoon angelica powder

FILLING
¼ cup oil, butter, or ghee*
1 onion, peeled and thinly sliced
4 cloves garlic, peeled and sliced
1 cup shelled walnuts, coarsely chopped
1 teaspoon sea salt

½ teaspoon pepper
¼ teaspoon red pepper flakes
1 tablespoon sumac powder
3 tablespoons pomegranate molasses
1 tablespoon grape molasses

BASTE
¼ cup butter, ghee,* or oil
2 tablespoons fresh lime juice
¼ teaspoon ground saffron dissolved in 2 tablespoons hot water

GARNISH
1 teaspoon angelica powder *(gol-par)*
2 tablespoons chopped walnuts
¼ cup pomegranate seeds

1. Rinse fish in cold water. Pat dry with paper towel and rub inside and outside with a mixture of the salt, pepper, turmeric, and angelica powder.

2. To make the filling: Heat ¼ cup oil in a wide skillet over medium heat, and sauté onion and garlic. Add all the ingredients for the filling and stir-fry for 3 minutes. Remove from heat and allow to cool.

3. Preheat oven to 400°F (200°C). Place the fish in an oiled, nonreactive baking dish. Stuff the fish's cavity with the filling and pin or sew it shut. Mix the ingredients for the baste and pour over the fish.

4. Place the fish in the oven and bake for 30–45 minutes for the whole fish (until the fish flakes easily with a fork) or 10 to 15 minutes for fillets.

5. Arrange the fish on a serving platter. Pour the sauce from the baking dish over the fish. Garnish with angelica powder, walnuts, and pomegranate seeds.

6. Serve with saffron-steamed plain rice. *Nush-e Jan!*

NOTES

The fish in the photo is a whole John Dory.

If using fish fillets, place a layer of fish fillets in the greased baking dish and place a layer of stuffing on top and another layer of fish on top. Repeat for all the fish fillets. Pour the baste on top and bake for 10 to 15 minutes until the fish is flaky.

VARIATIONS

Caspian-Style Fish with Walnut and Bitter Orange Stuffing—Substitute pomegranate molasses with bitter orange molasses or 1 cup juice.

Caspian-Style Fish with a Walnut Vinegar Stuffing—Substitute pomegranate molasses with 1 cup sherry vinegar.

Caspian-Style Fish with Sweet and Sour Fruit Stuffing—Substitute the pomegranate molasses with ¼ cup prunes, ¼ cup apricots, and ¼ cup raisins, all finely chopped.

Persian Gulf-Style Fish with Walnut and Tamarind Stuffing—Substitute pomegranate molasses with 3 tablespoons tamarind molasses.

Seared Fish with Sumac

Makes 4 servings
Preparation time: 10 minutes
Cooking time: 5–7 minutes

ماهی باسماق

Mahi-ye kababi ba somaq

VARIATION

If using whole fish, as shown in the photo, instead of sautéing, bake in a 400°F (200°C) oven for 35–45 minutes. Or grill the fish.

GARNISH:
¼ toasted walnuts
1 cup parsley
¼ chopped fresh mint
4 cloves garlic, peeled and chopped
1 tablespoon lime juice
½ teaspoon sea salt
¼ teaspoon pepper
2 tablespoons olive oil

DUSTING MIXTURE
1 teaspoon sea salt
¼ teaspoon freshly ground pepper
1 teaspoon turmeric
¼ cup sumac powder
1 tablespoon flour

FISH
4 thick firm-fleshed white fish fillets or 1 large, whole fish
2 tablespoons oil, butter, or ghee*
Juice of 1 lime

1. In a food processor, pulse all the garnish ingredients until you have a grainy mixture (not a paste). Keep chilled in an airtight container.

2. In a bowl, mix all the ingredients for dusting and set aside.

3. Wash the fish and pat dry with a paper towel. Brush it on both sides with 2 tablespoons olive oil and the lime juice. Cover it with the dusting mixture. Arrange in a baking sheet lined with parchment paper and keep chilled until ready to cook.

4. Heat a wide skillet over high heat until hot. Add 1 tablespoon oil and brown the fish (2 fillets at a time) for 2 to 3 minutes on each side. Add remaining oil and repeat for the other 2 fillets. Place 2 tablespoons of garnish on each fillet and serve with plain rice (*kateh*). *Nush-e Jan!*

Platonic Fish

Makes 4 servings
Preparation time: 20 minutes
Cooking time: 5–10 minutes

ماهی افلاطونی

Mahi-ye aflatuni

SWEET AND SOUR SAUCE
2 tablespoons oil, butter, or ghee*
4 cloves garlic, peeled and thinly sliced
1 cup pomegranate juice
½ cup verjuice (*ab-ghureh*, unripe grape juice)*
1 cup bitter orange juice
1 teaspoon sea salt
2 teaspoons *advieh* (Persian spice mix)*
1 tablespoon angelica powder *(gol-par)*
½ teaspoon cayenne
1 tablespoon honey or grape molasses

FISH
4 thick fish fillets (about 2 pounds)
2 tablespoons oil, butter, or ghee*

DUSTING MIXTURE
½ teaspoon sea salt
¼ teaspoon freshly ground pepper
1 teaspoon turmeric
1 tablespoon flour

GARNISH
½ cup pomegranate seeds
4 spring onions, chopped (use green and white parts)

1. Heat 2 tablespoons oil in a medium saucepan and brown the garlic. Add the rest of the ingredients for the sauce. Bring to a boil and adjust seasoning to taste (it should be sweet and sour). If necessary, add more honey. Set aside.

2. Wash the fish and pat dry. Dredge in the dusting mixture.

3. In a wide skillet, heat 2 tablespoons oil over medium-high heat until very hot and brown the fish on both sides. Add the sauce to the fish. Reduce heat to low, cover, and simmer for 5 to 10 minutes until the fish is tender. Garnish with pomegranate seeds and spring onions. Serve with plain rice (*kateh*). *Nush-e Jan!*

Sautéed Fish with Garlic and Bitter Orange

Makes 4 servings
Preparation time: 30 minutes
Cooking time: 30 minutes

FISH
4 thick fillets of rockfish (or catfish, or tilapia), about 2 pounds

DUSTING
1 teaspoon sea salt
¼ teaspoon freshly ground black pepper
1 teaspoon ground turmeric
1 tablespoon all-purpose flour
1 tablespoon ground angelica petals

FOR COOKING THE FISH
¼ cup oil, butter, or ghee*
10 cloves garlic, peeled
1 cup bitter orange juice or mixture of ½ cup fresh squeezed orange juice and ½ cup lime juice
1 teaspoon grape molasses or honey

ماهی سیر داغ با نارنج

Mahi-ye sir-dagh ba narenj

1. Wash the fish and pat dry. Set aside.

2. In a small bowl, mix all the dusting ingredients and set aside.

3. Dredge both sides of the fish fillets in the dusting mixture.

4. Heat 2 tablespoons oil in a wide skillet over medium heat, add the garlic, and sauté until golden brown. Remove the garlic with a slotted spoon and set aside.

5. In the same skillet, heat 2 tablespoons oil over medium-high heat until hot. Sear the fish until brown on each side. Return the garlic to the skillet, add the bitter orange juice, and grape molasses.

6. Cover and simmer for 3 to 5 minutes or until fish is tender. Adjust seasoning to taste. Add more bitter orange juice or grape molasses as needed. Keep warm.

7. When ready to serve, transfer to a serving platter and serve with plain rice *(kateh)* and fresh herbs. *Nush-e Jan!*

First millennium BCE bas-relief of a woman being fanned. She has a spindle in her hand and a fish in a bowl in front of her.

Smoked White Fish

1 whole Canadian smoked white fish, between 4–5 pounds
4 bitter oranges (2 for juicing, 2 for garnish) or fresh limes

2 tablespoons olive oil
½ teaspoon sea salt
1 teaspoon freshly ground pepper
3 cloves garlic, peeled and crushed

Makes 6 servings
Preparation time: 10 minutes
Cooking time: 55 minutes

ماهی دودی

Mahi-ye dudi

Smoked fish is traditionally served with herb rice (sabzi polow) *as the main meal on Nowruz, the Persian New Year. It never fails to remind me of the annual visit of Khanum Rashty, the "lady from Rasht," a town near the Caspian Sea. She was an old family retainer who would suddenly appear in our garden two weeks before the New Year. There she would be, a short, wiry woman with two gray braids tied on top of her head, her colorful scarf falling down around her neck. She always offered us a large, two-handled wicker basket filled with wonderful spring treasures. Around its edges were bunches of violets, my mother's favorite flower; there was always an enormous bouquet of yellow-centered, double-petaled wild narcissus as well. Within were bitter oranges nestled in their green leaves. And hidden among them, its head and tail peeking out at us, was a large smoked white fish. This, Khanum Rashty always said, was her New Year's gift to us. My mother saw to it that she was handsomely looked after in return, and we all enjoyed the presents. The flowers filled the house with the scent of spring all through the days that followed. As for the fish, we ate it with the fragrant herb rice.*

1. Preheat oven to 400°F (200°C). Line a rimmed baking sheet with a layer of aluminum foil and a layer of parchment paper (large enough to overhang the baking sheet). Place the fish on top, open its cavity, squeeze in the bitter orange juice, drizzle with olive oil, and sprinkle with salt, pepper, and crushed garlic. Wrap the fish with the parchment paper and the aluminum foil. Place in the oven and bake for 55 minutes.

2. Remove fish from oven and gently transfer to a serving dish. Open up the aluminum foil and parchment paper, peel back the skin from the top of the fish, and squeeze some bitter orange juice over it. *Nush-e Jan!*

VARIATION

Caspian-Style Smoked Fish Steamed in Rice—Follow the recipe for Fresh Herb Rice on page 286. Set the smoked fish fillet on a deep plate that will fit inside the rice pot. Once the rice has been formed into a mound in the pot, place the fish plate on top of it. Cover and cook for 10 minutes over high heat, reduce heat to medium, and cook for another 50 minutes. Take out the plate with the fish and discard the juices in the plate. Squeeze fresh bitter orange over the fish and serve with the rice.

Fish with Fresh Herb and Barberry Stuffing

Makes 6 servings
Preparation time: 30 minutes
Cooking time: 20–30 minutes,
* depending on the size of fish*

FISH
1 large whole fish (striped bass or
  rockfish), between 3–4 pounds,
  scaled, butterflied, and skin scored, or
  2 thick fillets of fish, about 2 pounds
1 teaspoon sea salt
½ teaspoon pepper
1 teaspoon turmeric

FILLING
½ cup oil, butter, or ghee*
4 cloves garlic, peeled and sliced
½ cup chopped fresh parsley
2 tablespoons chopped fresh tarragon
4 spring onions, chopped
1 tablespoon chopped fresh cilantro

¼ cup chopped fresh mint or 2
  tablespoons dried mint
1 cup finely ground walnuts
½ cup dried barberries, cleaned, soaked
  for 10 minutes in cold water, drained,
  and rinsed
½ cup raisins
¼ cup fresh lime juice
1 teaspoon sea salt
¼ teaspoon freshly ground
  black pepper
¼ teaspoon ground saffron dissolved
  in 2 tablespoons hot water (optional)

ماهی تو پُر با سبزی

Mahi-ye tu por ba sabzi

1. Rinse fish in cold water. Pat dry with towel and rub inside and out with a mixture of the salt, pepper, and turmeric.

2. Heat 2 tablespoons oil in a wide skillet and sauté the garlic for 1 minute. Add the parsley, tarragon, spring onions, cilantro, mint, walnuts, barberries, raisins, lime juice, salt, and pepper and sauté for 2 minutes longer. Remove from heat and set aside to cool.

3. Preheat oven to 400°F (200°C). Lay the fish in a oiled baking dish. Stuff it with the filling and sew or pin cavity shut. Drizzle the remaining oil and saffron water over the fish.

4. Place in the oven and bake for 20 to 30 minutes (depending on the size of the fish) until the fish flakes easily with a fork. Remove from the oven and baste with pan juices.

5. Serve from the baking dish or arrange it on a serving platter.

6. Serve with saffron-steamed plain rice.

THE STORY OF SAFFRON

Long treasured as a medicine, perfume, dye, and seasoning, saffron consists of the golden stigmas of the autumn-flowering purple crocus, *Crocus sativus*. It takes the stigmas of 50,000 to 75,000 blossoms—an acre of flowers—to make one pound of the spice. These must be picked from the crocus by hand, making Iranian sargol saffron threads, currently selling for about $100 an ounce, the most expensive spice in the world.

The beautiful little saffron crocus is native to Iran and Southwest Asia. The name comes from the Arabic *za`faran*, meaning "yellow," which may be the Arabized form of the Persian word *zarparan*, meaning "golden stamens (golden feathers)." It has been cultivated throughout the region since ancient times. The Persians' Sumerian predecessors, from the third millennium BCE, called saffron "the perfume of the gods"; in fact, there exists a Sumerian recipe for beer, intended no doubt for the most exalted of drinkers, that includes toasted pomegranate seeds, myrtle, oak, sumac, cumin, and, most importantly, saffron.

Like the Sumerians before them, the Persians valued the spice as a medicine. It still is made into a tea that is said to suppress coughs and induce sleep; on the other hand, saffron may be used as an antidepressant, and too much is said to induce madness. As crocus cultivation spread north and east into the Mediterranean and India, so did medicinal claims for the spice. It was, it seems, almost a universal panacea. Thus the medieval physicians of Salerno, who created the medical regimen named after that city, wrote:

> *Saffron arouses joy in every breast,*
> *Settles the stomach, gives the liver rest.*

In the classical world and later, saffron was considered an aphrodisiac, which is perhaps why it was used to perfume Greek halls and baths, not to mention the villas of the famous courtesans known as hetaerae. It was also said to have been sprinkled on the streets of Rome to welcome Emperor Nero in the first century—less as an aphrodisiac, perhaps, than as an extravagant compliment to that most extravagant of rulers.

This rare spice's reputation followed it as cultivation spread along the trade routes into Kashmir and farther east. Golden yellow became a royal color—and a sacred one. Shortly after the Buddha

Saffron threads

died in the fifth century BCE, his priests chose saffron dye to color their robes. (The distinctive golden color remains, although the dye is now usually made from cheaper turmeric.) Perhaps in token of its erotic associations, saffron was also used to dye the veils of brides in ancient Tyre as well as the breasts and arms of newly married Indian women. All of these virtues aside, saffron remains a wonderful seasoning and coloring for food, especially grain. This is a fact long appreciated in the traditions of Iran and beyond, for the cultivation of saffron spread not only to India but also to Italy, Spain, France, and even England. As you will see in this book the spice enhances the rice dishes of Iran. And fortunately for the modern cook's pocketbook, when used properly (see How To section, page , 536) only the tiniest amount will produce a remarkable fragrance, flavor, and color.

Ground saffron

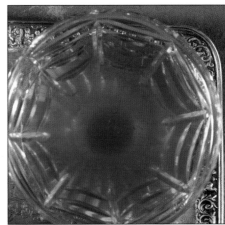

Saffron water

RICE DISHES CHELOWS & POLOWS

RICE DISHES, CHELOWS & POLOWS

THE FOOD OF THE CLOAK

Mulla Nasruddin heard that there was a party being held in the nearby town, and that everyone was invited. He made his way there as quickly as he could. When the master of ceremonies saw him in his ragged cloak, he seated him in the most inconspicuous place, far from the great table where the most important people were being waited on hand and foot.

Mulla saw that it would be at least an hour before the waiters reached the place where he was sitting. So he got up, went home, and dressed himself in a magnificent sable cloak and turban and returned to the feast. As soon as his host's heralds saw this splendid sight they started to beat the drum of welcome and sound the trumpets in a manner consistent with a visitor of high rank.

The Chamberlain himself came out of the palace, and conducted the magnificent Nasruddin to a place almost next to the Emir. A dish of wonderful food was immediately placed before him. Without a pause, Nasruddin began to rub handfuls of it into his turban and cloak.

"Your Eminence," said the prince, "I am curious as to your eating habits, which are new to me."

"Nothing special," said Mulla, "the cloak got me in here. Surely it deserves its share!"

*A*ccording to ancient texts, the Chinese began to grow domesticated rice about eight to ten thousand years ago. The Persian word for rice, *berenj,* is related to the old Indo-Iranian *vrihi.* From this root comes the Greek *oruza,* the Arabic *al ruzz,* the Spanish *arroz,* the French *riz,* and, of course, the English rice. Rice was probably brought to Iran from southeast Asia or the Indian subcontinent and possibly first cultivated in the Caspian area around the fourth century BCE. (although written evidence of rice farming in Iran did no appear for another millennium or so). There are five major varieties of rice in Iran: *champa* (short and thick, probably from the ancient Indonesian kingdom of Champa); *rasmi* (longer and wider); *anbarbu, mowla'i,* and *sadri* (a variety brought to Gilan from Peshawar in 1850 by the grand vazir Mirza Aqa Khan Nuri Sadr-e A'zam). Other varieties have names based on their shape, perfume, or taste: *khanjari,* dagger-shaped; *anbarbu,* amber-perfumed; *shekari,* sweet; *dom-siyah,* black-tailed. Today in the West, basmati rice from India and Afghanistan is readily available and are close to Persian rice. When basmati rice is cooked, it fills the air with a delightful aroma similar to that of flowers (basmati literally means "the fragrant one"). Other kinds of long-grain rice may also be used for Persian rice dishes, but never the so-called converted rice.

COOKED RICE

Rice is eaten in great quantities in the Caspian region, but elsewhere in Iran bread is the main staple. Rice is considered a luxury by villagers or the urban poor to be eaten only on special occasions or served to guests. There are four major types of cooked rice in Iran: *kateh, dami, chelow,* and *polow.* Though various *polows* were first mentioned in Persian literature by Obeyd-e Zakani in his *Mush-o Gorbeh* around 1350 (see page 23), and although Boshaq Atameh wrote a long poem around 1400 about the battle between saffroned rice and pasta (saffron rice is the eventual winner), the present refined versions were developed in the 1600s in the Safavid courts and in the 1800s by the Qajars.

Kateh is the traditional dish of Gilan and is the simplest way of cooking Persian rice. Rice, water, and salt are cooked until the water is absorbed. Butter or vegetable oil is added, the pot is covered, and the rice is allowed to cook. The rice becomes compact with a crusty surface. In the Caspian region, *kateh* is eaten for breakfast heated with milk and jam, or cold with cheese and garlic. For lunch and dinner, it is eaten with meat, fowl, fish, or *khoresh* (a delicate braise).

Dami is a type of *kateh* cooked with herbs or vegetables. It is similar to *kateh* except that the heat is reduced to low immediately after the rice starts to boil. The lid of the pot is then wrapped with a dish towel *(dam-koni)* to prevent steam from escaping. After 40 minutes, remove the cover, pour oil or butter on top of the rice, re-cover, and continue cooking for another 20 minutes.

Chelow has the same ingredients as *kateh* except that more care is taken in the cooking process, including presoaking, parboiling, and steaming. This results in a fluffy rice with each grain separate, and the bottom of the pot has a crisp golden brown crust, *tah-dig*. *Tah-dig* should be a golden color, never scorched or dark brown. The reputation of Iranian cooks rests on the quality of their *tah-dig*. *Chelow* is then eaten with *khoresh*, called *chelow-khoresh*, or with *kabab*, called *chelow-kabab*.

Polow is initially cooked in the same way as *chelow*. The meat, fruit, herbs and vegetables are fried together and then arranged in alternating layers with the rice. They are then steamed together.

Rice is, of course, also used in many other dishes in Persian cuisine, including soups, *oshes*, meatballs *(kufte-berenji),* and stuffed vegetables *(dolmeh).* There are also many sweets and cookies made using rice flour: *tar-halva, fereni, shirberenj,* and *nan-e berenji*. It is also used as a type of popcorn, by roasting *(berenj-e budadeh* or *berenjak),* and deep-fried as a candy *(reshteh bereshteh).*

CLEANING, WASHING, AND SOAKING RICE

Basmati rice contains many small, solid particles. This grit must be removed by picking over the rice carefully by hand. Then the rice is washed thoroughly in lukewarm water. Place the rice in a large pot and cover with lukewarm water. Agitate gently with your hand without breaking the rice, then pour off the water. Repeat 5 times until the rice is completely clean. If you use an ordinary colander to drain your rice, you may lose some rice through the holes. A fine-mesh, free-standing colander is needed so the water can drain from the rice. When properly washed rice is cooked, it gives off a delightful perfume that unwashed rice can never have. In Gilan, rice would often be soaked in salt water in large quantities and used for cooking as needed. Soaking and cooking in salt water seems to help firm up the rice, lengthen it, and keep it separated and fluffy after the cooking process.

Throughout this book I have used cooking times for basmati rice, which I recommend. However, if you use American long-grain rice it is not necessary to wash the rice 5 times. Just place it in a fine-mesh colander and rinse with water.

POTS FOR COOKING RICE

A deep, non-stick pot must be used for the rice grains to swell properly and for a good crust to form without sticking. I use a 5-quart (4.7-liter) Anolon pot. Rice cookers are a wonderful invention for cooking rice Persian-style because the non-stick coated mold allows for a golden crust (*tah-dig*) and the unvarying temperature produces consistently good rice. However, each type of rice cooker seems to have its own temperature setting; therefore the timing must be experimented with to get the best results. Step-by-step instructions are given for Steamed Plain Rice and Rice with Lentils using the Pars electric rice cooker. Other rice recipes can be carried out similarly. Electric rice cookers and non-stick pots that are helpful in making and unmolding the golden crust are available at Iranian grocers in the U. S. or through the internet (see list of stores on page 616).

SELECTING RICE

Iranian rices are not available in the U.S. at this time, but Indian and Afghan basmati rice, which is like the Persian varieties and gives off much the same flowery scent during cooking, is sold even in supermarkets these days. My favorite rice is the hard-to-find Domsiyah Iranian rice, available at some Persian markets, Aahu Barah and Lal Quilla basmati brands are also good for accomplishing the long, separated pearls of rice appreciated by Iranians. Basmati is usually not pre-washed and should be well cleaned and washed before cooking.

COOKING OIL & FAT

I have given you the option of oil, butter, or clarified butter *(ghee)* for you to choose according to your fancy. I cook mostly with canola oil these days because it has a neutral flavor, a high smoke point, and it might be healthier for your body. In Iran, rice is traditionally cooked in one of three types of oil or fat:

SEMISOLID VEGETABLE OIL—*Roghan-e nabati*
Semisolid or liquid vegetable oil is a relative newcomer to Iranian cookery, and canola oil (a rapeseed oil low in saturated fats) makes excellent, tasty, and aromatic rice.

CLARIFIED UNSALTED BUTTER *(ghee)*—*Roghan-e kareh* or *Roghan-e khub*
Ghee, which means "clarified butter," was the traditional favorite for cooking rice. It gives rice a wonderful nutty flavor. To make and store your own clarified butter, see "How to Make and Store Kitchen Ingredients" on page 533.

SHEEP-TAIL FAT—*Roghan-e donbeh*

Fat-tailed sheep are prevalent in Iran and have a long history. They have distinctive large tails in which fat is stored. Marco Polo, who traveled through Iran in the thirteenth century, wrote: "Then there are sheep here as big as asses; and their tails are so large and fat, that one tail shall weigh some 30 lb. They are fine fat beasts, and afford capital mutton." Fat-tailed sheep are rare in the U.S., though small farmers are starting to breed the Karakul variety. In Iran the use of tail fat for cooking is also waning. When being melted, tail fat has an unpleasant smell; once melted, however, it gives a pleasing fragrance and a delicate flavor to many Persian dishes, especially rice.

COOKING WITH SAFFRON

When buying saffron, choose threads rather than powder, which is too often adulterated with turmeric. Threads should be ground with a cube of sugar, which helps the grinding process (use a spice grinder or mortar and pestle), then dissolved in hot water for use in recipes (see page 536). Saffron water will keep well in an airtight jar in the refrigerator for up to 3 weeks.

SALT

I cook with a fine-grain sea salt. Keep in mind that coarse grains salt less because there are fewer of them in a given measure. Ordinary Morton iodized salt tends to salt more. More or less salt is up to you, but rice dishes in particular need the minimum recommended amount of salt for both taste and texture. For "finishing" the flavor upon serving, or for adding texture (for kababs, for example), I recommend a delicately coarse-grain sea salt, such as a *fleur de sel* or Maldon Sea Salt.

THE TRAVELS OF JEAN CHARDIN, 1686

They served up the dinner after this manner: There were spread before all the company, cloths of gold brocade, and upon them, all along, there was bread of three or four sorts, very good, and well made; this done, they immediately brought eleven great basins of that sort of food called pilau, which is rice baked with meat: There was of it, of all colors, and of all sorts of tastes, with sugar, with the juice of pomegranates, the juice of citrons, and with saffron: each dish weighed above fourscore pounds, and had alone been sufficient to satisfy the whole assembly. The four first had twelve fowls in each; the four next had a lamb in each; in the others there was only some mutton: with these basins, were served up four flat kettles, so large and heavy, that it was necessary to help to unload those that brought them. One of them was full of eggs made into a pudding; another of soup with herbs; another was filled with herbage and hashed meat; and the last with fried fish. All this being served upon the table, a porringer was set before each person, which was four times deeper than ours, filled with sherbet of a tartish sweet taste, and a plate of winter and summer sallets: After which, the carvers began to serve all the company out of each dish, in china plates. As for us Frenchmen, who were habituated to the country of Persia, we ate heartily at this feast, but the freshcomers fed upon the admiration of the magnificence of this service, which as all of fine gold, and which (for certain) was worth above a million.

A banquet scene in Tiflis under the Safavids circa 1670

Saffron-Flavored Steamed Rice with Golden Crust

Makes 6 servings
Preparation time: 15 minutes
Cooking time: 1 hour 30 minutes

Chelow

NOTE

In step 2, you can flavor your rice with any one of the following (or you can mix and match according to your fancy): 4 cardamom pods, 1 cinnamon stick, 2 cloves, 2 bay leaves, a few kaffir lime leaves, or a tablespoon of rose or orange blossom water. I like to mix cardamom, kaffir lime leaves, and rose water. This gives the rice a heavenly aroma and also improves the taste.

RICE
4 cups long-grain basmati rice
10 cups water
2 tablespoons sea salt
4 cardamom pods
1 tablespoon rose water

TAH-DIG
1 cup oil, melted butter or ghee*
1 teaspoon ground saffron dissolved in 4 tablespoons rose water or hot water
2 tablespoons plain yogurt
1 teaspoon cumin seeds (or nigella seeds, or coriander seeds), optional

1. Pick over the rice. Basmati rice like any other old rice contains many small solid particles. This grit must be removed by picking over the rice carefully by hand. Wash the rice by placing it in a large container and covering it with *lukewarm water*. Agitate gently with your hand, then pour off the water. Repeat 5 times until the rice is completely clean. When washed rice is cooked it gives off a delightful perfume that unwashed rice does not have. *If using long-grain American or Texmati rice, it is not necessary to wash or soak the rice.* After washing the rice it is then desirable but not essential to soak it in 8 cups water with 2 tablespoons salt for 2 to 24 hours. Soaking and cooking rice with plenty of salt firms it up to support the long cooking time and prevents the rice from breaking up. The grains swell individually without sticking together. The result is a light and fluffy rice known as "the pearls of Persian cuisine."

2. In a large, non-stick pot, bring 10 cups water to a boil over high heat. Add the salt, cardamom, and rose water. Pour the washed and drained rice into the pot.

3. Boil briskly over high heat for 6 to 10 minutes (depends on the kind of rice you are using), gently stirring twice with a wooden spoon to loosen any grains that may have stuck to the bottom. Bite a few grains. If the rice feels soft, and all the rice has risen to the top, it is ready.

4. Drain rice in a large, fine-mesh colander and rinse with 2 or 3 cups cold water.

5. To make golden crust (*tah-dig*): In a mixing bowl, whisk together ½ cup oil, ½ cup water, a few drops of saffron water, 2 tablespoons yogurt, 3 spatulas of rice, and the cumin seeds.

6. Spread the yogurt-rice mixture over the bottom of the pot, give it a shake to even it out, and pack it down. This will help to create a tender golden crust when the rice is cooked.

7. Take one spatula full of drained rice at a time and gently place it on top of the yogurt and rice mixture, gradually shaping the rice into a pyramid. This shape leaves room for the rice to expand and enlarge.

1. WASHING

2. ADDING DRAINED RICE TO BOILING WATER

3. BRISKLY PARBOILING RICE

4. DRAINING AND RINSING RICE

5. PREPARING SAFFRON YOGURT MIX FOR THE BASE

6. SPREADING BASE FOR *TAH-DIG*

7a. PLACING RICE OVER THE BASE

7b. MOUNDING THE RICE

8. Cover and cook rice for 10 minutes over medium-high heat to form a golden crust.

9. Mix the remaining oil with ½ cup hot water and pour over the rice pyramid. Drizzle the rest of the saffron water over the top. Wrap the lid with a clean dish towel and cover firmly to prevent steam from escaping. Cook for 70 minutes longer over medium-low heat (this is for a gas flame; adjust according to your cooktop).

10. Remove the pot from heat. Allow to cool on a damp surface for 5 minutes without uncovering it. This helps to free the crust from the bottom of the pot. Uncover and loosen the edges with a wooden spatula.

11. There are two ways to unmold and serve the rice. The first is to hold the serving platter tightly over the uncovered pot and invert the two together, unmolding the rice onto the platter. The rice will emerge as a golden-crusted cake. Serve in wedges.

12. The second way is to take 2 tablespoons of the saffron rice from the top and set aside for garnish. Gently taking one spatula full of rice at a time, place it on a serving platter without disturbing the crust. Mound the rice into a cone. Garnish with the saffron rice on top. Detach the layer of crust from the bottom using a wooden spatula. Place the pieces of crust into a small platter and serve on the side or arrange the crust around the rice platter. *Nush-e Jan!*

BROWN RICE VARIATION

To make *chelow* with long grain brown basmati rice, in step 3, boil the rice for 12 to 15 minutes then proceed with the recipe as above. For *tah-dig*, use a bread crust.

QUICK CHELOW VARIATION

To make this rice, *chelow,* quickly without the golden crust—in step 9, instead of cooking the rice for 70 minutes, cook it for 15 minutes so that it is steamed.

REHEATING RICE

Chelow-ye do nameh—Leftover rice can be reheated and used again. Place the rice in a pot, add ½ to 1 cup water (depending on the amount of rice) by swirling it over the rice, cover, and cook over low heat for 15 to 20 minutes.

CHELOW COOKING TECHNIQUE FOR RESTAURANTS

Wash and boil rice for 8 to 10 minutes, drain, and spread in a pan sheet. Cover and seal with plastic wrap and keep in a cooler rack until needed. In a 5-quart pot, pour in ½ cup water and add enough rice to fill the pot, leaving a few inches on top for expansion. Whisk together ½ cup oil and ¼ cup water and swirl over the rice. Drizzle 2 tablespoons saffron-rose water on top. **Cover tightly** and steam over medium heat for 15 to 20 minutes until the rice is long and soft but not mushy.

8. SHORT-TERM COOKING OVER MEDIUM-HIGH HEAT FOR *TAH-DIG*

9. LONG-TERM STEAMING OVER MEDIUM-LOW HEAT

10. COOLING ON A DAMP SURFACE

11. INVERTING POT ON SERVING PLATTER

A PLAIN CRUST *TAH-DIG*

RICE CRUST VARIATIONS FOR STEPS 5–7 OF THIS RECIPE

ته دیگ ساده

Plain Crust—For this crust, in a mixing bowl, whisk together ½ cup oil, ½ cup water, a few drops of saffron water, and 3 spatulas of the parboiled rice. Spread the mixture in the bottom of the pot and mound the rest of the rice over it.

ته دیگ ماست

Yogurt Crust—In a mixing bowl, whisk together ½ cup oil, ½ cup water, a few drops of saffron water, 2 tablespoons yogurt, and 3 spatulas of the parboiled rice. Spread the mixture in the bottom of the pot and mound the rest of the rice over it.

ته دیگ شیری

Milk Crust—In a mixing bowl, whisk together ½ cup oil, ½ cup milk, a few drops of saffron water, and 3 spatulas of the parboiled rice. Spread the mixture in the bottom of the pot and mound the rest of the rice over it.

ته دیگ ماست و تخم مرغ

Egg Crust—In a mixing bowl, whisk together ½ cup oil, ½ cup water, a few drops of saffron water, 2 tablespoons yogurt, 2 egg yolks, and 3 spatulas of the parboiled rice. Spread the mixture in the bottom of the pot and mound the rest of the rice over it.

ته دیگ نان لواش

Lavash Crust—In a mixing bowl, whisk together ½ cup oil, ½ cup water, and a few drops of saffron water, and spread in the pot. Place a layer of *lavash* bread on top to fit the bottom of the pot and mound the rest of the rice over it. For this crust, in step 8 cook over medium heat (not medium-high heat) for 10 minutes.

ته دیگ سیب زمینی

Potato Crust—In a mixing bowl, whisk together ½ cup oil, ½ cup water, and a few drops of saffron water, and spread in the pot. Arrange slices of peeled ¼–inch thick rounds of Idaho russet potatoes (do not wash the potatoes, the starch helps to bind the *tah-dig*) to fit the bottom of the pot. Place a thin layer of rice over the potatoes and press down firmly with your hands. Mound the rest of the rice on top.

ته دیگ به

Quince Crust—In a mixing bowl, whisk together ½ cup oil, ½ cup water, and a few drops of saffron water, and spread in the pot. Arrange ¼-inch thick rounds of cored quinces to fit the bottom of the pot. Place a thin layer of rice over the quinces and press down firmly with your hands. Mound the rest of the rice on top.

NOTE

I am giving you guidelines and proportions for making your favorite tah-dig. However, you should experiment and practice using your stovetop (I am using a gas flame) and the type of basmati rice you have. Making good rice with a perfect golden crust, tah-dig, is all about the combination of the temperature and the cooking time.

Traditionally, Iranians use a ready-made padded lid (damkoni) to cover the rice pot to prevent steam from escaping during long-term steaming. You can buy one or make your own. Otherwise, wrap a clean dish towel over the lid of the pot, as shown in the previous page, to prevent steam from escaping when the lid covers the pot.

A POTATO CRUST *TAH-DIG*

A *LAVASH* BREAD CRUST *TAH-DIG*

Rice Cooker-Style Saffron-Flavored Rice

3 cups long-grain white basmati rice
4 cups water
1 tablespoon sea salt
¾ cup oil, butter, or ghee*
¼ teaspoon ground saffron dissolved
   in 1 tablespoon hot water or
   rose water

Makes 6 servings
Preparation time: 10 minutes
Cooking time: 1 hour

Chelow ba polow paz

1. Wash the rice by placing it in a large container and covering it with *lukewarm water.* Agitate gently with your hand, then pour off the water. Repeat 5 times until the rice is completely clean. *If using long-grain American or Texmati rice, it is not necessary to wash the rice.*

2. Combine all the ingredients except the saffron water in the rice cook. Gently stir with a wooden spoon and start the cooker.

3. After 1 hour, pour saffron water over the top of the rice and unplug the rice cooker.

4. Allow to cool for 10 minutes without uncovering the pot.

5. Remove lid and place a round serving dish over the pot. Hold the dish and the pot tightly together and turn them over to unmold the rice. The rice will be like a cake. Cut into wedges and serve. *Nush-e Jan!*

NOTE

These cooking times are for the Pars rice cooker. The cooking time for rice may vary depending on the various brands of rice cookers on the market. You should experiment with yours from anywhere between 60 and 90 minutes to achieve the best results.

Among other long-grained types of rice, choose those that are long, thick, and sleek at the tip. For American long-grain rice, as opposed to basmati, use only 3 cups water and rinse the rice once.

For brown basmati rice, use 3 cups rice and 5 cups water.

In step 2, you can flavor your rice with any one of the following (or you can mix and match according to your fancy): 4 cardamom pods, 1 cinnamon stick, 2 cloves, 2 bay leaves, a few kaffir lime leaves, or a tablespoon of rose or orange blossom water. I like to mix cardamom, kaffir lime leaves, and rose water. This gives the rice a heavenly aroma and also improves the taste.

Smothered Rice

3 cups long-grain basmati rice
1 tablespoon sea salt
6 cups water
½ cup oil, melted butter or ghee*

Makes 6 servings
Preparation time: 5 minutes
Cooking time: 1 hour

Kateh

NOTE

In step 2, you can flavor your rice with any one of the following, (or you can mix and match according to your fancy): 4 cardamom pods, 1 cinnamon stick, 2 cloves, 2 bay leaves, a few kaffir lime leaves, or 1 tablespoon of rose or orange blossom water. I like to mix cardamom, kaffir lime leaves and rose water. This gives the rice a heavenly aroma and also improves the taste.

1. Wash the rice by placing it in a large container and covering it with *lukewarm water.* Agitate gently with your hand, then pour off the water. Repeat 5 times until the rice is completely clean. *If using long-grain American or Texmati rice, it is not necessary to wash the rice.*

2. Place rice, salt, and water in a deep, non-stick pot. Bring to a boil over high heat, reduce heat, and simmer for 20 minutes over medium heat (do not cover). Gently stir the rice with a wooden spoon a few times while it boils.

3. When the rice has absorbed all the water, swirl the oil over the rice. Reduce heat to low.

4. Wrap the lid of the pot with a clean dish towel and cover firmly to prevent steam from escaping. Cook 40 minutes over low heat. Remove the pot from heat and allow to cool for 5 minutes on a damp surface without uncovering it.

5. Gently taking one skimmer or spatula full of rice at a time, place it on a serving platter without disturbing the crust. Mound rice in shape of a cone.

6. Detach the crust from the bottom of the pot using a wooden spatula. Place onto a small platter and serve on side. *Nush-e Jan!*

VARIATIONS

Kermani-Style Cumin Smothered Rice *(Zireh polow-ye Kermani)*—Replace the water with chicken broth and 1 teaspoon turmeric. In step 3, when the rice has absorbed all the broth, add 3 tablespoons cumin seeds and swirl the oil over the rice. Proceed with step 4.

Saffron Milk Steamed Rice *(Shir pilau)*—Replace the water with milk. In step 3 add 1 cup dates and 1 cup raisins. Swirl the oil over the rice and proceed with the recipe.

Oven-Baked Rice

Makes 6 servings
Preparation time: 1 hour
40 minutes
Cooking time 2 hours

شیرازی پلو

Shirazi polow-ye qalebi

VEGETARIAN VARIATION

Eliminate the chicken from
step 1 and increase the number
of eggplants from 3 to 6.

NOTE

*If you do not have barberries,
you may replace the barberries
with cranberries, dried
tart cherries or grapes.*

CHICKEN
1 chicken, about 2 pounds, with excess
 fat removed
1 large onion, peeled and thinly sliced
1 teaspoon sea salt
½ teaspoon pepper
¼ teaspoon turmeric
2 tablespoon fresh lime juice

RICE
3 cups long-grain basmati rice
3 medium seedless Japanese or
 Italian eggplants

½ cup oil
2 large onions, peeled and thinly sliced
1 cup dried barberries *(zereshk),**
 cleaned and washed
3 tablespoons sugar
1 teaspoon toasted cumin seeds
2 tablespoons orange zest (3 oranges)
1 teaspoon ground saffron dissolved in
 ¼ cup orange blossom water
1 cup butter, ghee* or oil
3 egg yolks
2 cups plain yogurt

1. Place the chicken, onion, salt, pepper, turmeric, and lime juice in a medium-sized saucepan. Do not add water. Cover and simmer for 1 hour over low heat. Bone the chicken and cut into pieces. Set aside, reserving juices.

2. To cook the rice: Clean and wash 3 cups rice 5 times in warm water. It is then desirable but not essential to soak the rice in 8 cups water with 2 tablespoons salt for at least 2 hours.

3. Peel and cut eggplants lengthwise in ½-inch-thick slices. To remove bitterness from the eggplants, place slices in a container, cover with water, sprinkle with 1 tablespoon salt, let stand for 20 minutes, drain, and rinse with cold water. ***Blot dry thoroughly.*** Heat 4 tablespoons oil In a wide skillet over medium heat and brown eggplant slices. Remove eggplant and set aside. Add 2 tablespoons oil to the same skillet and brown the onions. Remove the onions from the skillet and set aside.

4. In the same skillet, heat 2 tablespoon oil, add the barberries and sugar, and stir-fry for 1 minute (beware, barberries burn easily; do not overcook). Add the cumin, orange zest, 1 tablespoon saffron water, and stir-fry for 20 seconds. Remove from heat and set aside.

5. Bring 8 cups water and 2 tablespoons salt to a boil in a large, non-stick pot. Pour the washed and drained rice into the pot. Boil briskly for 6 minutes, gently stirring twice to loosen any grains that may have stuck to the bottom. Drain rice in a large, fine-mesh colander and rinse with 2 or 3 cups water.

6. Place the oven rack in the middle. Preheat oven to 375°F (190°C). Melt ½ cup butter in a 4-quart, Pyrex dish. Spread the butter evenly over the base and sides of the dish.

7. In a mixing bowl, whisk the egg yolks, yogurt, 2 tablespoons saffron-orange blossom water, and 4 full spatulas of the rice. Place this rice mixture in the oven-proof dish. Arrange chicken pieces on top. Spread the barberry mixture over the chicken (reserve 2 tablespoons of the barberries for the garnish). Arrange a few slices of eggplant-onion mixture on top (reserve 2 slices of eggplant for the garnish). Cover with remaining rice and *pack down* using a rubber spatula. Pour remaining butter, saffron-orange blossom water and chicken juice over the top of the rice. Cover with a layer of oiled parchment paper and a layer of aluminum

foil on top, and *press down* evenly with your hands (this will help the unmolding process later on). Seal tightly around the rim so that steam cannot escape.

8. Bake in the preheated oven for 1½ to 2 hours or until the crust is golden brown (a glass ovenproof dish allows you to see through).

9. Remove the dish from oven *(do not uncover)* and allow to cool for 15 minutes on a damp surface. Uncover and loosen the rice around the edges of the dish with the point of a knife. Place a serving platter (larger than the rice mold) on top of the dish. Hold the dish and platter firmly together and turn over in a single motion with a jolt to unmold the rice. Allow to rest for a moment, then gently lift the ovenproof dish. Garnish with the reserved eggplant slices and spoon barberries on top of the rice. Serve hot. *Nush-e Jan!*

Rice with Lentils

Makes 6 servings
Preparation time: 35 minutes
Cooking time: 2 hours

Adas polow

VEGETARIAN VARIATION

Eliminate all the ingredients for the meat and skip step 1 and proceed with step 2. Garnish with 1 cup toasted almonds, ½ cup toasted sunflower seeds, ½ cup toasted chopped walnuts.

COOKING VARIATION

Cook lentils for 25 to 35 minutes until tender. Drain and set aside. Chop and sauté 2 onions, mixed with raisins, dates, and orange zest, until golden brown and set aside. Make the rice as directed without adding the lentils. Before serving, place a spatula of rice on a serving platter, then alternate with layers of lentils, the onions, raisins, and dates mixture, and rice.

MEAT
2 tablespoons oil
2 onions, peeled and thinly sliced
5 cloves of garlic, peeled and crushed
4 pounds leg of lamb, or lamb shanks (or 3 young chickens)
1½ teaspoons sea salt
½ teaspoon freshly ground black pepper
1 teaspoon turmeric
1 teaspoon *advieh* (Persian spice mix)*
¼ cup fresh lime juice
¼ teaspoon ground saffron dissolved in 2 tablespoons rose water

RICE
3 cups long-grain basmati rice
2 cups lentils
1½ teaspoons sea salt
1 cup oil, butter, or ghee*
2 onions, peeled and thinly sliced
2 cups raisins
2 cups pitted dates
¼ cup orange zest (6 oranges)
½ teaspoon freshly ground pepper
2 teaspoons *advieh* (Persian spice mix)*
1 teaspoon ground saffron dissolved in ¼ cup orange blossom water
2 tablespoons plain yogurt

1. To cook the meat: Preheat the oven to 375°F (190°C) and oil a baking dish. Spread the onions and garlic in the baking dish, and place the lamb on top. Season with salt, pepper, turmeric, *advieh*, and lime juice. Cover tightly and bake in the oven for 1½ to 2 hours until the lamb is tender. Add the saffron-rose water, cover, and set aside.

2. Clean and wash 3 cups rice 5 times in warm water.

3. In a medium saucepan, place the lentils, 6 cups water, and 1 teaspoon salt, and cook for 10 minutes. Drain and set aside.

4. In a wide skillet, heat 3 tablespoons oil and brown the onions. Add raisins, dates, orange zest, ½ teaspoon salt, pepper, *advieh,* and a few drops of the saffron-orange blossom water. Stir-fry for 20 seconds and set aside.

5. Bring 8 cups water and 2 tablespoons salt to a boil in a large non-stick pot. Pour the washed and drained rice into the pot. Boil briskly for 6 to 10 minutes, gently stirring twice to loosen any grains that may have stuck to the bottom. Bite a few grains. If the rice feels soft, and all of it has risen to the surface, it is ready to be drained. Drain rice in a large, fine-mesh colander and rinse with 2 or 3 cups water.

6. To make the golden crust *(tah-dig):* In a mixing bowl, whisk together ½ cup oil, ¼ cup water, and a few drops of saffron-orange blossom water, the yogurt, and 2 spatulas of rice, and spread the mixture over the bottom of the pot.

7. Place 2 spatulas full of rice in the pot. Add a spatula full of lentils and a spatula of the onions, raisins, and dates mixture. Repeat, mounding in the shape of a pyramid.

8. Cover and cook the rice for 10 minutes over medium heat. Pour the remaining oil, ½ cup water, and the remaining saffron-orange blossom water over the pyramid. Wrap the lid of the pot with a clean dish towel and cover the pot firmly to prevent steam from escaping. Cook for 70 minutes longer over low heat.

9. Remove the pot from heat and allow to cool for 5 minutes on a damp surface without uncovering it. This will help to free the crust from the bottom of the pot.

10. Uncover the pot, take out 2 tablespoons of the saffron-flavored rice, and set aside for garnishing.

11. Gently take 1 spatula full of rice at a time and place it on a serving platter without disturbing the crust. Mound the rice in the shape of a cone. Arrange meat around rice. Decorate with saffron-flavored rice.

12. Detach the crust from the bottom of pot using a wooden spatula. Unmold onto a small platter and serve on the side with Persian pickles (*torshi*) and fresh herbs. *Nush-e Jan!*

Rice Cooker-Style Rice with Lentils

Makes 6 servings
Preparation time: 20 minutes
Cooking time: 1 hour

RICE
3 cups long-grain basmati rice
3 ½ cups water
1 tablespoon sea salt
½ cup oil, melted butter, or ghee*

LENTILS
1½ cups lentils
1 teaspoon salt

RAISINS AND DATES MIXTURE
¼ cup oil, butter, or ghee*
2 onions, peeled and thinly sliced
2 cups raisins
2 cups pitted dates, halved
4 tablespoons orange zest
¼ teaspoon freshly ground
   black pepper
2 teaspoons *advieh* (Persian spice mix)*
½ teaspoon ground saffron dissolved in
   2 tablespoons orange blossom water

Adas polow ba
polow paz

1. To cook the rice: Clean and wash 3 cups rice 5 times in warm water, drain the rice.

2. In an electric rice cooker, combine 3½ cups of water, the washed and drained rice, 1 tablespoon salt, and ½ cup oil. Gently stir with a wooden spoon.

3. Start the electric rice cooker. Cover and cook for 15 minutes.

4. To cook the lentils: Clean and wash lentils and boil in 4 cups water and 1 teaspoon salt for 15 minutes over high heat. Drain.

5. Hollow out the middle of the rice mound and add the lentils.

6. In a wide skillet, heat ¼ cup oil and brown the onion. Add raisins, dates, orange zest, pepper, *advieh,* and saffron-orange blossom water, and stir-fry for 20 seconds. Add to the rice and gently stir with a wooden spoon.

7. Cover and cook for 45 minutes longer, then unplug the rice cooker and let stand for 10 minutes without uncovering it.

8. Remove lid and place a large serving dish on top of the rice cooker mold. Grasp them together firmly and turn pot upside down to unmold rice onto the dish. Cut into wedges to serve with leg of lamb. *Nush-e Jan!*

Rice with Dried Yellow Fava Beans

Makes 6 servings
Preparation time: 45 minutes,
* plus 2 hours of soaking time*
* for the beans*
Cooking time: 1 hour

Dampokhtak

NOTE

Yellow fava beans with skins removed are available at Iranian specialty stores.

To cook sunny-side up eggs: In a large skillet, heat 4 tablespoons oil over medium-low heat. Break each egg into the skillet. Sprinkle with salt and pepper. Cook for about 1 minute until whites begin to set. Cover and cook over medium-low heat for about 2 to 4 minutes until you have gentle whites and creamy yolks.

3 cups long-grain basmati rice
3 large onions, peeled and thinly sliced
1 cup oil, butter, or ghee*
1 tablespoon turmeric
2 cups dried yellow fava beans with
  skins removed, cleaned, washed,
  soaked in 2 cups water for 2 hours,
  and drained
1 tablespoon sea salt
¼ teaspoon freshly ground
  black pepper

½ teaspoon ground cinnamon
2 teaspoons *advieh* (Persian spice mix)*

GARNISH (OPTIONAL)
½ cup raisins
½ cup pitted dates, cut in half
6 eggs, fried sunny-side up*

1. To cook the rice: Clean and wash 3 cups rice 5 times in warm water. It is then desirable but not essential to soak the rice in 8 cups water with 2 tablespoons salt for at least 2 hours.

2. In a deep, non-stick pot, heat ½ cup oil over medium heat and sauté the onions until golden brown. Add the salt, pepper, turmeric, cinnamon, and fava beans, and sauté for a few minutes. Add 7 cups warm water and bring to a boil, stir with a wooden spoon, reduce heat, cover, and simmer over medium heat for 45 minutes.

3. Add the rice to the pot, cover, and simmer 20 minutes over medium heat. As soon as the water has evaporated, sprinkle the *advieh* and add the rest of the oil on top.

4. Wrap the lid of the pot with a clean dish towel and cover the pot firmly to prevent steam from escaping. Cook 50 minutes over low heat. Remove the pot from heat and allow to cool for 5 minutes on a damp surface without uncovering it.

5. Gently taking 1 spatula full at a time, place rice in a serving platter without disturbing the crust. Mound the rice in the shape of a cone. Garnish with raisins, dates, and sunny-side-up fried eggs.

6. Using a wooden spatula, detach the crust from the bottom of the pot. Unmold onto a small platter and serve on the side. Serve immediately with Persian pickles, (*torshi*) and fresh herb platter (*sabzi-khordan*) *Nush-e Jan!*

VARIATIONS

Smothered Bulgur with Dried Yellow Fava Beans *(Dami-e balghur ba baghali khoshk)*— For this recipe the rice is replaced with bulgur. Bulgur (cracked wheat grains) is popular in southern Iran, where it is more plentiful than rice. In the above recipe replace the rice with 4 cups coarse wheat bulgur. First toast the bulgur in a large frying pan then in step 3 add it to the fava beans and stir gently once. Continue with step 4 but reduce the cooking time from 50 to 20 minutes. This *dami* can be made with various beans by replacing the fava beans with mung beans or lentils.

Smothered Lentil and Millet *(dami-e balghur ba arzan)*—Replace the yellow fava beans with lentils and replace the rice with millet. Just before serving add 3 cloves fried garlic, ½ cup chopped parsley, and 1 cup liquid *kashk* (sun-dried yogurt) to the pot.

Rice with Toasted Noodles and Dates with Bread Crust

Makes 6 servings
Preparation time: 15 minutes
Cooking time: 2 hours

رشته پلو

Reshteh polow

Eliminate all the ingredients for the meat and skip step 1. In step 10 garnish the rice with ½ cup toasted almonds, ½ cup sunflower seeds, ½ cup pine nuts, and ½ cup chopped walnuts.

NOTE

If you cannot find toasted noodles, in a wide skillet over medium heat, toast the noodles for a few minutes until golden.

MEAT
3 tablespoons oil
1 onion, peeled and thinly sliced
1½ pounds boned leg of lamb, or chicken thighs, cut into 1-inch cubes
1 teaspoon sea salt
½ teaspoon pepper
½ teaspoon turmeric
1 teaspoon *advieh* (Persian spice mix)*
2 tablespoons fresh lime juice
¼ teaspoon ground saffron dissolved in 2 tablespoons rose water

RICE
2 cups long-grain basmati rice
½ pound toasted Persian noodles *(reshteh),* cut into 3-inch lengths
½ cup oil, butter, or ghee*
2 onions, peeled and thinly sliced
1 cup pitted dates, cut in halves
1 cup raisins or currants
¼ cup orange zest (about 6 oranges)
1 teaspoon ground saffron dissolved in 4 tablespoons orange-blossom water
2 teaspoons *advieh* (Persian spice mix)*

TAH-DIG
Lavash bread to fit the bottom of pot

1. To cook the lamb: Heat 3 tablespoons oil in a medium-sized pot, and brown the onion and lamb. Season with salt, pepper, turmeric, *advieh,* and lime juice. Pour in 1½ cups water. Cover and simmer for 45 to 55 minutes over medium heat until the lamb is almost tender. Add the saffron-rose water, cover, and set aside.

2. For the rice: Clean and wash 2 cups rice 5 times in warm water. It is then desirable but not essential to soak the rice in 8 cups water with 2 tablespoons salt for at least 2 hours.

3. Bring 10 cups water and 2 tablespoons salt to a boil in a large, non-stick pot. Pour the rice into the pot. Add the noodles. Boil briskly for 6 to 10 minutes, gently stirring twice with a wooden spoon to loosen any grains that may have stuck to the bottom. Bite a few grains of the rice. If it feels soft and all of it has risen to the surface, it is ready. Drain the rice and noodles in a large, fine-mesh colander and rinse with 2 or 3 cups water.

4. Heat ¼ cup oil in a wide skillet over medium heat and brown the onions. Add the dates, raisins, orange zest, a few drops of the saffron-orange blossom water, and *advieh,* and stir-fry for 20 seconds. Set aside.

5. To make the bread crust *(tah-dig-e nun,* see photo on page 243): In a mixing bowl, whisk together ¼ cup oil, ½ cup water, and a drop of saffron-orange blossom water. Spread this mixture in the pot. Place a layer of *lavash* bread on top to fit the bottom of the pot.

6. Place 2 spatulas full of the rice and noodle mixture in the pot. Add a spatula of the raisins, orange zest, and dates mixture. Add a spatula of the meat mixture. Repeat this process, arranging the layers in the shape of a pyramid.

7. Cover and cook rice and noodle mixture for 10 minutes over medium heat. Mix the remaining oil, ¼ cup water, and saffron-orange blossom water, and pour over the rice and noodle pyramid. Wrap the lid of the pot with a clean dish towel and cover firmly to prevent steam from escaping. Cook for 50 minutes over low heat.

8. Remove rice and noodle from heat and allow to cool for 5 minutes on a damp surface without uncovering. This helps free the crust from the bottom of the pot.

9. There are two ways to unmold and serve the rice. The first is to hold the serving platter tightly over the uncovered pot and invert the two together, unmolding the rice onto the platter. The rice will emerge as a golden-crusted cake. Serve in wedges.

10. The second way is to take 2 tablespoons of the saffron rice from the top and set aside for garnish. Gently taking one spatula full of rice at a time, place it on a serving platter without disturbing the crust. Mound the rice into a cone. Garnish with the saffron rice on top. Detach the layer of crust from the bottom using a wooden spatula. Place the pieces of crust into a small platter and serve on the side. *Nush-e Jan!*

VARIATION

Cook toasted Persian noodles (*reshteh*) for 10 to 15 minutes in 3 cups water, 1 tablespoon oil, and ½ teaspoon salt until tender. Drain and set aside. Make your rice as directed without adding the noodles. Before serving, place a spatula of rice on a serving platter, then alternate with layers of noodles, and the raisins and dates mixture.

Rice with Apricots

Makes 6 servings
Preparation time: 15 minutes
Cooking time: 1 hour 30 minutes

Qeysi polow

VEGETARIAN VARIATION
Eliminate the meat from the ingredients and step 1. Cook 2 cups mung beans in 6 cups water and 1 teaspoon salt over medium heat for 15 minutes. Drain and add at the end of step 3 together with 2 teaspoons ground cumin.

NOTE
You may replace the chicken pieces with roasted chicken pieces on the bone (opposite).

MEAT
3 tablespoons oil
1 onion, peeled and thinly sliced
1½ pounds boned leg or shoulder of lamb or boneless, skinless chicken thighs, cut into 1-inch cubes
1 teaspoon sea salt
½ teaspoon freshly ground black pepper
1 teaspoon turmeric
1 teaspoon *advieh* (Persian spice mix)*
¼ cup lime juice
¼ teaspoon ground saffron dissolved in 1 tablespoon rose water

RICE
3 cups long-grain basmati rice
¾ cup oil, butter, or ghee*
2 onions, peeled and thinly sliced
2¼ cups dried apricots, quartered
1 cup pitted dates
1 cup golden raisins
1 teaspoon cinnamon
½ teaspoon nutmeg
½ teaspoon ground saffron dissolved in 2 tablespoons rose water
2 tablespoons plain yogurt

1. In a sauté pan, heat 3 tablespoons oil over medium heat and brown the onion and meat. Season with salt, pepper, turmeric, *advieh,* and lime juice. Pour in 1½ cups water. Cover and simmer for 55 minutes over low heat until the meat is almost tender. Add the saffron-rose water and set aside.

2. To cook the rice: Clean and wash 3 cups rice 5 times in warm water. It is then desirable but not essential to soak the rice in 8 cups water with 2 tablespoons of salt for at least 2 hours.

3. In a wide skillet, heat 2 tablespoons oil and brown the onions. Add apricots, dates, and raisins, and sauté for several minutes. Add the cinnamon and nutmeg and sauté for 1 minute longer. Set aside.

4. Bring 8 cups water and 2 tablespoons salt to a boil in a large, non-stick pot. Pour the washed and drained rice into the pot. Boil briskly for 6 to 10 minutes, gently stirring twice with a wooden spoon to loosen any grains that may have stuck to the bottom. Bite a few grains of the rice. If it feels soft and all of it has risen to the surface, it is ready. Drain in a large, fine-mesh colander and rinse with 2 or 3 cups water.

5. To make the golden crust *(tah-dig):* In a mixing bowl, whisk together ½ cup oil, ¼ cup water, a few drops of the saffron-rose water, the yogurt, and 2 spatulas of rice. Spread the mixture over the bottom of the pot.

6. Place 2 spatulas full of rice in the pot. Add 1 spatula full of the meat, raisins, apricots, and dates mixture. Repeat, alternating the rice with the meat, and the fruit mixture. Mound into the shape of a pyramid.

7. Cover and cook for 10 minutes over medium heat.

8. Mix the remaining oil and ½ cup of the meat juices and pour over the rice. Pour the remaining saffron-rose water over the top.

9. Wrap the lid of the pot with a clean dish towel and cover firmly to prevent steam from escaping. Cook another 70 minutes over low heat. Remove from heat and allow to cool for 5 minutes on a damp surface without uncovering.

10. Uncover the pot, remove 2 tablespoons of the saffron-flavored rice, and set aside for garnishing.

11. Gently, taking 1 spatula full at a time, place rice on a serving platter without disturbing the crust. Place the meat on the platter. Mound the rice in the shape of a cone. Decorate with the saffron-flavored rice.

12. Detach the crust from the bottom of the pot using a wooden spatula. Unmold onto a small platter and serve on the side. Serve hot with fresh herbs and salad. *Nush-e Jan!*

VARIATIONS

Rice with Turnips *(Shalgham polow)*—In step 3, replace the apricots, cinnamon, and nutmeg with 1 pound turnips, peeled, cut into 1-inch cubes, and fried until golden brown. Add 2 teaspoons ground ginger and 2 teaspoons ground cumin.

Rice with Quince *(Beh polow)*—In step 3 replace the apricots with 2 pounds quince, cored, cut into 1-inch cubes, and fried until golden brown. Remove from the skillet and fry the onion as per step 3. Then return the quince back to the skillet and add the rest of the ingredients.

Rice with Fresh Fava Beans

Makes 6 servings
Preparation time: 20 minutes
Cooking time: 3 hours

با قلا پلو

Baqala polow

VEGETARIAN VARIATION

Eliminate all the ingredients for the meat and step 1.
In step 4, replace the fava beans with 2 pounds fresh or frozen shelled soya beans.

NOTE

For a fresher, greener looking baqala polow, *in step 9 cook only for 15 minutes, remove the bulk of the rice leaving a layer for the* tah-dig. *Keep the rice warm and continue to cook the* tah-dig *for another 50 minutes.*

MEAT
6 lamb shanks
2 teaspoons sea salt
½ teaspoon ground black pepper
½ teaspoon turmeric
2 tablespoons flour
6 tablespoons oil
2 large onions, peeled and thinly sliced
8 cloves garlic, peeled and chopped
1 tablespoon honey
2 tablespoons orange zest
2 tablespoons fresh lime juice
½ teaspoon ground saffron dissolved in 4 tablespoons rose water
2 teaspoons *advieh* (Persian spice mix)*
1 cup water

RICE
3 cups long-grain basmati rice
2 pounds fresh or 1 pound frozen fava beans, shelled
½ teaspoon turmeric
1 cup oil, butter, or ghee*
½ cup milk
1 teaspoons ground saffron dissolved in ¼ cup rose water
6 cups fresh dill weed, washed and finely chopped
6 baby green garlic, trimmed
2 teaspoons ground cinnamon

1. To cook the lamb shanks: Preheat the oven to 325°F (165°C). Wash lamb shanks, pat dry, and dust with a mixture of salt, pepper, turmeric, and flour. Heat 3 tablespoons oil in an ovenproof baking dish to fit 6 lamb shanks. Sauté the shanks on all sides until golden brown. Remove from the pan and set aside. In the same baking dish, add 3 tablespoons oil and sauté the onions and garlic. Add the honey, orange zest, lime juice, saffron-rose water, and *advieh*, and stir-fry for 20 seconds. Return the lamb shanks back to the pan, add 1 cup water, cover tightly with a layer of parchment paper and aluminum foil on top, and bake in the preheated oven for about 3 hours or until the lamb is tender. Remove from heat and keep warm.

2. To cook the rice: Clean and wash 3 cups basmati rice 5 times in warm water.

3. Shell beans and remove outer layer of skin. If using frozen fava beans, soak in warm water for a few minutes, then remove the second skin.

4. Bring 10 cups water and 2 tablespoons salt to a boil in a large, non-stick pot. Pour the washed and drained rice into the pot. Add the fava beans and turmeric to the pot while water is boiling (turmeric helps to keep the green color).

5. Boil briskly for 6 to 10 minutes, stirring gently with a wooden spoon to loosen any stuck grains. Bite a few grains. If rice feels soft and all of it has risen to the surface, it is ready to be drained. Remove from heat and drain in a large, fine-mesh colander; rinse with 2 or 3 cups water.

6. To form a tender golden crust (*tah-dig*): In a mixing bowl, whisk together ½ cup oil, the milk, a few drops of saffron-rose water, and 3 spatulas of rice, and spread the mixture over the bottom of the pot.

7. Taking a spatula full of rice and beans, begin to form a pyramid by alternating layers of rice with dill weed, the garlic, and cinnamon. Repeat these layers. Cover and cook over medium-high heat for 10 minutes.

VARIATION

Pistachio Rice *(Pesteh polow)* —Replace the fava beans with raw, shelled pistachios. Soak 1 pound raw, shelled pistachios in water overnight and drain. In step 4 replace the fava beans with the pistachios.

VARIATION

8. Mix the remaining oil and ½ cup warm water and pour over the rice. Pour the remaining saffron-rose water over the top.

9. Wrap the lid of the pot with a clean dish towel and cover firmly to prevent steam from escaping. Cook another 70 minutes over low heat. Remove from heat and allow to cool for 5 minutes on a damp surface without uncovering.

10. Remove lid and take out 2 tablespoons of the saffron-flavored rice and set aside for garnish. Gently taking 1 spatula of rice at a time, mound the rice in the shape of a pyramid. Arrange the lamb around the rice and garnish with saffron-flavored rice.

11. Detach the crust from the bottom of the pot with a wooden spatula. Unmold onto a small platter. Serve this rice with yogurt or *torshi* (pickle) or sometimes *khoresh-e qeymeh* (potato *khoresh*). *Nush-e Jan!*

Braised Leg of Lamb *(Run-e barreh)* —This is a substitute for the lamb shanks—a trimmed leg of lamb (about 6–7 pounds) baked in the oven. Rinse and pat dry. Using the point of a small knife, make 10 slits all over the leg of lamb and insert a peeled clove of garlic in each slit. Peel and thinly slice 2 onions and spread them in a deep baking dish. Place leg of lamb on the onions. Sprinkle the lamb with 2 tablespoons sea salt, 1 teaspoon pepper, 2 tablespoons *advieh*, 2 tablespoons candied orange peel, 1 teaspoon ground saffron dissolved in ¼ cup rose water. Pour ¼ cup fresh lime juice all over it. Cover with a layer of parchment paper and then a layer of foil, seal tightly, and roast in a preheated 350°F (180°C) oven for 3 to 3½ hours, uncovering for the last half hour of cooking. Check your lamb. A well-done lamb tends to be more tender. When it is done, place it on a board and slice and serve along with your rice.

Rice with Shrimp and Fresh Herbs Persian Gulf-Style

Makes: 6 servings
Preparation time: 20 minutes
Cooking time: 1 hour 15 minutes

میگو پلو

Maygu polow

RICE
3 cups basmati rice
8 cloves garlic, peeled and sliced
3 cups freshly chopped cilantro
1 cup fresh chopped dill
2 cups fresh chopped spring onions
1 tablespoons dried fenugreek or,
    ½ cup fresh chopped fenugreek
1 teaspoon sea salt
½ teaspoon pepper
2 teaspoons red pepper flakes
4 teaspoons hot curry powder
1 tablespoon angelica powder *(gol-par)*
1 cup oil, melted butter, or ghee*
½ teaspoon saffron, dissolved in
    2 tablespoons hot water

SHRIMP
2 tablespoons oil
1 pound raw shrimp, butterflied, or
    1 pound white fish fillets,
    4-inch lengths
1 teaspoon lime powder
1 teaspoon curry powder
½ teaspoon sea salt
1 tablespoon fresh chopped cilantro

VEGETARIAN VARIATION

Eliminate the shrimp from the ingredients and replace it with 2 cups raw cashew nuts. Dust the cashew nuts as for the shrimp, sauté in oil, and add to the rice in step 9.

VARIATION

Replace the shrimp with six 4-inch salmon fillets. In step 4 combine ½ cup oil and ¼ cup water and spread over the bottom of the pot. Arrange the salmon fillets on top and mound the rice over them. In step 5 cook for 10 minutes over medium heat and proceed with step 6.

1. Pick over and wash the rice 5 times in warm water and drain. In a large, non-stick pot, bring 8 cups water and 2 tablespoons salt to a boil.

2. Pour the washed and drained rice into the pot. Boil briskly for 6 to 10 minutes, stirring gently with a wooden spoon to loosen any stuck grains. Bite a few grains. If rice feels soft and all of it has risen to the surface, it is ready to be drained. Remove from heat and drain in a large, fine-mesh colander. Rinse with 2 or 3 cups water.

3. In a mixing bowl, toss together the garlic, all the herbs, salt, pepper, pepper flakes, curry, and angelica powder. Set aside.

4. To form a tender golden crust *(tah-dig)*: In a mixing bowl, whisk together ½ cup oil, ¼ cup water, a few drops of saffron water, and 2 spatulas of rice. Spread this mixture over the bottom of the pot. Then mound alternating layers of rice and the herb and spice mixture to form a pyramid.

5. Cover and cook for 10 minutes over medium-high heat.

6. Mix the rest of the oil with ½ cup water and pour over the rice. Pour the saffron water on top. Wrap the lid of the pot with a clean dish towel and cover firmly to prevent steam from escaping. Cook another 50 minutes over low heat.

7. Remove from heat and allow to cool for 5 minutes on a damp surface without uncovering it.

8. Heat 2 tablespoons oil in a wide skillet until very hot. Dust the shrimp with the mixture of lime powder, curry powder, salt, and cilantro. Sear the shrimp for a 1 minute on each side or until the shrimp change color, and then remove from heat.

9. Uncover pot and gently taking one spatula of rice at a time, mound it on a serving dish without disturbing the crust in the pot. Place the shrimp on top. Finally detach the crust from the bottom of the pot using a wooden spatula and serve on the side. *Nush-e Jan!*

THE STORY OF THE BARBER'S SIXTH BROTHER

In the stories from the *Thousand and One Nights,* the calif takes a girl each evening and then has her killed in the morning, until Shahrzad (the noble daughter of the Vazir) agrees to be the calif's wife for one night. However, she devises a plan of starting a story each evening, refusing to finish it until the next night. Her plan is successful and the khalifeh ultimately abandons his murderous way with women.

In the story "The Barber's Sixth Brother," the barber's poor brother visits the mansion of a rich man with a sense of humor. The rich man treats the poor brother to a magnificent make-believe feast. While no food is actually served, the rich man describes a host of exotic dishes on the table in elaborate detail, beginning with all kinds of appetizers and then going on to rice with candied orange peel and carrots, and garnished with slivered pistachios and almonds, served with lamb stuffed with pistachios.

By this time the poor brother is almost dead with hunger, but the rich man, who does not do anything in half measures, continues with *khoreshes* of meat, fruit, vegetables and nuts flavored with *advieh,* cloves, nutmeg, ginger, pepper, and sweet herbs.

Finally come the desserts of date cake, almond cookies, chickpea cookies, and honey almonds.

The poor brother is also a man of some wit and pretends to go along with all this while getting drunk on the make-believe wine. Then, pretending to have lost his senses, he gives the rich man a heavy blow. The rich man, a little upset at first, eventually catches on and, in appreciation of the poor brother's sense of humor, makes him his right-hand man.

From A Thousand and One Nights

Sweet Rice with Candied Orange Peel

Makes 6 servings
Preparation time: 40 minutes
Cooking time: 2 hours

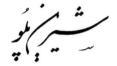

Shirin polow

VEGETARIAN VARIATION

Eliminate all the ingredients for the chicken and step 1. Increase the pistachios and almonds to 2 cups each.

VARIATION

Sweet Rice with Meatballs— You may use ground meatballs in place of the chicken by combining 1 pound ground meat with 1 peeled and grated onion. Season with 1 teaspoon salt and ½ teaspoon pepper, ½ teaspoon cinnamon, ½ teaspoon cardamom, and ½ teaspoon turmeric. Knead well and form the mixture into meatballs the size of hazelnuts. Brown in a wide skillet over medium heat with 2 tablespoons butter. Add the carrot mixture, mix well, and set aside. Alternate layers of the mixture with layers of rice in step 8.

CHICKEN
2 young chickens, about 3 pounds
2 teaspoons sea salt
1 teaspoon freshly ground black pepper
1 teaspoon turmeric
¼ cup lime juice
2 large onions, peeled and cut in 4
2 cloves garlic, peeled
¼ teaspoon ground saffron dissolved in 2 tablespoons rose water

RICE
3 cups long-grain basmati rice

2 cups slivered orange peel
⅔ cup oil, melted butter, or ghee*
2 cups carrots, peeled and cut into thin strips
1 teaspoon ground saffron dissolved in 4 tablespoons orange blossom water
2 cups sugar
1 cup slivered pistachios, toasted
1 cup slivered almonds, toasted
1 teaspoon ground cinnamon
2 teaspoons ground cardamom
lavash bread to fit bottom of pot

1. To cook the chicken: Preheat the oven to 425°F (220°C). Rub each chicken, inside and outside, with a mixture of the salt, pepper, turmeric, and lime juice. Stuff each chicken with 1 onion and 1 clove of garlic. Place in an oiled baking dish, and cover tightly with a layer of parchment paper and a layer of aluminum foil on top. Bake for 1½ hours or until the chicken is tender. Add the saffron-rose water, cover, and set aside.

2. Clean and wash 3 cups rice 5 times in warm water. It is desirable but not essential to soak the rice in 8 cups water with 2 tablespoons salt for at least 2 hours.

3. To remove the bitterness from the orange peel: Place the orange peel and 6 cups water in a saucepan, bring to a boil, boil for 5 minutes, and drain. Rinse with cold water and set aside.

4. In a wide skillet, heat 3 tablespoons oil over medium heat and sauté the carrots for 5 minutes. Add the orange peel, 2 tablespoons of the saffron-orange blossom water, and sugar, and stir-fry for 1 minute. Add 2 cups water and bring to boil. Simmer over medium heat for 15 to 20 minutes until lightly caramelized. Drain the syrup off into a separate bowl and save for later use.

5. Add the pistachios and almonds to the carrot mixture and set aside.

6. Bring 8 cups water and 2 tablespoons salt to a boil in a large, non-stick pot. Pour the washed and drained rice into the pot. Boil briskly for 6 to 10 minutes, gently stirring twice to loosen any grains that may have stuck to the bottom. Bite a few grains. If the rice feels soft and all of it has risen to the surface, it is ready. Drain rice in a large, fine-mesh colander and rinse with 2 or 3 cups water.

7. To make a bread crust (*tah-dig*): In a mixing bowl, whisk together ¼ cup oil, ½ cup water, and a few drops of saffron-orange blossom water. Spread it in the same pot. Cut and place a disk of *lavash* bread on top so that it fits the bottom of the pot.

8. Place 1 spatula full of rice in the pot, add 1 spatula of the carrot mixture, and then sprinkle with a some of the cinnamon and cardamom. Repeat these steps, arranging the rice in the shape of a pyramid (reserve 2 tablespoons of the carrot mixture for the garnish).

9. Cover and cook rice for 10 minutes over medium heat.

10. Mix the remaining oil with ½ cup water, and pour over the rice. Then pour ½ cup syrup that was set aside in step 4. Wrap the lid of the pot with a clean dish towel and cover firmly to prevent steam from escaping. Cook for 50 minutes longer over low heat. Remove the pot from heat and allow to cool for 5 minutes on a damp surface without uncovering it.

11. Gently taking 1 spatula full of rice at a time, place it on a serving platter. Be careful not to disturb the crust on the bottom of the pot. Mound the rice in the shape of a cone. Garnish with some of the carrot mixture.

12. Remove the chicken from the oven and allow to rest, covered, for 5 minutes. Cut chicken into pieces and arrange it around the rice.

13. Detach the crust from the bottom of the pot using a wooden spatula and serve on a small platter on the side. Serve this rice with fresh herbs. *Nush-e Jan!*

Rice with Eggplant and Pomegranate

Makes 6 servings
Preparation time: 1 hour
Cooking time: 1 hour

بادمجان پلو

Bademjan polow

NOTE

Sadaf's California-made pomegranate molasses has an excellent balance of sweet and sour.

MEAT

3 tablespoons oil
2 pounds stew meat (lamb or beef), or boneless chicken thighs, cut into 1-inch cubes
2 onions, peeled and thinly sliced
1 teaspoon sea salt
½ teaspoon freshly ground pepper
1 teaspoon red pepper flakes
1 teaspoon turmeric
2 large fresh tomatoes, peeled and finely chopped (about 2 cups), or ½ pound chopped canned tomatoes, drained
3 tablespoons pomegranate molasses

EGGPLANT

¼ cup oil
2 pounds Japanese eggplants, peeled and cut into 2-inch strips

RICE

3 cups long-grain basmati rice
1 cup oil, melted butter, or ghee*
1 teaspoon ground saffron dissolved in 4 tablespoons hot water
3 teaspoons *advieh* (Persian spice mix)*

GARNISH

1 cup fresh chopped dill
1 cup fresh pomegranate arils

1. To cook the meat: Heat 3 tablespoons oil in a medium saucepan over medium heat and sauté the meat and onion until brown. Then add the salt, pepper, red pepper flakes, and turmeric, and sauté for a few minutes longer. Add the tomatoes and pomegranate molasses. Cover and simmer for 40 minutes over low heat.

2. Rinse the eggplants and *blot* dry. Heat ¼ cup oil in a wide skillet over high heat until hot. Sauté the eggplant on all sides until golden brown (in batches, add more oil if necessary). Add the eggplant to the meat mixture, remove from heat and set aside.

3. To cook the rice: Clean and wash 3 cups rice 5 times in warm water and drain.

4. Bring 8 cups water and 2 tablespoons salt to a boil in a large, non-stick pot. Pour the washed and drained rice into the pot. Boil briskly for 6 to 10 minutes, gently stirring twice with a wooden spoon to loosen any grains that may have stuck to the bottom. Bite a few grains of the rice. If the rice feels soft and all of it has risen to the surface, it is ready. Drain rice in a large, fine-mesh colander and rinse with 2 or 3 cups water.

5. To make the golden crust *(tah-dig)*: In a mixing bowl, whisk together ½ cup oil, ¼ cup water, a few drops of saffron water, and 2 spatulas of rice. Spread the mixture over the bottom of the pot.

6. Place 2 spatulas full of rice in the pot, then layer with some of the meat and eggplant mixture, a sprinkle of *advieh*. Repeat, alternating the rice with the meat, and *advieh* to form a pyramid.

7. Cover and cook rice for 10 minutes over medium heat.

8. Swirl the remaining oil and saffron water (and any juices remaining from the meat mixture) over the rice pyramid. Wrap the lid with a clean dish towel and cover

the pot firmly to prevent steam from escaping. Cook for another 50 minutes over low heat. Remove rice pot from heat and allow to cool for 5 minutes on a damp surface without uncovering it.

9. Gently taking 1 spatula full of rice at a time without disturbing the crust, place it on a serving platter. Mound the rice in the shape of a cone. Garnish with the dill and pomegranate arils.

10. Detach the crust from the bottom of the pot using a wooden spatula. Place the pieces on a small platter and serve on the side *Nush-e Jan!*

VARIATIONS

Rice with Green Peas and Dill *(Nokhod-sabz polow)*—Eliminate the pomegranate molasses in step 1. In step 2 replace the eggplant with 1 pound shelled or frozen peas. Add 2 tablespoons curry powder and 1 tablespoon *limu-omani* powder (Persian lime powder) in step 1. Add 5 cups chopped fresh dill in between the layers in step 6. Eliminate the garnish.

Rice with Mung Beans *(Maash polow)*—In step 2 replace the eggplant with 1½ cups mung beans (cooked in 4 cups water and 1 teaspoon salt and then drained).

Barberry Rice

Makes 6 servings
Preparation time: 40 minutes
Cooking time: 2 hours 5 minutes

رزشک پلو

Zereshk polow

VEGETARIAN VARIATION
Eliminate all the ingredients
for the chicken and step 1.
Add 2 cups each of toasted
pistachios and almonds in
step 11.

NOTE
*You may place the barberries
in the rice and steam them
together, but the color of
barberries will not be as red
as when you layer them with
the rice at the last minute. If
using fresh barberries, clean
by removing the stems and
rinse with cold water.*

CHICKEN

2 young chickens, about 3 pounds
2 teaspoons sea salt
1 teaspoon freshly ground black pepper
1 teaspoon turmeric
¼ cup lime juice
2 onions, peeled and cut in 4
2 cloves garlic, peeled
¼ teaspoon ground saffron dissolved in 2 tablespoons rose water

RICE

3 cups long-grain basmati rice
2 cups dried barberries *(zereshk),* cleaned, washed, and drained
1 cup oil, melted butter, or ghee*
2 tablespoons yogurt
1 onion, peeled and thinly sliced
4 tablespoons sugar
1 teaspoon ground saffron dissolved in 4 tablespoons rose water
4 tablespoons toasted cumin seeds

1. To cook the chicken: Preheat the oven to 425°F (220°C). Rub each chicken, inside and outside, with a mixture of the salt, pepper, turmeric, and lime juice. Stuff each chicken with 1 onion and 1 clove of garlic. Place in a greased baking dish, cover tightly with a layer of parchment paper and a layer of aluminum foil, and bake for 1½ hours or until the chicken is tender. Add the saffron-rose water, cover, and set aside.

2. To cook the rice: Clean and wash 3 cups rice 5 times in warm water. It is then desirable but not essential to soak the rice in 8 cups water with 2 tablespoons of salt for at least 2 hours.

3. To prepare the barberries: Clean the barberries by removing their stems and placing the berries in a colander. Place colander in a large container full of cold water and allow barberries to soak for 20 minutes. The sand will settle to the bottom. Take the colander out of the container and run cold water over the barberries. Drain and set aside.

4. In a wide skillet, heat 2 tablespoons oil over medium heat and sauté the onions until golden brown. Add the barberries, sugar, 1 tablespoon saffron-rose water, and stir-fry for 1 minute (beware, barberries burn very easily!). Remove from heat and set aside.

5. Bring 8 cups water and 2 tablespoons salt to a boil in a large, non-stick pot. Pour the washed and drained rice into the pot. Boil briskly for 6 to 10 minutes, gently stirring twice to loosen any grains that may have stuck to the bottom. Bite a few grains. If the rice feels soft and all of it has risen to the surface, it is ready to be drained. Drain rice in a large, fine-mesh colander and rinse with 2 or 3 cups water.

6. To make a golden crust (*tah-dig*): In a mixing bowl, whisk together ½ cup oil, ¼ cup water, yogurt, a few drops of saffron-rose water, and 3 spatulas of rice. Spread the mixture evenly over the bottom of the pot.

7. Place 1 spatula full of rice in the pot, then sprinkle the cumin over the rice. Repeat these steps, arranging the rice in the shape of a pyramid. This shape allows room for the rice to expand and enlarge. Cover and cook for 10 minutes over medium-high heat.

8. Mix the remaining oil with ½ cup water and pour over the pyramid. Pour the remaining saffron-rose water over the rice. Wrap the lid of the pot with a clean dish towel and cover firmly to prevent steam from escaping. Cook for 70 minutes longer over low heat.

9. Remove the pot from heat and allow to cool, covered, for 5 minutes on a damp surface to free crust from the bottom of the pot.

10. Remove lid and take out 2 tablespoons of saffron-flavored rice and set aside for use as garnish.

11. Then, gently take 1 spatula full of rice at a time, and place it on a serving platter in alternating layers with the barberry mixture. Mound the rice in the shape of a cone. Arrange the chicken around the platter. Finally, decorate the top of the mound with the saffron-flavored rice and some of the barberry mixture. Detach the crust and serve on the side. *Nush-e Jan!*

Barberries (Berberis vulgaris) *during the harvest season in Birjand, eastern Iran.*

Jeweled Rice

Makes 6 servings
Preparation time: 40 minutes
Cooking time: 1 hour 30 minutes

جواهر پلو

Javaher polow

NOTE

To make orange slivers, take a large, firm orange and use a peeler to peel thick layers of the skin together with some of the white pith. With a sharp knife, cut these peels into thin strips as shown in photos 5a and 5b.

To make carrot strips, use large carrots. Peel and cut them into 3-inch lengths. Then cut each length vertically into slices, and finally cut each slice into strips as shown in photo 6a.

4 cups long-grain white basmati rice
1 cup dried barberries
1¼ cups oil, butter or ghee*
½ cup sliced raw almonds
¼ cup sliced raw pistachios
½ cup seedless raisins
1 teaspoon ground saffron dissolved in ¼ cup orange blossom water
1 cup plus 2 tablespoons granulated sugar
3 large oranges (1 cup slivered orange peel)
2–3 large carrots (2 cups peeled and cut 3-inch strips
½ teaspoon ground cinnamon
2 teaspoons cardamom powder

Considered the king of Persian dishes, Javaher Polow is made of orange peels, almonds, sugar, barberries, and pistachios. As a wedding dish it represents gold, rubies, emeralds, and pearls. I like to serve this rice with chicken kabab and a meatless pomegranate khoresh (fesenjan).

1. Clean and wash 4 cups rice 5 times in warm water. Drain in a large, mesh colander and set aside

2. Clean barberries by removing their stems and any grit. Place the barberries in a fine-mesh colander, and place the colander in a large container full of cold water. Allow barberries to soak for 20 minutes. Any sand will settle to the bottom. Take the colander out of the container and run cold water over the barberries. Drain and set aside.

3. Heat 1 tablespoon oil in a wide skillet over medium heat. Add the almonds, pistachios, and raisins, and stir-fry for 20 seconds. Remove the almond and raisin mixture from the skillet and set aside.

4. In the same skillet, heat 2 tablespoons oil over medium heat, add the barberries, a few drops of saffron-orange blossom water, and 2 tablespoons sugar, and stir-fry for 1 minute. Remove from the heat and set aside (beware, barberries burn very easily!).

5. To remove the bitterness from the orange peel: Drop the orange peel in a saucepan of boiling water and cook for 5 minutes. Drain and rinse with cold water.

6. Heat 4 tablespoons oil in a wide skillet over medium heat. Add the carrots and the orange peel, stir-fry for 2 minutes. Add 1 cup sugar, a drop of saffron-orange blossom water, the cinnamon, and the cardamom, and stir-fry for 1 minute. Add 1 cup water, bring to a boil, and cook over medium high heat for 15 minutes until lightly caramelized. Drain, reserving the syrup. Set aside.

7. In a large nonstick pot, add 10 cups water and 2 tablespoons salt, and bring to a boil. Pour the washed and drained rice into the pot. Boil briskly for 6 to 10 minutes (depending on the type of basmati rice you are using). Bite a few grains of rice. If the rice feels soft and all of it has risen to the surface, it is ready. Drain the rice in a large, fine-mesh colander and rinse with 2 cups water.

2. WASHING THE BARBERRIES

3. STIR-FRYING ALMONDS AND PISTACHIOS AND ADDING RAISINS

4. STIR-FRYING BARBERRIES, SAFFRON WATER AND SUGAR

5a: SLIVERING ORANGE PEEL

5b. SLIVERING ORANGE PEEL

5c. REMOVING BITTERNESS FROM ORANGE PEEL

6a. CUTTING CARROTS INTO STRIPS

6b. CARAMELIZING THE CARROTS AND ORANGE PEEL

NOTE

*If you are cooking
this rice for a
wedding or if you
don't want the
golden crust tah-dig,
in step 9 eliminate
the cooking over
medium-high heat
for 10 minutes and
continue with step
10. In step 11, steam
the rice, over
medium heat, for
only 20 minutes.
Keep warm until
ready to serve.*

8. To make a golden crust *(tah-dig):* In a mixing bowl, whisk together ½ cup oil, ½ cup water, a few drops of saffron-orange blossom water, 3 spatulas of rice, and spread the mixture over the bottom of the pot. Give the pot a shake to even out the base.

9. Take one spatula full of rice at a time and gently place it on top of the saffron-rice mixture, gradually shaping the rice into a pyramid. This shape leaves room for the rice to expand and enlarge. Cover and cook for 10 minutes over medium-high heat.

10. Swirl ½ cup water, the remaining oil, and the reserved syrup from step 6 over the rice.

11. Wrap the lid of the pot with a clean dish towel and cover firmly to prevent steam from escaping. Cook for 70 minutes longer over low heat.

12. Remove the pot from heat. Allow to cool on a damp surface for 5 minutes without uncovering it. This helps to free the crust from the bottom of the pot. Uncover and loosen the edges with a wooden spoon.

13. Gently taking 1 spatula full of rice (about 1 cup of cooked rice) at a time, place it on a serving platter in alternating layers with the caramelized carrot mixture, caramelized barberries, and the almonds, pistachio, and raisin mixture. Mound the rice in the shape of a cone.

14. Detach the crust from the bottom of the pot using a wooden spatula, place on a small platter, and serve on the side. *Nush-e Jan!*

PHOTO CAPTIONS:

8. Spreading base for crust (tah-dig).

9a. Mounding rice over the base.

9b. 10 minute medium-high heat cooking to start the crust.

11. 70 minute low heat steaming for fluffy rice.

13a, b. Alternating layers of the rice with the caramelized and toasted mixtures

13c. Jeweled rice

14. Jeweled rice crust.

8.

9a.

9b.

11.

13a.

13b.

13c.

13d.

13.

Rice with Split Peas

Makes 6 servings
Preparation time: 55 minutes
Cooking time: 1 hour

MEAT

3 tablespoons oil
3 onions, peeled and thinly sliced
2 pounds stew meat—lamb, beef, or
   chicken thighs—cut into ½-inch pieces
½ cup yellow split peas
½ teaspoon freshly ground pepper
1 teaspoon turmeric
2 teaspoons sea salt
2 cups fresh tomatoes, chopped (3
   tomatoes
4 whole *limu-omani* (dried Persian
   limes)*, pierced, or 2 tablespoons
   powdered
¼ cup orange zest (6 oranges)
¼ teaspoon ground saffron dissolved in
   1 tablespoon hot water

RICE

3 cups long-grain basmati rice
¾ cup oil, melted butter, or ghee*
½ cup milk
1 teaspoon ground saffron dissolved in
   4 tablespoons orange blossom water
1 tablespoon *advieh* (Persian spice mix)*
1 teaspoon ground cardamom

GARNISH

1 tablespoon oil
1 cup barberries (cleaned)*,
   or tart cherries
2 tablespoons sugar

Qeymeh polow

VEGETARIAN VARIATION

Eliminate the meat from the
ingredients and from step 1,
and increase the amount of
yellow split peas from ½ cup to
1 cup, and the water from
2 cups to 4 cups. Everything
else remains the same.

1. To cook the meat: Heat the oil in a medium-sized saucepan over medium-high heat, and brown the onions and meat. Add the salt, pepper, turmeric, and split peas, and sauté for a few minutes. Add the tomatoes and 2 cups water. Bring to a boil, cover, and simmer over medium heat for 20 minutes. Add the dried limes, orange zest, and saffron-water. Cover and simmer over low heat for 10 to 20 minutes, depending on the type and quality of split peas you use. Be sure the split peas are cooked but not mushy. Set aside.

2. To cook the rice: Clean and wash 3 cups rice 5 times in warm water. It is then desirable but not essential to soak the rice in 8 cups water with 2 tablespoons of salt for at least 2 hours.

3. Bring 8 cups water, 2 tablespoons salt, and the orange blossom water to a boil in a large, non-stick pot. Pour the washed and drained rice into the pot. Boil briskly for 6 to 10 minutes, gently stirring twice to loosen any grains that may have stuck to the bottom. Bite a few grains. If the rice feels soft and all of it has risen to the surface, it is ready to be drained. Drain rice in a large, fine-mesh colander and rinse with 2 or 3 cups water.

4. To make a golden crust *(tah-dig):* In a mixing bowl, whisk together ¼ cup oil, ½ cup milk, a few drops of saffron-orange blossom water, and 2 spatulas of rice, and spread the mixture evenly over the bottom of the pot.

5. Place 3 spatulas full of rice in the pot, then add a layer of the meat and split pea mixture. Repeat these steps, sprinkle some *advieh* and cardamom between each layer, and mound the layers in the shape of a pyramid. Cover and cook for 10 minutes over medium heat.

6. Pour the remaining oil and ¼ cup water over the rice. Add the remaining saffron-orange blossom water on top.

7. Wrap the lid of the pot with a clean dish towel and cover firmly to prevent steam from escaping. Cook for 50 minutes longer over low heat. Remove the pot from heat and allow to cool for 5 minutes on a damp surface without uncovering.

8. Meanwhile, to make the garnish: Heat the oil in a wide skillet, add the barberries and sugar and stir-fry for 2 minutes over low heat (beware, barberries burn easily!).

9. To serve the rice: Take out 2 tablespoons of saffron-flavored rice from the top and set aside for the garnish. Then, gently taking 1 spatula full of rice at a time, place rice on a serving platter without disturbing the crust. Mound the rice in the shape of a cone and garnish with the saffron-flavored rice and the barberries.

10. Detach the crust from the bottom of the pot using a wooden spatula, place on a small platter, and serve on the side with fresh herbs, yogurt, or *torshi* (Persian pickles). *Nush-e Jan!*

Spiced Yogurt Rice

Makes 6 servings
Preparation time: 55 minutes
Cooking time: 1 hour 10 minutes

CHICKEN
2 tablespoons oil, butter, or ghee*
2 young chickens (3 pounds), butterflied and cut up
1 medium onion, peeled and thinly slice
4 garlic cloves, peeled and thinly sliced
1 teaspoon sea salt
½ teaspoon freshly ground black pepper
½ teaspoon turmeric
2 teaspoons ground coriander
2 teaspoons ground cumin
2 teaspoons ground cardamom
1 serrano chili, finely chopped, or 1 teaspoon red chili flakes
1-inch ginger, peeled and grated
2 bay leaves
2 tablespoons *limu-omani* (dried Persian lime powder)*, or 4 whole limes, pierced
1 teaspoon angelica powder *(gol-par)*

2 large tomatoes, peeled and chopped
1 cup plain yogurt
½ teaspoon saffron dissolved in ¼ cup rose water

NUTS
2 tablespoons oil, butter, or ghee*
2 medium onions, peeled and thinly sliced
1 cup raw whole almonds or cashews
1 cup raisins

RICE
2 cups long-grain basmati rice
½ cup oil, melted butter, or ghee*
2 Idaho russet potatoes peeled and ¼ inch round sliced

مات پلو

Mast polow

1. For the chicken: Heat 2 tablespoons oil in a medium-sized pot over medium heat and sauté the chicken. Add the onion and garlic, and sauté until golden brown. Add the rest of the ingredients for the chicken except the yogurt and saffron-rose water, and give it a gentle stir. Cover and cook over low heat for 55 minutes.

2. Beat the yogurt with the saffron-rose water for 5 minutes. Add it to the chicken and stir gently. Remove from heat.

3. For the nuts: In a wide skillet, heat 2 tablespoons oil over medium heat. Add the onions and cook until golden brown. Add the almonds and stir-fry for 1 minute. Add the raisins and stir-fry for 20 seconds. Remove from heat and set aside

4. To cook the rice: Clean and wash 3 cups rice 5 times in warm water, drain. Bring 8 cups water and 2 tablespoons salt to a boil in a large, non-stick pot. Boil briskly for 6 to 10 minutes, gently stirring twice to loosen any grains that may have stuck to the bottom. Bite a few grains. If the rice feels soft and all of it has risen to the surface, it is ready to be drained. Drain in a large, fine-mesh colander and rinse with 3 cups cold water.

VEGETARIAN VARIATION

Replace the chicken with two pounds of zucchini cut into 4-inch lengths. Reduce the cooking time in step 1 from 55 minutes to 5 minutes. All other ingredients and steps remain the same.

5. In the same pot heat ¼ cup oil with ¼ cup water and arrange a layer of potato slices side by side, overlapping them to fit the bottom of the pot. Place 2 spatulas of the rice in the pot. Add a spatula of the chicken mixture and some of the onion and almond mixture. Alternate layers of the rice with the chicken mixture and onion and almonds, and mound the layers to form a pyramid. Cover and cook over medium heat for 10 minutes.

6. Drizzle ¼ cup oil on top of the rice. Wrap the lid with a clean dish towel and cover the pot firmly to prevent steam from escaping. Cook for another 70 minutes over low heat. Remove from heat and place on a damp cloth. Allow to cool for 5 minutes without uncovering.

7. Gently take 1 spatula at a time of the rice mixture, without disturbing the crust, and place it on a serving platter. Detach the potato crust from the bottom of the pot using a wooden spatula and place it around the rice. Serve with fresh basil and yogurt. *Nush-e jan!*

FAIR EXCHANGE

The mulla was on a journey with a number of companions, and they paused to have lunch. They spread a cloth and sat about it, and each of them put a little round of bread on the cloth. The mulla said, "I'm really not hungry, so I'll give my whole round of bread to you, and each of you just give me half of yours in exchange."

Rice with Green Cabbage

Makes 6 servings
Preparation time: 30 minutes
Cooking time: 1 hour

Kalam polow

MEATBALLS
1 pound ground meat: lamb, beef, or chicken thighs
1 onion, peeled and grated
1 teaspoon sea salt
½ teaspoon freshly ground pepper
½ teaspoon turmeric
½ teaspoon cayenne
¼ teaspoon smoked paprika

CABBAGE MIXTURE
5 tablespoons oil
1 large head green cabbage, washed and cut into 1-inch pieces
1 teaspoon sea salt
½ teaspoon cayenne

2 tablespoons *limu-omani* (Persian lime powder)*
6 medium fresh tomatoes, peeled and finely chopped

RICE
3 cups long-grain basmati rice
¾ cup oil, melted butter, or ghee*
1 teaspoon ground saffron dissolved in 2 tablespoons hot water
1 tablespoon ground cumin seed
1 tablespoon *advieh* (Persian spice mix)*

GARNISH
2 tablespoons oil
1 large onion, peeled and thinly sliced

1. To cook the meatballs: Combine meat with onion, salt, pepper, turmeric, cayenne, and paprika. Knead lightly to form a paste. With damp hands form the paste into meatballs the size of hazelnuts. Place in a baking sheet lined with parchment paper.

2. To make the cabbage mixture: In a wide sauté pan, heat 5 tablespoons oil over medium heat and carefully add the meatballs. Swirl and shake the pan back and forth to brown meatballs all over —a spatula might break the meatballs—until the meatballs are golden brown. Add the cabbage and sauté over medium heat for a few minutes. Add the salt, cayenne, lime powder, and the tomatoes, cover, and cook over medium heat for 20 minutes. Remove from heat, and set aside.

3. To make the garnish: Heat 2 tablespoons oil in a wide skillet over medium heat, add the onions and brown, and then set aside.

4. To cook the rice: Clean and wash 3 cups rice 5 times in warm water. It is then desirable but not essential to soak the rice in 8 cups water with 2 tablespoons of salt for at least 2 hours.

5. Bring 8 cups water and 2 tablespoons salt to a boil in a large pot. Pour the washed and drained rice into the pot. Boil briskly for 6 to 10 minutes, gently stirring twice to loosen any grains that may have stuck to the bottom. Bite a few grains. If the rice feels soft and all of it has risen to the surface, it is ready to be drained. Drain rice in a large, fine-mesh colander and rinse with 2 or 3 cups water.

6. To make the golden crust *(tah-dig)*: In a mixing bowl, whisk together ½ cup oil, ¼ cup water, a few drops of saffron water, and 3 spatulas of rice. Spread the mixture over the bottom of the pot.

7. Place 2 spatulas full of rice in the pot, then add a layer of the cabbage and meatball mixture. Repeat, alternating layers, sprinkling some of the cumin and *advieh* between the layers. Mound the rice in the form of a pyramid.

8. Cover and cook rice for 10 minutes over medium heat to form a golden crust.

9. Mix the remaining oil, saffron water, and any juices left from the meat, and pour over the pyramid. Add the fried onion on top. Wrap the lid of the pot with a clean dish and cover the pot firmly to prevent steam from escaping. Cook for 70 minutes longer over low heat. Remove the pot from heat and allow to cool for 5 minutes on a damp surface without uncovering it.

10. Take 2 tablespoons of saffron-flavored rice from the top for use as a garnish. Then, gently taking 1 spatula full at a time, place rice on a serving platter without disturbing the crust. Mound the rice in the shape of a cone. Garnish with the saffron-flavored rice and fried onion.

11. Detach the crust from the bottom of the pot using a wooden spatula. Place on a small platter and serve on the side. *Nush-e Jan!*

Rice with Green Beans

Makes 6 servings
Preparation time: 45 minutes
Cooking time: 1 hour

Lubia polow

MEAT
3 tablespoons oil
2 large onions, peeled and thinly sliced
2 cloves garlic, peeled and crushed
2 pounds stew meat, lamb, beef, or chicken thighs, cut into 1-inch cubes
1½ pounds fresh green beans, cleaned and cut into ½-inch pieces
1½ teaspoons sea salt
½ teaspoon freshly ground pepper
½ teaspoon turmeric
½ teaspoon cayenne (optional)
1 teaspoon ground cinnamon
1 teaspoon *advieh* (Persian spice mix)*
1 teaspoon *limu-omani* (dried Persian lime powder)*
6 large fresh tomatoes, peeled and finely chopped, or one 14.5-ounce can of chopped tomatoes, drained

RICE
3 cups long-grain basmati rice
¾ oil, melted butter, or ghee*
½ teaspoon ground saffron dissolved in 2 tablespoons hot water
½ teaspoon *advieh* (Persian spice mix)*
1 teaspoon *limu-omani* (dried Persian lime powder)*

1. To cook the meat: In a medium saucepan, heat 3 tablespoons oil over medium heat and brown the onions, garlic, and meat. Add green beans, salt, pepper, turmeric, cayenne, cinnamon, *advieh*, and *limu-omani*. Sauté for a few minutes and add the tomatoes. If using canned tomatoes, make sure they are completely drained. Cover and simmer over low heat for 40 minutes.

2. To cook the rice: Clean and wash 3 cups rice 5 times in warm water. It is then desirable but not essential to soak the rice in 8 cups water with 2 tablespoons of salt for at least 2 hours.

3. Bring 8 cups water and 2 tablespoons salt to a boil in a large, non-stick pot. Pour the washed and drained rice into the pot. Boil briskly for 6 to 10 minutes, gently stirring twice to loosen any grains that may have stuck to the bottom. Bite a few grains. If the rice feels soft and all of it has risen to the surface, it is ready to be drained. Drain rice in a large, fine-mesh colander and rinse with 2 or 3 cups water.

4. To make a golden crust *(tah-dig):* In a mixing bowl, whisk together ½ cup oil, ¼ cup water, a few drops of saffron water, and 2 spatulas rice. Spread this mixture evenly over the bottom of the pot.

5. Place 2 spatulas full of rice in the pot, then add a layer of the green bean and meat mixture (use a slotted spatula to avoid bringing in the juices and reserve any remaining juice to use later on). Sprinkle with *advieh* and *limu-omani* between the layers. Repeat, alternating layers to form a pyramid. Cover and cook for 10 minutes over medium heat.

6. Pour the remaining oil, saffron water, and meat juices over the rice. Wrap the lid with a clean dish towel and cover the pot firmly with the lid to prevent steam from escaping. Cook 50 minutes longer over low heat. Remove the pot from heat and allow to cool for 5 minutes on a damp surface without uncovering it (this helps to free the crust from the bottom of the pot).

7. Take out 2 tablespoons of the saffron-flavored rice from the top and set aside for garnishing.

8. Gently taking 1 spatula full of rice at a time, place it on a serving platter without disturbing the crust. Mound the rice in the shape of a cone. Garnish with the saffron-flavored rice.

9. Detach the crust from the bottom of the pot using a wooden spatula. Place the pieces of the crust on a small platter and serve on the side. Serve rice with a fresh herb platter *(sabzi-khordan)*, cucumber salad *(salad shirazi)*, and Persian pickles *(torshi). Nush-e Jan!*

Rice with Tomato Sauce

Makes 6 servings
Preparation time: 20 minutes
Cooking time: 1 hour

اسلامبو پلو

Eslamboli polow

VEGETARIAN VARIATION

Eliminate the meat from the ingredients and from step 1. In step 1, add 1 cup mung beans cooked in 4 cups water and 1 teaspoon salt for 15 minutes and drained. Then add 2 bell peppers, seeded and diced, and 1 tablespoon ground cumin, and reduce cooking time to 10 minutes. Proceed with the recipe.

SAUCE
5 tablespoons oil
1 large onion, peeled and thinly sliced
4 cloves garlic
2 pounds stew meat (lamb, veal, or beef, or boned chicken thighs), cut into ½-inch cubes
1½ teaspoons sea salt
1 teaspoon freshly ground black pepper
½ teaspoon cayenne
1 teaspoon turmeric
3 tablespoons tomato paste
1 teaspoon ground cinnamon
6 medium, fresh tomatoes, peeled and finely chopped, or one 12-ounce can tomatoes, drained and diced

RICE
3 cups long-grain basmati rice
½ cup oil, butter, or ghee*
¼ teaspoon ground saffron dissolved in 2 tablespoons hot water (optional)

1. In a medium saucepan, heat the oil and brown the onion, garlic and meat. Add salt, pepper, cayenne, turmeric, cinnamon, and tomato paste. Sauté for a few minutes and add the tomatoes. Cover and simmer over low heat for about 40 minutes.

2. To cook the rice: Clean and wash 3 cups rice 5 times in warm water, then drain in a fine-mesh colander in the sink.

3. Bring 8 cups water and 2 tablespoons salt to a boil in a large, non-stick pot. Pour the washed and drained rice into the pot. Boil briskly for 6 to 10 minutes, gently stirring twice to loosen any grains that may have stuck to the bottom. Bite a few grains. If the rice feels soft and all of it has risen to the surface, it is ready to be drained. Drain rice in a large, fine-mesh colander and rinse with 2 or 3 cups water.

4. To make the crust *(tah-dig)*: In a mixing bowl, whisk together ½ cup oil, ¼ cup water, a few drops of saffron water, and 2 spatulas of rice. Spread this mixture evenly in the same pot.

5. Place 2 spatulas full of rice in the pot; then use a slotted spoon (to avoid bringing in the juices) to add a layer of the meat-and-tomato mixture. Repeat, alternating layers in the shape of a pyramid. Cover and cook rice for 10 minutes over medium heat in order to form a golden crust.

6. Pour the remaining oil, meat juices and saffron water over the rice. Wrap the lid of the pot with a clean dish towel and cover pot firmly to prevent steam from escaping. Cook for 50 minutes longer over low heat.

7. Remove the pot from heat and allow to cool for 5 minutes on a damp surface without uncovering it.

8. Gently taking 1 spatula full of rice at a time, place it on a serving platter without disturbing the crust. Mound the rice in the shape of a cone.

9. Detach the crust from the bottom of the pot using a wooden spatula. Unmold onto a small platter and serve on the side.

10. Serve immediately with cucumber and tomato salad (*salad shirazi*), Persian pickles (*torshi*), and a fresh herb platter (*sabzi-khordan*). *Nush-e Jan!*

RICE COOKER VARIATION

In a rice cooker, heat 3 tablespoons oil and brown onion, garlic, and 1 pound ground
meat. Add 1½ tablespoons salt, 1 teaspoon black pepper, 1 teaspoon cinnamon,
2 tablespoons tomato paste, and the rice, and sauté for a few minutes longer. Add
4 cups of the peeled and finely chopped tomatoes and stir gently. Cover and cook
for 30 minutes. Unplug the rice cooker and allow to sit for 10 minutes. Remove lid
and place a round serving dish over the pot. Hold the serving dish and pot together
tightly and flip them to unmold the rice. The rice will be like a cake. Cut into slices
and serve.

Baked Saffron Yogurt Rice with Lamb

Makes 6 servings
Preparation time: 1 hour plus
 30 minutes of marinating
Cooking time: 2 hours

تَه چین برّه

Tah-chin-e barreh

VEGETARIAN VARIATION

Remove the meat from the ingredients, eliminate step 1 totally, and eliminate the meat and the marination time from step 2. Add 1 cup toasted almonds and ½ cup raisins on top of the yogurt mixture in step 6.

NOTE

For a damp surface: Line a baking sheet with a wet kitchen towel. Place the Pyrex dish coming out of the oven on top in order for it to cool. This helps with the unmolding process. Do not uncover while dish cools..

MEAT

2 pounds boned leg or shoulder of lamb, or chicken thighs, cut in 2-inch cubes
1 onion, peeled and thinly sliced
2 cloves garlic, peeled and sliced
1 teaspoon sea salt
½ teaspoon freshly ground pepper

YOGURT MARINATION

2½ cups plain yogurt
1 teaspoon ground saffron dissolved in 4 tablespoons rose water
1 teaspoon sea salt
½ teaspoon freshly ground pepper
¼ cup orange zest (6 oranges)
1 teaspoon sugar

RICE

3 cups long-grain basmati rice
1 cup and 2 tablespoons oil, melted butter, or ghee*
1 cup seedless raisins
1 onion, peeled and thinly sliced
2 egg yolks
2 teaspoons ground cumin
1 teaspoon *advieh* (Persian spice mix)*

1. For the meat: Preheat the oven to 350°F (180°C). Place the meat, onion, garlic, salt, and pepper in an ovenproof baking dish. Cover and bake for 1 hour, drain, keeping the juice to use later, and allow to cool.

2. For the yogurt marination: In a large bowl, combine the yogurt, 2 tablespoons saffron-rose water, salt, pepper, orange zest, and sugar. Add the lamb, toss, cover, and marinate for at least 30 minutes and up to 24 hours.

3. To cook the rice: Clean and wash 3 cups rice 5 times in warm water and drain in a fine-mesh colander in the sink.

4. Bring 8 cups water and 2 tablespoons salt to a boil in a large pot. Pour the washed and drained rice into the pot. Boil briskly for 6 to 10 minutes, gently stirring twice to loosen any grains that may have stuck to the bottom. Bite a few grains. If the rice feels soft and all of it has risen to the surface, it is ready to be drained. Drain in a large, fine-mesh colander and rinse with 2 to 3 cups water.

5. Heat 2 tablespoons oil in a wide skillet and sauté 1 onion until golden brown. Add the raisins and set aside.

6. Place the oven rack in the middle and preheat oven to 375°F (190°C). Place ½ cup oil in a 4-quart Pyrex baking and heat in the oven.

7. Remove the lamb from the marinade and set aside. In the same bowl with the marinade, whisk together the egg yolks and 4 spatulas of rice.

8. Remove the hot baking dish from the oven. Add the mixture of rice and marinade, spreading it across the bottom and up the sides of the baking dish. Place the meat pieces on top, cover with the remaining rice and sautéed onion and raisin mixture, cumin, and *advieh*. Pour the remaining saffron water, oil, and the juice reserved from the lamb over the rice. Pack firmly with a wooden spoon and cover with oiled parchment paper and a layer of aluminum foil on top of it. Use the palms of both hands to firmly *press the rice down,* compacting it evenly throughout (this helps the unmolding later on). Seal thoroughly.

9. Bake in the middle rack of the oven for 1½ to 2 hours or until the crust is golden brown (look through the Pyrex glass to check color).

10. Remove baking dish from oven. Allow to cool on a damp surface for 15 minutes (do not uncover). Then loosen the rice around the edges of the baking dish with the point of a knife. Place a large serving dish over the baking dish. Hold both dishes firmly together with two hands and turn them upside down. Allow to rest for 5 minutes. Tap and gently unmold the rice by lifting up the Pyrex dish.

11. Serve hot with fresh herbs, yogurt, and Persian pickles *(torshi)*. *Nush-e Jan!*

STOVETOP VARIATION

Stovetop Saffron Yogurt Rice with Lamb *(tah-chin-e kham)*—For this variation, the lamb or chicken is cut into thin slices and is not cooked prior to marination. Marinate only for 30 minutes. In step 6 use a 5-quart non-stick pot. In step 9 instead of cooking in the oven, cook on the stove for 10 minutes over medium heat and for 1½ hours over low heat. Otherwise, the recipe remains the same for unmolding the rice.

A first millennium BCE bas-relief showing soldiers preparing meals in tents while the king sits on his throne.

Baked Saffron Yogurt Rice with Spinach

Makes 6 servings
Preparation time: 1 hour
  30 minutes
Cooking time: 2 hours
  30 minutes

MEAT
2 pounds boned leg or shoulder of
  lamb, or chicken thighs, cut in 2-inch
  pieces
1 large onion, peeled and sliced
2 cloves garlic, peeled and sliced
1 teaspoon sea salt
½ teaspoon freshly ground pepper
1 teaspoon turmeric

FOR THE YOGURT MARINATION
1½ cups plain yogurt
1 teaspoon saffron dissolved in ¼ cup
  orange blossom water

½ teaspoon sea salt
½ teaspoon freshly ground pepper

RICE
1 cup oil, butter, or ghee*
1 large onion, peeled and sliced
2 pounds fresh spinach, chopped,
  or 1 pound frozen
1 teaspoon sea salt
½ teaspoon freshly ground pepper
3 cups pitted prunes
2 cups long-grain basmati rice
2 egg yolks

Tah-chin-e esfenaj

VEGETARIAN VARIATION
Eliminate all the ingredients
for the meat mixture and
begin by making the yogurt
marinade mixture in step 2.
Proceed with the recipe.

NOTE
*This dish can also be prepared
on a stovetop instead of in the
oven.*

*For a damp surface: Line a
baking sheet with a wet kitchen
towel. Place the Pyrex dish
coming out of the oven on top
in order for it to cool. This helps
with the unmolding process. Do
not uncover while dish cools.*

1. To cook the meat: Preheat the oven to 375°F (190°C). In a medium-sized ovenproof baking dish, combine the meat with the onion, garlic, salt, pepper, and turmeric. Cover and bake for 1 hour. Remove from heat, drain, and allow to cool. Reserve the juice to use later.

2. To marinate the cooked meat: In a bowl, beat the yogurt, saffron-orange blossom water, salt, and pepper. Toss the lamb in this marination, cover, and place in the refrigerator for at least 30 minutes and up to 24 hours.

3. Heat 3 tablespoons oil in a wide skillet over medium heat. Brown onions, add the spinach and 1 teaspoon salt, cover, and cook for 5 minutes over low heat to steam the spinach. Add the prunes and cook, uncovered, for about 3 minutes or until water is absorbed.

4. Clean and wash 2 cups rice a few times in water until the water is clear. Bring 8 cups water and 2 tablespoons salt to a boil in a large pot. Add the rice. Boil briskly for 6 to 10 minutes, gently stirring twice to loosen any grains that may have stuck to the bottom. Bite a few grains. If the rice feels soft and all of it has risen to the surface, it is ready to be drained. Drain rice in a large, fine-mesh colander and rinse with 2 cups water.

5. Place rack in center of the oven, and preheat oven to 375°F (190°C). Heat ½ cup oil in a 4-quart Pyrex baking dish in the oven.

6. Remove the meat from the yogurt marinade and set aside. In the same bowl with the marinade, whisk together the egg yolks and 4 spatulas of the rice.

7. Place the Pyrex dish on the counter. Spread the mixture of rice and marinade across the bottom of the dish and up the sides. Place the pieces of lamb on top and add a layer of spinach and prunes. Cover with the remaining rice. Pour the remaining

saffron water, oil, and the juice reserved from the lamb over the rice. Pack firmly with a wooden spoon and cover with oiled parchment paper and a layer of aluminum foil on top. Use the palms of both hands to *firmly press the rice down* compacting it evenly throughout (this helps the unmolding later on). Seal thoroughly.

8. Bake for 1½ to 2 hours or until the crust is golden brown (look through the Pyrex glass to check color).

9. Remove baking dish from oven. To unmold, keep it covered and allow to cool on a damp surface for 10 to 15 minutes. Then loosen the rice around the edge of the baking dish with the point of a knife. Place a large serving dish over the baking dish. Hold both dishes firmly together with your hands and turn them upside down. Allow to rest for 5 minutes then lift Pyrex dish gently to unmold the rice. Serve hot. *Nush-e Jan!*

Rice with Fresh Herbs and Fish

Makes 6 servings
Preparation time: 45 minutes
Cooking time: 1 hour

Sabzi polow ba mahi

VEGETARIAN VARIATION

Eliminate the fish from the ingredients and from the steps. Serve the rice in wedges with a sunny-side up egg with each wedge.

VARIATION

Rice with Spring Ramps (Valak polow)—Replace all the herbs with ramps. Use the green leaves of the ramps and discard the bulbs. Replace the herbs with 6 cups cleaned, washed, and coarsely chopped ramp leaves. Continue from step 4.

Valak, called ramp and also wild leek, is a wonderful, strong-flavored mountain bulb that is available fresh in the spring. Nowadays, in the U.S. it is popular in farmers' markets.

RICE

3 cups long-grain basmati rice
½ cup chopped fresh chives or spring onions
2 cups coarsely chopped fresh dill
2½ cups coarsely chopped fresh parsley
2 cups chopped fresh cilantro
¾ cup oil, melted butter, or ghee*
1 teaspoon ground saffron dissolved in 4 tablespoons hot water or rose water
Lavash bread for the crust
1 teaspoon ground cinnamon
8 green garlics, trimmed, or 3 cloves garlic, peeled and thinly sliced

FISH

1 large white-fleshed fish (striped bass, rockfish, 4–5 pounds), scaled and cleaned, or 3 pounds catfish fillets

DUSTING

½ cup flour combined with 1 teaspoon sea salt, ½ teaspoon turmeric, and ½ teaspoon cinnamon

4 tablespoons oil for frying fish
4 small bitter oranges or limes for garnish

1. To cook the rice: Clean and wash 3 cups rice 5 times in warm water. It is then desirable but not essential to soak the rice in 8 cups water with 2 tablespoons of salt for at least 2 hours.

2. Bring 8 cups water and 2 tablespoons salt to a boil in a large, non-stick pot. Pour the washed and drained rice into the pot. Boil briskly for 6 to 10 minutes, gently stirring twice to loosen any grains that may have stuck to the bottom. Bite a few grains. If the rice feels soft and all of it has risen to the top, it is ready to be drained. Drain rice in a large, fine-mesh colander and rinse with 2 or 3 cups water.

3. In a bowl, toss the chopped herbs together and set aside.

4. To make the bread crust: In a mixing bowl, whisk together ¼ cup oil, ½ cup water, and a few drops of saffron water. Pour this mixture in the same pot. Place a layer of *lavash* bread on top to fit the bottom of the pot.

5. Place 2 spatulas full of rice in the pot, then add one spatula full of herbs. Repeat, alternating layers of the rice and herbs, sprinkling the cinnamon between the layers. Form the rice into the shape of a pyramid (this shape allows room for the rice to expand and enlarge). Cover and cook for 10 minutes over medium heat.

6. Pour the remaining oil, ½ cup hot water, and a drop of saffron water over this pyramid. Arrange the green garlics on top. Wrap the lid with a clean dish towel and cover the pot firmly to prevent steam from escaping. Cook for 50 minutes longer over low heat.

7. While the rice is cooking, cut the fresh fish down the center lengthwise without removing the backbone. Slice across into 6 pieces. Wash and pat dry. Dredge in the dusting mixture.

If using dried herbs, reduce the amount used to ¼ of the fresh herbs. Place a sieve in a bowl of lukewarm water and soak the dried herbs for 20 minutes. Remove the sieve from the bowl and use the herbs.

8. Just before serving, heat 4 tablespoon oil in a wide skillet over medium heat until very hot, and brown the fish pieces on both sides. Add more oil if necessary. Sprinkle each piece of fish with a squeeze of bitter orange and a dash of the saffron water.

9. Remove rice pot from heat and allow to cool for 5 minutes on a damp surface without uncovering it. This frees the crust from the bottom of the pot. Unmold the rice onto a serving platter and serve on the side.

10. Arrange fish on a serving platter and pour the remaining saffron water over it. Garnish with the baby green garlics. Serve hot with *torshi. Nush-e Jan!*

Rice with Sour Cherries

Makes 6 servings
Preparation time: 35 minutes
Cooking time: 1 hour

Albalu polow

VEGETARIAN VARIATION

Remove all the ingredients for the chicken and eliminate step 1. Increase the quantity of almonds and pistachios to 1 cup each.

NOTES

I prefer to use fresh sour cherries in season, but you can use sour cherries in syrup or dried (all available in Persian stores) all year round.

If you use sour or Morello cherries in light syrup, use 3 jars (8 ounce each, drain the cherries, and discard any liquid. Place cherries and 1 cup sugar in a saucepan. Cook for 35 minutes over high heat. Drain the cherries over a bowl. Save the syrup. Add 2 tablespoons oil, cinnamon, and saffron. Proceed as you would for fresh sour cherries.

If you use dried sour cherries, use 4 cups, add 2 tablespoons oil and 1 cup ready-made sour cherry syrup, and cook over medium heat for 5 minutes. Proceed with the recipe.

CHICKEN
1 tablespoon oil
2 young chickens, butterflied with backbones removed
2 large onions, peeled and sliced
1 teaspoon sea salt
½ teaspoon freshly ground pepper
1 teaspoon turmeric
2 tablespoons lime juice
¼ teaspoon ground saffron dissolved in 2 tablespoons rose water

RICE
4 pounds fresh sour cherries,* or 2 pounds pitted frozen
1¼ cups sugar
1 teaspoon fresh lime juice
1 cup oil, melted butter, or ghee*
½ teaspoon cinnamon
1 teaspoon ground saffron dissolved in 2 tablespoons rose water
3 cups long-grain basmati rice
Lavash bread for the crust

GARNISH
2 tablespoons slivered almonds, toasted
2 tablespoons slivered pistachios
½ cup cherry syrup *
2 tablespoons oil, butter or ghee*

1. To cook the chicken: In a medium sauté pan, heat 1 tablespoon oil until hot and sear the chicken. Add the onions, salt, pepper, turmeric, lime juice, and ¼ cup water. Cover and cook over low heat for 1½ hours. Add the saffron-rose water, 2 tablespoons cherry syrup, cover, and set aside.

2. Gently rinse the cherries in a colander, remove stems, pit them, and place in a medium saucepan with the sugar and lime juice. Bring to a boil and cook for 10 minutes over high heat. Drain over a bowl and save the syrup for later use. Return cherries to the saucepan and add 2 tablespoons oil, the cinnamon, and a few drops of saffron-rose water. Stir gently but do not crush the cherries. Set aside.

3. To cook the rice: Clean and wash 3 cups rice 5 times in warm water.

4. Bring 8 cups water and 2 tablespoons salt to a boil in a large, non-stick pot. Pour the rice into the pot. Boil briskly for 6 to 10 minutes, gently stirring twice to loosen any grains that may have stuck to the bottom. Bite a few grains. If the rice feels soft and all of it has risen to the top, it is ready to be drained. Drain in a large, fine-mesh colander and rinse with 2 or 3 cups water.

5. To make the bread crust *(tah-dig):* In a mixing bowl, whisk together ¼ cup oil, ½ cup water, and a few drops of saffron-rose water. Pour this mixture into the same pot. Place a layer of *lavash* bread on top to fit the bottom of the pot.

6. Place 2 spatulas of rice in the pot, then add 1 slotted spatula of cherries. ***Do not add any of the syrup***. (Set aside 2 spatulas of cherries for garnish.) Repeat, alternating layers of rice and cherries to mound the rice in the shape of a pyramid.

7. Cover and cook over medium heat for 10 minutes. Pour the remaining saffron-rose water over the pyramid and reduce the heat to low.

8. Wrap the lid of the pot with a clean dish towel and cover firmly to prevent steam from escaping. Cook 40 minutes longer over low heat. Remove the lid and pour a mixture of ½ cup cherry syrup and ½ cup oil over the rice. Cover and cook for another 10 minutes.

9. Remove the pot from heat and allow to cool on a damp surface for 5 minutes without uncovering it. Take out 2 tablespoons of saffron-flavored rice and set aside with the rest of the garnish.

10. Gently taking 1 spatula at a time, place the rice on a serving platter without disturbing the crust. Mound the rice in the shape of a pyramid. Remove the chicken from the pot, cut into pieces, and place around the rice. Garnish with the saffron rice, cherries, almonds, and pistachios. In a small saucepan, heat ½ cup hot cherry syrup and 2 tablespoon oil and drizzle over the rice. Detach crust from the bottom of the pot with a wooden spatula and serve on the side. *Nush-e Jan!*

VARIATION

Sour Cherry Rice with Tiny Meatballs *(albalu polow ba kufteh ghelgheli)*—You may substitute meatballs for the chicken. In a mixing bowl, combine 1 pound ground lamb, 1 grated onion, 1 teaspoon salt, ½ teaspoon pepper, ½ teaspoon turmeric, and ½ teaspoon cinnamon, and knead well. Moisten your hands and shape the paste into balls the size of hazelnuts. Heat 2 tablespoons oil in a wide skillet over low heat and brown the meatballs while shaking the skillet constantly. Add 2 tablespoons sour cherry syrup to the meatballs and set aside.

Rice Veiled in Pastry

Makes 6 servings
Preparation time: 20 minutes
Cooking time: 1 hour 25 minutes

پرده دار پلو

Polow-ye pardehi

NOTE
You can also use ready-made frozen puff pastry to replace the filo. Roll out 1 thawed package of puff pastry on a floured surface to 16x16 inches square. Use it in step 5 by placing it in the pan with the edges overhanging. Place the chicken in the center, cover with rice (shaping it into a dome), then bring the four corners of the pastry on top of the rice, and pinch the corners together to enclose the rice. Seal the seams and use glaze to smooth out the dome. Continue with step 7.

MEAT
3 tablespoons oil, butter, or ghee*
2 pounds boneless, skinless chicken thighs
1 large onion, peeled and thinly sliced
½ teaspoon sea salt
½ teaspoon freshly ground pepper
½ teaspoon ground saffron dissolved in 2 tablespoons orange blossom water

RICE
3 tablespoons oil, melted butter, or ghee*
2 cups white basmati rice
1 teaspoon sea salt
3 cups chicken broth

CARROTS AND NUTS MIXTURE
¼ cup oil, butter, or ghee*
1 medium onion, peeled and thinly sliced
2 carrots, peeled and thinly sliced
2 cups dried apricots, chopped
¼ cup raw, shelled pistachios
¼ cup raw almonds
2 cups raisins
Zest of 1 orange
2 tablespoons sugar
1 teaspoon sea salt
2 teaspoons ground cardamom
1 teaspoon ground cinnamon

PASTRY
10-inch spring form cake pan
1 cup oil, butter or ghee*
1 package frozen filo pastry sheets (take the package out of the freezer and leave at room temperature for 2 hours); cover the filo while working to prevent it from drying
1 egg yolk mixed with a splash of water for the glaze

1. To make the chicken: In a sauté pan, heat the oil over medium heat and sauté the chicken, onion, salt and pepper for a few minutes. Add the saffron-orange blossom water, cover, and cook over low heat for 30 minutes or until the chicken is almost tender.

2. To cook the rice: Heat the oil in a medium saucepan over medium heat and sauté the rice for 2 minutes. Add the salt and broth, and bring to a boil. Reduce heat, cover, and simmer for 20 minutes over low heat. Remove from heat and allow to cool.

3. To cook the carrots and nuts mixture: In a wide skillet, heat the oil over medium heat and sauté the onion until golden brown. Add the rest of ingredients and sauté for 2 minutes. Add this mixture to the rice, use a fork to gently combine it evenly with the rice, and allow to cool.

4. Preheat oven to 400°F (200°C). Brush a 10-inch-diameter baking pan with some oil.

5. Lay the first sheet of filo pastry in the baking pan (allow the ends to hang well over the edges) and brush it with oil. Repeat this for 10 more sheets of filo, laying one over the other.

6. Place the chicken in the center of the filo on the baking pan. Cover it with the rice mixture. Fold the filo layers across and over the top of the filling. Place a sheet of filo over the top and tuck in any overlapping edges. Use your hands to form a round, smooth surface and brush the top of the pastry with the oil and the glaze.

7. Bake in the center of the preheated oven for 40 minutes or until the crust is crisp and golden.

8. Remove from the oven and allow to cool for 5 minutes. Unclip the side of the pan. Use an offset spatula to transfer to a round platter larger than the pastry. Cut into wedges and serve hot with a green salad. *Nush-e Jan!*

BRAISES & KHORESHES

BRAISES & KHORESHES

*K*horeshes are delicate and refined braises. A *koresh* is a combination of meat (lamb, beef, or veal), poultry or fish with vegetables, herbs, fruits, beans, grains, and sometimes nuts. It is seasoned subtly with fresh herbs and spices, then simmered for a long time over low heat. To achieve the slow fusing of flavors that characterizes a *khoresh,* it is best to cook it in a heavy pot (cast iron if possible). I recommend a classic Dutch oven (called *cocotte* in French, see page 312 for a classic Dutch oven), but any heavy-bottomed, medium-sized pot will do.

Khoresh is first mentioned in the *Shahnameh* to refer to food in general, while *khoresh khaneh* literally "the house where the khoresh is made" meant the kitchen (see page 172).

Khoreshes can be made in advance and reheated just before serving; in fact, it often improves after sitting for a while. To obtain a wonderful *khoresh,* brown your meat and onion very well. Don't use too much water.

The good Persian cook always uses whatever vegetables and fruits are in season when preparing *khoresh,* not only because it is more economical to do so, but because their freshness enhances the flavor of the dish. For every recipe, I have specified options for the meat. In the case of lamb, use the leg or shanks for exceptionally good results; for veal or beef use eye round, and carefully monitor the cooking period. I use fine-grind sea salt. If you use regular iodized salt, be careful because it tends to be sharper and salt more. If you use coarse sea salt, remember that it tends to salt less because there is less of it in a measure. I have also suggested using grape molasses, an ancient Persian sweetening agent, as an alternative to sugar. I have also found, in thirty years of testing, that a pinch of cayenne and smoked paprika, brings out the best in *khoreshes,* especially the Green Bean Khoresh and the Tomato Khoresh.

In this edition, I have also given vegetarian variations as an alternative for those who might prefer their *khoreshes* without meat.

Khoresh is always served with *chelow* (saffron-steamed rice), which is heaped on each dinner plate with the *khoresh* served beside it or on top of it. This is called *chelow khoresh.*

Photo left: Yogurt Khoresh with rice and golden crust, *Chelow khoresh-e mast ba tah-dig,* recipe on page 345

MEMORIES OF QORMEH SABZI

Few dishes are so evocative of the Persian love of fragrance as the delicate braise known as *khoresh*. The one I remember most from my childhood is *Qormeh sabzi* (fresh herb khoresh, photo left). Its preparation would begin early in the morning when, while picking up *barbari* bread for breakfast, we would visit the market to buy the fresh herbs: parsley, chives, cilantro, and, most important because of the scent, fenugreek. Then all the women of the house would gather around a table with a large copper basin and tray on it. There they chatted companionably while they cleaned and washed the herbs before arranging them in flat woven baskets and setting them in the sun to dry. My mother, who emphasized the importance of even, clean chopping, would do it alone. She would stand over a large oak chopping board, seize a handful of each herb in one hand, and set to work with a large cleaver at a rhythmic, fast, even, slanting stroke. I can see and smell and hear it still: the various greens of the herbs, the sharp steel of the cleaver with droplets of herb juice on it, the lovely aroma, the faraway, trancelike concentration on my mother's angelic face, her strong body adorned with a turquoise necklace—she never wore her rings when she cooked—the even, quick blows of the cleaver. Never was I allowed to try it. After college, she said, there would be plenty of time for me to try my hand at cooking.

After the herbs were chopped, they were stir-fried, their heavenly scent drifting through the house and even across the neighborhood. Then the other ingredients added their own notes—the lamb we always used in this dish, the onion, the garlic, and the saffron, added at the end to preserve its scent, and finally the gnarled whole dried limes. All morning the *khoresh* would simmer, perfuming our house until lunchtime. I recall those days every time I visit people who are making this dish, especially if they live in apartment buildings: The haunting scent greets us in the elevator and drifts up long corridors, drawing us to friends' doors.

Okra Khoresh

Makes 4 servings
Preparation time: 30 minutes
Cooking time: 2 hours 30 minutes

5 tablespoons oil, butter, or ghee*
2 medium onions, peeled and thinly
  sliced
2 cloves garlic, peeled and sliced
1 pound stew meat (lamb or beef), or
  boneless, skinless chicken thighs, cut
  into 2-inch cubes, or 2 pounds
  veal shank
1 teaspoon sea salt
½ teaspoon freshly ground pepper

1 teaspoon turmeric
½ teaspoon red pepper flakes
½ red bell pepper, chopped
3 tablespoons tomato paste
1 tomato, peeled and chopped
1 pound fresh or frozen okra
3 tablespoons fresh lime juice
1 tablespoon grape molasses

Khoresh-e bamieh

VEGETARIAN VARIATION

Eliminate the meat from the
ingredients and from step 1
and replace it with 1 cup
mung beans. In step 2, pour in
3 cups water. Cover and
simmer for 30 minutes.
Proceed with step 3.

1. In a Dutch oven, heat 3 tablespoons oil over medium heat and brown onions, garlic, and meat. Sprinkle with salt, pepper, turmeric, red pepper flakes, and bell peppers, and sauté for 2 minutes. Add the tomato paste and fresh tomato, and sauté for 1 minute.

2. Pour in water—2 cups for meat and 1½ cups for chicken. Cover and simmer over low heat for 2 hours for meat or 1½ hours for chicken until the meat is tender, stirring occasionally.

3. Cut the okra into 1-inch lengths and sauté in a wide skillet in 2 tablespoons oil over medium heat (if you use baby okra, there is no need to cut them). Set aside.

4. When the meat is tender, add the lime juice, grape molasses, and okra. Cover and simmer for 15 to 20 minutes over low heat until the okra is tender.

5. Check to see if the okra is tender. Taste the *khoresh* and adjust the seasoning by adding more lime juice or salt.

6. Transfer the *khoresh* to a deep casserole. Cover and place in a warm oven until ready to serve. Serve hot with *chelow* (saffron-steamed rice). *Nush-e Jan!*

NOTE

If you don't want to fry the okra, in step 3, instead of sautéing it, you can parboil the okra for 10 minutes in salted water. Drain and add it to step 4.

Instead of lime juice, add 2 tablespoons tamarind paste and 1 teaspoon hot curry powder.

Carrot and Prune Khoresh

Makes 6 servings
Preparation time: 20 minutes
Cooking time: 2 hours
  10 minutes

6 tablespoons oil, butter, or ghee*
2 large onions, peeled and thinly sliced
1 clove garlic, peeled and sliced
1 pound boneless, skinless chicken
  thighs, or stew meat (lamb, veal, or
  beef), cut into 2-inch cubes, or 2
  pounds veal shanks
1 teaspoon sea salt
½ teaspoon freshly ground
  black pepper

½ teaspoon turmeric
1 teaspoon ground cinnamon
1 teaspoon ground cardamom
1 pound carrots, peeled and sliced
½ cup freshly squeezed lime juice
2 tablespoons wine vinegar
½ cup brown sugar
2 cups pitted prunes or golden plums
¼ teaspoon ground saffron dissolved
  in 1 tablespoon hot water

Khoresh-e havij-o alu

1. In a Dutch oven, heat 3 tablespoons oil over medium heat and brown the onions, garlic, and chicken. Add salt, pepper, turmeric, cinnamon, and cardamom, and sauté for 1 minute.

2. Pour in water—1½ cups for chicken, 2½ cups for stew meat. Cover and simmer over low heat for 40 minutes for chicken or 1¼ hours for meat, stirring occasionally.

3. In a wide skillet, sauté the carrots in 3 tablespoons oil over medium heat. Add it to the chicken. Add lime juice, vinegar, sugar, prunes, and saffron water. Cover and simmer for 50 minutes longer over low heat.

4. Check to see if chicken and prunes are tender. Taste the *khoresh* and adjust seasoning. The sauce should be sweet and sour. Add more sugar or lime juice as desired.

5. Transfer to a deep, ovenproof casserole. Cover and place in a warm oven until ready to serve. Serve hot with *chelow* (saffron-steamed rice). *Nush-e Jan!*

VEGETARIAN VARIATION

Eliminate the meat from the ingredients and from step 1. Reduce the water in step 2 to 1 cup and the cooking time to 5 minutes. Add all the ingredients in step 3 but reduce cooking time to 30 minutes. In step 4, just before serving, make 6 shallow wells in the carrot sauce, drop ½ teaspoon oil and 1/8 teaspoon grated garlic in each well, and break an egg in each. Cover and cook for 5 minutes over low heat until eggs are set.

VARIATION

You can replace the lime juice and vinegar with ¼ cup pomegranate molasses and 1 teaspoon advieh.

Butternut Squash and Prune Khoresh

Makes 6 servings
Preparation time: 35 minutes
Cooking time: 2 hours
40 minutes

خورش کدو حلوائی وآلو

Khoresh-e kadu
halvai-o alu

VEGETARIAN VARIATION

Eliminate the meat. Replace it with 1 cup dried chickpeas soaked for at least 4 hours in water, and then drained. In step 1 brown the onions and add the broad beans with the rest of the ingredients for step 1. In step 2 add 4 cups water and cook over medium heat for 1 hour or until beans are tender. Proceed with the recipe from step 3.

6 tablespoons oil, butter, or ghee*
2 large onions, peeled and thinly sliced
1 pound stew meat (lamb or beef), cut up, or 2 pounds veal shanks, or 2 pounds chicken legs, cut up
1 teaspoon sea salt
½ teaspoon freshly ground black pepper
½ teaspoon turmeric
1 teaspoon ground cinnamon

2 pounds fresh butternut squash
2 tablespoons brown sugar or grape molasses
¼ cup fresh lime juice
¼ teaspoon ground saffron dissolved in 1 tablespoon hot water
2 cups dried golden plums *(alu zard)** or pitted dried prunes

1. In a Dutch oven, heat 3 tablespoons oil over medium heat and brown the onions and meat or chicken. Add salt, pepper, turmeric, and cinnamon, and sauté for 1 minute.

2. Pour in water—2½ cups for meat, 1½ cups for chicken. Cover and simmer over low heat for about 1¼ hours for meat or 30 minutes for chicken, stirring occasionally.

3. Meanwhile, peel and cut the squash into 3-inch cubes. Heat 3 tablespoons oil in a wide skillet over medium heat and brown squash on all sides for 15 to 20 minutes.

4. When the meat is almost tender, add 2 tablespoons sugar, lime juice, saffron water, plums, and butternut squash cubes. Cover and simmer over low heat for 45 to 55 minutes until the meat and butternut squash are tender.

5. Check the taste of the *khoresh* and adjust seasoning. Add more lime juice or sugar according to your taste.

6. Transfer the *khoresh* to a deep casserole, carefully arrange the butternut squash then the meat, and spoon in the broth. Cover and place in a warm oven until ready to serve. Serve hot from the same dish with *chelow* (saffron-steamed rice). *Nush-e Jan!*

Cardoon or Artichoke Khoresh

Makes 6 servings
Preparation time: 35 minutes
Cooking time: 2 hours 15 minutes

1 pound fresh cardoon stalks,* or
  12 baby artichokes,
1 teaspoon vinegar or lemon juice
6 tablespoons oil, butter, or ghee*
2 large onions, peeled and thinly sliced
1 pound stew meat (lamb, veal, or beef),
  or boneless, skinless chicken thighs,
  cut into 2-inch cubes, or 2 pounds
  veal shanks
1 teaspoon sea salt

¼ teaspoon freshly ground pepper
½ teaspoon turmeric
2 cups chopped fresh parsley
1 cup chopped fresh dill
½ cup chopped fresh mint
4 tablespoons fresh lime juice or
  ½ cup verjuice (*ab-ghureh*, unripe
  grape juice)*
¼ teaspoon ground saffron dissolved
  in 1 tablespoon hot water

Khoresh-e kangar

1. To clean the cardoon: Carefully remove and discard prickly parts of cardoon stalks after removing leafy heads. Be sure to remove strings by lifting them with the tip of a knife and peeling them off. Cut into pieces 2 inches long. To prevent them from discoloring and to keep them tender, soak peeled cardoon pieces in a bowl of water with a splash of vinegar until ready to use.

2. In a Dutch oven, heat 3 tablespoons oil over medium heat and brown the onions and meat. Add salt, pepper, and turmeric, and sauté for 1 minute.

3. Pour in water—2½ cups for meat, 1½ cups for chicken. Cover and simmer over low heat for about 1¼ hours for meat or 30 minutes for chicken, stirring occasionally.

4. Drain the cardoon. In a wide skillet, sauté the cardoon pieces in the remaining oil. Add parsley, dill, and mint, and sauté for 10 minutes longer.

5. When the meat is tender, add lime juice, saffron water, and the cardoon. Cover and simmer for 1 hour over low heat (if using artichokes, simmer for only 45 minutes).

6. Check to see if the cardoon pieces are tender. Taste the *khoresh* and adjust seasoning. Transfer it to a deep casserole. Cover and place in a warm oven until ready to serve.

7. Serve hot from the same dish with *chelow* (saffron-steamed rice). *Nush-e Jan!*

VEGETARIAN VARIATION

Eliminate the meat from the ingredients and from step 2. Replace it with 1 cup dried white broad beans soaked in water for at least 4 hours, and then drain. In step 2 brown the onions and add the broad beans with the rest of the ingredients. In step 3 add 4 cups water and cook over medium heat for 1 hour or until beans are tender. Proceed with the recipe from step 4.

NOTES

Cardoon is a vegetable from the artichoke family and is available these days at farmers' markets in the U. S. between May and July.

To clean artichokes: If you use baby artichokes, place a container of water with the juice and the halves of 1 lemon next to you. One at a time, remove the outer leaves of each artichoke until you reach the tender yellow leaves. Cut about 1 inch off the top of the artichoke. Cut off the stem. Use a paring knife to cut off the dark outer layer from the sides of the bottom of the artichoke. Halve the artichoke lengthwise. Place the halves in the water with lemon juice to keep them from discoloring while you work. For regular artichokes, use only the hearts, removing the hairy interior.

Celery Khoresh

Makes 6 servings
Preparation time: 30 minutes
Cooking time: 2 hours
  25 minutes

6 tablespoons oil, butter, or ghee*
2 large onions, peeled and thinly sliced
1 pound stew meat (lamb, veal, or beef),
   or boneless, skinless chicken thighs,
   cut into 2-inch cubes, or 2 pounds
   veal shanks
1 teaspoon sea salt
½ teaspoon freshly ground
   black pepper
½ teaspoon turmeric
1 bunch or 8 stalks celery, washed and

chopped into 1-inch lengths
3 cups chopped fresh parsley
½ cup chopped fresh mint, or 2
   tablespoons dried
½ cup fresh squeezed lime juice or
   1 cup baby green plums (*gojeh sabz*),*
   or 4 whole *limu-omani* (dried Persian
   limes),* pierced
½ teaspoon ground saffron dissolved
   in 2 tablespoons hot water

Khoresh-e karafs

VEGETARIAN VARIATION

Eliminate the meat. Replace it with 1 cup white broad beans (soaked in water for at least 4 hours, and then drained). In step 1 brown the onions and add the broad beans with the rest of the ingredients. In step 2 add 4 cups water. Cook over medium heat for 1 hour or until beans are tender. Proceed with the recipe from step 3.

1. In a Dutch oven, heat 3 tablespoons oil over medium heat and brown the onions and meat. Add salt, pepper, and turmeric, and sauté for 1 minute.

2. Pour in water—2½ cups for meat, 2 cups for chicken. Cover and simmer over low heat for about 30 minutes for meat or 10 minutes for chicken.

3. In a wide skillet, sauté the celery in 3 tablespoons oil for 10 minutes, stirring occasionally. Add chopped herbs and sauté for 10 minutes longer.

4. Add the mixture of celery and herbs, the lime juice, and the saffron water to the meat. Cover and simmer over low heat for 1½ hours longer or until the meat and celery are tender.

5. Taste the *khoresh* and adjust seasoning to taste by adding more salt or lime juice. Transfer it to a deep casserole. Cover and place in a warm oven until ready to serve.

6. Serve hot from the same dish with *chelow* (saffron-steamed rice). *Nush-e Jan!*

Unripe Grape Khoresh with Meatballs

Servings: 6
Preparation time: 30 minutes
Cooking time: 1 hour 30 minutes

خورش غوره

Khoresh-e ghureh

VEGETARIAN VARIATION
Eliminate the meat from the ingredients and from step 1. In step 1, replace it with 1 pound firm tofu (water squeezed out and minced) and 1½ cups ground almonds and 2 eggs. Proceed with the recipe.

MEATBALLS
1 pound ground meat (lamb, beef, or chicken)
1 onion, peeled and grated
1 teaspoon sea salt
½ teaspoon freshly ground pepper
1 tablespoon hot curry powder
¼ cup bread crumbs
2 tablespoons chopped fresh parsley
2 tablespoons oil, butter, or ghee*

SAUCE
4 tablespoon oil, butter, or ghee*
2 medium onions, peeled and thinly sliced
2 cloves garlic, peeled and sliced
1 bunch or 8 stalks celery, washed and chopped into 1-inch lengths
2 green chilies, chopped
1 teaspoon sea salt
½ teaspoon fresh ground pepper
1 cup fresh chopped cilantro
1 cup chopped fresh parsley
1 cup chopped fresh mint, or 2 tablespoons dried
2 tablespoons dried fenugreek leaves
1 tablespoon tomato paste
2 large fresh tomatoes, peeled and chopped
1 cup fresh unripe grapes, stems removed, or canned in brine, drained
1 teaspoon honey
2 tablespoons fresh lime juice

I was inspired to make this recipe from a seventeenth-century Safavid cookbook.

1. In a mixing bowl combine all the ingredients for the meatballs. Knead lightly and with moistened hands shape into hazelnut-sized meatballs. Place on a pan sheet lined with parchment paper.

2. In a wide skillet heat 2 tablespoons oil over medium heat and carefully add the meatballs, swirl and shake the skillet back and forth to brown meatballs on all sides. Set aside.

3. In a medium-sized sauté pan, heat 4 tablespoons oil and add the onions, garlic, celery, chilies, salt, and pepper. Sauté for 10 minutes until the celery is translucent. Add cilantro, parsley, mint, and fenugreek, and sauté for 5 minutes. Add the tomato paste and sauté for another 1 minute.

4. Add the fresh tomatoes, unripe grapes, honey, lime juice, and 1 cup water to the sauté pan. Bring to a boil. Add the meatballs. Reduce heat to low, cover, and simmer heat for 1¼ hours or until the celery is tender.

5. Taste the *khoresh* and adjust seasoning to taste. Transfer the *khoresh* to an ovenproof casserole, cover, and place in a warm oven until ready to serve.

6. Serve hot from the same dish with *chelow* (saffron-steamed rice). *Nush-e Jan!*

Mushroom Khoresh

Makes 6 servings
Preparation time: 30 minutes
Cooking time: 2 hours

Khoresh-e qarch

VEGETARIAN VARIATION

Eliminate the meat from the ingredients and from step 1, add 1½ cups water, and reduce cooking time to 15 minutes. Proceed with the recipe.

6 tablespoons oil, butter, or ghee*
2 large onions, peeled and thinly sliced
2 cloves of garlic, peeled and sliced
1 pound stew meat (lamb, veal, or beef), or boneless, skinless chicken thighs, cut into 2-inch cubes
1 teaspoon sea salt
½ teaspoon freshly ground pepper
½ teaspoon turmeric

1 pound fresh mushrooms
1 tablespoon flour
2 tablespoons chopped fresh parsley
2 tablespoons fresh lime juice
¼ teaspoon ground saffron dissolved in 1 tablespoon hot water
2 egg yolks, beaten
1 teaspoon ground cumin

1. In a Dutch oven, heat 3 tablespoons oil over medium heat and brown onions, garlic, and meat. Add salt, pepper, and turmeric, and sauté for 1 minute. Pour in water—3 cups for meat, 2 cups for chicken. Cover and simmer over low heat for 1½ hours for meat or 55 minutes for chicken, stirring occasionally.

2. Clean mushrooms using a damp cloth, cut off stems, and slice. Sprinkle with flour and parsley, and sauté in 3 tablespoons oil.

3. Add mushrooms, lime juice, and saffron water to the meat. Cover and simmer 35 minutes over low heat.

4. Taste the *khoresh* and adjust seasoning. Add beaten egg yolks and cumin, stirring gently. Simmer for 5 minutes over low heat.

5. Transfer the *khoresh* to an ovenproof casserole. Cover and place in a warm oven until ready to serve. Serve hot from the same dish with *chelow* (saffron-steamed rice). *Nush-e Jan!*

Jujube Khoresh

Makes 6 servings
Preparation time: 20 minutes
Cooking time: 1 hour

Khoresh-e anab

MEAT
1 pound ground meat (lamb, beef, or chicken)
1 medium onion, grated
1 teaspoon sea salt
½ teaspoon freshly ground black pepper
1 teaspoon *advieh* (Persian spice mix)*
1 tablespoon all-purpose flour
2 tablespoons oil, butter, or ghee*

SAUCE
2 tablespoons oil, butter, or ghee*
1 medium onion, sliced
2 cloves garlic, peeled and sliced
2 tablespoons dried mint
1 cup finely ground walnuts
⅓ cup yellow split peas
1 cup jujubes*
3 tablespoons grape molasses
4 cups pomegranate juice

1. To make the meatballs: Knead together the meat, grated onion, salt, pepper, *advieh*, and flour, and make hazelnut-sized meatballs.

2. In a Dutch oven, heat 2 tablespoons oil over medium heat and brown the meatballs. Remove the meatballs from the pot and set aside. In the same pot, heat 2 tablespoons oil and brown the sliced onion and garlic. Add the mint and walnuts and sauté for 1 minute. Add the split-peas, jujubes, grape molasses, and pomegranate juice, and bring to a boil. Return the meatballs to the pot and bring back to a boil. Reduce heat to low, cover, and simmer for 30 minutes or until the split peas are tender. Adjust seasoning to taste. *Nush-e Jan!*

Fava Bean and Dill Khoresh

Makes 6 servings
Preparation time: 30 minutes
Cooking time: 1 hour 40 minutes

خورش گل در چمن

Khoresh-e gol dar chaman

MEAT

3 tablespoons oil, butter, or ghee*
1 pound stew meat (lamb, veal or beef), or 2 pounds chicken thighs cut up
2 medium onions, peeled and thinly sliced
10 cloves garlic, peeled and thinly sliced
1 teaspoon sea salt
½ teaspoon freshly ground pepper
1 teaspoon turmeric

FAVA BEANS

2 pounds fresh fava beans in the pod, or 1 pound shelled, fresh or frozen
3 tablespoons oil, butter, or ghee*
½ teaspoon sea salt
½ teaspoon turmeric
2 cups fresh chopped dill weed or chives
¼ cup verjuice (ab-ghureh, unripe grape juice)*
½ teaspoon ground saffron dissolved in 2 tablespoons rose water
3 eggs

VEGETARIAN VARIATION

Eliminate the meat from the ingredients and from steps 1 and 5. In step 1 brown the onions and garlic. In step 2 reduce the water to 2 cups and the cooking time to 10 minutes. Proceed with the recipe from step 3. In step 5 add the fava beans and saffron-rose water to the onion and garlic mixture. Increase the number of eggs to 6.

1. In a Dutch oven, heat 3 tablespoons oil over medium heat and brown meat, onions, and garlic. Add salt, pepper, and turmeric, and sauté for 1 minute.

2. Pour in water—3 cups for meat, 2 cups for chicken. Cover and simmer over low heat for 1½ hours for meat or 1 hour for chicken.

3. To remove the second skins from the fava beans: In a medium saucepan, bring 6 cups water and 1 teaspoon salt to a boil over high heat. Add the shelled fava beans, bring back to a boil, use a slotted spoon to remove the fava beans, and place in a bowl of ice water. Remove the second skins, drain, and set aside.

4. In a wide skillet, sauté the fava beans in 3 tablespoons oil over medium heat for 2 minutes, stirring gently and occasionally. Add the salt, turmeric, and dill weed, and sauté for 3 minutes longer.

5. Check to see if the meat is tender. Add the fava bean mixture, verjuice, and the saffron-rose water to the meat. Cover and simmer over low heat for 2 to 5 minutes until fava beans are tender, but not falling apart.

6. Taste the *khoresh* and adjust seasoning to taste.

7. Just before serving, break the eggs, one by one, into the *khoresh* and allow to simmer, undisturbed, for 1 minute. Stir gently once spreading the eggs to create yellow and white ribbons.

8. Serve hot with *kateh* (smothered rice), *mast-e khiki* (drained yogurt), and *Zeytun parvardeh* (Caspian tapenade). *Nush-e Jan!*

NOTE

In step 7 there are several ways of adding the eggs to the khoresh: *you can add the eggs all at once, allow for them to simmer over low heat for 1 minute, then gently stir for a few seconds to create yellow and white ribbons. You can whisk the eggs and add them to the* khoresh, *stirring gently for 20 seconds. Or you can fry the eggs separately and garnish the top of the* khoresh *with them.*

Green Bean Khoresh

Makes 4 servings
Preparation time: 30 minutes
Cooking time: 2 hours

6 tablespoons oil, butter, or ghee*
1 pound stew meat (lamb, veal, or beef),
  or boneless, skinless chicken thighs,
  cut into 2-inch cubes
2 large onions, peeled and thinly sliced
1 clove garlic, peeled and sliced
1 teaspoon sea salt
½ teaspoon freshly ground
  black pepper
½ teaspoon turmeric
½ teaspoon cayenne (optional)

½ teaspoon ground cinnamon
1 pound fresh green beans, trimmed, or
  1 pound frozen
3 tablespoons tomato paste
1 medium fresh tomato, peeled
  and chopped
2 tablespoons fresh lime juice
¼ teaspoon ground saffron dissolved
  in 1 tablespoon rose water

Khoresh-e lubia sabz

VEGETARIAN VARIATION

Eliminate the meat from the ingredients and from step 1. Eliminate step 2 and proceed with step 3 and the rest of the recipe. This recipe makes a perfect meatless green bean and tomato braise.

1. In a Dutch oven, heat 3 tablespoons oil over medium heat and brown meat, onions, and garlic. Add salt, pepper, turmeric, cayenne, and cinnamon, and sauté for 1 minute.

2. Pour in water—2 cups for meat, 1 cup for chicken—cover, and cook over low heat for 45 minutes for meat or 15 minutes for chicken, stirring occasionally.

3. Cut green beans into 1-inch lengths (or keep whole).

4. In a wide skillet, heat 3 tablespoons oil over medium heat. Add the green beans and sauté for 2 minutes. Add the tomato paste and sauté for 1 minute longer.

5. Add the green beans, tomato, lime juice, and saffron-rose water to the pot. Cover and simmer over low heat for 1¼ hours or until the meat and beans are tender .

6. Adjust seasoning to taste. Transfer the *khoresh* to an ovenproof casserole, cover, and place in a warm oven until ready to serve.

7. Serve hot from the same dish with *chelow* (saffron-steamed rice), cucumber and tomato salad, and a fresh herb platter. *Nush-e Jan!*

Spinach and Plum Khoresh

Makes 6 servings
Preparation time: 20 minutes
Cooking time: 2 hours 15 minutes

MEAT

3 tablespoons oil, butter, or ghee*
1 large onion, peeled and thinly sliced
1 pound leg of lamb, cut into 2-inch cubes, or 2 pounds veal shanks, or 1 pound boneless, skinless chicken thighs, cut into 2-inch cubes
1½ teaspoons sea salt
½ teaspoon freshly ground pepper
½ teaspoon turmeric

SPINACH

3 tablespoons oil, butter, or ghee*
2 large onions, peeled and thinly sliced
2 pounds fresh spinach, washed and coarsely chopped, or 1 pound frozen chopped spinach
3 cups golden dried plums *(alu zard)** or pitted prunes
1 tablespoon brown sugar or grape molasses
¼ cup verjuice (*ab-ghureh*, unripe grape juice)* or bitter orange juice*

Khoresh-e esfenaj-o alu

1. To cook the meat: In a Dutch oven, heat 3 tablespoons oil over medium heat and brown the onion and the meat. Add salt, pepper, and turmeric, and sauté for 1 minute.

2. Pour in water—2½ cups for meat, 1½ cups for chicken. Cover and simmer 45 minutes for meat or 10 minutes for chicken over low heat.

3. To cook the spinach: Place the spinach in a large steamer, cover and steam over high heat for 10 minutes until wilted. In a wide skillet, heat 3 tablespoons oil over medium heat and brown the onions. Add the spinach and sauté for 1 minute.

4. Add the spinach and onion mixture to the Dutch oven. Add the plums, sugar, and verjuice. Cover and simmer 1½ hours over low heat.

5. Check to see that meat is cooked. Taste the *khoresh* and adjust seasoning. Transfer to a deep casserole. Cover and place in a warm oven until ready to serve.

6. Serve hot from the same dish with *chelow* (saffron-steamed rice). *Nush-e Jan!*

VEGETARIAN VARIATION

Khoresh-e torsh tareh—Eliminate the meat. Brown all the 1 onion and garlic with the seasoning in step 1. In step 2, dissolve 2 tablespoons rice flour in 2½ cups water and cook for 5 minutes over low heat. In step 3 reduce the spinach to 1 cup, and add 1 cup fresh chopped parsley, 1 cup fresh chopped cilantro, 1 cup fresh chopped dill, 1 cup fresh chopped spring onion, and 1 teaspoon *advieh*, and sauté for 10 minutes over medium heat. Add this with the plum, sugar, and verjuice to the Dutch oven in step 4 and cook over low heat for 30 minutes. In step 5, add 6 eggs and 2 cloves garlic (peeled and grated), and cook for 5 minutes, stirring constantly until the *khoresh* becomes thick. This dish is popular in Gilan by the Caspian.

Pomegranate Khoresh with Chicken

Makes 4 servings
Preparation time: 30 minutes
Cooking time: 1 hour 30 minutes

خورش فسنجان با جوجه

*Khoresh-e fesenjan
ba jujeh*

VEGETARIAN VARIATION
Vegetarian Pomegranate and Eggplant Khoresh, *(Shishandaz)*. Eliminate the chicken from the ingredients. In step 1, replace the butternut squash with 2 pounds slim eggplants, peeled and chopped into 2-inch pieces, and sauté with the onions. Proceed with the recipe from step 2.

NOTE
The butternut squash can be replaced with 2 cups peeled and cubed beets, quinces, carrots, or prunes.

5 tablespoons oil, butter, or ghee*
2 large onions, peeled and thinly sliced
2 pounds chicken legs, cut up
1 pound butternut squash, peeled and cut into 2-inch cubes*
½ pound (2 cups) shelled walnuts
4 cups pure pomegranate juice
2 tablespoons pomegranate molasses
½ teaspoon sea salt
¼ teaspoon freshly ground pepper

¼ teaspoon turmeric
½ teaspoon cinnamon
¼ teaspoon ground saffron dissolved in 1 tablespoon hot water
2 tablespoons grape molasses or sugar (optional)

GARNISH
Arils of 1 fresh pomegranate
2 tablespoons toasted walnuts

1. In a Dutch oven, heat 3 tablespoons oil over medium heat until very hot, and sauté the onions. Remove from pot with a slotted spoon and set aside. Add 2 tablespoons oil and brown the chicken. Add the butternut squash and sauté for a few minutes.

2. To toast the walnuts: Preheat the oven to 350°F (180°C). Spread the walnuts in a pan sheet and bake for 10 minutes. Set aside.

3. In a food processor, finely grind the sautéd onions with the toasted walnuts (set aside a few walnuts for the garnish), add 1 cup pomegranate juice, the pomegranate molasses, salt, pepper, turmeric, cinnamon, saffron water, and grape molasses, and mix well to create a creamy paste.

4. Add the creamy walnut paste and the remaining pomegranate juice to the Dutch oven, stirring gently. Cover and simmer over *low heat* for 1½ hours, stirring occasionally with a wooden spoon to prevent the walnuts from burning.

5. The *khoresh* should be sweet and sour and have the consistency of heavy cream. Adjust to taste by adding pomegranate molasses for sourness or grape molasses for sweetness. If the sauce is too thick, thin it with more pomegranate juice.

6. Transfer the *khoresh* from the Dutch oven to a deep, ovenproof casserole. Cover and place in a warm oven until ready to serve with *chelow* (saffron-steamed rice). Just prior to serving, sprinkle with fresh pomegranate arils and walnuts. *Nush-e Jan!*

VARIATIONS

Caspian-Style Pomegranate Khoresh with Fish—Eliminate the chicken in step 1 and replace it with 2 pounds of white fish fillets, cut into 3-inch lengths and seared in 2 tablespoons oil in a wide skillet over medium heat. Add it to the *khoresh* in step 5.

Pistachio Khoresh-e Fesenjan—In Kerman, the walnuts are replaced with shelled pistachio kernels to make a pistachio *fesenjan*.

Pomegranate Khoresh with Roasted Duck—Make a vegetarian version and serve it with duck. Rub a duck, inside and out, with 1 tablespoon salt, 1 tablespoon black pepper. Stuff it with 2 cloves garlic and 2 spring onions, and roast at 350°F (180°C) for 3 hours. Just before serving, carve or serve whole with *khoresh*.

Pomegranate Khoresh with Meatballs—As an alternative to chicken, you may use 1 pound ground meat mixed with 1 grated onion, 1 teaspoon salt, ½ teaspoon pepper, ½ teaspoon turmeric, and ½ teaspoon cinnamon. Knead lightly with moist hands and shape into hazelnut-sized meatballs. In a wide skillet heat 2 tablespoons oil over medium heat, carefully add the meatballs, swirl, and shake the skillet back and forth to brown meatballs on all sides. Add them to the Dutch oven in step 4.

Pomegranate Khoresh with Turkey—Replace the chicken with 2 pounds turkey thighs, cut up. In step 4 increase the cooking time to 3 hours or until tender.

THE TURQUOISE-BLUE DOME

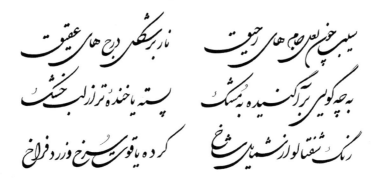

The Haft Paykar *describes in verse the life and adventures of King Bahram and his seven princesses. Each princess comes from a different region of the world and represents the climes into which the habitable world is divided. Each lives in a separate symbolically colored dome and palace that Bahram has had built for her. Bahram then visits them on seven successive nights. Here is a section from the story told by the princess from the turquoise-blue dome of mercury, visited by Bahram on Wednesday night.*

Mahan enlarged the hole and put his head through it; there he saw a garden, not an earthly one, but a part of paradise, a garden of Eram.

Its fruit trees were bent to the ground in adoration. There were apples like goblets filled with ruby-red wine, pomegranates like jewel-boxes made of agate; the quinces looked like balls stuffed with musk and the pistachio nuts smiled with juice. Then there were peaches, like red hyacinths on one side, like yellow suns on the other. Next to them bananas, dates, pears, and figs—a vine, wearing its cap of leaves askew, was watching over its subordinates, light ones and dark ones—a sight of unparalleled splendor. Soon the memory of yesterday's hell faded. Mahan walked around quietly—plucking a rose here, picking an apple there, tasting peaches, and cracking nuts.

In this paradise Mahan encounters an old man who loves him as a son from first sight. And then Mahan is tempted by a band of beautiful girls who prepare a banquet for him: A pomegranate *khoresh* flavored with saffron, sugar, and honey, scented with musk, aloe, and rose water served with saffron flavored rice. And range chicken kabab with plenty of circular *lavash* bread loaves, soft and tender like the backs and breasts of the girls who unwrapped them. And finally the sweets: *halva* in candied sugar and a thousand different types of pastries and cookies.

From the *Haft Paykar* of Nezami Ganjavi

Barberry Khoresh

Makes 6 servings
Preparation time: 30 minutes
Cooking time: 2 hours

Khoresh-e zereshk

Barberry Khoresh with Whole Roast Duck—Replace chicken pieces with a whole duck. Stuff a whole duck with 2 cloves garlic, 2 spring onions, 1 tablespoon salt, 1 teaspoon black pepper, ¼ teaspoon turmeric, 1 teaspoon cardamom, ½ teaspoon cinnamon, and 2 peeled and sliced fried onions. Roast at 350°F (180°C) for 3 hours. Prepare the vegetarian *khoresh* and, just before serving it, either cut up the duck or carve it, and serve it with the *khoresh*. Garnish with barberries and nuts prepared in step 3.

6 tablespoons oil, butter, or ghee*
2 large onions, peeled and thinly sliced
1½ pounds boneless chicken thighs (or lamb or beef), cut into 2-inch cubes
1 teaspoon sea salt
½ teaspoon freshly ground black pepper
¼ teaspoon turmeric
½ teaspoon ground cinnamon
1 teaspoon ground cardamom
¼ teaspoon ground saffron dissolved in 1 tablespoon rose water
2½ cups apple cider

GARNISH
2 tablespoons oil
¼ cup slivered almonds
¼ cup raw shelled pistachios

BARBERRY SAUCE
1 cup dried barberries, cleaned and drained *(zereshk)**
¼ cup grape molasses or brown sugar
¼ teaspoon ground saffron dissolved in 1 tablespoon rose water
2 tablespoons fresh lime juice

1. In a Dutch oven, heat 2 tablespoons oil over medium heat and brown the onions and chicken. Add salt, pepper, turmeric, cinnamon, cardamom, saffron-rose water and sauté for 1 minute.

2. Add apple cider—1½ cups for chicken or 2½ cups for meat—and bring to a boil. Reduce heat, cover, and simmer over medium heat for 1 hour for chicken or 2 hours for meat or until the meat is tender.

3. Meanwhile, to make the garnish: Heat 2 tablespoons oil in a wide skillet over medium-low heat, add the nuts, and stir-fry for 20 seconds. Remove the nuts from the skillet and set aside (for garnish later).

4. In the same skillet, heat another 2 tablespoons oil. Add the barberries, grape molasses, saffron-rose water, and lime juice. Stir-fry for 1 minute (beware, barberries burn easily; do not overcook). Set aside.

5. Check to be sure the meat is tender. Transfer the *khoresh* from the Dutch oven to a deep, ovenproof casserole. Add barberries on top and keep warm until ready to serve. Just before serving, add the nuts and serve with *chelow* (saffron-steamed rice). *Nush-e Jan!*

VARIATIONS

Barberry Khoresh with Meatballs—Use 1½ pounds of ground meat or chicken thighs to make meatballs. Mix with 1 grated onion, ½ teaspoon salt, ½ teaspoon pepper, ½ teaspoon turmeric, 1 teaspoon ground cardamom, and ½ teaspoon cinnamon. Knead lightly and shape into hazelnut-sized meatballs. In a wide skillet heat 2 tablespoons oil over medium heat, carefully add the meatballs, then swirl and shake the skillet back and forth to brown meatballs all over. Add to the Dutch oven in step 2.

Spinach and Bitter Orange Khoresh

Makes 6 servings
Preparation time: 30 minutes
Cooking time: 2 hours

MEATBALLS
1 pound ground chicken thigh
  (or lamb or beef)
1 onion, peeled and grated
1 teaspoon sea salt
½ teaspoon freshly ground
  black pepper
½ teaspoon turmeric
2 teaspoons chopped fresh parsley
3 tablespoons oil, butter, or ghee*

SPINACH SAUCE
3 tablespoons oil, butter, or ghee*
1 large onion, peeled and thinly sliced

2 cloves garlic, peeled and sliced
2 pounds fresh chopped baby spinach,
  or 1 pound frozen chopped spinach
1 cup chopped fresh parsley
1 teaspoon sea salt
¼ teaspoon freshly ground pepper
¼ teaspoon turmeric
3 cups bitter orange juice *(narenj)**
1 tablespoon rice flour
½ teaspoon ground saffron dissolved in
  2 tablespoons orange blossom water
1 tablespoon grape molasses or brown
  sugar (if bitter orange is too sour)

Esfenaj-o narenj (saak)

VEGETARIAN VARIATION

To make vegetarian balls: Eliminate the meat from the ingredients and from step 1. Replace it with ½ cup kidney beans cooked with 4 cups water and 1 teaspoon salt for 45 minutes over medium heat. Add ½ cup rice and cook for another 45 minutes until tender. Drain. In a food processor, combine all the remaining ingredients for the meatballs and the beans and rice, then pulse until you have a paste. Moisten your hands and shape into balls the size of hazelnuts. Proceed with the recipe from step 2. Eliminate the rice flour from step 4.

1. To make the meatballs: In a mixing bowl, combine the meat, onion, salt, pepper, turmeric, and parsley. Knead lightly to create a paste. Use moist hands to shape the paste into small meatballs the size of hazelnuts.

2. In a wide skillet heat 3 tablespoons oil over medium heat and carefully add the meatballs. Swirl and shake the skillet back and forth to brown meatballs on all sides—a spatula might break the meatballs. Set aside.

3. In a Dutch oven, heat 3 tablespoons oil over medium heat and brown onion and garlic. Add spinach and parsley. Cover and cook over low heat for 10 minutes. Add salt, pepper, and turmeric, and sauté for 2 minutes. Add 1 cup of bitter orange juice and the meatballs. Cover and cook over low heat for 15 minutes.

4. Meanwhile, in a mixing bowl, whisk together the rest of the bitter orange juice, rice flour, and saffron-orange blossom water. Add this mixture to Dutch oven. Cover and simmer for 1 hour over low heat.

5. Adjust seasoning to taste. This *khoresh* should be sweet and sour—add grape molasses if too sour. Transfer it to a deep ovenproof casserole. Cover and place in a warm oven until ready to serve.

6. Serve hot from the same dish with saffron-steamed rice. *Nush-e Jan!*

NOTE

Bitter oranges are available at Iranian markets from December to March. You can substitute 1½ cups orange juice and ½ cup lime juice, or 2 cups verjuice (ab-ghureh, unripe grape juice),* for the bitter orange juice.

A SWEET & SOUR STORY

The orange has a most exotic and well-traveled past. The wild parent, *C. aurantium,* is native to the Caspian and southeast Asia; its name derives from the Sanskrit nareng. This orange is a late traveler. Its first mention west of China doesn't appear until 100 CE, in an Indian religious text. It seems to have moved slowly west along overland trade routes and then north into Europe with the Arab diaspora. By the eleventh century the bitter orange was growing in Sicily, and by the end of the twelfth, in Spain.

As for the sweet orange, it was developed by the Chinese. It did not appear in the West until the end of the fifteenth century. While some seeds came through Genoa into Italy, most seem to have arrived in Portugal with Vasco da Gama following his discovery of the sea route to India. The Portuguese were soon exporting this delicious fruit both east and west, which is why it is called by a variant of the word "Portugal" in countries ranging from Greece to Iran, Turkey, and Romania.

It is the older, bitter orange, known to Iranians as narenj and to Westerners as the Seville or bitter orange, that most interests me in cooking. Westerners know this orange primarily as a component of marmalade. Cooks in Iran, however, value it for its aromatic skin, flowers, leaves, and juice.

The juice, for instance, serves as a subtle souring agent in many recipes. For more intense flavor, it may be reduced to a molasses *(rob-e narenj).* It may also be cooked with sugar to make a syrup that is the basis for a tasty soft drink *(sharbat-e najenj).*

Bitter orange leaves are particularly aromatic. They make an excellent tea, said to have both a digestive and calming effect.

As for the peel, when dried it may be combined with bay leaves to make another tea that is an excellent cold remedy. Or the peel may be candied for used in rice dishes, stuffings, and desserts (see Orange Peel, Candied).

Last there are fragrant orange blossoms. These may be distilled into orange flower water, widely available, for use as a flavoring. The distilling process also produces the much more intense orange flower essence, which is used to scent perfumes and liqueurs.

Until recently, almost all bitter oranges in the West were made into marmalade: The fruit itself was quite hard to find. At least one English food writer was reduced to stealing oranges from the public parks in Seville; many Iranians had to take the same expedient in California. Today, however, bitter oranges are available during the winter months at Persian markets; the slivered and dried (or candied) peel is sold all year round, as is bitter orange molasses.

Orange Khoresh

Makes 6 servings
Preparation time: 30 minutes
Cooking time: 2 hours

6 tablespoons oil, butter, or ghee*
2 large onions, peeled and thinly sliced
2 pounds chicken legs, cut up, or 1
  pound boneless, skinless chicken
  thighs, cut into 2-inch cubes
1 tablespoon all-purpose flour
Zest of 4 oranges
1 teaspoon *advieh* (Persian spice mix)*
1 teaspoon sea salt
½ teaspoon freshly ground
  black pepper
½ teaspoon turmeric
1½ cups freshly squeezed orange juice

2 large carrots
4 large oranges (used for zest),
  segmented*
2 tablespoons wine vinegar
¼ cup fresh lime juice
½ cup brown sugar or grape molasses
¼ teaspoon ground saffron dissolved
  in 1 tablespoon orange blossom water

GARNISH
2 teaspoons slivered pistachios
2 teaspoons slivered almonds

خورش پرتقال

Khoresh-e porteqal

VEGETARIAN VARIATION
Eliminate the meat from the
ingredients and from step 1.
Replace it with 1 cup dried
white broad beans (soaked in
water for 4 hours and drained).
In step 2 add 3 cups water with
the orange juice and cook for
1½ hours. Proceed with step 3.

1. In a Dutch oven, heat 3 tablespoons oil over medium heat and brown the onions and chicken. Sprinkle in flour, orange zest, *advieh*, salt, and pepper, and sauté for 1 minute.

2. Pour in the orange juice. Cover and simmer over low heat for 35 minutes.

3. Meanwhile, peel the carrots and slice into thin slivers. Sauté in 2 tablespoons oil for a few minutes. Add the carrot to the chicken, cover, and simmer for 1 hour.

4. Peel the oranges, separate them into segments, and peel the membrane from each segment.

5. In a saucepan, combine the vinegar, lime juice, sugar, and saffron-orange blossom water. Simmer for 10 minutes over low heat. Remove from heat, add the orange segments, and set aside to macerate for 10 minutes.

6. Transfer the *khoresh* to a deep, ovenproof casserole, carefully arrange the orange segments with the sauce on the top, cover, and place in a warm oven until ready to serve.

7. Check to see if the chicken is tender. Taste and adjust seasoning. Add more sugar or lime juice according to your taste.

8. Just before serving, sprinkle the *khoresh* with pistachios and almonds. Serve hot from same dish with *chelow* (saffron-steamed rice). *Nush-e Jan!*

A VERBAL CONTEST BETWEEN A DATE PALM AND A GOAT

As early as the second century BCE Iranians were considering the benefits of an agricultural life versus a pastoral one—and possibly vegetarianism versus meat eating. This is played out in a poem (that starts as a riddle) written in the Parthian language (an Iranian language preceding Middle Persian) by an anonymous poet, who sets up a verbal dialogue between a palm tree and a goat. The tree lists for the goat all the benefits it provides:

> A palm tree in the land of Assyria: its trunk is dry; its top is moist; its leaves resemble canes; its fruits resemble grapes; and it bears sweet fruits for a people. In summer I am shade over the heads of rulers. I am vinegar for farmers, honey for noblemen; I am a nest for little birds and shade for travelers, who eat fruit from me until they become full.

The goat challenges and ridicules it and lists its own benefits:

> They make my skin into water bags; in the plain and desert, on a hot day and at noon, cold water is from me. They make tablecloths of me, on which they arrange meals. The opulent great feast they adorn with my meat. Bread and roasted flour and cheese, and all the pastries. They make trimmings from me for beer, kumis, and wine. I am milk and cheese; they dry my yogurt for palaces. Harp and lyre and lute and cither, every instrument they play, they play on me. Since the beginning that is primeval creation I go pasturing on the mountains, the sweet-smelling mountains; I eat fresh grass and drink cool water from springs.

In the end, the poet proclaims the goat the winner.

Many of the words for the food items remain the same or close to those used in Persian today: milk *(shir)*, cheese *(panir)*, churned sour milk *(dugh)*, yogurt *(mast)*, sun-dried yogurt *(kashk)*, honey *(angabin)*, vinegar *(sik)*, bread *(nan)*, roasted flour *(pist)*, appetizers *(pish parag)*, pastries *(royn khowrag)*, beer *(washag)*, wine *(mey)*.

From *Drakht-e Asurik*, circa second century BCE

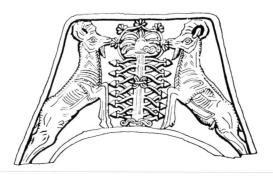

Kermani-Style Goat and Kashk Khoresh

Makes 6 servings
Preparation time: 25 minutes
Cooking time: 3 hours

GOAT
½ cup oil , butter, or ghee*
5 medium onions, peeled and thinly sliced
2 pounds boned leg of goat, or lamb, or skinless, boneless chicken thighs, cut into 2-inch pieces
1 teaspoon sea salt
1 teaspoon freshly ground black pepper
1 teaspoon turmeric
5 cloves garlic, peeled and sliced
1 tablespoon dried tarragon

1 cup dried chickpeas, soaked in water for at least 4 hours, drained

KASHK SAUCE
1½ cups liquid *kashk* (sun-dried yogurt)
5 cloves garlic, peeled and grated
½ teaspoon ground saffron dissolved in 2 tablespoons rose water

CROUTON GARNISH
1 large *sangak* bread for croutons
1 clove garlic, grated
¼ cup fresh tarragon leaves
2 tablespoons olive oil

خورش بز قورمه کرمانی

Boz-qormeh,
Khoresh-e Kashk

VEGETARIAN VARIATION
Eliminate the meat from the ingredients and replace it with 2 cups coarsely chopped, toasted walnuts in step 1. Proceed with step 2 and the rest of the recipe.

1. In a Dutch oven, heat 3 tablespoons oil over medium heat and brown the onions and goat meat. Add salt, pepper, turmeric, garlic, tarragon, and the drained chick-peas, and sauté for 1 minute.

2. Pour in 4 cups water and bring to a boil, cover, and simmer for 2½ to 3 hours over low heat until the goat and chickpeas are tender, stirring occasionally.

3. Add the *kashk* and garlic. Cover and simmer for 5 to 10 minutes until the *kashk* has warmed through (it should not come to a boil). Adjust seasoning to taste.

4. Transfer to a deep casserole. Garnish on top with the saffron-rose water, cover, and place in a warm oven until ready to serve.

5. To make the croutons: Cut the bread into ½-inch squares. Spread on a pan sheet, add the grated garlic and fresh tarragon leaves, pour the oil on top, and toss well. Toast under the broiler for a few minutes. Transfer to a serving bowl.

6. Serve the *khoresh* from the same dish with a few *sangak* bread croutons on top, and accompanied with a fresh herb platter *(sabzi khordan)* on the side. *Nush-e Jan!*

VARIATION

This *khoresh* can also be garnished with the following: ½ cup chopped walnuts (or almonds, pistachios, or hazel nuts) sautéd with 2 tablespoons oil and ½ teaspoon turmeric for 1 minute. Remove from heat, add 2 tablespoons dried mint and stir for a few seconds *(na'na daq)*.

Peach Khoresh

Makes 6 servings
Preparation time: 30 minutes
Cooking time: 2 hours

6 tablespoons oil, butter, or ghee*
2 large onions, peeled and thinly sliced
1 pound boneless, skinless chicken
   thighs, cut into 2-inch cubes, or stew
   meat (lamb, veal, or beef),
1 teaspoon sea salt
½ teaspoon freshly ground pepper
¼ teaspoon turmeric
1 teaspoon *advieh* (Persian spice mix)*
½ cup fresh lime juice

½ cup light brown sugar or grape
   molasses
¼ teaspoon ground saffron dissolved
   in 1 tablespoon rose water
5 firm peaches (not ripe)

GARNISH
2 tablespoons chopped fresh mint

Khoresh-e hulu

VEGETARIAN VARIATION
Eliminate the meat from the
ingredients . In step 1 brown
the onions, then add 1 cup
white broad beans that have
been soaked for at least
4 hours and drained. Add the
salt, pepper, turmeric, and
advieh, and sauté for 1 minute.
In step 2, pour in 4 cups water,
cover, and simmer for
45 minutes over low heat.
Proceed with the recipe.

Peaches originally came from China to ancient Persia, and were distributed to the West from there. Many languages refer to peaches as a Persian fruit: in French, pêche; *in Russian,* persik; *in Italian,* pesca; *and in German,* pfirsich.

1. In a Dutch oven, heat 3 tablespoons oil over medium heat and brown the onions and meat. Add salt, pepper, turmeric, and *advieh*, and sauté for 1 minute.

2. Pour in water—1 cup for chicken, 2 cups for meat. Cover and simmer over low heat for 1 hour for meat or 30 minutes for chicken.

3. In a mixing bowl, whisk together the lime juice, sugar, and saffron water, and add it to the meat. Cover and simmer 45 minutes longer over low heat.

4. To remove fuzz, wash the peaches well. Remove pits and cut peaches into ½-inch wedges. Brown in a skillet in 3 tablespoons oil until golden brown. Add the peaches to the Dutch oven, cover, and simmer 25 minutes longer

5. Check to see if meat is tender. Taste and adjust seasoning. Transfer the *khoresh* to a deep, ovenproof casserole. Cover and place in a warm oven until ready to serve.

6. Just before serving, garnish with the mint and serve hot from the same dish with *chelow* (saffron-steamed rice). *Nush-e Jan!*

NOTE
You may use 3 cups sliced frozen peaches or 3 cups canned sliced peaches in heavy syrup in place of fresh peaches. Just eliminate the ½ cup sugar and add peaches, without the syrup, in the last 10 minutes of cooking. Or you may use 2 cups sliced dried peaches soaked in ½ cup water for 30 minutes and added in step 2.

Quince Khoresh

Makes 6 servings
Preparation time: 20 minutes
Cooking time: 2 hours

6 tablespoons oil, butter, or ghee*
2 large onions, peeled and thinly sliced
1 pound stew meat (lamb, veal, or beef),
   or boneless, skinless chicken thighs,
   cut into 2-inch cubes, or 2 pounds
   chicken legs, cut up
1 teaspoon sea salt
½ teaspoon freshly ground
   black pepper

½ teaspoon turmeric
¼ teaspoon ground cinnamon
3 medium quinces (about 2 pounds)
½ cup grape molasses or brown sugar
¼ cup wine vinegar
¼ cup fresh lime juice
½ teaspoon ground saffron dissolved in
   2 tablespoons rose water
⅓ cup yellow split peas

Khoresh-e beh

Wild quince trees are found in the Caspian region of Iran, and the cultivated variety probably originated thereabouts. These days the best quinces come from Isfahan, where they are large and juicy, and can be eaten raw. Quince was valued for its aphrodisiac powers and was customarily given to brides on their wedding nights. The seeds continue to be used in herbal teas to soothe coughs. Quince is also used in Persian cuisine as a paste (loz-e beh *or* halva-ye beh), *for jam and custard, and as a syrup with lime to make a sherbet drink* (beh limu).

1. In a Dutch oven, heat 3 tablespoons oil over medium heat and brown the onions and meat. Add salt, pepper, turmeric, and cinnamon, and sauté for 1 minute.

2. Pour in water—3 cups for meat or 2½ cups for chicken. Cover and simmer—1¼ hours for meat or 30 minutes for chicken—over low heat, stirring occasionally.

3. Meanwhile, prepare the quinces. Wash but *do not peel* the quinces. Core using an apple corer, cut into quarters, and remove seeds. Cut into cubes or wedges.

4. Heat 3 tablespoons oil in a wide skillet over medium heat. Sauté the quinces, shaking the skillet often, for about 15 to 20 minutes until golden brown. Add to the meat.

5. Add the grape molasses, vinegar, lime juice, saffron-rose water, and yellow split peas to the Dutch oven. Cover and simmer for 30 to 45 minutes longer over low heat (the cooking time depends on the type of yellow split peas used).

6. Taste the *khoresh* and adjust seasoning. Transfer to a deep, ovenproof casserole. Cover and place in a warm oven until ready to serve.

7. Serve hot with *chelow* (saffron-steamed rice). *Nush-e Jan!*

VEGETARIAN VARIATION
Eliminate the meat from the ingredients. In step 1 brown the onions. Add the salt, pepper, turmeric, and cinnamon, and sauté for 1 minute. In step 2, pour in 4 cups water, cover, and simmer for 10 minutes over low heat. Proceed with step 5, except increase the yellow split peas to ½ cup in step 5.

Apple Khoresh

Makes 4 servings
Preparation time: 20 minutes
Cooking time: 2 hours 15 minutes

6 tablespoons oil, butter or ghee*
2 large onions, peeled and thinly sliced
1 pound stew meat (lamb, veal, or beef), or boneless, skinless chicken thighs, cut into 2-inch cubes, or 2 pounds chicken legs, cut up
1 teaspoon sea salt
¼ teaspoon freshly ground pepper
½ teaspoon turmeric

½ teaspoon ground cinnamon
⅓ cup yellow split peas
1 tablespoon tomato paste
3 tablespoons brown sugar or grape molasses
3 tablespoons apple cider vinegar
½ teaspoon ground saffron dissolved in 2 tablespoons rose water
5 tart cooking apples

Khoresh-e sib

1. In a Dutch oven, heat 3 tablespoons oil over medium heat and brown the onions and meat. Sprinkle with salt, pepper, turmeric, and cinnamon, and sauté for 1 minute.

2. Pour in water—3 cups for meat and 2 cups for chicken. Cover and simmer over low heat for 1¼ hours for meat or 30 minutes for chicken.

3. Add yellow split peas, tomato paste, sugar, vinegar, and saffron-rose water. Cover and simmer for 30 minutes longer.

4. Core and peel the apples and cut into wedges. In a wide skillet, heat 3 tablespoons oil over medium heat, and sauté the apples for 10 to 15 minutes, shaking skillet back and forth until golden brown.

5. Preheat oven to 350°F (180°C). Transfer the *khoresh* to a deep casserole and arrange the apples on the top. Cover and place in the oven. Cook for 45 minutes longer.

6. Taste the *khoresh* and correct seasoning. Add either more sugar or vinegar if necessary. The *khoresh* should be sweet and sour.

7. Serve from the same dish with *chelow* (saffron-flavored steamed rice), green salad, and a platter of fresh herbs on the side. *Nush-e Jan!*

VEGETARIAN VARIATION

Eliminate the meat from the ingredients and from step 1. Add 4 cups water in step 2. In step 3, increase split peas to ½ cup. Proceed with the recipe.

VARIATION

Apple Khoresh with Sour Cherries *(Khoresh-e sib ba albalu)*—In step 2, reduce water to 2 cups for meat or 1½ cups for chicken. Eliminate the split peas from step 3. Add 1 cup pitted, dried tart (sour) cherries or 2 cups fresh, pitted tart (sour) cherries with the apples in step 6.

Shiraz when spring is here – what pleasure equals this?
With streams to sit by, wine to drink and lips to kiss,
With mingled sounds of drums and lutes and harps and flutes;
Then, with a nice young lover near, Shiraz is bliss.

Jahan Malek Khatun

شیراز خوش است این خطه در فصل بهار

وانگه لب گلب جوی و لب جام و لب یار

آواز دف و چنگ و نی و عود و رباب

اینها همه بانگ کی شیرین کار

Baby Green Almond Khoresh

Makes 6 servings
Preparation time: 30 minutes
Cooking time: 2 hours 30 minutes

6 tablespoons oil, butter, or ghee*
2 onions, peeled and thinly sliced
1 pound stew meat (lamb, veal, or beef), or boneless, skinless chicken thighs, cut into 2-inch cubes, or 2 pounds veal shank
1 teaspoon sea salt
½ teaspoon freshly ground black pepper
½ teaspoon turmeric
½ pound baby green almonds*

3 cups chopped fresh parsley
½ cup chopped fresh mint, or 2 tablespoons dried mint
½ cup verjuice *(ab-ghureh,* unripe grape juice)*, or ⅓ cup fresh lime juice
1 tablespoon grape molasses or light brown sugar
¼ teaspoon ground saffron dissolved in 1 tablespoon rose water

خورش چغاله با دام

Khoresh-e chaghaleh badam

VEGETARIAN VARIATION

Eliminate the meat from the ingredients. In step 2 reduce the water to 1½ cups and the cooking time to 10 minutes. Proceed with the recipe. Garnish with 1 cup toasted almonds.

1. In a Dutch oven, heat 3 tablespoons oil over medium heat and brown onions and meat. Add salt, pepper, and turmeric, and sauté for 1 minute.

2. Pour in water—2½ cups for meat and 1½ cups for chicken. Bring to a boil. Cover and simmer over low heat for 1 hour for meat and 30 minutes for chicken.

3. To remove the bitterness from the almonds: In a medium saucepan, bring 6 cups water and 1 tablespoon salt to a boil. Add the almonds, bring back to a boil, and boil for 1 minute. Drain and rinse with cold water to stop the cooking.

4. In a wide skillet heat 3 tablespoons oil over medium heat and sauté the almonds, parsley, and mint for 10 minutes, and add this mixture to the Dutch oven.

5. Add the verjuice, grape molasses, and saffron-rose water. Cover and simmer over low heat for 1 hour longer.

6. Check to see if the meat and almonds are tender. Taste and adjust seasoning by adding more salt, verjuice for sourness, or grape molasses for sweetness.

7. Transfer the *khoresh* to a deep casserole. Cover and place in warm oven until ready to serve. Serve hot from the same dish with *chelow* (saffron-steamed rice). *Nush-e Jan!*

NOTES

Baby green almonds have a short season and are available in the springtime in Iranian markets.

You can also make khoresh *with baby green plums* (gojeh sabz) *by replacing the almonds with ½ pound baby green plums and eliminating the verjuice.*

Fresh Herb Khoresh

Makes 6 servings
Preparation time: 25 minutes
Cooking time: 3 hours

خورش قرمه سبزی

Khoresh-e qormeh sabzi

6 tablespoons oil, butter, or ghee*
2 large onions, peeled and thinly sliced
2 pounds lamb shank or 1½ pounds
  boned leg of lamb cut into 2-inch pieces
2 teaspoons sea salt
1 teaspoon freshly ground black pepper
1 teaspoon turmeric
½ cup dried kidney beans, soaked in
  warm water for at least 30 minutes,
  drained
4 whole *limu-omani* (dried Persian
  limes),* pierced

4 cups finely chopped fresh parsley,
  or 1 cup dried
1 cup finely chopped fresh chives, or
  spring onions or ¼ cup dried chives
1 cup finely chopped fresh cilantro
3 tablespoons dried fenugreek leaves,
  or 1 cup chopped fresh fenugreek
¼ cup freshly squeezed lime juice
1 teaspoon ground cardamom
½ teaspoon ground saffron dissolved in
  2 tablespoons rose water

1. In a Dutch oven, heat 3 tablespoons oil over medium heat and brown the onions and meat. Add salt, pepper, and turmeric, and sauté for 1 minute.

2. Pour in 4½ cups water. Add the drained kidney beans and whole *limu-omani*. Bring to a boil, cover, and simmer for 30 minutes over low heat, stirring occasionally.

3. Meanwhile, in a wide skillet, heat 3 tablespoons oil over medium heat and sauté parsley, chives, cilantro, and fenugreek for about 20 to 25 minutes, stirring frequently *until the aroma of frying herbs rises* (this stage is very important to the taste of the *khoresh*. Be careful not to burn the herbs).

4. Add the sautéed herbs, lime juice, cardamom, and saffron-rose water to the pot. Cover and simmer for another 2½ hours over low heat, stirring occasionally.

5. Check to see if meat and beans are tender. Taste the *khoresh* and adjust seasoning, adding more salt or lime juice to taste. Transfer to a deep casserole. Cover and place in a warm oven until ready to serve.

6. Serve hot from the same dish with *chelow* (saffron-steamed rice). *Nush-e Jan!*

VEGETARIAN VARIATION

Eliminate the meat from the ingredients and increase the kidney beans to 1 cup. Proceed with the recipe.

VARIATION

Fresh Herb Khoresh with Fish *(Qormeh mahi)*—Replace meat with 2 pounds white, firm fish fillets cut into 4-inch lengths. Dust with salt, pepper, turmeric, and flour, and brown both sides in a wide skillet in 3 tablespoons oil over medium-high heat. Just before serving, add the fish, and 4 cloves garlic, peeled and grated, to the *khoresh*.

NOTE

For this recipe you cannot substitute the fenugreek leaves with anything else—if you don't have fenugreek, don't make this recipe (and don't use more than 3 tablespoons, dried, as it is very strong and will make the khoresh *bitter). Dried fenugreek leaves and dried Persian limes are available at Iranian markets. The fried and frozen mixture of the herbs for this recipe can also sometimes be found at Iranian markets.*

A ready-made dried mixture of herbs for this khoresh *is also available at Iranian markets. If using dried herbs, place a sieve in a bowl of lukewarm water and soak the herbs for 20 minutes. Remove the sieve from the bowl and add it in step 3.*

آن غذائی که مرا چون جان است

غوره و جوجه و بادمجان است

That food which I most cherish is the sour grape, spring chicken and eggplant dish.
—Bos'haq Ata'meh of Shiraz, circa 1400

Eggplant Khoresh

Makes 6 servings
Preparation time: 20 minutes
Cooking time: 2 hours
*   15 minutes*

½ cup oil, butter, or ghee*
2 pounds chicken legs, cut up, or
   2 pounds lamb shanks
4 medium onions, thinly sliced
2 cloves garlic, peeled and thinly sliced
1 teaspoon sea salt
½ teaspoon freshly ground pepper
1 teaspoon turmeric
1 teaspoon cinnamon
1 teaspoon ground saffron dissolved in
   4 tablespoons rose water

6 fresh tomatoes, peeled and chopped
1 cup *ghureh* (unripe grapes)*
¼ cup lime juice
9 slim eggplants, or slim green zucchini
1 egg white

GARNISH
2 tablespoons oil
1 onion, peeled and thinly sliced
3 cherry tomatoes

خورشٹ بادمجان

Khoresh-e bademjan

VEGETARIAN VARIATION

Eliminate the meat. In step 1 (after browning the onions), add 2 cups ground walnuts, 1 cup chopped cilantro, 4 cloves garlic, and sauté with the rest of the ingredients. In step 2 add 2 cups water. Cover and cook for 30 minutes. Proceed with the recipe from step 3.

VARIATION

Khoresh-e qeymeh bademjan—
Replace the cutup chicken or lamb shanks with 1 pound boned lamb or skinless, boneless chicken thighs cut into ½-inch cubes. Brown with the onions. Add 2 cups water; 4 tomatoes, peeled and chopped; 1 tablespoon tomato paste; 4 whole pierced *limu-omani* (dried Persian limes). Add ⅓ cup yellow split peas cooked in 3 cups water for 30 minutes, drain, and add them to the casserole in step 7.

1. In a Dutch oven, heat 3 tablespoons oil over medium heat and brown the chicken, onion, and garlic. Add salt, pepper, turmeric, cinnamon, and saffron-rose water, and sauté for 1 minute.

2. Add tomatoes, unripe grapes, and lime juice (if using lamb shanks, add 2 cups water). Cover and simmer over low heat—30 minutes for chicken and 1½ hours for lamb.

3. Meanwhile, peel eggplants and cut into halves if too long. To remove the bitterness from the eggplant, place them in a colander in the sink, sprinkle with water and 2 tablespoons salt, and allow to sit for 20 minutes. Rinse and ***blot dry***.

4. Preheat the oven to 350°F (180°C).

5. Brush each eggplant on all sides with egg white (so eggplants will absorb less oil). In a wide skillet, heat 3 tablespoons oil over medium heat until very hot. Brown the eggplants on all sides in batches, add more oil if necessary. Set aside on paper towels.

6. To make the garnish: In a wide skillet, heat 2 tablespoons oil over medium heat and brown the onion. Remove from skillet and set aside. In the same skillet sauté the tomato. Set aside.

7. Transfer the chicken and sauce to a deep, ovenproof casserole. Arrange the eggplant on top and garnish with the onion and tomato. Cover (if the casserole does not have its own lid, cover with a layer of parchment paper and a layer of aluminum foil on top and seal tightly). Bake for 45 minutes. Uncover and bake for another 15 minutes or until the eggplant is tender. Adjust seasoning to taste by adding more lime juice or salt.

8. Serve immediately from the same dish or keep warm until ready to serve. Serve with saffron-steamed rice, a fresh herb platter with Persian basil, and cucumber and tomato salad. *Nush-e Jan!*

If you use zucchini, there is no need to peel it or to remove bitterness in step 3. Just trim it.

Potato Khoresh

Makes 6 servings
Preparation time: 20 minutes
Cooking time: 2 hours
*   15 minutes*

3 tablespoons oil, butter, or ghee*
2 large onions, peeled and thinly sliced
1 pound stew meat (lamb, veal, or beef),
  or boneless, skinless chicken thighs,
  cut into ½-inch cubes
4 whole *limu-omani* (dried Persian
  limes)*, pierced
1 teaspoon sea salt
½ teaspoon freshly ground
  black pepper
½ teaspoon turmeric
1 teaspoon *advieh* (Persian spice mix)*
1 large tomato, peeled and chopped
1 tablespoon tomato paste

¼ cup orange zest (6–8 oranges)
½ teaspoon ground saffron dissolved
  in 2 tablespoons orange blossom
  water
1 pound or 2 large potatoes, peeled and
  cut into matchsticks and soaked in
  cold water
⅓ cup yellow split peas

DEEP FRYING THE POTATOES
2 cups canola oil for deep frying
¼ teaspoon coarse sea salt
1 teaspoon *limu-omani* powder (dried
  Persian lime powder)*

Khoresh-e qeymeh

1. In a Dutch oven, heat 3 tablespoons oil over medium heat and brown the onions and meat. Add the *limu-omani,* salt, pepper, and turmeric. Sauté for 2 minutes longer.

2. Pour in water—2 cups for meat, 1½ cups for chicken—and bring to a boil. Cover and simmer over low heat for 55 minutes for meat or 10 minute for chicken, stirring occasionally.

3. Add the *advieh,* tomato, tomato paste, orange zest, and saffron-orange blossom water. Cover and cook for another 45 minutes.

4. Meanwhile, drain and rinse the potatoes and *dry thoroughly.* In a deep skillet, heat 2 cups oil until hot (350°F/180°C), add the potatoes, and deep-fry until golden. Use a slotted spoon to remove the potatoes and place them on paper towels. Sprinkle with coarse sea salt and *limu-omani* powder, and set aside.

5. In a saucepan, cook the yellow split peas in 3 cups water and ½ teaspoon salt for 30 minutes. Drain and add to the Dutch oven.

6. Check to see if meat and peas are tender. Taste the *khoresh* and adjust seasoning to taste by adding lime juice or salt. Transfer to a deep casserole, cover, and place in a warm oven until ready to serve.

7. Just before serving add the potatoes on top of the *khoresh.* Serve with *chelow* (saffron-steamed rice), *torshi* (Persian pickles), and *sabzi-khordan* (fresh herb platter) on the side. *Nush-e Jan!*

VEGETARIAN VARIATION
Eliminate the meat from the
ingredients. Increase the
split peas to ½ cup and add
them in step 1 (instead of
step 5). In step 2, increase the
water to 4 cups and reduce
the cooking time to 30
minutes. Proceed with the
recipe from step 3, but
eliminate step 5 altogether.

NOTE

Qeymeh—*This* khoresh *without the potato is called* qeymeh. *It often accompanies thick Persian soups* (oshes) *and rice with fresh fava beans,* (baqala polow).

Yogurt Khoresh

Makes 6 servings
Preparation time: 15 minutes
Cooking time: 2 hours

Khoresh-e mast

VEGETARIAN VARIATION

Eliminate the meat and replace it with 1 pound of your favorite mushrooms. In step 2 after frying the onion and spices, add 1 cup water and reduce the cooking time to 15 minutes. Proceed with step 3. Add 3 peeled hard-boiled eggs (cut in halves) to the *khoresh* in step 5.

NOTE

Also see photo of this polow khoresh *with tah-dig on page 296*

GARNISH
2 tablespoons oil
1 cup whole raw almonds
¼ cup raisins
1 cup fresh basil leaves

CHICKEN
4 tablespoons oil, butter, or ghee*
1 onion, peeled and thinly sliced
2 cloves garlic, peeled and grated
1-inch fresh ginger, peeled and grated
1 green bird chili, finely chopped, or ½ teaspoon red pepper flakes
1 stalk celery, finely chopped
2 pounds boneless chicken thigh or leg of lamb, cut into 2-inch pieces

1 teaspoon sea salt
½ teaspoon freshly ground pepper
½ teaspoon turmeric
2 teaspoons ground coriander
2 teaspoons ground cumin
2 teaspoons ground cardamom
½ teaspoon ground cloves
½ teaspoon cinnamon
2 bay leaves
2 large tomatoes, peeled and chopped

YOGURT SAUCE
4 tablespoons raw almonds
3 tablespoons raisins
1½ cups whole plain yogurt
2 tablespoons fresh lime juice

1. To make the garnish: In a wide skillet, heat 2 tablespoons oil over medium heat until hot. Add the almonds and stir-fry for about 1 minute until slightly browned. Add raisins, give it a stir, and transfer to a small serving bowl. Set aside.

2. To cook the chicken: In a Dutch oven heat 2 tablespoons oil until very hot. Add the onion, garlic, ginger, chili, and celery. Sauté for 5 minutes. Add the chicken and remaining spices, and sauté until brown. Add the tomatoes (if using lamb add 1 cup water). Cover and simmer over low heat for 30 minutes for chicken or 1½ hours for lamb.

3. To make the yogurt sauce: In a food processor, grind the almond and raisins, add the yogurt and lime juice, and mix for 5 minutes. The almond acts as a thickening agent and when mixed with the yogurt prevents the yogurt from curdling.

4. When the chicken is cooked, gradually add the yogurt mixture while stirring gently. Cover and simmer over very low heat for another 30 minutes, stirring occasionally. Adjust seasoning to taste by adding lime juice, salt, or chili.

5. Serve with plain rice, barberry chutney, fresh basil, and the garnish. *Nush-e Jan*

VARIATION

Yogurt Khoresh with Lamb Necks—In a Dutch oven, place 2 *whole* lamb necks, 1 large chopped onion, 2 teaspoons salt, 1 teaspoon pepper, 1 teaspoon turmeric, 1 teaspoon cinnamon, and 4 cups water. Bring to a boil, reduce to low, cover, and cook for 3 hours until the lamb is tender (turn the necks once after 2 hours). Separate the meat and discard the bones (be sure to get rid of them all). In a food processor, grind 3 tablespoons almonds, and 3 tablespoons raisins. Add ½ teaspoon ground saffron dissolved in 2 tablespoons rose water, zest of 2 oranges, and 1 cup yogurt. Mix for 5 minutes. Add this mixture gradually to the meat—stirring clockwise. Cook for 10 to 15 minutes over low heat until the mixture becomes a thick, elastic puree. Adjust seasoning to taste and keep warm. Serve with steamed plain rice, barberry chutney, and fresh Persian basil.

Kermani Pistachio Khoresh

Makes 6 servings
Preparation time: 15 minutes plus
  24 hours of soaking time
Cooking time: 1 hour 40 minutes

خورش پسته کرمانی

Khoresh-e pesteh-ye Kermani

VEGETARIAN VARIATION

Eliminate the meat from the ingredients and in step 2, reduce the water to 1¼ cups, and simmer for 30 minutes. Proceed with the recipe.

1 pound (4 cups of kernels) raw shelled pistachios
3 tablespoons oil, butter, or ghee*
2 medium onions, thinly sliced
1 pound boneless leg of lamb, or chicken thighs, cut into 2-inch pieces
1 teaspoon sea salt

½ teaspoon ground black pepper
½ teaspoon turmeric
½ cup verjuice (ab-ghureh, unripe grape juice)*
1 teaspoon ground saffron dissolved in ¼ cup rose water

This recipe is inspired by a family favorite dish given to me by Shohreh Amin.

1. Soak the pistachios in a container of cold water for 24 hours, changing the water twice. Drain, spread on a clean kitchen towel, pat dry, and remove any skin that remains stuck to the kernels.

2. In a Dutch oven, heat 3 tablespoons oil over medium heat and brown the onions and meat. Add the salt, pepper, and turmeric. Sauté for 2 minutes. Pour in water—2½ cups for lamb and 1½ cups for chicken—and bring to a boil. Cover and simmer over low heat—1½ hours for lamb and 30 minutes for chicken—stirring occasionally.

3. Add the verjuice, saffron-rose water, and pistachios, and bring back to boil.

4. Preheat the oven to 350°F (180°C).

5. Transfer the khoresh to a deep, ovenproof casserole, cover, and place in the middle rack of the oven. Bake for 30 to 45 minutes until the lamb is tender.

6. Adjust seasoning to taste, adding more verjuice or salt. Serve with chelow (saffron-steamed rice) and sabzi-khordan (fresh herb platter) on the side. Nush-e Jan!

Plum and Apricot Khoresh

Makes 4 servings
Preparation time: 20 minutes
Cooking time: 1 hour 30 minutes

خورش آلو

Khoresh-e alu
  qormeh qeisi

3 tablespoons oil, butter, or ghee*
1 pound stew lamb, or skinless, boneless chicken thighs, cut into 2-inch pieces
2 large onions, peeled and sliced
1 teaspoon sea salt
½ teaspoon freshly ground pepper
½ teaspoon turmeric

¼ teaspoon grated nutmeg
½ teaspoon ground saffron dissolved in 2 tablespoons rose water
⅓ cup yellow split peas
2 tablespoons dried fenugreek leaves
½ cup dried plums
½ cup dried apricots, cut into quarters
1 teaspoon brown sugar (optional)

1. In a Dutch oven, heat the oil over medium heat and brown the lamb and onions. Add the salt, pepper, turmeric, nutmeg, and saffron water. Sauté for 1 minute. Add the yellow split peas and fenugreek, and sauté for 20 seconds.

2. Add the plums, apricots, and 3 cups water. Bring to a boil, reduce heat to low. Cover and cook for 1½ hours for meat or 45 minutes for chicken until the meat is tender.

3. Adjust seasoning to taste; add sugar if too sour. Transfer to a deep casserole, cover, and keep warm in the oven until ready to serve. Serve from the same dish with chelow (saffron-flavored steamed rice). Nush-e Jan!

Rhubarb Khoresh

Makes 6 servings
Preparation time: 30 minutes
Cooking time: 2 hour 15 minutes

6 tablespoons oil, butter, or ghee*
2 onions, peeled and thinly sliced
1 pound stew meat (lamb, veal, or beef),
　or boneless, skinless chicken thighs,
　cut into 2-inch cubes, or 2 pounds
　veal shank
1½ teaspoons sea salt
½ teaspoon freshly ground
　black pepper
½ teaspoon turmeric

3 cups chopped fresh parsley
½ cup chopped fresh mint, or 2
　tablespoons dried
¼ teaspoon ground saffron dissolved
　in 1 tablespoon rose water
1 tablespoon tomato paste
2 tablespoons fresh lime juice
1 pound fresh or frozen rhubarb,
　cut into 1-inch pieces

Khoresh-e rivas

From ancient times rhubarb has been known for cleansing the blood and purifying the system.

1. In a Dutch oven, heat 3 tablespoons oil over medium heat and brown onions and meat. Add salt, pepper, and turmeric, and sauté for 1 minute.

2. Pour in water—2½ cups for meat and 1½ cups for chicken. Cover and cook for 1 hour for meat and 15 minutes for chicken over low heat, stirring occasionally.

3. In a wide skillet, sauté parsley and mint in 3 tablespoons oil over medium heat for 10 to 15 minutes until aromatic.

4. Add parsley and mint mixture, saffron-rose water, tomato paste, and lime juice to the Dutch oven. Cover and simmer 55 minutes longer over low heat.

5. Preheat oven to 350°F (180°C). Transfer the *khoresh* to a deep, ovenproof casserole. Arrange the rhubarb on the top, cover, and seal tight the casserole with a layer of parchment paper and a layer of aluminum foil. Pierce several holes in the cover (the foil and parchment paper) and place the casserole in the oven. Cook for 25 to 35 minutes or until the rhubarb is tender.

6. Adjust seasoning. If the *khoresh* is too sour, add 1 tablespoon sugar. If the rhubarb needs more cooking, continue until done. Remember, rhubarb is fragile; the pieces must be cooked but not to the point of dissolving or falling apart.

7. Serve hot from the same dish with *chelow* (saffron-flavored steamed rice). *Nush-e Jan!*

VEGETARIAN VARIATION

Eliminate the meat from the ingredients and replace it with ½ cup yellow split peas. In step 1 brown the onions, add split peas and the rest of the ingredients for step 1, and sauté for 1 minute. In step 2, pour in 3 cups water, cover, and simmer for only 20 minutes over low heat. Proceed with the recipe from step 3.

Persian Gulf-Style Shrimp with Herbs and Tamarind

Makes 4 servings
Preparation time: 25 minutes
Cooking time: 45 minutes

TAMARIND SAUCE
2 tablespoons oil
½ cup chopped fresh spring onions
6 cloves garlic, peeled and sliced
3 cups fresh chopped cilantro
1 cup fresh chopped parsley
1 tablespoon dried or 1 cup fresh chopped fenugreek
1 teaspoon sea salt
½ teaspoon freshly ground pepper
½ teaspoon turmeric
1 teaspoon ground coriander
½ teaspoon red pepper flakes
1 tablespoon flour
½ cup homemade tamarind paste, or 2 tablespoons commercial

1 teaspoon grape molasses or brown sugar
2 cups fish stock or water

DUSTING
1 tablespoon flour
½ teaspoon red pepper flakes
½ teaspoon turmeric
1 teaspoon ground cumin
1 teaspoon ground coriander
¼ teaspoon cinnamon
¼ teaspoon ground cloves
1 teaspoon sea salt
½ teaspoon freshly ground pepper

SHRIMP
1 tablespoon oil
1 tablespoon butter
1½ pounds raw shrimp, butterflied

میگو با تمر هندی

Ghalieh maygu

VEGETARIAN VARIATION

Replace the shrimp with 2 cups raw cashew nuts. Just before serving, dust the cashews with the dusting mixture and sauté in oil and butter until golden. Add them to the tamarind sauce in step 4.

NOTE

Store-bought tamarind paste is very sour and concentrated. I prefer to use homemade tamarind paste (see page 535 for making homemade tamarind paste).

1. Heat 2 tablespoons oil in a medium-sized sauté pan and sauté the spring onions and garlic over medium heat, until translucent. Add cilantro, parsley, and fenugreek, and sauté 2 minutes longer.

2. Add the salt, pepper, turmeric, coriander, red pepper flakes, and flour, and sauté for 1 minute. Add the tamarind paste, grape molasses, and fish stock. Stir well and bring to a boil. Reduce heat to low, cover, and simmer for 20 minutes. Adjust seasoning to taste. Keep warm.

3. In a bowl, mix together all the dusting ingredients. Dust all sides of the shrimps and set aside.

4. Just before serving, in a large skillet, heat the oil and butter over medium-high heat until *very hot* and sauté the shrimp on both sides, shaking the pan, for a few minutes until they change color. Be careful not to overcook—shrimp loses its tenderness when overcooked. Add to the tamarind sauce.

5. Serve with *chelow* (saffron-flavored steamed rice). *Nush-e Jan!*

VARIATION

Fish Khoresh *(Ghalieh-ye mahi)*—Replace the shrimp with fish fillets. In step 3 use 2 pounds of firm white fish fillets (rockfish or catfish) cut into 3-inch lengths. Proceed with step 4, searing both sides of the fillets. Add to the sauce just before serving.

Caspian Fish Khoresh *(Khoresh-e anar avij)*—Replace the tamarind paste with 2 tablespoons pomegranate molasses or bitter orange paste.

DESSERTS, PASTRIES & CANDIES

دسرها و یا غذاهای شیرین

DESSERTS, PASTRIES & CANDIES

The desserts of Iran are served at any time of the day, not just at the end of a meal. Some are associated with special events.

Katchi, a saffron cream, for example, is eaten by new mothers on the first and fifth days after giving birth as part of a ceremony in which a holy person whispers the newborn child's name in her or his ear. It is also very good for nursing mothers.

Halva, a saffron brownie, is prepared during the first three days after a death and after the eve of the seventh and fortieth days of mourning. It is offered to family, friends, and the poor.

Sholeh zard, a saffron pudding (photo left), is reserved for the holiday in remembrance of the dead. It also serves as an offering to the poor or as thanksgiving for a wish come true.

All of these dishes may be eaten hot or cold. I prefer to serve them well chilled. They may be presented in individual dishes or in a large serving bowl.

Iranian pastries were refined during a period of much experimentation in the nineteenth century. Although these pastries are delicate, the recipes that follow are simple and well worth trying.

The English word "candy" comes from the Arabic *"qandi,"* which came from the Persian word for cane sugar *"qand."* Persian candies are easy to make, not overly sweet, and well worth trying.

Saffron Pudding

Makes 8 servings
Preparation time: 5 minutes
Cooking time: 1 hour
*   40 minutes*

شله‌زرد

Sholeh zard

1 cup rice
½ teaspoon sea salt
7 cups water
2 cups sugar
¼ cup oil or unsalted butter
½ cup raw blanched almonds
½ teaspoon ground saffron dissolved
   in 2 tablespoons hot water
1 tablespoon ground cardamom
½ cup rose water

GARNISH
2 teaspoons ground cinnamon
2 teaspoons slivered almonds
¼ cup candied orange peel,* chopped
2 teaspoons slivered pistachios

This rich, delicious saffron pudding is associated with sofrehs *and the giving of alms during religious ceremonies. It also makes a wonderful dessert in small portions.*

1. Clean and wash the rice, changing the water several times. Drain.

2. In a large pot, combine the rice and salt with 7 cups water, and bring to a boil, skimming the foam as it rises. Cover and simmer for 35 minutes over medium heat, stirring occasionally, until the rice is quite soft.

3. Add the sugar, stirring constantly with a long, wooden spoon for 5 minutes until the sugar has dissolved. Add the oil, almonds, saffron water, cardamom, and rose water. Stir well. Reduce heat to low, cover, and simmer for 50 to 60 minutes or until you have thick, smooth pudding.

4. Remove from heat and immediately spoon the pudding into individual serving bowls or a large bowl. Decorate right away (before the pudding has cooled) with cinnamon, almonds, orange peel, and pistachios. Allow to cool at room temperature, then chill in refrigerator.

5. Serve the pudding chilled. *Nush-e Jan!*

Saffron Brownie

SYRUP
1½ cups water
1½ cups sugar
1 teaspoon ground saffron dissolved in
  1 cup rose water
1 teaspoon ground cardamom

DOUGH
½ cup unsalted butter or ghee*
1½ cups canola oil
1 cup all-purpose flour
1 cup whole wheat flour

GARNISH
¼ cup raw pistachios, almonds, or
  walnuts, chopped

Makes 6 servings
Preparation time: 10 minutes
Cooking time: 30 minutes

Halva

Lavash Halva Rolls—Place a piece of 9x9-inch Cellophane wrap on the counter. Place a 7x7-inch piece of *lavash* bread over it. Spread a layer of the *halva* over the bread. Roll up the bread tightly, wrap the Cellophane around the roll, and seal the two ends. Store in a covered container and keep chilled until ready to serve. Just before serving, unwrap the Cellophane and slice the roll.

This dish is associated with Sofreh's *or the giving of alms during religious ceremonies. Zoroastrians make this* halva *white for the New Year by not using saffron.*

1. Bring the water and sugar to a boil in a saucepan. Remove from heat and add the saffron-rose water and ground cardamom. Mix well and set aside.

2. In a wide, shallow, non-stick pot, heat the butter and oil over medium heat until hot. Add both types of flour. Stir constantly with a long, wooden spoon for about 20 to 25 minutes or until golden brown. (This stage is very important: Be careful that the flour is not overcooked or undercooked.) Remove the pot from heat.

3. Wear mittens. Carefully and gradually stir the syrup into the hot flour mixture, stirring quickly and constantly with the wooden spoon for about 5 minutes. Continue stirring until you get a thick, smooth paste.

4. Hold the pot by both handles and rock it from side to side for a few minutes. This helps develop the texture and taste of the *halva* (see photos below).

5. Transfer onto a flat dish and pack firmly and quickly with a spoon. Decorate by making geometric patterns and garnish with pistachios.

6. Allow to cool, cover, and chill in the refrigerator. Cut it into small pieces and serve cold with *lavash* bread, or alone as a dessert. *Nush-e Jan!*

VARIATION

Bite-Sized Halva—Spread the chilled paste on a flat surface then stamp out shapes using small cookie cutters and place in petit four cases (see photo on page 352).

Paradise Custard

½ cup rice flour
1 cup cold water
¾ cup corn starch
4 cups milk or almond milk
1 cup sugar
5 cardamom pods, peeled and seeded
¼ cup rose water

GARNISH
⅓ cup sliced almonds, toasted, or ground raw pistachios

Makes 6 servings
Preparation time: 10 minutes
  plus 2 hours of setting time
Cooking time: 40 minutes

Yakh dar behesht

1. In a medium-sized, heavy-bottom saucepan whisk together the rice flour and water, and cook over low heat for 10 to 15 minutes.

2. In a separate bowl whisk together the corn starch and milk, and gradually add it to the rice flour in the saucepan. Add the sugar and whisk together until smooth.

3. Cook over low heat for about 10 to 15 minutes, stirring constantly until the mixture has thickened.

4. Add the cardamom seeds and rose water. Cook for 5 to 10 minutes longer, stirring constantly to prevent sticking and lumping, until the mixture reaches the consistency of a smooth, glossy custard (and you are able to draw a line on the surface). Remove the saucepan from the heat.

5. Transfer the custard to a serving dish. Garnish immediately while the custard is hot. Allow to cool at room temperature, then chill in the refrigerator for at least 2 hours. Serve cold. *Nush-e Jan!*

VARIATION

Custard on Ice *(Ru yakhi)*—Cook in the same way as above except you should eliminate the sugar. Serve with grape molasses *(shireh-ye angur)*.

Wheat Pudding

1 cup wheat or corn starch
6 cups water
2 cup sugar
2 tablespoons rose water
¼ cup sliced almonds

¼ cup oil

GARNISH
2 tablespoons ground pistachios
2 tablespoons dried rose petals

Makes 6 servings
Preparation time: 10 minutes
  plus 2 hours of setting time
Cooking time: 20 minutes

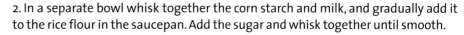

Masqati

1. In a mixing bowl, dissolve the starch in the water and pass through a sieve. Pour into a heavy-bottomed saucepan and bring to a boil. Reduce heat to medium and simmer for 15 minutes, stirring occasionally. Add the sugar, rose water, and almonds, and simmer for 5 minutes, stirring constantly, until thick enough to coat the back of a spoon.

2. Heat the oil in a small saucepan and add it to the pudding, stirring until all the oil is absorbed and the mixture is smooth and glossy. Spread on an oiled, rimmed half-baking sheet. Garnish and allow to cool. Chill and cut into diamonds.

Carrot Halva

Makes 12 servings
Preparation time: 15 minutes
Cooking time: 40 minutes

CARROT HALVA WITH RICE FLOUR
2 pounds carrots
1½ cups sugar or grape molasses
1 cup canola oil or unsalted butter
2 cups sifted rice flour
½ teaspoon ground saffron dissolved in
  ½ cup rose water
1 tablespoon ground cardamom

GARNISH
2 tablespoons ground pistachios
2 tablespoons ground walnuts
2 tablespoons dried rose petals, crushed
¼ teaspoon ground cinnamon

VARIATION WITHOUT RICE FLOUR
2 pounds carrots, peeled and grated
6 cups whole milk
1½ cups sugar
1 tablespoon cardamom powder
½ teaspoon ground saffron dissolved in
  2 tablespoons rose water
½ cup canola oil, butter, ghee*

حلوای هویج

Halva-ye havij

NOTE
You may use a food processor on pulse to grate the carrots (do not purée)

Photo shows the halva made with rice flour.

This sweet, nutritional, and comforting dish is associated with the Winter Festival, Shab-e Yalda.

1. Wash, peel, and grate the carrots. Place in a saucepan and add 2 cups water and the sugar. Bring to a boil stirring constantly until the sugar completely dissolves. Reduce heat to low, cover, and simmer for 30 minutes.

2. In a large Dutch oven, heat the oil over high heat and gradually add the rice flour while stirring constantly. Cook for 5 to 8 minutes or until the mixture turns lightly golden.

3. Reduce heat to low. Wear oven mitts and carefully add the cooked carrot to the hot rice flour(step back to avoid getting splashed). Add saffron-rose water and cardamom, and cook over low heat for another 15 to 20 minutes, stirring quickly and constantly with a wooden spoon to make a thick, smooth halva.

4. Place a ring on a flat serving platter and spoon the halva into it; pack firmly with a spoon. Garnish with ground pistachios, walnuts, rose petals and cinnamon. Allow to cool, lift up the ring, then cover and chill in the refrigerator. Serve either as a main dish with *lavash* bread or alone as a dessert. *Nush-e Jan!*

VARIATION

Carrot Halva without Rice Flour—In a medium saucepan, combine the carrots and milk and cook over medium heat for 55 minutes, stirring occasionally until the carrots have absorbed all the milk. Add the sugar, cardamom, saffron-rose water, and butter, stirring frequently for 20 to 25 minutes until you have a pudding. Remove from heat, transfer to a dish, and garnish. Allow to cool and chill in the refrigerator.

Rice Pudding

Makes 6 servings
Preparation time: 5 minutes
Cooking time: 1 hour 30 minutes

شیربرنج

Shir berenj

½ cup rice, cleaned and washed
2 cups water
¼ teaspoon sea salt
3 cups milk or almond milk
½ cup half-and-half or cream
  (optional)

¼ cup rose water
1 teaspoon ground cardamom

TOPPING
½ cup grape molasses or honey
1 cup pomegranate arils (in season)

1. Place the rice in a saucepan with 2 cups water and ¼ teaspoon salt. Bring to a boil and reduce the heat. Cover and cook over medium heat for 20 minutes or until the rice is tender.

2. Add the milk and half-and-half. Bring to a boil and reduce the heat. Cover and cook over low heat for about 55 minutes or until the mixture has thickened to a pudding consistency. Add rose water and cardamom, and cook over low heat for 10 minutes longer.

3. Remove from heat, spoon into individual bowls, and chill. Just before serving top with a tablespoon of grape molasses (or honey) and pomegranate arils. *Nush-e Jan!*

Saffron Cream

Makes 6 servings
Preparation time: 10 minutes
Cooking time: 45 minutes

Katchi

NOTES

Katchi is given to new mothers to restore their strength and during breast-feeding.

Katchi is a liquid form of halva, with three times the amount of water. It is best served warm.

SYRUP
5½ cups water
2½ cups sugar
1 teaspoon ground saffron dissolved in
  ¼ cup hot water
¼ cup rose water
½ teaspoon ground cardamom

ROUX
1 cup unsalted butter or oil
2 cups sifted all-purpose flour

GARNISH
2 tablespoons slivered almonds
2 tablespoons slivered pistachios

1. To make the syrup: Bring the water and sugar to a boil in a saucepan. Add the saffron water, rose water, and cardamom. Set aside.

2. In a large, deep skillet, melt the butter and gradually add the flour, stirring constantly with a wooden spoon. Cook over medium heat for about 20 to 25 minutes or until it is golden brown.

3. Add the saffron syrup, stirring quickly and constantly with a wooden spoon. Simmer until the mixture reaches a creamy consistency. Add more warm water if too thick.

4. Transfer the saffron cream to a serving bowl. Garnish it with almonds and pistachios and serve warm. *Nush-e Jan!*

VARIATION

Saffron Rice Cream *(Tar halva)*—Replace the flour with rice flour.

Quince Paste

Makes 6 servings
Preparation time: 15 minutes
Cooking time: 4½ hours plus
* 24 hours rest at room*
* temperature*

Loz-e beh

6 pounds quinces
  (about 8 medium quinces)
4 cups sugar
2 tablespoons fresh lime juice

5 cardamom pods, peeled and seeded

GARNISH
1 cup ground raw pistachios or almonds

This dish is often associated with the Winter Festival, Shab-e Yalda.

1. Wash and peel the quinces. Place in a container of water with a splash of vinegar to prevent discoloration.

2. Grate the quinces. Remove the quince seeds from the core and place in a cheese-cloth. Tie the cheesecloth in a knot so the seeds are held inside (the seeds have some natural pectin, which will help form the paste).

3. Transfer the quinces to a pot (preferably copper), cover with 3 cups water, add ½ cup sugar and the wrapped quince seeds, and bring to a boil. Reduce heat, cover, and simmer over low heat for about 2 hours or until tender, stirring occasionally with a wooden spoon.

4. Squeeze and then remove the wrapped quince seeds from the pot and discard. Add remaining sugar, lime juice, and cardamom seeds. Use a handheld mixer to puree the quinces. Cover and simmer over low heat for 2½ hours or until you have a thick reddish paste, stirring occasionally with a wooden spoon. Transfer to a 2-inch-deep oiled container. Garnish with pistachios. Leave uncovered at room temperature overnight, or longer, until firm. Cover and keep chilled.

Quince-Blossom Paste

Makes 2 servings
Preparation time: 35 minutes
Cooking time: 25 minutes plus
* cooling at room temperature*
* for 8 hours*

Loz-e gol-e beh

4 cups fresh quince blossoms,
  or 1 cup dried blossoms soaked in
  2 cups water for 2 hours, drained

2 cups water
4 cups confectioners' sugar
½ cup raw shelled pistachios

This is a spring dish prepared during the quince blossom season. It is very nutritious as well as delicious.

1. Carefully rinse the quince blossoms in a colander and separate the petals. Place the petals in a saucepan with 2 cup water and cook over low heat for 15 minutes until tender.

2. Transfer petals to a food processor and grind with confectioners' sugar.

3. Transfer the petal mixture to a skillet. Cook over low heat for about 20 minutes or until the sugar dissolves completely. Stir constantly to obtain the consistency of a paste. Add the pistachios and stir for 1 minute. Remove from heat.

4. Transfer the quince-blossom paste to an oiled, 2-inch-deep, rimmed half-sheet pan and pack it down firmly with a spoon. Allow to cool at room temperature. Chill in refrigerator. Cut into diamond shapes and serve as a dessert. *Nush-e Jan!*

Rice Cream

¼ cup rice flour (ground rice)
4 cups milk
2 tablespoons rose water
½ cup sugar

Makes 6 servings
Preparation time: 5 minutes
Cooking time: 25 minutes

Fereni

This dish is favored in Iran for the very young and the very old.

1. In a saucepan, combine the rice flour, milk, rose water, and sugar. Cook for 20 to 25 minutes over low heat, stirring frequently with a wooden spoon, until the mixture has thickened and reaches a creamy consistency.

2. Remove the cream from the heat. Ladle it into a serving bowl or individual bowls. Chill in the refrigerator. *Nush-e Jan!*

Coconut Paste

1 pound grated frozen coconut
½ pound confectioners' sugar
1 tablespoon rose water

GARNISH
½ cup ground raw pistachios

Makes 6 servings
Preparation time: 20 minutes
Cooking time: none, setting at
  room temperature overnight

Loz-e Nargil

1. In a mixing bowl, mix all the ingredients and spread evenly on an oiled, rimmed half baking sheet. Pack down well using your hands. Spread a sheet of parchment paper over it and roll over it with a rolling pin. Even out the surface and pack it down well.

2. Cut into diamond shapes and garnish with the pistachios.

3. Leave out at room temperature overnight to dry out. *Nush-e Jan!*

Cantaloupe and Peach Cocktail

Makes 2 servings
Preparation time: 15 minutes
plus 30 minutes to chill

کمپوت هلو و طالبی

Compot-e hulu va talebi

2 peaches
1 cantaloupe or honeydew melon
2 tablespoons sugar
1 tablespoon fresh lime juice

2 tablespoons rose water or orange
  blossom water
½ cup fresh mint leaves

1. Peel and slice the peaches into 1-inch pieces (or cut each peach in half, remove stone, and use a melon baller).

2. Peel and slice the cantaloupe into 1-inch pieces (or cut the cantaloup in half, remove seeds, and use a melon baller).

3. In a glass bowl, combine all the ingredients and stir gently. Adjust the taste by adding more sugar if necessary. Cover and chill. Just before serving, garnish with mint leaves. *Nush-e Jan!*

VARIATIONS

Cantaloupe and Peach Sorbet *(Paloodeh-ye hulu-o talebi)*—Combine all the ingredients in a blender and chill in the refrigerator. Pour the mixture into a sorbet maker. Follow your machine's instructions.

Cantaloupe Smoothie *(Paloodeh-ye talebi)*—Puree the cantaloupe with sugar and 3 ice cubes in a blender. Add a few drops of rose water, and decorate with mint leaves and rose petals.

Dried Fruit Cocktail

Makes 2 servings
Preparation time: 30 minutes
Cooking time: 30 minutes

خوشاب میوه های خشک

Khoshab-e miveh-ye khoshk

1 cup dried apricots
1 cup pitted prunes
2 sticks cinnamon
2 whole cloves
2 tablespoons honey

1 teaspoon chopped candied
  orange peel*
2 tablespoons raw pistachios
2 tablespoons slivered almonds
Fresh mint leaves for garnish

1. Rinse and drain the dried fruit.

2. Place the fruit in a saucepan and add 3 cups water. Bring to a boil, cover, and simmer for 20 minutes. Remove from heat and transfer to glass bowl. Add spices, honey, and orange peel, and stir well. Taste and add more honey if needed.

3. Cover and refrigerate for 30 minutes or until chilled.

4. Just before serving, add pistachios and almonds, and stir well. Serve in individual serving dishes. Decorate with mint leaves. *Nush-e Jan!*

General Rules for Compotes—For every pound of fresh sweet fruit, use ½ cup sugar and 6 cups water; for every pound of sour fresh fruit, use ½ cup sugar and 5 cups water. There are two ways to prepare the fruit cocktail. First method: Combine the sugar and water in a pot, bringing it to a boil, and then adding fruit. Simmer for 5 more minutes over medium heat. Second method: Combine the sugar and water in a pot, bringing it to a boil to produce a syrup. Place the fruit in sterilized jars, fill the jars to within 2 inches of the top with the syrup, and then seal. Place the jars upright in a large pot and fill the pot with water up to the neck of the jars. Bring to a boil, reduce heat, and simmer for 10 minutes.

Pomegranate Jelly

Makes 6 servings
Preparation time: 15 minutes
Setting time: 8 hours

4 envelopes unflavored gelatin
4 cups freshly squeezed or bottled
  pomegranate juice*
2 tablespoons sugar or honey
  (if pomegranates are too sour)
2 tablespoons fresh lime juice
  (if pomegranates are too sweet)
Seeds of 4 fresh pomegranates

GARNISH
2 tablespoons raw pistachios

رُله انار

Jeleh-ye anar

NOTE
You can also make individual servings of this jelly.

1. In a large bowl, thoroughly dissolve the unflavored gelatin in 1 cup cold pomegranate juice by stirring well. Let stand for 1 minute.

2. In a saucepan, warm 3 cups pomegranate juice.

3. Add the softened gelatin to the saucepan. Stir constantly for 5 minutes.

4. Adjust to taste by adding sugar or lime juice. Pour the pomegranate juice mixture into a laminated mold or a bowl. Allow to cool.

5. Scatter the pomegranate seeds on top of the mixture. Chill it in the refrigerator until firm.

6. Serve pomegranate jelly with whipped cream, ice cream, or drained yogurt, and garnish with pistachios. *Nush-e Jan!*

VARIATIONS

Sour-Cherry Jelly—You may substitute the pomegranate juice with sour cherry juice.

Rhubarb Jelly—You may substitute the pomegranate juice with rhubarb juice.

Baked Candied Quince with Walnuts

Makes 4 servings
Preparation time: 15 minutes
Cooking time: 4 hours

مربای به درسته

Moraba-ye beh-e dorosteh

SYRUP
2 cups water
¾ cup sugar
4 tablespoons fresh lime juice
1 vanilla bean, split and scraped out, or
   ½ teaspoon vanilla extract

QUINCE
2 medium-sized quinces
4 cinnamon sticks (1-inch long)
4 bay leaves

GARNISH
½ cup fresh pomegranate arils*
½ cup toasted walnuts, chopped
   (optional)
Vanilla ice cream, whipped cream, or
   drained yogurt

1. Preheat oven to 350°F (180°C).

2. In a mixing bowl, combine the water, sugar, lime juice, and vanilla. Stir well until the sugar has completely dissolved.

3. Wash and rub off the fuzz from the quinces. Peel and core the quinces and cut into halves.

4. Place the quince halves face up in a deep, 9-inch baking dish.

5. Lay a cinnamon stick and a bay leaf inside the hollow of each quince.

6. Pour the syrup over the quinces. Cover and seal with a layer of parchment paper and a layer of aluminum foil on top. Bake for 3 hours. Uncover and continue to bake for 1 more hour, basting occasionally, until the quinces are orange-red.

7. Remove from the oven and transfer to individual serving dishes. Garnish with pomegranate arils and walnuts, and serve with vanilla ice cream. *Nush-e Jan!*

VARIATIONS

Candied Quince in Pomegranate Juice—Follow the recipe above, but substitute 3 cups pomegranate juice and ½ cup sugar for the water. The flavor will be distinctly different and the color ruby-red.

Spiced Quince Dessert—Follow the recipe above and add 3 cloves and 1 star anise, cover and bake for 3 hours, then bake uncovered for 1 more hour. Once cooked, the quinces will turn into a orange-red color.

Baked Candied Apples—You may substitute full-flavored, firm apples, such as Rome or Empire, for the quinces, in which case reduce the baking time in step 6 to 45 minutes.

STOVETOP COOKING VARIATION
Place the quince halves, side by side, in a medium-sized pot. Lay cinnamon sticks and bay leaves on top and pour the syrup over the quinces. Cover tightly and cook over medium-low heat for 1½ to 2 hours until the quinces are orange-red.

Orange and Pomegranate Dessert

Makes 4 servings
Preparation time: 20 minutes,
*   plus 30 minutes for*
*   refrigeration*

خوشاب پرتقال و انار

Khoshab-e
*   porteqal-o anar*

2 cups pomegranate arils (about 2
   pomegranates)*
4 large chilled oranges, peeled and
   sliced (with membrane removed)*
¼ cup candied orange peel*
½ cup fresh orange juice (use the juice
   from segmenting oranges)
1 tablespoon fresh lime juice
1 teaspoon orange blossom water*

GARNISH
6 orange blossoms (optional)
6 orange leaves (optional)

1. Combine the pomegranate arils, orange slices, candied orange peel, orange and lime juices, and orange blossom water in a glass bowl. Cover and chill in the refrigerator for at least 30 minutes.

2. Serve chilled in individual glasses, and garnish each glass with an orange blossom and an orange tree leaf. *Nush-e Jan!*

___
VARIATION

You can replace the pomegranates with 2 cups dates, pitted and halved. Garnish with
   ½ cup blanched almonds and ½ cup raw shelled pistachios.

Saffron Ice Cream

Makes 4 servings
Preparation time: 20 minutes
Ice cream making: 40 minutes
   plus 1 hour to develop taste

بستنی زعفران

Bastani-e gol-o bolbol

NOTES

You can make round ice cream sandwiches, similar to those made in Iran and Turkey, using torte wafers available at Middle Eastern grocery stores. They come in 8½x11-inch sheets. Use a cookie cutter to make 4-inch disks. Or you can buy both the ice cream and the wafers, in various sizes, ready-made from Mashti Malone's Ice Cream in Los Angeles (www.mashti.com).

Sahlab is a starch made from a powdered root. The sahlab available in the U.S. is mixed with cornstarch, which is why 4 tablespoons are necessary. If you have pure sahlab, use only 2 teaspoons ground sahlab.

Mastic is a resin from the mastic tree (Pistacia Lentiscus).

CRUNCHY FROZEN HEAVY CREAM
1 cup heavy cream

ICE CREAM
4 tablespoons *sahlab* mixture (Cortas)*
4 cups whole milk
1 cup sugar
½ teaspoon salt
½ teaspoon ground saffron threads,
   dissolved in 2 tablespoons rose water

¼ teaspoon ground cardamom
   (optional)
½ teaspoon mastic* ground with
   1 teaspoon sugar
¼ cup shelled, raw pistachios

WAFERS
8 ice cream wafers, (3 inch, round)

In my childhood in Iran, our favorite summer treat was a creamy, elastic, sweet ice cream flavored with rose water and saffron, and garnished with pistachios. After a siesta on a long, hot summer afternoon, my three sisters and I were happiest when we could soak all our senses in an ice cream sandwich costing ten cents. We held in both hands a scoop of ice cream between two round crispy wafers. Eating it was an art we perfected with practice. We would begin by turning it around clockwise, gently and systematically, as we sucked and licked while squeezing the wafers with just the right amount of pressure. The idea was to make the ice cream last the longest amount of time possible without it melting or dripping. Each lick would bring to our mouths a cold, creamy, perfumed delight with chunks of solid, frozen cream. It was both delicious and sensuous. Once you know the taste of a Persian ice cream (bastani-e nuni) eaten in this way, you can never again see a good-looking scoop of ice cream between two wafers without wanting to take a lick of it.

1. Pour the cream into a 9-inch freezer-proof pie dish and place in the freezer. In a small bowl, dissolve the *sahlab* in 1 cup milk until quite smooth. Set aside.

2. To make the ice cream: In a medium saucepan, bring 3 cups milk and the sugar to boil, and reduce heat to very low. Add the sahlab mixture, salt, saffron-rose water, and mastic, and bring back to a boil. Reduce heat to low and simmer, whisking constantly, for 10 to 20 minutes until thick enough for the mixture to coat the back of a spoon. Remove from heat and allow to cool then chill in refrigerator. Pour into a chilled ice cream maker and follow the manufacturer's instructions for making ice cream (in my machine it takes about 1 hour 40 minutes).

3. Remove the cream from the freezer. Unmold it from the pan and break it into ¼-inch pieces. Add it to the ice cream in the machine. Add the pistachios and continue to turn in the machine for another 20 seconds.

4. Pour the ice cream into a freezer-proof glass container with a press-in-place lid. Cover tightly (uncovered ice cream develops an unpleasant taste). Freeze the ice cream for at least 1 hour to allow it to develop texture and flavor.

5. Twenty minutes before serving, remove the ice cream from the freezer and refrigerate. Serve by placing 3 scoops of ice cream into individual glass containers or use 2 wafers to make an ice cream sandwich. *Nush-e Jan!*

Rice Stick Sorbet with Sour Cherries

Makes 6 servings
Preparation time: 15 minutes
Cooking time: 5 minutes
Setting time: 3 hours in freezer

4 ounces thin rice-stick noodles or rice vermicelli, snipped into 3-inch lengths using scissors, soaked in warm water for 30 minutes, drained
¼ teaspoon sea salt
2½ cups water
2 cups sugar
2 tablespoons light corn syrup
¼ cup fresh lime juice
1 tablespoon cooking rose water

GARNISH
2 tablespoons pistachios
¼ cup fresh sour cherry preserve
4 tablespoons fresh lime juice

HOMEMADE RICE STICK NOODLES
These noodles can be made from rice or wheat starch (see below).*

فالوده شیرازی

Paludeh-ye shirazi

1. Bring 8 cups water to a boil and drop in the noodles. Boil for 5 minutes, drain, and rinse with cold water.

2. Combine 2½ cups water and the sugar, and stir well until the sugar has completely dissolved. Add the remaining ingredients, except the noodles, and stir well.

3. This stage is important. The mixture has to have an icy consistency before adding the noodles, and the noodles have to be added gradually so they are frozen. Pour the mixture into an ice cream maker and start the machine. When the mixture has an icy consistency, add the noodles a little at a time, allowing them to freeze before adding the next batch. When the noodles freeze properly, they will not have a rubbery texture.

4. Scoop some rice noodle *granita* into individual dishes and garnish with pistachios. Top with sour cherry preserve and fresh lime juice. *Nush-e Jan!*

Homemade Rice Noodles: To prepare your own noodles, slowly blend 1 cup rice starch with 9 cups water in a saucepan. Stir well until smooth, pass through a metal colander, then bring to a boil over medium heat, stirring constantly until the mixture reaches the consistency of rich, smooth white cream (or until thick enough to coat the back of a spoon). Let it stand for a few minutes. Gently strain through a metal sieve over a bowl of ice water, then proceed with step 3.

THE STORY OF THE ROSE

چوکه گل رفت و گلستان درگذشت   نشنوی زان پس زبلبل سرگذشت

چوکه گل رفت و گلستان شد خراب   بوی گل را از که جوئیم از گلاب

When the rose is withered and the garden is gone
You will hear no more the nightingale's song;
When the rose is withered and the garden laid bare
In attar of roses the scent is still there.

Roses began their slow journey to the West in the third century BCE, when they appeared in the botanical garden of Aristotle, in Athens. They had been sent from Persia, along with other specimen plants that might prove useful to medicine, by Alexander the Great. The conqueror, once a pupil of Aristotle, was always interested in the flora and fauna of the countries that fell to him.

During the centuries that followed, as roses spread north into Europe, Westerners began to use the beautiful flowers in the same way as Persians . Roses were (and still are) given as gifts, scattered on fountains or walkways during festivities—perhaps this is the parent of the red carpet—and fashioned into decorations for dining tables.

The culinary delights of the rose, however, never assumed the central importance that they have in Persian cooking. I hope they will. The flower's delicate fragrance and taste is something worth exploring.

Fresh rose petals, for instance, may be used in salads, used to make a strong wine, steeped to produce rose tea (and the fruit, or hip, may be turned into rose hip tea), cooked into jam, or used to scent honey. The fresh petals may also be mixed with stored sugar to make rose petal sugar, infused with the subtle taste and memorable aroma of the flower.

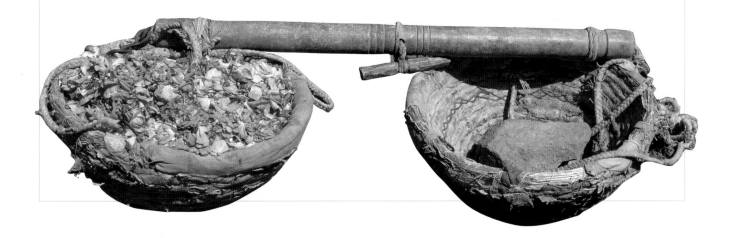

Dried rose petals more intense in flavor, can be put to any of these uses. Most important—dried petals with cinnamon, cardamom, and cumin—form the delicate Persian spice mix called *advieh*, which gives many dishes their distinctive flavor.

In other forms—as rose water and oil or attar of roses—the flowers have given savor at least since 500 BCE. At around that time, if not earlier, Persians began to extract both water and essential oil from the petals of that same damask rose that Omar Khayyam loved.

Look to the rose that blows about us—"Lo, Laughing," she says, "into the world I blow:
At once the silken tassel of my purse
Tear, and its treasure on the garden throw."

In Iran, rose water and oil still are produced by ancient methods, primarily at Qamsar and Naysar, two small towns near Kashan in the center of the country. Workers pick the roses in the early morning, when the scent is at its peak. The flowers are transferred to a rose water factory, where they are spread over the floor of a cool room and sorted. Then the fresh petals are steamed in a clay-sealed cauldron; the perfumed vapor rises through a bamboo pipe into a second pot set in cold running water.

Cooling condenses the vapors into liquid rose water and more intense oil. The first is bottled for cooking; the second is used for

perfume (*"atr"* in Persian, which is the source of the English "attar"); and the leftover petals are fed to animals.

Few scents are more characteristic of Iran than that of rose water. Even thousands of years ago, Zoroastrians used it in their purification rites. Today it is still found everywhere: One offers it to guests to dip their fingers in before and after meals, for instance. It serves as an air freshener both at home and in public places. It is part of every woman's makeup, and men use it to clean their mustaches and beards. And, of course, it is essential to Persian cooking. It is used to flavor rice pudding, baklava, and the wonderful Persian chewy ice cream, for instance. And it makes a very good *sharbat*.

Its name in Persian, *golab* (literally "rose water") has its own history. In the seventh century, Arabs borrowed the word as a term for a drink with water and honey or syrup. In English, *golab* became julep, originally used for any sweet drink that helped medicines go down, then for any comforting drink. *Golab's* latest incarnation was in Kentucky, in the mint and whiskey mixture known as the mint julep.

With rose water and attar of roses, you might say, the practical cook answers the poet's lament for the brevity of beauty:

When the rose is withered and the garden is gone
You will hear no more the nightingale's song;
When the rose is withered and the garden laid bare
In attar of roses the scent is still there.

Rice Cookies

Makes 36 pieces
Preparation time: 30 minutes
  plus 2 to 4 hours of resting time
Cooking time: 15–20 minutes

SYRUP
1½ cups sugar
½ cup water
¼ cup rose water
½ teaspoon lime juice

BATTER
4 egg yolks, at room temperature
1 cup canola oil or clarified butter*
2 teaspoons cardamom powder
¼ teaspoon sea salt
3 cups rice flour
syrup (made in step 2)

DECORATION
2 tablespoons poppy seeds
2 tablespoons dried rose petals,
  crushed
2 tablespoons ground raw pistachios

ﻧﺎن ﺑﺮﻧﺠﯽ

Nan-e berenji

1. Prepare the syrup by combining sugar and water in a saucepan. Stir well until the sugar dissolves completely. Bring to a boil and simmer for 2 minutes *(be careful not to over boil)*, remove from heat, add rose water and lime juice, and set aside to cool. It should be at room temperature and not too thick.

2. In a warm mixing bowl, whisk the egg yolks until creamy. Add the cooled syrup from step 1 and whisk for 1 minute. Set aside.

3. In another mixing bowl, whisk together the oil, cardamom, salt, and rice flour until you have a creamy batter.

4. Add egg yolk mixture to the rice flour mixture. Use a rubber spatula to fold in until you have a soft, snow-white dough. Cover and chill in the refrigerator.

5. Place the oven rack in the center and preheat oven to 350°F (180°C). Line several baking sheets with a baking mats.

6. Use an ice cream scoop to scoop up a walnut-sized amount of dough. Place it on the baking mat. Flatten slightly using an offset spatula. Repeat, leaving 2½ inches between each cookie. With a fork or the open end of a thimble, draw geometric patterns on the cookies and sprinkle with poppy seeds, rose petals, and pistachios.

7. Bake the cookies for 10 to 15 minutes. Keep in mind that the cookies should be white when they are done.

8. Remove cookies from the oven and allow to cool. These cookies crumble very easily; remove them carefully from the baking mat using an offset spatula.

9. Arrange the cookies in a pyramid on a footed cake dish. If you are not using them immediately, store in a airtight glass container. *Nush-e Jan!*

NOTE

To clarify the butter, bring it to a boil over very low heat. Simmer for 10 minutes. Remove foam as it rises, then remove from heat and let it stand until the milk solids settle. Decant the clear yellow liquid (clarified butter) from the top.

AN UNINVITED GUEST

The mulla went to a party, although he hadn't been invited. Someone asked him what he was doing there without an invitation. He smiled and said, "If the host forgets his social obligations, that's no reason for me to neglect mine."

Chickpea Cookies

Makes 40 pieces
Preparation time: 30 minutes
Cooking time: 30 minutes

Nan-e nokhodchi

1 cup canola oil or clarified butter*
1½ cups confectioners' sugar
4 teaspoons ground cardamom
¼ teaspoon sea salt
1 tablespoon rose water
3½–4½ cups triple-sifted roasted
  chickpea flour

DECORATION
4 tablespoons slivered raw pistachios

1. Combine oil, sugar, cardamom, salt, and rose water in mixing bowl, and mix for 2 minutes until white and creamy. Add 3½ cups chickpea flour and mix for 1 minute until dough is no longer sticky. Add more chickpea flour if necessary.

2. Line a baking sheet with a baking mat and dust it with chickpea flour. Place the dough on top and knead it well until soft and pliable.

3. Flatten the dough and shape it to a ¾-inch thick square. Cover the entire baking sheet with plastic wrap and use a rolling pin, gently, to even out the dough. Chill for 1 to 24 hours in the refrigerator (the resulting cool, flat, and even dough will be easier to cut).

4. Line 2 baking sheets with parchment paper. Place the oven rack in the center and preheat the oven to 300°F (150°C).

5. Unwrap the dough. Use a cloverleaf cookie cutter to cut out the dough. Place cookies on the lined baking sheet, leaving 1 inch between pieces. Decorate each cookie with slivered pistachios.

6. Bake for 25 to 30 minutes or until base of cookies is a light golden color. Remove baking sheet from oven and place on a cooling rack. When cookies have thoroughly cooled, carefully lift using an offset spatula (be careful, these cookies crumble very easily). Arrange the cookies on a platter. *Nush-e Jan!*

Roasted Chickpea Cake

Preparation time: 10 minutes
Cooking time: 15 minutes

Bereshtook-e nokhodchi

To make Roasted Chickpea Cake (quick and easy), heat 2 cups canola oil over medium-low in a large wide skillet until very hot. Add 4 cups sifted chickpea flour and stir-fry for 5 to 10 minutes until golden. Remove from heat and add 2 cups confectioners' sugar, 1 tablespoon ground cardamom, and 2 tablespoons rose water. Mix thoroughly for 5 minutes (you may use a food processor). Spread evenly on a half baking sheet lined with parchment. Spread another sheet of parchment paper on top and use a rolling pin to even out, firm up, and pack down the dough well. Cut into diamond shapes, garnish with raw pistachio slivers, and allow to cool at room temperature.

Almond Cookies

Makes 20 pieces
Preparation time: 40 minutes
Cooking time: 15–20 minutes

DOUGH #1
4 cups raw almonds, ground
2 egg whites
1½ cups confectioners' sugar
¼ teaspoon sea salt
2 tablespoons rose water
1 teaspoon ground cardamom

DECORATION
¼ cup almond slices
2 tablespoons dried rose petals,
 crushed

DOUGH # 2 (*Badam pulaki*)
4 cups sliced raw almonds
2 egg whites
¾ cup confectioners' sugar
2 tablespoons rose water
1 teaspoon ground cardamom

DOUGH # 3 (*Haji-badami*)
4 cups blanched almonds
2½ cups sugar
1 teaspoon baking soda
3 tablespoons ground cardamom
2 tablespoons rose water
5 egg yolks

Nan-e badami

For Dough #1

1. Place the oven rack in the center and preheat oven to 350°F (180°C). Line 2 baking sheets with parchment paper or baking mats.

2. In a mixing bowl, lightly beat the egg whites, sugar, salt, and rose water until frothy.

3. Fold in the almond and cardamom with a rubber spatula until a soft dough is formed.

4. Use an ice cream scoop to scoop up some of the dough (the size of a walnut). Drop it on the baking sheet. Continue, leaving 2½ inches between each piece for expansion. Decorate each piece with a few almond slices and rose petals.

5. Bake for 15 to 20 minutes until the cookies are lightly golden.

6. Remove baking sheet from the oven and allow to cool on a cooling rack. Remove the cookies from the baking sheet using an offset spatula. Serve or store in an airtight glass container.

7. Serve with tea. *Nush-e Jan!*

VARIATIONS

Sliced Almond Cookies *(Badam-e pulaki)*—Use dough # 2: In a mixing bowl lightly combine all the ingredients for dough# 2 using a rubber spatula. All other steps remain as the recipe above.

Yazdi Almond Cookies *(Haji-badami)*—Use dough # 3: Combine all the ingredients in a food processor. Pulse until a dough forms. Continue with step 5 above, except preheat the oven to 375°F (190°C) and bake for 7 to 10 minutes until the cookie bases are lightly brown.

Pistachio Cookies *(Nan-e pestehi)*—In dough# 1, replace the raw almonds with 4 cups raw pistachios.

Walnut Cookies

Makes 20 pieces
Preparation time: 30 minutes
Cooking time: 15–20 minutes

Nan-e gerdui

5 egg yolks
¾ cup confectioners' sugar
¼ teaspoon sea salt
1 teaspoon vanilla extract
2 tablespoons rose water

4 cups raw ground walnuts or raw
  ground pistachios

DECORATION
¼ cup raw whole shelled pistachios

1. Place the oven rack in the center and preheat oven to 300°F (150°C). Line 2 cookie sheets with parchment paper or baking mats.

2. In a mixing bowl, whisk together the egg yolks, confectioners' sugar, salt, vanilla, and rose water until creamy. Fold in the walnuts using a rubber spatula until you have a soft dough.

3. Use an ice cream scoop to pick up round spoonfuls of dough and drop them on the lined cookie sheets, leaving about 2½ inches between cookies. Decorate with pistachios.

4. Bake for 15 to 20 minutes until the edges of the cookies are brown. Remove cookie sheets from the oven and allow to cool on a cooling rack. Lift the cookies off the sheets using an offset spatula. Arrange the cookies on a serving dish or store in an airtight, glass container. *Nush-e Jan!*

Coconut Cookies

Makes 20 pieces
Preparation time: 30 minutes
Cooking time: 10–15 minutes

Nan-e nargili

4 eggs
2 cups confectioners' sugar
¼ teaspoon sea salt
1 teaspoon ground cardamom
2 tablespoons rose water
½ cup all-purpose flour, sifted
2 cups dried grated coconut

DECORATION
¼ cup ground raw pistachios

1. Place the oven rack in the center and preheat oven to 350°F (180°C). Line 2 cookie sheets with parchment paper or baking mats.

2. In a mixing bowl, whisk together the eggs, confectioners' sugar, salt, cardamom, and rose water until creamy. Fold in the flour and coconut until a light and soft dough is formed. Use an ice cream scoop to pick up and drop round spoonfuls of dough on the lined cookie sheets, leaving about 2½ inches between cookies. Decorate with ground pistachios.

3. Bake 10 to 15 minutes in the center rack of the oven. Remove cookie sheets from the oven and place on a cooling rack. Allow to cool.

4. Lift the cookies off the sheets using an offset spatula. Arrange the cookies on serving dish or store in an airtight, glass container. *Nush-e Jan!*

Rice Noodle Sweet

Makes 8 servings
Preparation time: 15 minutes
Cooking time: 30 minutes

رشته برشته

Reshteh bereshteh

NOTE

To make colored noodles that look like great fun, place a drop of food coloring on different portions before frying.

4 cups oil for frying
¼ pound rice sticks
 (thin rice noodles)

DUSTING
1 cup confectioners' sugar
1 tablespoon cardamom powder

1. Line a baking sheet with a few layers of paper towels.

2. Heat 4 cups oil in a deep-fat fryer to 350°F (180°C).

3. Divide the rice sticks into ½-ounce portions (you can use scissors).

4. Drop each rice stick portion into the hot oil. Fry it for 2 seconds until it rises to the surface and turns a white color. With a skimmer, remove the rice noodles from the oil and place them on the paper towels. Repeat the process until all the rice noodles are fried.

5. Combine the sugar and cardamom dusting mixture. While the rice noodles are hot, sprinkle them on both sides with dusting mixture. *Nush-e Jan!*

VARIATION

Gilani-Style Noodles in Syrup *(Reshteh-ye khoshkar)*—Make a syrup by bringing to a boil 1 cup water, 2 cups sugar, 2 tablespoons rose water, and 1 teaspoon cardamom powder. Reduce heat and simmer for 3 minutes. Prepare the noodles as above but eliminate the dusting. Dip the noodles in the syrup and allow to soak for 1 minute. Remove with a slotted spoon and arrange on a dish.

Sugar-Coated Almonds

Makes 1 cup
Preparation time: 20 minutes
Cooking time: 20 minutes

نُقل

Noghl

2¼ cups sugar
¼ cup water

¼ cup rose water
1 cup blanched slivered almonds

1. Line a cookie sheet with parchment paper. In a saucepan, bring the sugar and water to a boil and add the rose water. Bring back to boil and boil over high heat for 10 to 15 minutes until elastic. When a drop is placed on a plate, it should congeal. This stage is very important. If overboiled, almonds will stick together; if under-boiled, it will not coat the almonds. Remove from heat.

2. Roast ½ cup of the almonds at a time in a large skillet. Very gradually add half of the syrup, shaking and tossing the almonds constantly until they are thickly coated. Spread on the lined cookie sheet. Repeat for the remaining almonds. When completely cool separate from each other. *Nush-e Jan!*

Raisin Cookies

1 cup canola oil or unsalted
  butter, softened
1 teaspoon vanilla extract
2 tablespoons rose water
¼ teaspoon sea salt
1¼ cup sugar
4 large eggs
1¼ cups raisins
2 cups unbleached all-purpose flour

Makes 32 cookies
Preparation time: 15 minutes
Cooking time: 10–15 minutes

Nan-e keshmeshy

1. Place the oven rack in the center and preheat oven to 350°F (180°C). Line several cookie sheets with parchment paper or baking mats.

2. In a large mixing bowl whisk together the oil, vanilla, rose water, salt, and sugar until smooth. Then whisk in the eggs one at a time. Stir until the mixture is creamy.

3. Stir in the raisins. Fold in the flour using a rubber spatula until a thick batter forms.

4. Use a small ice cream scoop to pick up spoonfuls of the batter and place on the lined cookie sheets, leaving about 2 inches between each scoop.

5. Bake for 10 to 15 minutes until the edges of the cookies are golden brown.

6. Remove cookie sheets from the oven and place on a cooling rack. When cool, loosen the cookies from the parchment paper with an offset spatula.

7. Transfer the raisin cookies to a serving platter. To store, place them in an airtight glass container and refrigerate until ready to serve. *Nush-e Jan!*

Baklava

Makes 1 full sheet
Preparation time: 35 minutes
Cooking time: 35 minutes

SYRUP
2½ cups sugar
1½ cups water
½ cup rose water
2 tablespoons fresh lime juice

DOUGH
¼ cup milk
½ cup canola oil
1 tablespoon syrup (prepared below)
¼ cup rose water
1 egg
2½ cups unbleached all-purpose
  flour, sifted

FILLING
2 pounds ground blanched almonds
2 cups sugar
3 tablespoons ground cardamom
1 tablespoon rose water

BAKING
½ cup canola oil for baking

DECORATION
2 tablespoons slivered raw pistachios
2 tablespoons dried rose petals

Baqlava

NOTES

A thin, long dough roller or tool handle available at hardware stores makes a perfect rolling pin.

The dough can be divided into 3 layers with 1 layer of pistachios and 1 layer of almonds. You can also substitute honey for the syrup.

1. Prepare the syrup by combining the sugar and water in a saucepan. Bring to a boil *(do not overboil),* add the rose water and lime juice, and set aside.

2. For the dough, combine the milk, oil, syrup, rose water, and egg in a food processor mixing bowl. Add the flour and mix well for 5 to 10 minutes to form a dough that does not stick to your hands. Divide the dough into 2 balls of equal size and immediately wrap in plastic. Set aside.

3. For the filling, *finely grind* the almonds, sugar, cardamom, and rose water in a food processor. Set aside.

4. Brush a 17x11x1-inch rimmed baking sheet with ¼ cup oil. Place the oven rack in the center and preheat oven to 350°F (180°C).

5. Prepare and dust with flour a large, wide surface for rolling out the dough. Unwrap 1 ball of dough and roll out into a very thin rectangular layer with a thin wooden rolling pin (the rolled dough should be thinner than a pie crust). Roll dough from the center to the outside edge in all directions, giving it a quarter turn occasionally for an even thickness—dust the dough with flour as necessary. The finished dough should be larger than the baking sheet.

6. Roll the thin layer of dough around the wooden rolling pin and transfer it to the oiled baking sheet and unroll the dough until it covers the whole baking sheet. Do not cut off the excess dough; let the dough hang over the edge of the baking sheet, 1 inch on all sides.

7. Spread all the almond-filling mixture on top of the dough. Spread, press down, and smooth it out using your hands. Use a small rolling pin to even it out and to *pack it down firmly* (this is important to achieve a tight, firm baklava when baked).

8. Roll out the second ball of dough into a very thin rectangular layer as you did in step 5 for the first one. Transfer dough sheet on top of the filling, allowing it to hang over all sides like the bottom layer. Press down on the dough evenly with your hands and smooth out the surface of the dough.

9. Fold and roll the overhanging dough from the top layer under the dough from the bottom layer. Press together and pinch the top and bottom edges together to seal like a pie, forming a rim around the edge of the baking pan.

10. Hold down the dough with one hand, pressing down with your palm while cutting the dough with a sharp knife (all the way through) into diamond shapes. Use a brush to paint the dough with ¼ cup oil.

11. Place the baking pan in the middle of the preheated oven and bake for 25 to 35 minutes (depending on your oven) until the baklava is golden or pinkish in color.

12. Spread a damp towel on the counter. When the baklava is pink, remove it from the oven and place it on the towel. Evenly pour 2 cups of the syrup all over the top (I prefer a less syrupy baklava, use more syrup if you prefer it more moist).

13. Decorate the baklava with pistachios and rose petals. Cover immediately with a layer of plastic wrap and a layer of aluminum foil and seal tightly. Let stand at room temperature for at least 4 hours. It is important that the baklava be covered at all times because it dries out very easily.

14. When ready to serve, use a sharp knife to lift 2 of the diamond pieces out of the baking sheet (to create an opening), then carefully lift 1 diamond at a time and arrange on a serving dish. Or transfer to a covered glass container for storing in the refrigerator. *Nush-e Jan!*

PREPARING THE DOUGH

PREPARING THE FILLING

ROLLING DOUGH AROUND ROLLING PIN

PLACING DOUGH ON GREASED BAKING PAN

SPREADING ALMOND FILLING

ROLLING TO EVEN OUT AND PACK DOWN THE ALMOND FILLING

PAINTING DOUGH WITH OIL

DECORATING BAKLAVA WITH PISTACHIO SLIVERS AND ROSE PETALS

Baklava Cake

Makes a 9-inch cake
Preparation time: 20 minutes
Cooking time: 40 minutes

کیک باقلوا

Cayk-e Baqlava

GLAZE
1 cup honey
¼ cup rose water
Zest of 1 orange
1 tablespoon fresh lime juice

CAKE
3 eggs, separated (room temperature)
¾ cup sugar
2 teaspoons cardamom powder
2 tablespoons rose water
½ cup milk or almond milk
½ cup oil
1 cup unbleached all-purpose flour
    sifted with 1½ teaspoons
    baking powder
1½ cups ground almonds
1 apple, peeled, cored, and chopped
    (optional)

GARNISH
2 tablespoons raw pistachios
2 tablespoons blanched almonds
2 tablespoons dried rose petals

1. In a saucepan, combine all the ingredients for the glaze. Bring to a boil, stir gently, and set aside.

2. Preheat the oven to 350°F (180°C). Butter an 8-inch spring form cake pan and line the base with parchment paper. Then butter and dust the top of the parchment paper.

3. In a mixing bowl, whisk the egg yolks and sugar until creamy. Add the cardamom, rose water, milk, and oil, and whisk for 1 minute longer.

4. Add the flour, almonds, and apple, and fold in with a rubber spatula.

5. In a separate mixing bowl, whisk the egg whites until there are soft peaks. Fold into the flour mixture until you have a smooth, light batter.

6. Gently pour the batter into the cake pan and bake for 35 to 45 minutes until a tester comes out clean.

7. Remove the pan from the oven and place it on a cooling rack. Pour half of the glaze over the cake, and leave the cake in the pan until it has absorbed all the syrup. Tap the pan to release the cake and transfer to a serving dish.

8. Cut into diamond shapes, pour the remaining glaze over the cake, and decorate with pistachios, almonds, and rose petals. *Nush-e Jan!*

Yazdi Cupcakes

1 cup canola oil or butter
1½ cups light brown sugar
3 tablespoons rose water
4 eggs, separated (room temp.)
1 cup whole plain yogurt
1 teaspoon baking soda
2 teaspoons baking powder
¼ teaspoon sea salt
1 tablespoon ground cardamom
¼ cup rice flour
1¾ cups unbleached flour

GARNISH
¼ cup ground pistachios
2 tablespoons dried, crushed rose
    petals (optional)

Makes 24 cupcakes
Preparation time: 15 minutes
Cooking time: 25 minutes

کیک یزدی

Cayk-e yazdi

NOTE
This batter will also make an
excellent cake.

1. Place the oven rack in the center and preheat oven to 350°F (180°C). Line 2 muffin pans (capable of holding 12 muffins each) with paper cups.

2 In the mixing bowl of a mixer, blend the oil, sugar, and rose water. While mixer is running, add the egg yolks one by one. Add the yogurt and continue to blend until creamy.

3. Sift together the baking soda, baking powder, salt, cardamom, rice flour, and unbleached flour, and gradually add to the egg yolk mixture. Blend for a few minutes—do not overmix.

4. Beat the egg whites until stiff and fold into the flour mixture using a rubber spatula. Pour the batter into lined molds. Decorate each cupcake with the ground pistachios (and rose petals).

5. Place the pan in the center rack of the oven and bake for 20 to 22 minutes or until a tester comes out clean. Remove the pan from the oven and allow to cool on a cooling rack. Remove the cupcakes from the pan and allow to cool completely on a cooling rack.

6. When ready to serve, arrange the cupcakes on a footed cake dish. *Nush-e Jan!*

OPTIONAL FROSTING

In a mixing bowl, whisk together ½ cup butter and ½ cup cream cheese, at room temperature, for a few minutes. Add 2 tablespoons rose water, ½ teaspoon ground cardamom and 1 cup sifted confectioners' sugar, and continue to whisk until you have a smooth frosting. Use an offset spatula to spread the frosting on the cupcakes. Sprinkle ground pistachios and crushed rose petals on top.

Kermani Pistachio Cake

Makes 8 servings
Preparation time: 20 minutes
Cooking time: 40 minutes

1 cup sugar
1 cup raw shelled pistachios
4 eggs, separated (room temperature)
Zest of 1 orange
1 vanilla bean, split and scraped out, or
   ½ teaspoon vanilla extract
2 tablespoons rose water
1 cup plain yogurt
½ cup oil or unsalted butter
½ teaspoon sea salt

1 teaspoon baking powder
1 teaspoon baking soda
2 cups unbleached all-purpose flour

GARNISH
¼ cup ground raw pistachios
½ teaspoon cardamom powder
¼ cup confectioners' sugar

کیک پسته

Cayk-e pesteh

1. Place the oven rack in the center and preheat oven to 350°F (180°C).

2. Butter an 8-inch spring form cake pan and line the base with parchment paper. Then butter and dust the top of the parchment paper.

3. Pulse the sugar and pistachios in a food processor until finely ground.

4. In a mixing bowl, whisk together the egg yolks, orange zest, vanilla, rose water, yogurt, and oil for about 5 minutes until creamy. Fold in the sugar and pistachio mixture using a rubber spatula.

5. Sift together the salt, baking powder, baking soda, and flour onto a piece of wax paper. Use a rubber spatula to fold into the egg yolk mixture.

6. In a separate mixing bowl, beat the egg whites until they form soft peaks and fold into the flour mixture until you have smooth batter.

7. Gently pour the batter into the cake pan and bake in the preheated oven for 35 to 40 minutes until a tester comes out clean.

8. Remove from the oven and allow to cool on a rack for 10 minutes. Tap the pan to release the cake. Turn the cake out onto the rack and remove the mold, peel off the parchment paper, and turn the cake over. Sprinkle the top with ground pistachios, and dust with cardamom powder and confectioners' sugar. Allow to cool completely overnight, uncovered, to air-dry. Transfer to a serving platter. *Nush-e Jan!*

Life isn't empty:
There's kindness, there are apples, there's faith.
Yes,
While there's still an anemone one must live.
—Sohrab Sepehri

زندگی خالی نیست

مهربانی هست ، سیب هست ، ایمان هست

آری

تا شقایقی هست ، زندگی باید کرد

Date Pie

FILLING
1 cup coarsely chopped walnuts
3 cups pitted dates

ROUX
1 cup oil or unsalted butter
1½ cups unbleached all-purpose
   flour, sifted

DUSTING
1 teaspoon ground cinnamon
2 teaspoons ground cardamom
½ cup confectioners' sugar

GARNISH
1 cup ground raw pistachios or toasted
   shredded coconut

Makes 15 pieces
Preparation time: 30 minutes
Cooking time: 20 minutes

Ranginak

1. In a skillet, toast the walnuts over medium heat for 5 minutes, shaking the skillet back and forth. Set aside and allow to cool.

2. Place a few walnut pieces inside each date.

3. Arrange the dates, packed next to each other, in a flat 9-inch pie dish.

4. To make the roux: In a large deep skillet, heat the oil over medium heat, add the flour, and fry, stirring constantly for about 15 to 20 minutes until the mixture is a golden caramel color (beware to neither undercook nor overcook the flour).

5. Spread the hot roux over the dates, pack down, and smooth out with the back of a spoon to create an even surface.

6. Meanwhile, in a small bowl, mix together the cinnamon, cardamom, and confectioners' sugar. Sprinkle evenly over the pie.

7. Sprinkle the ground pistachios evenly over the surface. Allow to cool thoroughly.

8. Just before serving, cut in small pieces (traditionally diamond shaped). Carefully arrange these on a serving platter or serve on the same plate. *Nush-e Jan!*

Date Bun

Makes 8 scones (4-inches each)
Preparation time: 20 minutes
* plus 2 hours of resting time*
Cooking time: 25 minutes

گلوچه خرما

Kolucheh

SWEET DOUGHS, NO FILLING

Shushtari Bun—Combine 3½ cups unbleached all-purpose flour sifted with 1 teaspoon baking powder, 1 tablespoon nigella seeds, and 1½ cups oil. Cover and allow to rest overnight. Add 1½ cups sugar dissolved in 1½ cups warm water. Knead well (add more flour if necessary), divide into 8 balls, and proceed with step 4 without filling the buns in step 5.

Wheat Sprout Bun—Combine 4 cups wheat sprouts (malt wheat/*sahan*) and 1½ cups oil or sesame paste. Cover and allow to rest overnight. Add 1 cup honey dissolved in ½ cup boiling water. Knead well until you have soft dough (add more wheat flour if necessary. Divide into 8 balls and proceed with step 4 without filling in step 5.

NOTE

Wheat malt flour (sahan) *is flour made from partially germinated wheat grains, which give it a malty flavor.*

DOUGH

3½ cups unbleached all-purpose flour, sifted with 1 teaspoon ground cumin, 1 teaspoon baking powder, ½ teaspoon baking soda, and ½ teaspoon salt
1½ cup oil, butter, or ghee*
¼ cup milk
¼ cup yogurt
¼ cup rose water
2 tablespoons honey

DATE FILLING

2 cups pitted dates
2 cups walnuts
1 cup pistachios
1 teaspoon ground nutmeg
2 teaspoons ground cardamom
1 teaspoon ground cinnamon
1 tablespoon oil
2 tablespoons candied orange peel

GLAZE

½ cup oil

1. To make the dough: Place the sifted flour mixture in a mixing bowl, gradually add the oil, and mix until you have a crumbly dough. Cover the bowl with plastic wrap and allow to rest for 2 hours and up to 24 hours.

2. Gradually add the milk, yogurt, rose water, and honey, and knead for 5 minutes until you have a soft dough that does not stick to your hands (add more flour if necessary). Cover with plastic wrap and allow to rest at room temperature for 1 hour.

3. For the filling, combine all the filling ingredients in a food processor and pulse until you have a soft paste. Divide paste into 8 portions.

4. Place the oven rack in the center and preheat the oven to 350°F (180°C). Line 2 baking sheets with parchment paper. Divide the dough into 8 balls. On a cool, floured surface, roll out each ball into a ½-inch thick by 4-inch diameter disk.

5. Spread 1 portion of the filling over each of the 8 disks. Gently lift up each disk, gather, and pinch the edges to seal the filling inside. Turn disk over and gently press it down using a rolling pin to flatten it out. Use a stamp to decorate the top.

6. Lay the filled buns on the lined baking sheets, 2 inches apart. Brush each bun generously with oil. Repeat for all the buns. Keep chilled until ready to bake.

7. Place the baking sheets in the center rack of the preheated oven. Bake for 15 to 25 minutes until the buns are lightly brown.

8. Remove from the oven and allow to cool. Arrange in a basket and serve with tea. To keep for later use, store in the refrigerator in a covered glass container. *Nush-e Jan!*

VARIATIONS

Apricot Filling—Replace the dates with 2 cups dried apricots and 1 cup confectioners' sugar.

Apple Filling—Replace the dates with 5 peeled, cored apples, and 1 cup confectioners' sugar.

Orange Filling—Replace the dates with 2 cups orange peel (bitterness removed) and 2 cups confectioners' sugar.

Jam Filling—Replace the filling with 2 tablespoons of your favorite jam for each *kolucheh*.

Almond Sanbuseh

Makes 20 pieces
Preparation time: 1 hour plus
*   3 hours for dough to rise*
Cooking time: 20 minutes

DOUGH
Use ready-made puff pastry (thawed)
   or make your own dough (below)
2 egg yolks, beaten
1 cup plain yogurt or sour cream
½ cup oil
¼ cup milk
3 cups unbleached all-purpose flour,
   sifted with 1 teaspoon baking powder

FILLING
1 cup unsalted ground almonds or
   walnuts
½ cup sugar
1 tablespoon ground cardamom
1 tablespoon rose water

DUSTING AND DECORATION
½ cup confectioners' sugar
½ cup ground raw pistachios

Qotab

1. To make the homemade dough: In a mixing bowl, beat the egg yolks until creamy. Add yogurt, oil, and milk, and mix for 2 minutes. Gradually blend in 3 cups sifted flour mixture. Knead for about 5 minutes to produce a dough that does not stick to your hands (add more flour if necessary). Place the dough in a zip-lock bag, seal, and refrigerate for 3 hours.

2. Meanwhile, prepare the filling: In a wide skillet over medium heat, combine the ground almonds and sugar, and stir-fry for 1 minute. Add the cardamom and rose water, and stir-fry for 20 seconds. Set aside to cool.

3. Place the oven rack in the center and preheat oven to 400°F (200°C). Line 2 baking sheets with baking mats or parchment paper.

4. Dust a cool, floured surface. Knead the dough for 1 minute and roll it out to a ⅛-inch thick sheet (if using ready made, thawed puff pastry, spread it out on the floured surface). Use a cookie cutter or the open end of a glass, dipped in flour, to cut out 3-inch-diameter circles of dough. Fill each circle with 2 teaspoons of the almond mixture. Fold each circle into a crescent shape and close the edges with your fingers. Use a fork to crimp around the edges of the dough to double seal the filling inside.

5. Carefully transfer the *sanbusehs* one by one onto the baking sheet. Do not crowd. Bake until golden brown (about 15 to 20 minutes).

6. Remove from oven and place on a cooling rack. When they are cool enough to handle, dust them with confectioners' sugar mixture and sprinkle with pistachios.

7. Arrange the pastries in a pyramid on a serving platter and serve immediately, or store in the refrigerator in a covered glass container. *Nush-e Jan!*

NOTE

Sanbuseh or manti are Persian words that refers to turnovers with sweet or savory fillings They can be made by baking, frying, or steaming.

Rose Water Cream Roll

Makes 1 roll (10-inch)
Preparation time: 15 minutes
Cooking time: 12 minutes plus
  40 minutes of refrigeration

Rulet

BATTER
5 egg yolks
½ cup sugar
2 tablespoons rose water
1 vanilla bean, split and scraped, or
  1 teaspoon vanilla extract
2 tablespoons cake flour
5 egg whites

FILLING
1¼ cups heavy cream
3 tablespoons confectioners' sugar
1 tablespoon rose water
Zest of 1 orange

DECORATION
¼ cup confectioners' sugar for dusting
2 tablespoons dried rose petals
2 tablespoons ground raw pistachios

1. Oil a rimmed baking sheet and line it with parchment paper.

2. Preheat the oven to 400°F (200°C).

3. In a mixing bowl over a double boiler, beat the egg yolks with sugar, rose water, and vanilla for 5 minutes until the mixture is creamy and pale.

4. Fold in the flour using a rubber spatula. Set aside.

5. Whisk the egg whites in a mixing bowl until stiff but not dry. Fold it into the egg yolk mixture using a rubber spatula.

6. Spread the batter evenly on the lined baking sheet and bake for 10 to 12 minutes until lightly golden.

7. Remove from the oven, place on a cooking rack, cover with a damp kitchen towel, and allow to cool for 10 minutes.

8. Meanwhile, line another baking sheet with parchment paper and dust with confectioners' sugar.

9. Remove the kitchen towel and turn the pastry sheet out onto the dusted parchment paper. Peel off the parchment paper from the top and allow to cool.

10. To prepare the filling: Whip the cream, sugar, rose water, and orange zest in a chilled mixing bowl until you have soft peaks.

11. Spread the whipped cream evenly over the pastry sheet. Very gently and carefully, using the parchment paper to help lift it, roll up the pastry sheet from one of the long ends and wrap it in the parchment paper. Wrap in aluminum foil and seal the ends. Chill on a flat surface in the refrigerator for at least 40 minutes (it can also be frozen for later use).

12. Remove from the refrigerator and unwrap the parchment paper. Dust it with sugar and decorate with rose petals and pistachio. Keep chilled until ready to serve. *Nush-e Jan!*

Cream Puffs

Makes: 24 pieces
Preparation time: 20 minutes
Cooking time: 20 minutes

FILLING
1 cup heavy cream (8 ounces)
6 tablespoons sugar
1 tablespoon rose water
Zest of 1 orange

DOUGH
1 cup cold water
¼ teaspoon sea salt
6 tablespoons butter (unsalted), diced
  into small pieces

1 teaspoon vanilla extract
1 tablespoon rose water
1 cup unbleached all-purpose flour,
  triple sifted
4 eggs (room temperature)

DUSTING
1 cup confectioners' sugar
¼ cup ground pistachios
1 tablespoon dried rose petals

نان خامه ای

Nan-e khamehi

1. Line 2 baking sheets with baking mats or parchment paper. Place the oven rack in the middle and preheat oven to 425°F (220°C).

2. To prepare the filling, in a mixing bowl, combine the cream, sugar, rose water, and orange zest, and whip at high speed until soft peaks form. Cover and keep chilled.

3. For the dough, in a heavy-based medium saucepan over medium heat, combine the water, salt, and butter, and bring to a boil, stirring well with a wooden spoon. Add the vanilla and rose water. Reduce heat to *very low* and add the flour, all at once, stirring constantly (3 to 5 minutes) until you have a stiff paste.

4. Remove from heat and continue to stir for 4 to 5 minutes as the dough cools.

5. The temperature of the mixture at this stage is very important; use a candy thermometer to be sure it is around 150°F (65°C). Add 1 egg and stir for 1 minute. The dough becomes glossy and silky. Continue to stir for another minute until the egg has been absorbed and the dough is no longer glossy. Continue adding the eggs, 1 at a time, stirring each time an egg is added until the dough is *no longer glossy.* The dough should be light, smooth, and airy.

6. Use an ice cream scoop to drop the dough onto the prepared baking sheets, leaving 2 inches between each dollop to allow for expansion. Bake for 20 minutes.

7. *Without opening the oven door,* reduce heat to 350°F (180°C) and continue to bake for another 20 to 25 minutes or until the puff pastries are golden.

8. Remove from the oven, poke a whole in the pastry to allow steam to escape, and allow to cool thoroughly on a cooling rack.

9. Prior to serving, use a pastry bag or zip-lock bag to squeeze the chilled filling into the pastry until full. Repeat for all the pastry. Dust with confectioners' sugar, ground pistachios, and rose petals. *Nush-e Jan!*

Window Cookies

DUSTING
1 cup confectioners' sugar
1 teaspoon ground cardamom

½ cup raw ground pistachios

BATTER
5 eggs

½ cup milk
4 tablespoons rose water
½ cup unbleached all-purpose flour
½ cup rice flour
½ cup cornstarch
4 cups oil for frying

Makes 30 cookies
Preparation time: 10 minutes
Cooking time: 30 minutes

نان پنجره ای

Nan-e panjerehi

NOTES

It is important that the rosette iron (mold) be neither too hot nor too cold.

Traditionally, in Iran the mold for this cookie is square.

1. To make the dusting: In a small bowl, combine the confectioners' sugar with the cardamom, mix well, and set aside. Line a baking sheet with two layers of paper towels. Set aside.

2. In a mixing bowl, beat the eggs, milk, and rose water until creamy. Add the flour, rice flour, and cornstarch, and beat well to create a smooth batter. The batter should have the consistency of pancake batter—if it is too runny, add more flour.

3. Heat 4 cups oil over medium heat in a deep saucepan or deep-fat fryer to 375°F (190°C). Heat a rosette iron (mold) by dipping it into the hot oil. Shake the iron well and let the excess oil run off. Dip it immediately into the batter. It is essential to dip the mold into the batter to *just below the top edge.*

4. Plunge the batter-coated iron (mold) into the hot oil. Shake well, as this will help the cookie separate from the iron and lift out easily. Repeat and cook each cookie until golden. Stir the batter frequently to maintain proper consistency.

5. Remove the cookies from the oil with tongs. Place them on the baking sheet lined with paper towels to cool. Repeat this process until all the batter is used up.

6. When the cookies have *cooled*, use a sieve to sprinkle both sides with the dusting mixture. Arrange them on a serving platter. These cookies should be light, crisp, crunchy, and golden. *Nush-e Jan!*

Elephant Ears

DOUGH
2 eggs, ½ cup milk, ¼ cup oil,
3 teaspoons baking powder,

2 cups all-purpose flour, sifted. Or use a package of thawed puff pastry rolled out thin.

گوش فیل

Gush-e fil

NOTE

Use the same steps for frying and ingredients for dusting as for Window Cookies above.

1. In a mixing bowl, beat the eggs until creamy. Add milk, oil, baking powder, and flour, stirring constantly. Knead well on a lightly floured surface to produce a dough that does not stick to your hands (add more flour if necessary). Wrap the dough in plastic wrap and allow to rest in the refrigerator for 30 minutes.

2. Roll out the dough on a cool, floured surface until paper thin. Cut the dough into circles 3 inches in diameter, using a cookie cutter or the rim of a glass. Gather each circle around the middle with your fingers and pinch the center to make it hold its shape like a bow.

3. Drop the bows into the hot oil and fry until lightly golden—about 30 seconds on each side. Drain in a colander. When they are cool, sprinkle with the confectioners' sugar mixture and ground pistachios. *Nush-e Jan!*

Sweet Fritters

Makes 10 pieces
Preparation time: 1 hour
Cooking time: 20 minutes

زولبــیا

Zulbia

SYRUP
5 cups water
4 cups sugar
½ teaspoon alum* dissolved in
  1 tablespoon water, or 1 teaspoon cream
  of tartar, or 1 tablespoon lime juice
¼ cup rose water

BATTER
3 cups water
3¼ cups all-purpose flour, sifted with
  1½ teaspoons baking powder and
  ¼ teaspoon baking soda
2 cups wheat starch or cornstarch
½ cup plain yogurt

4 cups oil for frying

SPECIAL EQUIPMENT
3 large squeeze bottles, or pastry bags

1. To make the syrup: Place the water and sugar in a saucepan and stir well to dissolve the sugar. Bring to a boil over high heat and continue to boil for 2 minutes. Add alum and rose water, and stir well. Remove from heat and allow to cool completely.

2. To prepare batter: In a mixing bowl, thoroughly mix all the ingredients for the batter until smooth and creamy. Cover and set aside for 30 minutes. *Batter should not be too runny. If it is, add more flour—it should have the consistency of honey.*

3. Fill several clean squeeze bottles with batter. Heat the oil in a medium-sized saucepan to medium-high. To test the temperature of oil, drop a spoonful of the batter into the oil. If the batter rises to the top, the oil is ready for frying. If the batter does not hold together, add more flour and mix well.

4. Hold the bottle perpendicularly over the fryer. Squeeze batter into pretzel shapes by twirling it fast, clockwise, directly into the oil. Fry until golden brown on all sides. Use a slotted spoon to gently remove the fritters from the oil and drain. Dip them in the syrup, covering the entire surface.

5. Using another slotted spoon, remove the fritters from the syrup and arrange on a serving platter. (It is helpful to have 2 people cooking at this point, 1 person to place the batter into the oil and the other to remove it.) *Nush-e Jan!*

VARIATION

Ladyfingers *(Bamieh)*—In a small saucepan, combine 1 cup water, ¼ teaspoon salt, 6 tablespoons unsalted butter (diced), and ¼ teaspoon ground saffron dissolved in 2 tablespoons rose water. Bring to a boil over high heat, stirring constantly with a wooden spoon. Reduce heat to very low, add 1 cup flour, stirring constantly for 3 to 5 minutes until you have a stiff paste. Remove from heat and continue to stir for 4 to 5 minutes unit the candy thermometer shows 150°F (65°C). Add 4 eggs, 1 at a time. For each egg stir constantly until the egg is absorbed; repeat for all 4 eggs until the dough is no longer glossy. Transfer the batter to a pastry bag. Heat 4 cups oil in a medium saucepan over high heat until hot. Hold the pastry bag pipe perpendicular over the oil and squeeze out the batter, cutting off 2-inch lengths using scissors and dropping them in the oil. Fry all sides until golden brown, rotating with a slotted spoon. Drain and dip in the syrup from the recipe above. *Nush-e Jan!*

NOTES

Alum, which is aluminum potassium sulfate, which acts to give a glaze to the dough. It is available in Persian stores as zaaj.

Zulbia is associated with the fast-breaking ceremony during the month of Ramazan.

Facing page: Sixteenth-century street vendors making halvas *and fritters.*

White Mulberries

Makes 25 mulberries
Preparation time: 30 minutes

تت

Tut

1½ –2½ cups ground almonds
1 teaspoon ground cardamom
1 cup confectioners' sugar
2 tablespoons rose water

1 tablespoon orange flower water
1 cup sugar
2 tablespoons slivered pistachios

1. In a mixing bowl, combine 1½ cups ground almonds, cardamom, and sugar. Gradually blend in the rose water and orange flower water, stirring constantly to make a soft dough. Add more almonds, if necessary, until the dough no longer sticks to your hands.

2. Divide the dough into 2 balls and roll them out to ¾-inch-thick cords. Use a sharp knife to cut them into 1-inch lengths. Shape them into mulberries, tapering the ends, roll them in sugar, and insert a pistachio sliver in each as a stem.

3. Store them in a tightly covered glass container or cookie jar to avoid drying out. *Nush-e Jan!*

NOTE
You can use a few drops of red food coloring to make red mulberries.

Toasted Caramel Almonds

Makes 12 servings
Preparation time: 5 minutes
Cooking time: 25 minutes

بادام سوخته

Badam sukhteh

½ cup natural whole almonds
1 cup sugar or honey
2 tablespoons hot water

1. Oil a baking sheet and set aside.

2. Dry roast the almonds in a wide skillet over high heat for 1 minute by shaking the skillet. Reduce heat to medium and add the sugar.

3. Allow the sugar to melt over medium heat for 10 to 15 minutes or until it turns to a caramel color. Occasionally shake the skillet and toss the almonds to caramelize them evenly. Add 2 tablespoons hot water, stirring constantly for 5 minutes.

4. Remove from heat and immediately transfer onto the oiled baking sheet. Use two spoons to separate the almonds from each other while the caramel is still soft.

5. Allow to cool until hardened. Transfer to a bowl and serve immediately or keep in an airtight container. *Nush-e Jan!*

VARIATION

Toasted Caramel Walnuts (*Gerdu sukhteh*)—To make toasted caramel walnuts, in step 2 replace the almonds with 2 cups shelled walnuts. In step 3 replace the hot water with 1 cup hot milk. Add ¼ teaspoon ground ginger and ¼ teaspoon ground cinnamon, stirring for 5 to 10 minutes until the milk has evaporated completely. Continue from step 4 above.

Honey Almond Brittle

Makes 25 pieces
Preparation time: 15 minutes
Cooking time: 10 minutes

سوهان عسلی

Sohan asal

BATTER #1

1 cup sugar
3 tablespoons pure honey
4 tablespoons canola oil
1½ cups blanched slivered almonds
¼ teaspoon ground saffron
  dissolved in 2 tablespoons rose water

4 tablespoons chopped raw pistachios
  for decoration

BATTER #2*

½ cup unsalted melted butter
½ teaspoon saffron dissolved in
  ½ cup rose water
⅔ cup unsalted slivered almonds
8 tablespoons sugar
3 tablespoons pure honey

4 tablespoons chopped raw pistachios
  for decoration

Choose either batter #1 or batter #2 depending on which one appeals to you.

BATTER #1

1. Line 2 baking sheets with parchment paper. Place a bowl of ice water next to the stove. In a small, heavy bottomed saucepan, combine the sugar, honey, and oil, and cook over high heat for 5 minutes, *stirring occasionally* with a long wooden spoon. At this stage the sugar should be slightly discolored and foaming lightly around the edges.

2. Add the almonds to the mixture, giving them a quick stir. Continue to cook for 3 to 4 minutes until the mixture is firm, golden, and covered with bubbles.

3. Add the saffron-rose water mixture, gently stirring with a wooden spoon (be careful not to burn yourself). Cook for another 4 to 5 minutes, *stirring occasionally,* until the mixture is a golden brown. Be careful. It should not be dark brown.

4. To be sure the mixture is ready, drop a spoonful of the hot almond mixture in the water: If it hardens immediately and does not stick to your teeth when you try it, the brittle is ready. Remove from heat using a pot holder. Give it a stir, using a wooden spoon.

5. Place about a tablespoon of the mixture on the parchment paper, leaving a 1-inch space between each. Immediately garnish with pinches of pistachios.

6. Allow the brittle to cool completely (at least 1 hour). Remove them from the paper using an offset spatula.

7. Arrange on a serving platter or store in an airtight glass container in a cool place. *Nush-e Jan!*

BATTER #2

In a heavy saucepan, combine all the ingredients for batter #2. Boil over high heat for about 7 to 10 minutes. Stir occasionally with a wooden spoon until the mixture is golden brown. Proceed with step 4 in batter #1 instructions.

Saffron Almond Brittle

Makes 1 sheet
Preparation time: 5 minutes
Cooking time: 15 minutes plus
* 40 minutes for cooling*

½ cup unsalted butter cut into cubes,
  or ¼ cup canola oil
1 cup sugar
¼ cup heavy cream
¼ cup light corn syrup
2 tablespoons raw almonds
⅛ teaspoon ground saffron dissolved
  in 1 tablespoon rose water
½ teaspoon sea salt

GARNISH
2 tablespoons raw chopped pistachios
2 tablespoons barberries,
  rinsed and patted dry

Sohan-e qom

1. Line a baking sheet with parchment paper.

2. In a medium-sized, heavy-bottomed saucepan, combine the butter, sugar, cream, and corn syrup. Cook over medium heat stirring constantly with a wooden spoon and bring to a boil (about 5 minutes). Add the almonds, saffron-rose water mixture, and salt. Increase the heat to medium-high and cook without disturbing for about 7 minutes until the mixture is a deep, golden brown (the color of peanut butter), and the top is bubbling and getting thicker. Remove from heat immediately.

3. Pour out the mixture onto the lined baking sheet immediately. Sprinkle the top with pistachios and barberries. Press down with a large offset spatula. Allow to cool completely (about 40 minutes). Remove from parchment paper and break into pieces. Store in an airtight glass container. *Nush-e Jan!*

Rose Water Lokum

Makes 20 pieces
Preparation time: 15 minutes
Cooking time: 45 minutes, plus
   2 hours for setting

DUSTING
2 tablespoons confectioners' sugar
1 teaspoon ground cardamom
¼ cup cornstarch

SYRUP
2 cups water
2 cups sugar
1 tablespoon fresh lime juice
2 tablespoons rose water or
   1 tablespoon orange blossom water

GELATIN
4 envelopes unflavored gelatin (1 ounce)
¼ cup water
2 tablespoons rose water
½ teaspoon vanilla extract

FILLING
1 cup toasted raw pistachios, or walnuts

GARNISH
¼ cup dried rose petals, crushed
2 tablespoons ground pistachios

راحت الحلقوم

Rahat al-holqum

Rahat al-Lokum *in arabic and* rahat al-holqum *in Persian, means "contentment for the throat." It comes in many varieties, most flavored with lime or orange juice, but some with pomegranates, grapes, or mulberries. The pink type is usually scented with rose water and the green with mint*

1. In a small bowl, combine all the ingredients for the dusting.

2. Line a half pan sheet with parchment paper and sprinkle half of the dusting mixture over it evenly. Set aside.

3. To make the syrup, combine the water, sugar, lime juice, and rose water in a medium-sized, heavy-based saucepan. Bring to a boil over high heat, reduce heat to medium, and simmer for about 30 minutes, stirring occasionally, until the surface is full of bubbles. Remove from heat.

4. To make the gelatin: in a mixing bowl, dissolve the gelatin powder in ¼ cup water, add the rose water and vanilla, and stir well until smooth.

5. Gradually add the gelatin mixture to the syrup. Cook over low heat, stirring constantly with a whisk, for about 5 minutes until the mixture is smooth and has no lumps. Remove from heat. Add the filling and continue to stir for 20 seconds.

6. Spread the mixture in the prepared pan sheet. Sprinkle crushed rose petals over it evenly and dust with the remaining dusting mixture. Garnish it evenly with the ground pistachios.

7. Allow to set, at room temperature, for about 2 hours until set.

8. Cut the *lokum* into 1-inch squares with a sharp, oiled knife. Serve immediately, or store in an airtight glass container and keep refrigerated. *Nush-e Jan!*

Sequin Candies

1 cup sugar
1 tablespoon wine vinegar
Seeds of 2 cardamom pods
⅛ teaspoon ground saffron threads
  dissolved in 1 tablespoon hot water

Makes 20 pieces
Preparation time: 5 minutes
Cooking time: 5 minutes

Pulaki

NOTE
To add a slightly sour flavor, add 1 tablespoon ground lime or sumac powder with the saffron in step 2.

Traditionally these candies are colored with saffron and served with tea, but you can also replace the saffron with various food colorings to make the candies more festive looking.

1. Spread some parchment paper on the counter.

2. Melt the sugar in a small, heavy-bottomed saucepan over high heat. Add the vinegar, the cardamom seeds, and saffron water, and cook for 3 to 5 minutes until caramelized.

3. Once the syrup has caramelized, use a spoon to drip teaspoon-sized dollops of syrup on the paper, 2 inches apart from each other.

4. Allow to cool, peel off from the parchment paper, and serve with tea. These candies should be stored in an airtight glass container in a cool place.

Sesame Brittle

¾ cup sugar
3 tablespoons honey
1 tablespoon rose water
¾ natural or raw (hulled) sesame seeds
¼ teaspoon ground cinnamon
¼ teaspoon ground nutmeg

Makes 6 pieces
Preparation time: 10 minutes
Cooking time: 20 minutes plus
* 30 minutes for cooling*

mama jim jim

This type of brittle—made with honey, sugar, oil, and various nuts and seeds such as pistachios, almonds, and sesame—has been made throughout the Silk Road region since ancient times. In Italy, it is called croccant *(crunchy) and made with almonds; in Iran, it is called* sohan asali *and* mama jimjim *(honey crunch); and in Afghanistan, it is called* hasteh-ye shirin *(sweet kernel).*

1. Line a baking sheet with parchment paper.

2. In a small, heavy-based saucepan, melt the sugar, honey, and rose water over medium heat, stirring occasionally.

3. Add the sesame seeds, cinnamon, and nutmeg. Cook for 15 to 20 minutes, stirring occasionally, until golden brown and caramelized.

4. Pour onto the lined baking sheet and allow to cool. When the brittle has cooled, but before it is hard, use an offset spatula to ease it off the parchment paper and allow it to harden for about 30 minutes. Break off into pieces and store in a tightly covered glass container.

NOTE

Instead of using a baking sheet, you can use small, silver-dollar-sized individual-nonstick molds.

BREADS

مادرم ریحان می‌چیند .

نان و ریحان و پنیر ، آسمانی بی‌ابر ، اطلسی‌هایی تر .

رستگاری نزدیک : لای گل‌های حیاط .

نور در کاسه‌ی مس ، چه نوازش‌ها می‌ریزد !

My mother's picking basil.
Bread and basil and cheese, a
cloudless sky, wet petunias.
Salvation is near, amidst the flowers
in the courtyard.
What caresses the light pours into a
copper goblet!

Sohrab Sepehri

BREADS

A FRIENDLY COMPLAINT

بعد اگر شد ه ست ، اکنون شود   ملک با تو دیگر دوستی مانشود

تاکنایی یکنم ازتو دلم وانشود   دلم ازطینت پرین تو سخت گرفت

هیچ خوانی که خورد حضرت والا نشود   اسم نان بردم و گفتی که که نان داران

همه خوا هیم که بهترشود اما نشود   نان نمی گویم خوبست ولی پست نیست

نان نبود آنچه توی خوردی حاش نشود   اکیه بوی دو سه مه پیش درین ملک خراب

نان سنگک که دگر سبک و صلوا نشود   نان ازین تر تر و خوبتر و شیرین تر

کارین ملک دین و ما شود یا نشود   بس کن ایرج سخن ازنان و ذرباس نمی کردی

My friendship with you, Malek, is possible no longer.
    If it thrives later, so be it! But now its way is barred.
Your good-natured chariness has pained my heart,
    Which, till I voice this complaint, will find no ease.
I happened to mention "bread," provoking your response:
    "What others eat hardly compares to His Grace's bread."
The bread's not extraordinary, true, but neither is it bad;
    We all hope it were better, but hoping won't make it so.
O you who sojourned in this wasteland two months ago or three!
    It wasn't bread you ate then, that can't be denied.
What! Do you seek bread any crisper, sweeter, or finer than this?
    Do you think sangak can turn into cotton candy or halva?

Iraj Mirza

*B*read, called *nan* in Persian, is the staple food of Iran in all regions except around the Caspian, where rice supplants it. Bread is also, along with salt, treated with great respect. In my childhood growing up in Iran, it was considered a sin to let bread fall to the ground or for it to be thrown away.

The main Persian breads are flat breads, but they are well-leavened and light and usually eaten fresh daily. Leftover bread is often used like croutons in soups and with yogurt or milk as if a cereal.

In cities, several types of bread are prepared fresh daily—*barbari, sangak, lavash and taftun*—and every neighborhood has its own specialized bakers for each of these breads. Each type of bread is cooked at a different time of the day. Light and fluffy *barbari,* for example, is usually made in the early mornings and is a favorite breakfast bread (perhaps only the *baguette parisienne* can compete with *nan-e barbari*). Crispy *sangak,* on the other hand, is made throughout the day and is most popular for the evening meal. It is long and oval-shaped, and made with whole wheat flour, baked in a *tanur* (the name for an oven, known as *tandoor* in India) on very hot stones by indirect heat. *Lavash* bread is paper-thin, round, and pliable, and usually eaten at lunch time. It is perfect under and over kababs to keep them warm. In cities, it is made on the walls of *tanurs* by bakers, but in villages it is made on a *saj* (a heated, flat, or domed iron pan) in homes. *Taftun* is thicker than *lavash* and the easiest bread to make.

Several other types of breads, from various regions in Iran, are also made: one is, *nan-e shirmal,* sweet and made with milk; it is usually eaten at tea time. Another is *Nan-e zanjefil,* a thin, crispy, sweet bread made with ginger.

Barbari Bread

Makes 4 loaves
Preparation time: 40 minutes
plus 6 hours of rising time
Cooking time: 12 minutes for
each loaf

نان بربری

Nan-e barbari

NOTES

Barbari bread is a flat oval or round 1 to 1½-inch- thick loaf. It is at its best eaten fresh, as you would a French baguette.

You can also cook this bread without a baking stone by using a baking sheet. Dust it with cornmeal, place a loaf on it, and with damp hands dent the top and sprinkle with seeds. Bake for 12 minutes on one side and 6 minutes on the other.

VARIATION

If you'd like to make *Barbari* bread using whole wheat flour, use about ½ cup less flour.

DOUGH
1 package or 1 tablespoon dry active
  yeast
3 cups warm water
1 tablespoon sugar
2 teaspoons sea salt
6½–8½ cups unbleached all-purpose
  flour, sifted
4 tablespoons oil or butter

½ cup yellow cornmeal, for dusting

DECORATION AND SPECIAL EQUIPMENT
1 tablespoon sesame seeds or
  nigella seeds
Baking stone
Baker's peel

GLAZE
1 teaspoon baking soda
1 teaspoon flour
2 tablespoons warm water

1. In a wide mixing bowl, dissolve the yeast in 3 cups warm water. Add the sugar and set aside for 10 minutes.

2. Add the salt to the yeast mixture and mix well. Gradually add the flour and stir constantly. When 6 cups flour have been added and you have a sticky dough, add 1 tablespoon oil and mix for 2 minutes. Transfer the dough to a floured counter and knead for about 15 minutes, adding the rest of the flour if necessary, until the dough is no longer sticky.

3. Pour 3 tablespoons oil into another wide bowl and place the dough over it. Cover the bowl entirely with a clean damp towel or plastic wrap and allow the dough to rise for 4 hours, without moving it, in a warm, dark place (oven or pantry).

4. Punch the air out of the dough while it is still in the bowl and flip it over. Cover with a clean damp towel and allow to rise 2 more hours.

5. To cook the bread, place a baking stone in the lower level of the oven and preheat the oven to 500°F (260°C) for at least 20 minutes.

6. To make the glaze: In a small bowl, mix together the baking soda, flour, and warm water, and mix well until smooth.

7. With oily hands, divide the dough into 4 balls. Place each ball on a lightly oiled surface. Use an oiled rolling pin to roll each ball out to an approximately 14x8-inch oval shape. Place loaves on an oiled surface, cover with a towel, and leave at room temperature for 20 minutes.

8. Dust the baker's peel with the cornmeal and transfer a loaf to the baker's peel. Brush the glaze down the length of the dough. With damp fingers, make dents on the top of the loaf and sprinkle the tops with seeds.

9. Immediately slide the dough onto the hot baking stone in the oven, cornmeal side down, and bake for 8 minutes. Turn over and bake for 2 to 4 minutes longer. Continue for the remaining loaves.

10. Use the baker's peel to remove the bread from the oven and slide it onto cooling rack. Cover with a clean towel and serve hot. If you are not serving the bread fresh, wrap in aluminum foil and toast before serving. *Nush-e Jan!*

Lavash Bread

Makes: 6 to 8 loaves
Preparation time: 30 minutes,
*   plus 2 hours for dough to rise*
Cooking time: 20 minutes

Nan-e lavash

DOUGH #1
2 teaspoons dry yeast
½ cup warm water
2 tablespoons sugar
1 tablespoon sea salt
½ cup melted unsalted butter
  or oil
2 cups whole milk
5–7 cups unbleached all-purpose
  flour, sifted
2 tablespoons poppy or sesame seeds

DOUGH #2
2 teaspoons dry yeast
2½ cups warm water
2 tablespoons sugar
5–6 cups unbleached flour, sifted
1½ teaspoons sea salt
Oil for handling dough

SPECIAL EQUIPMENT AND DECORATION
Baker's cushion
Saj or wok
¼ cup sesame & nigella seeds

1. Make the baker's cushion by covering a large, round cushion with a clean cotton towel and tie the ends underneath tightly. It should be at least 10 inches in diameter.

2. To make dough #1, in a wide, shallow mixing bowl, dissolve the yeast in ½ cup warm water and add the sugar. Allow to ferment for 10 minutes.

3. Add the salt, butter, and milk, and stir well with a wooden spoon. Gradually add 5 cups flour, 1 cup at a time, stirring constantly for 15 to 20 minutes to make a soft dough. Turn the dough in a well-oiled, wide bowl, to coat it evenly. Cover with a damp towel or plastic wrap and allow to rise for 2 hours at room temperature.

4. Heat a *saj* (cast iron griddle that can be flat or convex) or an upside down wok over a gas flame. Place a plate of flour next to your work area for dipping the dough.

5. Place the dough on a floured surface and knead it for a few minutes. Divide it into 3-inch-diameter balls. Lightly dip a ball of dough in the flour, use a thin rolling pin to roll it out to a 6-inch disk, dip into the flour again, roll out further, and repeat until it is about 8 inches in diameter. Flip the dough across the back of your hand to stretch it a little (to about 10 inches in diameter).

6. Place the dough on the cushion so that it covers the top surface, then pull around the edges of the dough to further stretch it on the cushion and to make it nicely round. Quickly flip dough onto the hot *saj* and sprinkle the seeds on top.

7. Cook the *lavash* for 1 to 2 minutes. Remove from the *saj* and place on a round tray. Continue until all the loaves have been cooked. Cover the *lavash* with a clean towel. Serve it hot, otherwise, wrap the *lavash* in a clean cloth or in a plastic storage bag. *Nush-e Jan!*

VARIATION

Lavash without Milk—Make dough #2: Dissolve yeast in 2½ cups warm water and add the sugar. Allow to ferment for 10 minutes. Gradually add 4 cups flour and the salt, and mix for 5 minutes while adding the remaining flour if needed. This will create a dough that will not stick to your hand. Turn the dough in a well-oiled, wide bowl to coat it evenly in oil. Cover with a damp cloth and allow to rest for 2 hours. Divide the dough into 3-inch-diameter balls. Proceed with step 5 above.

Stone-Baked Bread

Makes 4 loaves
Preparation time: 30 minutes
* plus 1 hour of rising time*
Cooking time: 6–10 minutes for
* each loaf*

بان سنگگ

Nan-e sangak

2 teaspoons dry yeast
2½ cups warm water
1½ teaspoons sea salt
4 cups whole wheat flour mixed with
   1½ cups unbleached all-purpose
   white flour, sifted

GLAZE
2 tablespoons water
½ teaspoon baking soda

GARNISH
4 tablespoons sesame, poppy,
   cumin, or nigella seeds

Oil for handling dough

SPECIAL EQUIPMENT
Baking stone
Baker's peel

A sangak baker in Tehran told me that the secret to this bread is a very hot tanur. The bread is cooked by indirect heat on hot gravel. If he turns his tanur off, it takes 7 hours to get back to the right temperature. The amount of water is also dependent on the seasons (summer needs less water). The mother yeast for sangak bread is controlled by the bakers' union. The dough is prepared in wide clay containers (taghar).

1. In a wide, clay mixing bowl, dissolve the yeast in 2½ cups warm water and let stand for 10 minutes.

2. Add salt, mix well, and gradually add 4½ cups mixed flour, 1 cup at a time. Mix with a wooden spoon for 10 minutes to create a sticky dough (add more flour if necessary). Allow to rest for 10 minutes.

3. Turn the dough in a well-oiled, wide bowl to ensure it is evenly coated. Cover the bowl with a damp towel or plastic wrap and let the dough rise in a warm, dark place for 1 hour.

4. Place the baking stone in the lower level of the oven.

5. Preheat the oven to 500°F (260°C)—the stone needs to be good and hot. Remove the dough from the bowl and knead with oiled hands for another 10 to 15 minutes.

6. On an oiled surface, divide the dough into 4 balls.

7. Lightly flour the baker's peel, place a dough ball on the peel, and, using an oiled rolling pin, flatten each ball until it is ¼ inch thick. Perforate the top of each loaf with wet fingers. Mix the water and baking soda for the glaze and apply it to the dough with a brush. Sprinkle with seeds.

8. Pull out the oven rack with the stone. Slide 1 loaf on the hot stone and quickly return the rack to the oven. Bake for 1 minute, then press down on the dough with the baker's peel. Cook for 3 to 5 minutes until crisp and golden.

9. Remove the bread from the stone with the aid of a baker's peel. Cover it with a clean towel. Continue until all the loaves have been baked. Serve hot. If not serving right away, wrap in aluminum foil. Toast it just before serving. *Nush-e Jan!*

میوه کال شد را آن روز همی جویدم در خواب .

آب بی فلسفه می خوردم .

توت بی دانشی می چیدم .

تا نار ترکی برمی داشت ، دست فواره خواهش می شد .

In dreams that day I chewed on God's unripe fruit.
I drank a water without philosophy;
I picked a berry without knowledge.
No sooner did a pomegranate crack open than it became the
hand of yearning.

Sohrab Sepehri

WHAT A PLEASANT FRIDAY EVE IT WAS

چه صال خوش دشنه جمعهٔ خوشی دیدیم   چه بوی ارشب هر جمعه حال ما این بو

تمام حرف وفا دلبری وصفا در چشم   نه درسری هوی بد نه دردلی کین بو

انار وسیب و بهٔ و برتقال نارنگی   کبابی بس خوب و شرابی قزوین بو

معاشران همه خوش روی ومهربان بودند   یکی نبود که بدخوی ورشت آیین بو

بتول شور به مجلس فکند با ویلن   قمر مطابق او در غنا رشیرین بو

What good cheer! What a pleasant Friday eve it was!
Oh, if every Friday eve would find it so!
Only friendly words held sway, and glances of good will,
No mind was unfaithful, nor spiteful any heart.
There were pomegranates and apples, quinces and oranges and tangerines.
There was sumptuous lamb kabab and the wine of Qazvin.
Our companions were all personable and gentle;
Not one present was ill-disposed or disagreeable.
Batul and her violin raised a clamor in the crowd.
While Qamar, sitting across, sweetly crooned.

Iraj Mirza

Sweet Gingerbread

1 cup warm water
¼ cup vegetable oil
¼ cup molasses
¼ cup honey
3-inch fresh ginger, grated
¾ cup brown sugar
1 hot red chili, chopped, or ½ teaspoon
 chili paste

4–5 cups unbleached all-purpose flour
1 teaspoon baking powder
½ teaspoon baking soda
½ teaspoon sea salt
½ teaspoon ground cinnamon

DECORATION
¼ cup sesame seeds

Makes 4 loaves
Preparation time: 15 minutes plus
 20 minutes of resting time
Cooking time: 7–10 minutes for
 each loaf

Nan-e qandi

1. In a wide mixing bowl, combine the water, oil, molasses, honey, ginger, sugar, and chili, and stir well.

2. Sift together 4 cups flour, baking powder, baking soda, salt, and cinnamon onto a piece of wax paper, and gradually add it to the mixing bowl, one cup at a time. Mix with a wooden spoon, adding more flour as needed, until you have a soft dough (5 to 10 minutes).

3. Divide the dough into 4 equal balls, cover with a damp dish towel, and allow to rest for 20 minutes.

4. Preheat the oven to 400°F (200°C) and line a baking sheet with parchment paper.

5. Roll out 1 ball on a floured surface to form a 14x5x¼-inch-thick oval loaf.

6. Immediately place the rolled out dough on the baking sheet, paint the dough with water, stripe the surface with a fork, and sprinkle with sesame seeds. Bake for 7 to 10 minutes until a tester comes out clean. Repeat for all the dough.

7. Remove from the oven and allow to cool. This bread should be oval and brittle, and taste sweet and spicy. *Nush-e Jan!*

Saveh Sweet Saffron Bread

Makes 4 loaves
Preparation time: 15 minutes
plus 6–26 hours of resting
Cooking time: 25–30 minutes

1 package or 1 tablespoon active dry
  yeast
½ cup warm water
2 cups sugar
1½ cups warm milk
6½–8½ cups unbleached all-purpose
  flour
1 teaspoon baking soda
1 teaspoon salt
⅓ cup oil for handling dough

GLAZE
3 egg yolks
1 teaspoon ground saffron threads
  dissolved in 4 tablespoons rose water

DECORATION
2 tablespoons poppy, sesame, or
  nigella seeds

نان شیرمال

Nan-e shirmal

1. In a large mixing bowl, dissolve the yeast in ½ cup warm water. Add the sugar and allow to rest for 10 minutes undisturbed. Add the milk and stir with a wooden spoon until creamy.

2. Sift together the flour, baking soda, and salt into a bowl. Gradually add it, one cup at a time, to the yeast mixture, stirring constantly until 6 cups flour have been added and you have a sticky dough. Add 1 tablespoon oil and stir for 2 minutes longer.

3. Transfer the dough to a lightly floured work surface and knead dough for 15 minutes. Dust with more flour as needed.

4. Turn the dough in an oiled, wide bowl to ensure it is evenly coated. Cover with plastic wrap and allow to rise in a warm, dark place for 4 to 24 hours.

5. Punch the air out of the dough while it is still in the bowl. Flip it over, cover, and allow to rise for another 2 hours.

6. Preheat the oven to 350°F (180°C). Line 2 baking sheets with parchment paper.

7. Divide the dough into 4 balls. Use an oiled rolling pin to roll out each ball on a lightly oiled surface to 8-inch-diameter loaves. Transfer the loaves to the lined baking sheets.

8. Prepare the glaze by whisking together the egg yolks and saffron-rose water in a bowl. Generously brush the tops of each loaf with the glaze and sprinkle with poppy seeds.

9. Bake in the preheated oven for 25 to 30 minutes until a tester comes out clean.

10. Remove the baking sheets from the oven and allow to cool on a cooling rack. *Nush-e Jan!*

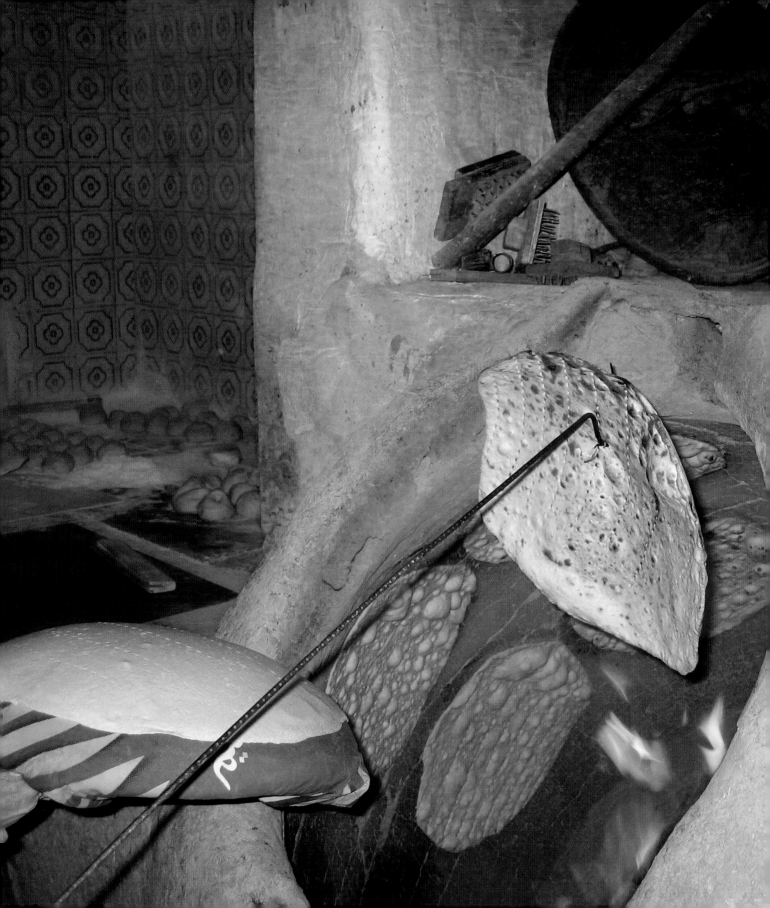

Taftun Flat Bread

2 teaspoons active dry yeast
1 cup warm milk or water
2 teaspoons sugar or honey
¼ cup plain yogurt beaten with 1 egg
¼ cup vegetable oil

2½–3½ cups unbleached all-purpose
flour mixed with 1½ teaspoons sea
salt and 1 teaspoon baking powder,
sifted into a bowl
2 tablespoons nigella seeds

Makes 4 loaves
Preparation time: 25 minutes
plus 4½ hours for the
dough to rise
Cooking time: 4 minutes for
each loaf

Nan-e taftun

1. In a small bowl, dissolve the yeast in the warm milk, add the sugar, and allow to rest for 10 minutes undisturbed.

2. Add the yogurt mixture and 2 tablespoons oil, and stir well.

3. Place 2½ cups flour, salt, and baking powder mixture in the mixing bowl of a dough maker. Gradually add the dissolved yeast while the machine is running. Continue to mix until dough forms into a ball (about 5 minutes). Allow to rest in the machine for 5 minutes, then continue to mix for another minute.

4. Turn out the dough onto a lightly floured work surface and knead in the nigella seeds. Continue to knead for 3 to 5 minutes until you have a smooth and elastic dough. Dust with more flour, if needed.

5. Turn the dough in a well-oiled bowl to ensure it is coated evenly with oil. Cover with plastic wrap and allow it to rise at room temperature for at least 4 hours (or overnight) until double in size (the dough should spring back when pushed in with your finger).

6. Turn out the dough onto a lightly floured work surface, punch down, cover and allow to rest for 30 minutes.

7. Divide the dough into 4 equal balls. Preheat the oven to 500°F (260°C).

8. Flatten 1 ball into an 8-inch circle and place it on an oiled baking sheet. Stripe the dough using a fork. Bake for 2 to 4 minutes until golden brown on top. Repeat for the remaining dough.

9. Make a pile and cover with a clean kitchen cloth until ready to eat. *Nush-e Jan!*

Armenian Sweet Bread

Makes 3 loaves
Preparation time: 20 minutes
* plus rising time overnight*
Cooking time: 35–40 minutes

1 package or 1 tablespoon dry yeast
¼ cup warm water
3 eggs
1½ cups sugar
1 tablespoon honey
2 teaspoons ground *mahlab*
1 cup whole milk
1 cup unsalted butter, melted, or oil

4½–5½ cups cake flour, sifted with
  1 teaspoon baking powder

GLAZE
2 egg yolks
1 tablespoon hot water

DECORATION
3 tablespoons poppy seeds or sugar

Nan-e gisu

NOTES

You could prepare the dough the night before. This sweet bread freezes well and comes in handy when you have unexpected guests. It goes well with butter, fig preserves, or by itself.

Mahlab powder is made from the ground seeds of the fruit of the mahlab tree, which is related to the rose family. It is used for aromatic flavor and is available in specialty food stores.

This bread, associated with Easter and made by our neighborhood Armenian bakery during my childhood, was a special breakfast treat for us, when we'd eat it with homemade fig jam.

1. In a wide mixing bowl, dissolve the yeast in ¼ cup warm water. Set aside for 10 minutes.

2. Add the eggs, sugar, honey, *mahlab*, milk, and butter, stirring constantly for 2 minutes with a wooden spoon.

3. Gradually add 4½ cups of the flour mixture, 1 cup at a time, stirring constantly for 10 to 15 minutes until you have a sticky dough.

4. Turn out the dough on a floured surface and knead for 5 to 10 minutes, adding more flour as needed. Turn the dough in a well-oiled bowl to ensure it is coated evenly in oil. Cover with plastic wrap and allow it to rise overnight.

5. On a floured surface, divide the dough into 3 balls. Working with 1 ball of dough at a time, divide it into 3 equal parts. Roll each part into a rope about 12 inches long. Secure the ropes at one end, then braid the 3 equal ropes together. Place this braid on a baking sheet lined with parchment paper.

6. Follow the same procedure to braid the 2 remaining dough balls. Cover and let the braids rise again for another hour.

7. Preheat oven to 350°F (180°C). Make the glaze in small bowl by mixing together the egg yolks and water. Brush the tops with the glaze and sprinkle the top with poppy seeds or sugar.

8. Place the baking sheets, 1 at a time, in the oven, and bake for 35 to 40 minutes until bread is golden brown and a tester comes out clean. Remove from the oven and allow to cool on a cooling rack. Serve either warm or at room temperature. *Nush-e Jan!*

Armenian Christmas Pastry

Makes: 24 pieces
Preparation time: 30 minutes
  plus overnight refrigeration
Cooking time: 30 minutes

Nazuk or Gata

1 package or 1 tablespoon dry yeast
1 cup sour cream
1 cup unsalted butter
1 egg
1 tablespoon vegetable oil
1 tablespoon vinegar
3–3½ cups all-purpose flour, sifted

FILLING
1 cup butter, melted
2 cups all-purpose flour, sifted
1¼ cups sugar
1 teaspoon vanilla

1 cup butter, melted

GLAZE
2 egg yolks, beaten
1 teaspoon yogurt

1. In a mixing bowl, combine the yeast with 1 cup sour cream and allow to rest for 10 minutes.

2. Add butter and stir well. Add the egg, oil, and vinegar, and stir well.

3. Gradually add 3 cups flour and continue to stir with a wooden spoon until a soft dough forms.

4. Turn out the dough onto a floured work surface and knead for 10 to 15 minutes. Add more flour as needed until dough is smooth and firm so that it does not stick to your hands. Gather dough into a ball, place it in a zip-lock storage bag, and refrigerate overnight.

5. To make the filling: In a wide mixing bowl, mix together all the ingredients for the filling and stir constantly for about 1 minute or until a soft dough is created. Cover and set aside.

6. Preheat oven to 350°F (180°C). Line a baking sheet with parchment paper.

7. Remove dough from the refrigerator and divide it into 8 equal balls. Place each ball on a lightly floured working surface.

8. Roll each ball out to as thin a rectangle as possible (about 10x6 inches). Paint each rectangle with melted butter.

9. Spread ¼ cup filling into the center of each rectangle and use a rolling pin to gently roll out the filling over the dough.

10. Fold in about ½ inch of the rectangle on each side. Roll up dough into a cylinder.

11. Place rolling pin on the pastry roll and flatten it slightly lengthwise. Cut the roll diagonally with a serrated knife into 2-inch slices.

12. Place pastry about 2 inches apart on a lined baking sheet.

13. In a small bowl, mix the egg yolks and yogurt to make the glaze. Paint the surface of each pastry with the glaze.

14. Place baking sheet in the middle rack of the oven and bake for 15 to 30 minutes or until golden brown. Transfer the baking sheet from oven and allow to cool on a cooling rack. *Nush-e Jan!*

KING KHOSROW AND HIS KNIGHT

In this tale, a youth named Vashpur presents himself to the greatest of Sasanian kings. Vashpur is well-born, well-schooled, skilled in the arts of war and peace alike, but his family has been ruined; he therefore asks King Khosrow to admit him to the royal court and volunteers for any test to prove his worth.

"My father died during my childhood, and I am the only son. I received from my parents my hereditary share, stately riches in cash and food of all kinds, and beautiful fine clothes. I have learned by heart all great works of literature and history and have become well versed in learned speech. My skill in riding, archery, and sword fighting is such that others must be fortunate to escape my arrow. I am also skillful in the *tar* and *dotar*. In the game of chess I am superior to my comrades. Now my family is ruined, and my mother has departed this life. If it pleases you put me to the test in anything whatsoever."

King Khosrow chooses to test the youth on his knowledge of cuisine (and of music, scents, women, and riding animals). Vashpur's answers provide hints of a very rarefied school of cookery, elements of which are recognizable in modern Iranian cuisine:

The king asks, "Which fowl is the finest and the most savory?" The boy replies: "May you be immortal! The pheasant, and the hen, and the gray partridge with the white tail and the red wings, and the lark, and the male crane. But with the male domestic fowl, that has been fed on hemp-seeds and the butter of olives, no fowl can contest. First, on the day it is killed one must chase and frighten it, and then must hang it up by its trunk, and on the second day must hang it by the neck, and roast it on a spit."

Among the best sweets are almond pastry and walnut pastry for summer, and almond and peach for winter, but the best dessert of all is a jelly made from the juice of the apple and the quince. The best shelled fruits include the coconut of India and Iran's own pistachios, and Vashpur praises dates stuffed with walnuts, pistachios, and peaches.

The king of kings was impressed and gave the boy a position with dignity.

From a fourth-century Sasanian coming-of-age manual

PRESERVES & PICKLES

مرباها

ترشی ها

PRESERVES & PICKLES

*P*ersian preserve recipes are special because they combine fruit, flower, and spice to create a perfect sweetness. Besides being eaten with bread and butter, which is most often the case, these preserves are good with yogurt, to sweeten tea, or to eat on their own as a dessert.

GOLDEN RULES FOR COOKING PRESERVES

1. Use good-quality fruit at the peak of the season.

2. Fruit should not be overripe and should have no bruises or blemishes.

3. Usually, for every pound of prepared fruit, you will need 1 pound of sugar.

4. Always store your preserves in a cool, dark place.

Photo left: Orange Peel Preserve, recipe on page 467

Sour Cherry Preserve

3 pounds sour cherries
 (or 2 pounds pitted sour cherries,
 fresh or frozen)
5 cups sugar
1 tablespoon lime juice
¼ teaspoon vanilla

Makes 2 jars (½ pint each)
Preparation time: 1 hour plus
 overnight macerating
Cooking time: 50 minutes

Moraba-ye albalu

NOTE

If using sour cherries in light syrup, drain the cherries first. Use ¼ cup sugar for every jar (1 pound) of cherries. Cook for 35 minutes over medium-high heat.

This preserve can also be made with unpitted sour cherries. I have fond childhood memories of coming home from school in the afternoon and putting spoonfuls of it in my tea instead of sugar (and then eating them with a spoon out of the tea glass, when I had drunk the tea). Sometimes, for a snack we'd put spoonfuls of the syrupy red sour cherry jewels over thick, white, creamy yogurt.

1. Wash cherries and remove stems and pits. Place the cherries and sugar in large laminated pot, cover, and allow to macerate overnight.

2. Place pot of cherries over high heat and bring to a boil. Skim the foam as it forms. Reduce heat to medium and simmer for about 35 minutes. Gently stir on occasion to prevent burning. Add the lime juice and vanilla, and simmer over medium heat for another 5 to 10 minutes until the syrup is thick enough to coat the back of a spoon. Remove from heat.

3. Sterilize jelly jars in boiling water, drain, and allow to dry thoroughly. Fill the jars with hot preserves and then seal the jars. Store in a cool, dark place. *Nush-e Jan!*

Quince Preserve

2 pounds quinces
  (3 medium-sized quinces)
1½ cups water
4 cups sugar
¼ teaspoon vanilla extract
1 cinnamon stick
4 tablespoons fresh lime juice

Makes 2 jars (½ pint each)
Preparation time: 25 minutes
Cooking time: 2 hours 45 minutes

Moraba-ye beh

1. Quarter the quinces and remove the cores. Slice the quarters into wedges. Place in a container full of cold water with a splash of vinegar to prevent the quince wedges from turning black. Drain and rinse.

2. Place quince wedges and 1½ cups water in a pot (copper pots are ideal for this). Bring to a boil over high heat, reduce heat to low, cover, and simmer for 15 minutes.

3. Add the sugar, vanilla extract, and cinnamon stick. To steep the quince, wrap the lid of the pot with a clean dish towel and cover firmly. Simmer over low heat for 1 hour.

4. Add lime juice. Cover and simmer for 1¼ to 1½ hours more over low heat, stirring gently from time to time, until the syrup has thickened and the quince has turned red. Remove from heat and allow to cool.

5. Sterilize jelly jars in boiling water, drain, and allow to dry. Fill the jars with hot preserves and then seal the jars. Store in a cool, dark place. *Nush-e Jan!*

PHOTO

Quince and Lime Syrup (Sharbat-e behlimu, *page 499*)
and Quince Preserve (Moraba-ye beh)

Fig Preserve

2 pounds firm, seedless, fresh green figs
3 cups sugar
2 cups water

2 tablespoons lime juice
½ teaspoon ground cardamom
2 tablespoons rose water
½ teaspoon vanilla extract

Makes 2 jars (½ pint each)
Preparation time: 5 minutes
  plus overnight macerating
Cooking time: 1 hour

1. Wash the figs, but *do not* remove the stems.

2. Place the figs and sugar in alternating layers in a laminated pot. Cover and macerate overnight.

3. Add the water to the pot, bring to a boil, cover, and let simmer for 45 minutes over medium heat. Add cardamom, vanilla extract, rose water, and lime juice. Simmer for 5 to 10 minutes over medium heat until syrup has thickened enough to coat the back of a spoon.

4. Sterilize jelly jars in boiling water, drain, and allow to dry. Fill the jars with hot preserves and then seal the jars. Store in a cool, dark place. *Nush-e Jan!*

Moraba-ye anjir

<hr />

VARIATION

Apricot Preserve—Replace figs with apricots (washed, halved, and stones removed). Continue with step 2.

Golden Plum Preserve

2 pounds golden plums
4 cups brown sugar
1 cup water

2 tablespoons lime juice
1 teaspoon ground cardamom
2 tablespoons rose water

Makes 2 jars (½ pint each)
Preparation time: 15 minutes
  plus overnight macerating
Cooking time: 55 minutes

1. Wash and peel plums, but do not remove stems (to peel plums more quickly, blanch them for 1 minute in boiling water, drain, and rinse in cold water—the skin will come off easily.)

2. Place the sugar and water in a laminated pot and bring to a boil. Reduce heat to medium and simmer for 10 minutes.

3. Add the plums and simmer uncovered for 30 to 35 minutes over medium heat (stirring gently from time to time) until the syrup has thickened enough to coat the back of a spoon. Add lime juice, cardamom, rose water, and vanilla extract, and simmer for 2 more minutes. Remove from heat.

4. Sterilize jelly jars in boiling water. Drain and allow to dry thoroughly. Fill the jars with jam and then seal the jars tightly. Store in a cool, dark place. *Nush-e Jan!*

Moraba-ye alu zard

Carrot Preserve

2 pounds carrots
½ cup slivered orange peel (optional)
5 cups sugar
2 cups water
2 tablespoons fresh lime juice

½ teaspoon ground cardamom
½ cup rose water
½ cup slivered pistachios

Makes 2 jars (½ pint each)
Preparation time: 25 minutes
Cooking time: 1 hour

مُربّای هویج

Moraba-ye havij

1. Scrape, wash, drain, and julienne the carrots.

2. To remove bitterness from the orange peel, place in a saucepan with water, cover, bring to a boil, and boil for 5 minutes, drain, and rinse in cold water.

3. In a heavy, laminated pot, combine the sugar, 2 cups water, orange peel, and carrots. Bring to a boil over high heat, reduce the heat to medium, and simmer for 35 minutes. Add the lime juice, cardamom, rose water, and pistachios, and simmer over medium heat for 5 to 10 minutes or until the syrup has thickened enough to coat the back of a spoon. Remove from heat.

4. Sterilize jelly jars in boiling water and dry them. Fill the jars with the hot preserve and then seal the jars. Store in a cool, dark place. *Nush-e Jan!*

Spring Pistachio Peel Preserve

1 pound fresh pistachio peels (hulls)
2 tablespoons fresh lime juice
2 cups sugar
1 cup water
1 tablespoon ground cardamom

Makes 1 jar (½ pint)
Preparation time: 35 minutes
* plus 24 hours soaking*
Cooking time: 1 hour

مربای پوست پسته

Moraba-ye pust-e pesteh

1. Select spotless, white, whole peels (for best results use Akbari pistachio peels if available). Place hulls in a container and cover with water. Let stand for 24 hours (changing the water twice). Drain and rinse thoroughly. Set aside.

2. Meanwhile, place sugar, water, and lime juice in a medium-sized pot and bring to a boil. Reduce heat to medium and simmer for about 5 minutes until the sugar has dissolved.

3. Add the pistachio peels and simmer for 30 to 40 minutes, or until the syrup is thick enough to coat the back of a spoon. Add the cardamom, remove from heat, and allow to cool.

4. Sterilize jelly jars in boiling water. Drain and let dry. Fill the jars with the hot jelly and the seal the jars. Store in a cool, dark place. *Nush-e Jan!*

Rose Petal Preserve

2 cups dried rose petals
¼ cup lime juice
2 cups sugar

2 cups water
2 tablespoons rose water
1 cup slivered pistachios

Makes 1 jar (½ pint)
Preparation time: 35 minutes
Cooking time: 1 hour

1. Place rose petals in a pot, cover with water, and bring to a boil. Drain in a colander. Sprinkle with 1 tablespoon lime juice and set aside.

2. Meanwhile, place sugar and water in a laminated pot. Bring to a boil, reduce the heat, and let simmer over medium heat for 40 minutes.

3. Dry roast the petals in a wide skillet for a few minutes, stirring constantly.

4. Add the petals to the syrup. Add the rest of the lime juice, rose water, and pistachios. Stir gently, cover, and simmer over medium heat for 5 minutes or until the syrup is thick enough to coat the back of a spoon. Remove from heat and allow to cool.

5. Sterilize jelly jars in boiling water. Drain and let dry. Fill the jars with the hot jelly and then seal the jars. Store in a cool, dark place. *Nush-e Jan!*

Moraba-ye gol-e Mohammadi

Orange Blossom Preserve

1 pound fresh or 2 cups dried orange
   blossoms
3½ cups sugar
3 cups water

2 tablespoons fresh lime juice
1 tablespoon orange blossom water (if
   using dried blossoms)

Makes 1 jar (½ pint)
Preparation time: 35 minutes
*   plus 1 day of marination*
Cooking time: 1 hour

1. Carefully wash the orange blossoms, separate the petals, and soak in a bowl of cold water. Set in refrigerator for a day, changing the water several times.

2. Bring 4 cups of water to a boil in a laminated pan over high heat. Add the blossoms, reduce heat, and simmer for 10 minutes. Drain in a colander and rinse with cold water. This step is essential to remove any traces of bitterness.

3. In a heavy saucepan, bring the sugar and 3 cups water to a boil. Add orange blossom petals, cover, and simmer for 45 minutes or until the syrup has thickened enough to coat the back of a spoon. Add lime juice (if using dried blossoms, add 1 tablespoon orange blossom water) and simmer for 5 more minutes. Remove from heat.

4. Sterilize jelly jars in boiling water. Drain and let dry. Fill the jars with the hot preserves and then seal the jars. Store in a cool, dark place. *Nush-e Jan!*

Moraba-ye bahar narenj

Whole Lady Apple Preserve

2 pounds Lady Apples with stems
2 cups water
4 cups sugar
½ teaspoon ground cardamom

¼ cup rose water
¼ cup fresh lime juice
2 tablespoons blanched almonds

Makes 1 jar (1 pint)
Preparation time: 15 minutes
Cooking time: 50 minutes

مربای سیب

Moraba-ye sib

1. Wash and peel the apples (keep them whole and do not remove the stems), core the apples from the bottom, and then place the cored apples in a large container of water with 2 tablespoons vinegar. Drain when ready to cook.

2. Place the apples in a laminated pot. Cover with 2 cups water. Bring to a boil. Reduce the heat to medium and simmer for about 5 minutes until the apples are tender. Use a skimmer to remove the apples from the pan. Set aside.

3. Add the sugar to the pot and bring to a boil. Simmer for 10 minutes over low heat.

4. Return the apples to the pan, then add cardamom and rose water. Cook for 30 minutes over medium heat. Add the lime juice and almonds, and simmer for 5 minutes, stirring gently from time to time, until the syrup has thickened enough to coat the back of a spoon. Remove from heat.

5. Sterilize jelly jars in boiling water. Drain and dry. Fill the jars with hot preserves and then seal the jars. Store in a cool, dark place. *Nush-e Jan!*

Barberry Preserve

2 cups dried barberries, washed
  and cleaned
2½ cups pure apple cider
2 cups brown sugar
½ teaspoon cinnamon

½ teaspoon cardamom powder
¼ teaspoon ground saffron dissolved in
  2 tablespoons rose water
2 tablespoons fresh lime juice

Makes 2 jars (less than 1 pint)
Preparation time: 30 minutes
Cooking time: 50 minutes

مربای زرشک

Moraba-ye zereshk

1. In a laminated pot, place the barberries and apple cider and bring to a boil over high heat.

2. Add the sugar, cinnamon, cardamom, saffron-rose water, and lime juice. Bring back to a boil, stirring frequently. Simmer over medium heat for 35 to 40 minutes until the syrup is thick enough to coat the back of a spoon.

3. Sterilize jelly jars in boiling water. Drain and dry thoroughly. Fill the jars with preserves and then seal the jars tightly. Store in a cool, dark place. *Nush-e Jan!*

Bitter Orange Preserve

Makes 2 jars (½ pint each)
Preparation time: 30 minutes
*   plus 24 hours of soaking*
Cooking time: 1 hour

مُربّای نارنج

Moraba-ye narenj

6 bitter oranges
1 tablespoon bitter orange seeds
3 cups water

8 cups sugar

GARNISH
¼ cup raw shelled pistachios

1. Scrub orange skins lightly so that they are smooth. Make sure that any black spots on the skin are removed.

2. Quarter each orange without entirely separating it—leave about ¼ inch intact at the bottom. Remove the seeds and place 1 tablespoon of them in a cheesecloth, tying the corners so that the seeds do not fall out. Soak in 3 cups water, setting aside for later use.

3. Soak the oranges in a container full of water for 24 hours, changing the water twice. In a saucepan, bring 8 cups water to a boil over high heat. Add the oranges, bring back to a boil, and boil for 15 minutes. Drain and rinse with cold water. Repeat 3 times (boil, drain and rinse) to soften the peels and remove any bitterness.

4. In a large, laminated pot, arrange the oranges side by side. Sprinkle the sugar all over the oranges. Squeeze out cheese cloth and discard it. Pour the water over the oranges. Partially cover and simmer for 30 to 45 minutes over low heat until the oranges become glossy and the syrup is thick enough to coat the back of a spoon. Add the pistachios. Remove from heat, cover, and allow to rest overnight.

5. Sterilize jars in boiling water. Drain and dry thoroughly. Place the oranges, 1 at a time, in the sterilized jars, leaving the syrup in the pot. Test the syrup. If it is not thick enough to coat the back of a spoon, simmer for 5 to 10 minutes until it has thickened. Fill the jars with the hot syrup.

6. Seal jars tightly and store in a cool, dark place. *Nush-e Jan!*

Bitter Orange Peel Preserve

Makes 1 jar (1 pint)
Preparation time: 30 minutes
*   plus soaking overnight*
Cooking time: 35 minutes

مُربّای خلال پوست نارنج

Moraba-ye khalal-e
*   pust-e narenj*

See photo on page 456

Peel of 9 bitter or sweet oranges
    (about ½ pound of peel)
Juice of 9 oranges (3 cups)

2 cups sugar
2 tablespoons lime juice
Seeds of 5 cardamom pods

1. Wash and peel oranges in a continuous strip using a peeler. In a medium sauce-pan, bring 8 cups water to a boil and add the peels. Boil for 15 minutes, drain, and rinse with cold water. Repeat 3 times (boil, drain and rinse—if using sweet oranges, once is enough) to soften the peels and remove bitterness. Roll each strip of orange peel into a rosebud shape. Use a toothpick to keep it together. Soak in a container of cold water overnight. Drain when ready to cook.

2. Bring the orange juice, 2 cups water, and sugar to a boil. Reduce heat to low. Add the lime juice, cardamom seeds, and orange buds, and simmer for 55 minutes or until the orange peel buds are glossy, transparent, and tender, and the syrup is thick enough to coat the back of a spoon.

3. Fill sterilized jar with hot preserves. Seal tightly and store. *Nush-e Jan!*

Watermelon Skin Preserve

1 large watermelon
  (2 pounds white flesh)
¼ cup pickling lime
8 cups water

SYRUP

3 cups water
5 cups sugar
Seeds of 5 cardamom pods
2 tablespoons fresh lime juice
¼ cup rose water

*Makes 2 jars (½ pint each)
Preparation time: 30 minutes
  plus 5 hours of soaking
Cooking time: 1 hour*

مربای پوست هندوانه

*Moraba-ye pust-e
hendevaneh*

1. Cut the watermelon into 4 equal quarters. Remove the red parts—enjoy eating them. Use a knife and then a peeler to cut off a thin layer of the shiny green rind and discard it, keeping the white flesh (2 pounds).

2. Place the white watermelon flesh on a flat surface. Stamp out shapes using your favorite cookie cutters or cut into 1-inch pieces.

3. In a laminated container (do not use aluminum), dissolve ¼ cup pickling lime in 8 cups water, stir well, and allow to sit for 10 minutes. Add the white watermelon flesh to the pickling lime and allow to soak for 2 hours or overnight (this helps to make it crisp). Remove the watermelon using a slotted spoon and discard the lime water. Rinse watermelon at least 3 times in cold water and drain.

4. In the same laminated pot, bring 8 cups water to a boil. Add the watermelon, reduce heat to medium, and boil for 15 minutes. Drain, rinse thoroughly with cold water, and set aside.

5. In the same pot, combine 3 cups water and 5 cups sugar and bring to a boil. Simmer for 10 minutes over medium heat until the sugar dissolves completely. Add the cardamom and watermelon, and simmer, uncovered, for 25 minutes over medium heat. Add the lime juice and rose water, and continue to cook for 15 to 20 minutes or until the syrup has thickened enough to coat the back of a spoon. Remove from heat.

6. Sterilize jelly jars in boiling water. Drain and dry. Fill the jars with hot preserves leaving ½ inch of head space and then seal the jars. Store in a cool, dark place. *Nush-e Jan!*

VARIATIONS

Pumpkin Preserve—Cut the pumpkin into 4 equal quarters. Use a spoon to remove the seeds and fibers. Cut off the shiny, hard orange rind and discard it, keeping the flesh. Continue with step 2 above, replacing the watermelon with the pumpkin flesh and replacing the cardamom with ¼ cup raw shelled pistachios.

Lime Skin Preserve—Use 2 pounds of limes, cut in half, juice (reserve juice), gently and carefully remove all pulp from the skin without breaking the skins. Proceed with step 2 above, replacing the watermelon with the lime skins (use 2 cups sugar for every pound of lime skins). Eliminate the cardamom.

Cucumber Preserve—Replace the watermelon flesh with 2 pounds Persian cucumbers, peeled, quartered lengthwise, and halved (8 pieces per cucumber). Proceed with step 3 above.

NOTE

Pickling lime or slaked lime is calcium hydroxide and the food grade powder is available at some drugstores and through the Internet (http://www.canningpantry.com/pickling-lime.html). It is used to make pickled fruit and vegetables more crisp.

Bergamot Preserve

2 pounds fresh bergamots
  or 1 pound dried
¼ cup pickling lime dissolved in
  8 cups water
3 cups water
4 pounds sugar

¼ teaspoon citric acid or ¼ cup
  lime juice
Seeds of 5 cardamom pods (optional)
2 tablespoons rose water

Makes 1 jar (1 pint)
Preparation time: 30 minutes
  plus 32 hours of standing time
Cooking time: 45 minutes

مربای بالرنگ

Moraba-ye baderang

Bergamot (baderang, Citrus bergamia) has a heavenly perfume, and the skin needs only to be scrubbed. I found some bergamots in the Santa Monica local farmers' market, from which I made the preserve in the photo on the facing page. A citrus fruit found around the Caspian and often confused with bergamot is Balang (Citrus medica cedrata). *It is somewhat similar to bergamot but much larger and more oval shaped, with a knobbly, thick yellow skin, which needs to be removed (as shown in the inset photos on the facing page) to make the preserve. The white pithy flesh inside is used to make a preserve.*

1. If using fresh bergamots, scrub the skin with a brush.

2. Cut the bergamots into 4 lengthwise slices. Remove the seeds and pulp. Cut the sliced bergamots into 4-inch pieces.

3. In a laminated container (do not use aluminum), dissolve ¼ cup pickling lime in 8 cups water, stir well, and allow to sit for 10 minutes. Add the bergamot slices to the pickling lime and allow to soak for 2 hours or overnight (this helps to make them crisp). Remove the bergamots using a slotted spoon and discard the lime water. Rinse at least 3 times in cold water and soak in ice water for 3 hours. Drain.

4. Place bergamot slices in a laminated pot and cover with cold water. Bring to a boil over high heat and boil for 15 minutes. Drain, rinse thoroughly, pat dry, and set aside.

5. Add 3 cups water and the sugar to the same pot, bring to a boil, reduce heat to medium, and simmer for 5 minutes or until the sugar has dissolved completely. Add the bergamots to the syrup and simmer over low heat, uncovered, for 15 minutes. Add the citric acid and simmer for another 5 minutes.

6. Remove from heat and let stand, covered, for about 24 hours. Remove the bergamots using a slotted spoon and set aside. Add cardamom and rose water to the syrup and simmer over medium heat for 5 to 10 minutes until syrup has thickened enough to coat the back of a spoon. Return the bergamots to the pot and remove from the heat.

7. Place hot preserves in a sterilized jar, leaving ½ inch head space. Seal the jar and store in a cool, dark place. *Nush-e Jan!*

NOTE

Pickling lime, also known as slaked lime, is food grade calcium hydroxide. Hard vegetables are soaked in a pickling lime solution before frying or pickling to keep them crisp. Pickling lime is sold at some drugstores and as a paste called "White Magic" at Vietnamese and Korean groceries. It is also available through the Internet at www.mrswages.com. Follow the package instructions for making soaking solutions.

Whenever the *sofreh* is spread for a meal, you will find a variety of pickles (*torshis*) accompanying the main course. Most of these *torshis* consist of vegetables or fruits and spices preserved in vinegar. For this chapter, I have selected only a few of the many kinds of *torshis* made in Iran. All are simple, traditional recipes.

Torshis are usually made by women; my mother used to say that some women have a special touch for making *torshis*. She herself was especially particular about the vinegar she used and who had made it. When I think back, it makes sense because good vinegar is the foundation of a good pickle.

Some pickles, such as garlic pickles, age very well. After about 7 years a good garlic pickle turns black and sweet, and becomes more like a preserve.

For a good *torshi,* use fresh ingredients, good vinegar, and pure salt. The fruits, vegetables, and herbs should be in season (they will be cheaper and tastier), without blemish, and thoroughly washed and dried. Not a trace of water can remain if the *torshi* is to keep well. After the jars have been sealed, they should be stored in a cool, dark place for aging. Once they are opened, they should be kept in the refrigerator.

I recommend using apple cider vinegar or malt vinegar with 5 percent acidity, and the salt should be as pure as possible (use pickling or canning salt).

ملّا نصر الدّین

SEVEN-YEAR-OLD TORSHI

Someone came to the mulla and said, "They say you have some torshi that's seven years old. Is that true?"

The mulla said, "Yes, it is."

The man said, "Would you please give me a dish of it?"

The mulla answered, "If I were to give everyone a dish of it, it wouldn't have gotten to be even one month old."

Fruit Chutney

Makes about 6 jars (1 pint each)
Preparation and cooking time:
3 hours
Storage: 10 days before using

CHUTNEY SPICE MIXTURE

2 teaspoons ground green cumin
1 teaspoon ground black cumin
3 teaspoons ground angelica
  powder *(gol-par)*
½ teaspoon freshly ground
  black pepper
½ teaspoon ground turmeric
3 teaspoons ground coriander seeds
2 teaspoons ground cinnamon
3 teaspoons ground ginger
1 tablespoon ground cardamom
1 tablespoon *limu-omani*
  (Persian lime powder)*

FRUIT AND VEGETABLES

¼ pound dried apricots, chopped
1 pound dried peaches, finely chopped
1 pound pitted dried tart cherries
½ pound dried tamarind*
2 pounds pitted dates, chopped
1 pound dried pitted prunes,
  finely chopped

1 cup grape molasses, or 1 pound
  seedless grapes, finely chopped
1 pound apples, cored
  and finely chopped
1 pound quinces, cored
  and finely chopped
1 pound persimmons, finely chopped
2 red peppers, seeds removed, and
  finely chopped
2 oranges, peeled, seeds removed and
  finely chopped
1 bulb of fresh garlic, peeled
  and crushed
5 pounds mangoes, peeled
  and chopped
2–3 quarts cider vinegar

SEASONING

2 teaspoons ground saffron
2 tablespoons nigella seeds
  (siah daneh)
2–4 tablespoons pickling salt
  (or sea salt)

Torshi-e miveh

NOTES

If you are using dried tamarind, cover it in vinegar overnight, then drain in a colander set over a bowl, and using the back of the spoon, press the tamarind to remove the stones, fiber, and pods.

To make less at a time, reduce quantities proportionally.

A food processor may be used to chop your fruit and vegetables.

1. Sterilize canning jars in boiling water. Drain and allow to dry thoroughly.

2. Prepare the chutney spice mixture by placing all the ground spice ingredients in a bowl and mixing well. Set aside.

3. Place all the prepared fruit and vegetables in a large laminated pot. Cover with the vinegar and simmer for 2 to 3 hours over low heat, stirring occasionally with a wooden spoon.

4. Remove the pot from heat. Add the chutney spice mixture prepared in step 2 to the pot and stir well. Allow to rest overnight. Adjust seasoning to taste by adding more vinegar, grape molasses, or salt (this chutney should be sweet and sour). Bring to a boil and simmer over medium heat for 10 minutes. Remove from heat.

5. Fill the jars to within ½ inch of the top with chutney, then end with a splash of vinegar and a bit of salt on top. Seal the jars.

6. Store the jars for at least 10 days in a cool, dark place before using. The result should be a healthful, sweet-and-sour chutney. *Nush-e Jan!*

Mango Pickle

7–8 cups cider vinegar
1 pound dried tamarind
4 firm mangoes, peeled and chopped
1 tablespoon pickling salt (or sea salt)
1 tablespoon Persian pickle spice mix*

½ teaspoon ground saffron
1 tablespoon sugar
1 tablespoon ground cardamom
1 tablespoon fenugreek seeds
1 tablespoon coriander seeds

Makes 2 jars (½ pint each)
Preparation time: 1 hour
Cooking time: 50 minutes
Storage: 6 weeks before using

1. Sterilize canning jars in boiling water. Drain and allow to dry thoroughly.

2. In a laminated pot, bring 4 cups vinegar and the tamarind to a boil. Reduce heat to medium and simmer for 30 minutes. Drain in a colander set over a bowl, and press with the back of a spoon to remove stones, pods, and fibers. Keep the liquid but discard the rest.

3. In the same laminated pot, place the mangoes, tamarind vinegar, the remaining vinegar, and bring to a boil over high heat. Reduce heat to medium and simmer for 15 minutes. Remove from heat and let cool.

4. Add salt, *advieh*, saffron, sugar, cardamom, fenugreek seeds, and coriander seeds, and simmer for 5 more minutes until you have thick chutney. Stir well. Adjust to taste by adding more salt, vinegar, or sugar.

Torshi-e anbeh

5. Fill jars within ½ inch of top, end with a bit of salt and a splash of vinegar, and seal. Store the jars in a cool, dark place for at least 6 weeks before using. *Nush-e Jan!*

Dates Pickled in Sumac

1 pound sumac berries or powder
1 pound dried tamarind
1 cup lime juice
1 clove garlic, peeled and crushed

1 tablespoon pickling salt (or sea salt)
2 tablespoons Persian pickle spice mix*
2 pounds pitted dates

Makes 2 jars (½ pint each)
Preparation time: 20 minutes
Cooking time: 1 hour 30 minutes
Storage: 10 days before using

1. Sterilize a large jar in boiling water. Drain and allow to dry thoroughly.

2. In a saucepan, bring 4 cups water and the sumac berries to a boil. Reduce heat and simmer over medium heat for 35 minutes. Drain through a strainer set over a bowl, keep the sumac water, and discard the rest.

3. In a laminated pot, bring 4 cups water and the tamarind to a boil. Reduce heat to medium and simmer for 30 minutes. Drain in a colander set over a bowl, and press with the back of a spoon to remove stones, pods, and fibers. Keep the liquid but discard the rest.

Torshi-e somaq-o khorma

4. In the same laminated pot, combine the sumac water, tamarind paste, lime juice, and garlic. Bring to a boil, reduce heat to low, and simmer for 15 minutes. Add salt and *advieh*, and simmer for 5 minutes. Remove from heat. Adjust seasoning to taste, adding more salt, vinegar or sugar.

5. Fill jar nearly to the top with dates and cover with the sumac-tamarind-lime juice mixture up to ½ inch from the top. Sprinkle the top with a bit of salt. Seal the jar. Keep in a cool, dark place. Store the jar for at least 10 days before using. *Nush-e Jan!*

I SAW A GARDEN PURE AS PARADISE

I saw a garden pure as paradise
Untouched by human dirt and human vice:
Thousands of blossoms bloomed, and small streams crept
So gently through the leaves you'd say they slept;
A myriad different hues lay mingled there,
A myriad scents drenched miles of perfumed air;
The rose lay in the hyacinth's embrace,
The jasmine nuzzled the carnation's face,
The blushing Judas blossoms kissed the grass—
The sand seemed glittering grains of polished glass,
The dust was camphor and the gravel lay
Like shining jewels strewn in the wanderer's way.
The flowing streams seemed rose-water that showed
Smooth beds where precious pearls and agates glowed—
Quick in their midst slim fish slipped playfully
Like silver coins in liquid mercury.
A massive rampart of bright emerald green
Ran round the garden and enclosed the scene;
Its slopes were covered with thick, shady trees,
Tall, noble poplars, slender cypresses.
(Its stones were rubies and when autumn came
The poplars' leaves glowed with the selfsame flame.)
Sweet sandalwood and aloe trees grew there
Censing with fragrance all the garden's air.
Finding this lovely place I knew the pleasure
Of one who stumbles on a hidden treasure:

Astonished by such gorgeous wealth I praised
The world's great God, and then explored—amazed
And feeding on delicious fruit—each sight
That opened like a vista of delight.
Until at last light-hearted, tired, I lay
Beneath a cypress; there I passed the day
Till nightfall came, surrounded by such beauties
That I forgot the world and all its duties;
I slept and ate, gave thanks to God, and then
Contentedly I slept and ate again.

From the *Black Dome* of Nezami Ganjavi

Mixed Vegetable Pickle

Makes about 4 jars (1 pint each)
Preparation and cooking
time: 2 hours 30 minutes
Storage: 10 days before using

½ cup chopped fresh mint leaves
½ cup chopped fresh parsley
½ cup chopped fresh cilantro
½ cup chopped fresh basil leaves
½ cup chopped fresh summer savory
½ cup chives, washed and chopped
½ cup chopped fresh tarragon
9 slim eggplants (about 2 pounds)
3–4 quarts apple cider vinegar
1 pound pickling cucumbers, washed, dried, and chopped
2 green peppers, cut into small pieces
1 pound carrots, scraped and finely chopped
½ pound turnips, peeled and chopped
2–3 stalks celery, chopped

10 cloves garlic, peeled and chopped
1 pound pearl onions
½ head cauliflower, separated into florets
2 tablespoons pickling salt (or sea salt)
1 tablespoon black pepper corns
1 tablespoon coriander seeds
2 tablespoon nigella seeds *(siah daneh)**
1 tablespoon dried mint
2 tablespoons dried fenugreek leaves
4 tablespoons angelica powder *(gol-par)*
2 tablespoons Persian pickle spice mix*
¼ teaspoon cayenne
½ cup grape molasses
½ cup tamarind paste

Torshi-e makhlut

1. Sterilize canning jars in boiling water. Drain and allow to dry thoroughly.

2. Wash the herbs and drain. Dry thoroughly and chop finely. Spread herbs on a pan sheet lined with towels (to dry them off).

3. Cut off eggplant tops (do not peel) and dice into 1-inch cubes. Place in a laminated pot, cover with vinegar, bring to a boil, reduce heat to medium, and simmer for 5 minutes. Drain in a colander, discarding the vinegar.

4. Place all chopped herbs and vegetables, including eggplants, in a large container and cover with 4 cups vinegar.

5. Add the rest of the ingredients. Stir well. Adjust seasoning, adding more salt, cayenne, or grape molasses to taste.

6. Fill the jars to within ½ inch of the top with the mixture. Sprinkle with salt and a splash of vinegar. Seal the jars.

7. Store for at least 10 days in a cool, dark place before using. *Nush-e Jan!*

Garlic Pickle

1 pound garlic bulbs
½ cup dried barberries, cleaned,
 soaked for 20 minutes in cold water,
 and drained
4–5 cups malt vinegar
1 tablespoon grape molasses
2 tablespoons pickling salt (or sea salt)

Makes 2 jars (½ pint each)
Preparation time: 20 minutes
Storage: 6 weeks before using

Torshi-e sir

3. Fill in the center of each bulb with 1 teaspoon barberries.

4. In a pitcher, mix the vinegar, grape molasses, and 1 tablespoon salt.

5. Fill the jars nearly to top with garlic bulbs. Fill the jar to within ½ inch of the top with the vinegar mixture. Add a pinch of salt on top. Seal the jars.

6. Store the jars in a cool, dark place for at least 6 weeks before using. Garlic pickle is at its best when 7 years old. It tastes sweet, like preserves. *Nush-e Jan!*

Onion Pickle

2 pounds pearl onions
1 tablespoon pickling salt (or sea salt)
6–8 cups apple cider vinegar
4 sprigs of fresh tarragon

Makes 2 jars (½ pint each)
Preparation and cooking time:
 30 minutes
Storage: 10 days before using

Torshi-e piaz

1. Sterilize the canning jars in boiling water. Drain and allow to dry thoroughly.

2. Wash and drain the onions. Peel the onions and remove the roots at the bottom. With the point of a paring knife cut a cross mark in the bottom of each onion so it will absorb vinegar. Leave onion tops intact.

3. In a large saucepan, bring salt and vinegar to a boil over high heat, then remove from heat.

4. Fill the jars almost to the top by layering onions and sprigs of fresh tarragon. Fill to within ½ inch of the top with the vinegar mixture. Seal the jars.

5. Store the jars for at least 10 days in a cool, dark place before using. Serve as a relish with meats. *Nush-e Jan!*

Vegetables in Brine

Makes about 4 jars (1 pint each)
Preparation time: 40 minutes
Storage: 3 weeks before using

AROMATIC HERBS
4 sprigs fresh dill
4 sprigs cilantro leaves
4 sprigs tarragon
4 bay leaves
4 fresh celery leaves

VEGETABLES
4 carrots
½ small head of cauliflower
1 stalk celery
4 turnips
2 red peppers

2 pounds small pickling cucumbers, blossoms removed
10 pearl onions, peeled
5 cloves garlic, peeled

SPICES
1 teaspoon coriander seeds
1 teaspoon nigella seeds

BRINE
8 cups water
4 tablespoons pickling salt (or sea salt)
1 teaspoon honey
½ cup cider vinegar

Torshi-e makhlut-e shur

1. Sterilize canning jars in boiling water. Drain and allow to dry thoroughly.

2. Clean, wash, and drain the herbs. Spread out on pan sheets lined with towels to air-dry them thoroughly.

3. Wash and drain the vegetables.

4. Peel carrots, cut in half lengthwise, and cut into 1-inch lengths.

5. Break the cauliflower into florets.

6. Remove the celery strings and cut into 1-inch lengths.

7. Peel the turnips, cut into quarters lengthwise, and cut into 1-inch lengths.

8. Seed the red peppers and cut into 1-inch lengths.

9. Leave pickling cucumbers, pearl onions, and garlic whole.

10. Combine all the vegetables in a large container.

11. Fill each jar almost to the top with alternating layers of herbs, some of the spices, and the vegetables.

12. To make the brine: In a large saucepan, bring water, salt, honey and vinegar to a boil. Use a ladle to fill each jar within ½ inch of the top with this hot liquid (top with a splash of vinegar). Seal jars immediately. Store the jars for at least 3 weeks in a cool, dark place before using. *Nush-e Jan!*

Eggplant Pickle

Makes 2 jars (1 pint each)
Preparation and cooking
time: 40 minutes
Storage: 40 days before using

Bademjan torshi

1½ pounds pickling eggplants
4 cups cider vinegar

FILLING
2 teaspoons pickling salt
2 cups chopped fresh mint
1 cup chopped fresh cilantro
½ cup chopped fresh parsley
½ cup basil
2 bulbs garlic, separated into cloves,
  peeled, and finely chopped
2 green bird chilies, finely chopped

VINEGAR BRINE
4–5 cups cider vinegar
1 tablespoon pickling salt (or sea salt)
2 teaspoons coriander seeds
2 teaspoons nigella seeds
1 tablespoon grape molasses or honey

1. Sterilize the canning jars in boiling water. Drain and allow to dry thoroughly.

2. Rinse the eggplants and remove the stems. Make a lengthwise slit on one side of each eggplant.

3. Place the eggplants in a laminated pot, cover with vinegar, bring to a boil, and simmer over medium heat for 5 to 10 minutes or until soft (do not overcook). Drain the eggplant, discarding the vinegar.

4. To make the filling: Combine all the ingredients for the filling. Stuff each of the eggplants with the herb mixture and gently press shut.

5. Gently fill each jar to within ½ inch of the top with stuffed eggplants.

6. To make the brine: In a saucepan, bring to a boil the vinegar, salt, coriander and nigella seeds, and grape molasses.

7. Use a ladle to fill each jar with the vinegar brine. Seal the jars. Store them in a cool, dark place for at least 40 days before using. *Nush-e Jan!*

NOTE
Autumn eggplants make excellent pickles.

Black and White Grape Pickle

Makes 2 jars (1 pint each)
Preparation time: 20 minutes
plus time to allow grapes to
dry completely
Storage: 40 days before using

ترشی انگور

Torshi-e angur

2 pounds black grapes (large, thick-skinned, and seedless)
2 pounds white grapes (large, thick-skinned, and seedless)

BRINE
2 quarts (8 cups) wine vinegar
2 tablespoons pickling salt (or sea salt)
  (1 tablespoon salt for every
  4 cups wine vinegar)
½ cup grape molasses
  (shireh-ye angur)

1. Sterilize canning jars in boiling water. Drain and allow to dry thoroughly.

2. Clip the grapes into small clusters. Fill a large container with cold water and add the grapes. Allow to rest for 5 minutes, then drain and spread on a pan sheet lined with towels for several hours or until all the clusters are completely dry.

3. Pack the jar almost to the top with black and white grapes, arranging them in alternating layers. In a medium-sized laminated saucepan bring vinegar, salt, and grape molasses to a boil over medium heat, reduce heat, and simmer for 5 minutes. Remove from heat and allow to cool.

4. Fill the jar to within ½ inch of the top with the vinegar mixture. Seal immediately. Store for at least 40 days in a cool, dark place before using. *Nush-e Jan!*

Unripe Grapes in Brine

Makes 2 jars (½ pint each)
Preparation time: 40 minutes
Storage time: at least 10 days

غوره ی شور

Ghureh-ye shur

2 pounds unripe grapes

BRINE
2 tablespoons pickling salt for every
  4 cups water
½ teaspoon sugar
½ cup wine vinegar

1. Sterilize canning jars in boiling water. Drain and allow to dry thoroughly.

2. Wash the unripe grapes and remove the stems.

3. Fill a large pot with water and bring to a boil. Blanch the grapes, drain, and set aside. Fill the jars almost to the top with grapes.

4. Bring 2 tablespoons salt, 4 cups water, sugar, and the vinegar to a boil, and fill the jars to within ½ inch of the top with this hot liquid mixture. Seal jars immediately.

5. Store for at least 10 days in a cool, dark place before using. Use these unripe grape pickles as a sour agent with fish or chicken, or in a braise. *Nush-e Jan!*

Photo on page 472

The Persian winter solstice festival is on the longest night of the year, December 21 or 22, and is called Shab-e Yalda, which means birthday eve [of the sun]. The ceremony can be traced back to the primal concept of Light and Good against Darkness and Evil in ancient Iran. From this night, when evil is at its zenith, light begins to triumph as days grow longer and give more light. In the autumn, during the grape harvest, the people of the grape-growing regions of Iran, such as Azerbaijan, select some of the choicest black and white grapes in order to make pickles. This symbolic delicacy of light and dark grapes is then served at the winter festival's dinner, where family and friends stay up all night, keeping fires burning and lights glowing to help the sun in its battle against darkness. They recite poetry and play music, tell jokes and stories, talk and eat and eat and talk until the sun triumphantly reappears in the morning. It is believed that in this way they help good conquer evil.

HOT & COLD DRINKS

HOT & COLD DRINKS

TEA

CHAI

We drank tea on the meadow of the table.
I opened the door: a piece of sky fell into my glass.
I drank the sky down with the water.

Sohrab Sepehri

چای را خوردیم روی سبزه زار میز.
در کشودم : قسمتی از آسمان افتاد در لیوان آبِ من.
آبی را با آسمان خوردم

Tea was discovered about five thousand years ago in China. In the early seventeenth century, tea was introduced to England and its Chinese name, *tay,* changed to the English name, tea. In England tea was brewed in china teapots. The English believed that a drop of milk in the teapot would prevent it from breaking and thus the tradition of drinking tea with milk started. Around 1868, an Iranian merchant, later nicknamed Chaikar, or "tea planter," brought tea from India to Iran. Tea became very popular in Iran and nowadays every Persian family has at least one samovar.

In most Iranian households, a samovar, a large metal container with three compartments—the top for keeping the teapot warm, the middle for water, and the bottom for hot coals (although today most samovars are electric)—sits on a large tray with a bowl called the *jaam* under the spout to catch the drips. The teapot, a jar of tea, and a covered bowl of sugar are set beside the samovar, which is kept steaming all day long. As soon as visitors step over the threshold, a small glass of tea with three lumps of sugar and a teaspoon is offered to them.

In Iran the color and appearance of tea is as important as its aroma and taste; therefore, tea is usually served in small glasses on saucers, or in *engareh,* silver or gold holders that hold the glass.

However, it is interesting that Iranian teahouses are still called *qahveh khaneh,* which literally means "coffeehouse." This name is left over from the time when coffee was served. Today the main drink served in these coffeehouses is tea! The *qahveh khaneh* are centers of social interaction.

In Iran tea is never drunk with milk. We take tea with sugar or with half a lime, honey, dates, raisins, or dried sweet white mulberries. A spoonful of sour cherry jam dropped into a glass of tea gives it an excellent taste. Tea should always be served hot. I still remember our afternoon teas in the summer of my golden childhood years in Iran. We would all sit on the colorful Persian carpets over wooden benches around a stone pool full of goldfish, with the fountain gently spraying, the pomegranate tree in full bloom, and the smell of the watered brick floor of our yard combined with the aroma of jasmines and gardenias floating through the air. Bronze samovars were lit, and a few tables were arranged with fruits and sweets. People would come and go, sitting near the pool and sometimes smoking the hookahs (*qalyan*). We drank tea, talked, and drank more tea. Sometimes even here at home, when I am alone and miss those childhood days, one of my sons might say, "Maman, don't be sad, let's have a chat over a glass of tea."

TO MAKE PERSIAN TEA

1. Bring water to a boil in a tea kettle. Warm a teapot by swirling some boiling water in it; pour out the water. Place 2 tablespoons Persian tea leaves in the pot, using perfumed Ghazal or any Persian blend black tea from an Iranian store, and 1 teaspoon orange blossom water for a delightful flavor, aroma and color.

2. Fill the teapot half full with boiling water. Replace the lid, cover the pot with a cozy, and let steep for 5 to 10 minutes—do not steep for more than 10 minutes as the quality will deteriorate. If you are using a samovar, steep the tea on top.

3. Pour a glassful of tea and return it to the pot to make sure the tea is evenly mixed.

4. Fill each glass or cup halfway with tea. Add boiling water from the kettle to dilute the tea to the desired color and taste: Some prefer their tea weak, some strong. Keep the pot covered with the cozy while you drink the first glasses. Persian-style tea should always be served good and hot. Refill the glass frequently (until you've had enough of company, and it's time for your guests to leave). *Nush-e Jan!*

COFFEE

QAHVEH

The Persian word for coffee is *qahveh* and comes from the Arabic meaning something undesirable; in the case of coffee, it removes the appetite for food and sleep. Its first recorded use in the Middle East was in fifteenth-century Yemen, but its origin can be traced to Ethiopia. It is said that a shepherd first discovered coffee when his sheep were eating beans under a coffee tree. Coffee was drunk in mystical Sufi orders, especially *zikrs*. Thus, it was initially seen as an aid to staying awake for pious purposes. Coffeehouses flourished in the sixteenth century because of the need at the time for social gathering places. With the competition among the various coffeehouses came the provision of entertainment such as storytelling, *naqali* (recitations from the *Shahnameh*, the Book of Kings), puppet shows, jugglers, tumblers, and music. Coffeehouses also provided a forum for poets and writers (the precursors of the French café society). Later in nineteenth-century Iran tea replaced coffee as the favorite drink and most coffeehouses were replaced by teahouses, yet the name in Persian continues to remain *qahveh khaneh* (coffeehouse).

Iranian coffee is like Turkish coffee, thick and very strong. In fact, in Iran it is called Turkish coffee. It is made from coffee beans ground to a very fine powder and then simmered with sugar. It is usually made in a long-handled copper ewer called an *ibriq* and then poured into very small cups. It is easy to make.

TO MAKE PERSIAN COFFEE

For each small cup (4 ounces—demitasse or espresso), put 1 teaspoon powdered coffee (very, very finely ground, available at Persian grocery stores), 1 teaspoon of sugar, a dash of ground cardamom (or rose water) and saffron, and 1 small cup water (4 ounces) into a small pan or *ibriq*. Stir with a spoon for a few minutes until the sugar has dissolved. Simmer over low heat until foam rises to the surface. Remove from the heat and stir until the foam subsides. Repeat this process 3 more times (don't walk away; this coffee needs supervision). To make sure that every cup of coffee has the same consistency, fill each cup a little at a time, until each is full. Sip the coffee carefully so as not to swallow any grounds. *Nush-e Jan!*

After drinking the coffee, remove the saucer and place it on top of the cup. Invert the cup and saucer away from yourself with your left hand (the hand of the heart) and let stand for 5 minutes without disturbing it. Then turn the cup over. A fortune-teller—or just a clever friend—can read your fate in the patterns of the grounds left behind in the cup.

Serve the coffee with pastries or fruit. Interestingly, for Armenian-Iranians coffee is a social drink associated with festivals, while for Muslim Iranians coffee is associated with funeral receptions and is served with *halva* and dates.

Iced Coffee

1½ cups cold milk
1 teaspoon sugar
1 cup strong brewed or instant coffee

4 scoops (about 1 cup) vanilla or
    coffee ice cream
2 tablespoons whipped cream

Makes 2 servings
Preparation time: 5 minutes,
  plus 1 hour of refrigeration

Café glacé

Slurping this ice cold drink imported to Iran from Belgium brings back wonderful memories of visiting Tehran cafés after school or during the summer holidays!

1. Bring milk and sugar to a boil. Remove from heat, add coffee, stir well, and allow to cool (chill in the refrigerator for an hour or so).

2. Just prior to serving, pour the coffee mixture into 2 tall glasses, filling them halfway. Place two scoops of ice cream and one spoon of whipped cream on top of each. Serve with a long spoon and straw. *Nush-e-Jan!*

Yogurt Drink

1 cup whole milk yogurt, well beaten
1 teaspoon chopped fresh mint or
    a dash of dried mint flakes, crushed
½ teaspoon sea salt

¼ teaspoon freshly ground
    black pepper
1½ cups club soda or spring water,
    chilled

Makes 2 servings
Preparation time: 10 minutes

Dugh

1. Pour yogurt, mint, salt, and pepper into a pitcher. Stir well.

2. Gradually add club soda, stirring constantly. Add 3 or 4 ice cubes and stir well.

3. Serve chilled. This drink is associated with Rice with Kabab.

NOTE

This refreshing yogurt drink is an excellent drink for travelers because yogurt has a cleansing power and disinfects your system.

Quince-Lime Syrup

Makes 1 pint
Preparation time: 10 minutes
Cooking time: 55 minutes

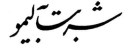

Sharbat-e beh limu

2 pounds quinces (about 2 cups juice)
4 cups sugar

2 cups water
½ cup fresh lime juice

1. Quarter the quinces and remove cores with a knife. Do not peel. Wash, pat dry, and process in a juicer.

2. Bring the sugar and water to a boil in a laminated pot. Add the quince juice and boil for 30 minutes over medium heat, stirring occasionally. Add the lime juice and cook for another 15 minutes or until the syrup thickens.

3. Remove from heat. Allow to cool. Pour the syrup into a clean, dry bottle and cork tightly.

4. In a pitcher, mix 1 part syrup, 3 parts water, and 2 ice cubes per person. Stir with a spoon. *Nush-e-Jan!*

_____

VARIATION

Tie the washed, cored, and sliced quinces in 2 layers of cheesecloth and place in a pot with 4 cups water. Bring to a boil. Reduce heat, cover, and simmer over low heat for 1½ hours until the quince is tender. Squeeze out and remove the cheesecloth, add 2 cups sugar, 2 cups water, and ½ cup fresh lime juice to the pot. Cover and simmer over medium heat for another 30 minutes. Continue with step 3 above.

Rhubarb Syrup

Makes 1 pint
Preparation time: 35 minutes
Cooking time: 30 minutes

Sharbat-e rivas

2 pounds rhubarb (about 2 cups rhubarb juice)
2 cups water

4 cups sugar
2 tablespoons lime juice

1. Wash and cut the rhubarb into ½-inch pieces. Process in a juicer.

2. Bring the water and sugar to a boil in a laminated pot. Add the rhubarb juice and lime juice, and simmer for 20 minutes over medium heat, stirring occasionally.

3. Allow to cool. Pour the syrup into a clean, dry bottle, and cork tightly.

4. In a pitcher, mix 1 part syrup, 3 parts water, and 2 ice cubes per person. Stir with a spoon and serve well chilled. *Nush-e-Jan!*

_____

VARIATION

In a pot, bring 4 cups sugar and 4 cups water to a boil. Tie up the rhubarb pieces in cheesecloth. Place the cheesecloth in the sugar and water, and simmer over medium heat for 30 minutes or until the syrup thickens. Squeeze out the cheesecloth and remove it. Pour the syrup into a clean, dry bottle, and cork tightly. Serve as in step 4 above.

JAMSHID SHAH AND THE DISCOVERY OF WINE

One day, as King Jamshid sat under his tent watching his archers practice, a large bird appeared in the sky. It seemed to be struggling to stay aloft. Jamshid saw that a snake was wrapped around the bird's neck and was threatening the bird with its fangs.

For Jamshid, this was a hateful sight. He could not stand by and allow the bird, a symbol of good, to be devoured by a snake, the symbol of evil.

Without hesitation, the king ordered his archer to kill the snake without harming the bird. A few moments later, the serpent fell to the ground, an arrow through its head.

The great bird soared toward the sun in homage to the triumph of good over evil, then swooped down and landed next to Jamshid. It opened its beak and dropped a few bright green seeds at the king's feet. Jamshid had never seen seeds like these. He looked up to question the bird, but it had already flown away.

When the king returned to his palace, he summoned his gardeners and consulted the wisest men in his kingdom, but not one was able to identify the strange seeds. Finally, he ordered that the seeds be planted in the most fertile soil of the royal gardens.

Some time later, a strange plant rose from the ground. During the warm season it proliferated, sending out long branches covered with many large leaves. But once winter arrived, it began to dry up and shrivel to the ground, as if to protect itself from the cold.

Finally, one spring the first of its fruit ripened. A gardener brought some of it to Jamshid, who examined them in wonder. The fruit was as strange as the plant that bore it. On each stem, there grew not one but twenty to forty dark blue, round berries. The skins burst easily, releasing the juice within. So that not a drop would be lost, the king ordered his servants to gather all the fruit and place it in large receptacles.

One evening the king returned to the palace very thirsty after a long day's hunt in the hot sun. He decided to try a glass of the mysterious juice, believing it would be a refreshing fermented drink. No sooner had he taken the first bitter sip than he spat it out.

"This must be a dreadful poison," he said. "I must make certain it does not fall into the hands of the wrong people."

He turned his attention to more pressing royal concerns and thought no more about the matter. Months passed.

Now as it happened, Jamshid had a beautiful favorite wife. One day while he was away, she fell violently ill, suffering from terrible headaches that none of the palace doctors could cure. The pain was so intense she decided to kill herself. Remembering the strange juice and the king's remark that it was poison, she drank one glass and was quite surprised to find that it did not have the bitter taste the king had complained of. To ensure that she would die, she drank a second, then a third glass, and finally fell into a deep sleep.

When she awoke, her terrible headache was gone. Although her mouth felt dry, she believed that she was healed.

When the king returned to the palace, she confessed what she had done and described the miraculous cure the drink had brought about. Jamshid asked to try the juice himself. He tasted it, cautiously at first, then with more and more pleasure. Unable to disguise his delight, he decreed the drink would be used as a remedy for all the people. The effect was so beneficial, especially among the elderly, that the liquid came to be called *daru-shah*, the "king's medicine."

That, according to legend, is the origin of the grapevine and the discovery of wine.

Cynics will probably question the truth of this tale, told by a Frenchman. In fact it was a Persian poet who once said, "Whoever seeks the origin of wine must be crazy." Nonetheless, it is certain that the grapevine originated somewhere between the Black Sea, the Caspian Sea, and the Zagros Mountains (in other words, the northwest of greater Iran), and it was there that, one long-forgotten day, the juice of the grapes turned into wine.

The Muslim religion forbids believers to seek paradise on Earth through artificial intoxication. The Koran promises its followers a far more precious nectar—but in another world.

HOW THE PERSIANS WENT FROM WINE TO SHERBET

As long ago as 5000 BCE, the inhabitants of Iran were wine drinkers, as archeologists investigating ancient sediments have attested. Outsiders like the Greek historian Herodotus, writing in the fifth century BCE, commented on the Persians' love of wine, and Persian poets then and later confirmed it in their verses. Hafez, for example, wrote:

بامی بکنارجوی می باید بو

With wine beside a gently flowing brook—this is best;

وغصه کن اژجوی می باید بو

Withdrawn from sorrow in some quiet nook—this is best;

این مت عمر ماحو گل ده رور

Our life is like a flower's that blooms for ten short days,

خندان لب ُ تازَروی می آیو

Bright laughing lips, a friendly, fresh-faced look—this is best.

With the advent of Islam, however, wine was forbidden, although courtiers (and poets) continued to enjoy it. They discarded the old Persian words for the drink *(badeh* and *mey)* and replaced them with *sharab,* Arabic for "sweet drink." That is the source of the English "syrup."

Renaming the forbidden was not enough. The Iranians needed a new, non-alcoholic drink, and *sharbat* was born. Its basis was the ice and snow that Iranians had learned to preserve during the hot summer months in spectacular domed ice wells on the edges of towns and along caravan routes. The flavorings were syrups, made by combining fruit or vegetable juice with honey, sugar, or date or grape molasses and boiling the mixture down to intensify the flavor. Sipped through a mound of crushed ice or snow, the syrup became a delightful drink.

Sharbats could be either sweet or savory. The Huguenot jeweler Jean Chardin, traveling in Iran, described a favorite of the Isfahanis: sugar, a pinch of salt, lemon or pomegranate juice, and a squeeze of garlic or lemon, all mixed with crushed ice. This sweet-sour mixture, he found, not only quenched the thirst but stimulated the appetite.

Such cool drinks traveled along the trade routes to become the *sharbats* of Turkey and Syria, the *sorbete* of Spain, the *sorbeto* of Italy, the *sorbet* of France, and the *sherbet* of England. The European versions were iced mixtures, usually based on fruit, that one ate with a spoon—merely a difference in the degree of freezing.

Such frozen desserts in Iran are made with lime juice, sour cherries or black mulberries and served with sweet rice vermicelli. They have their own name: *paludeh* or *faludeh.* A Persian *sharbat* remains a fruit drink with plenty of ice, often perfumed with rose water or orange blossoms and served in summer.

WHAT RUMI SAYS ABOUT WINE PROHIBITION

نه همه جانی خوی شر می کند   بر او دب سلامی چنان تری کند

دگر بو قتی نکو فہ می شقو   و رو بد خبی تہ می شقو

لیک اغلب چنن بد پذیرند   بر همہ می سلامحرم کہ از

Evil won't always come
> *From a loss of self-control*

Wine makes a person ruder
> *Who has rudeness in his soul;*

A wise man when he drinks
> *Will seem to grow more clever,*

An evil-natured man
> *Will turn out worse than ever;*

But since most men's behavior's
> *An absolute disgrace*

Wine has become forbidden
> *To everyone, just in case!*

Rose Water Syrup

2½ cups water
4 cups sugar
¼ cup fresh lime juice
½ cup rose water

Makes 1 pint
Preparation time: 5 minutes
Cooking time: 20 minutes

ﺷﺮﺑﺖ گﻞ ﻣﺤﻤﺪی

Sharbat-e gol-e Mohammadi

NOTES

Rose water (suitable for cooking) and most of the distillates (called araqs *in Persian) listed here are available in Persian stores (produced by Sadaf).*

Small copper distilling columns suitable for homemade flower and herb distillates are sold in the bazaars in Iran. In the U.S. they can be found at specialty stores or through the Internet. But remember, though you need only very little for home use, it takes about a million rose buds to make a kilo of attar.

1. In a laminated pot, bring the water and sugar to a boil. Simmer for 10 minutes. Add the lime juice and rose water, and cook 10 minutes longer, stirring occasionally.

2. Remove the pan from heat and allow to cool. Pour the syrup into a clean, dry bottle and cork tightly.

3. In a pitcher, mix 1 part syrup, 3 parts water, and 2 ice cubes per person. Stir with a spoon and serve well chilled. *Nush-e-Jan!*

VARIATIONS

Saffron Syrup—Add ½ teaspoon ground saffron threads diluted in 2 tablespoons hot water to the rose water syrup.

Barberry Syrup—Replace the lime juice in step 1 with barberry juice. (When fresh barberries are not available, barberry juice can be made from dried barberries. Pick over and thoroughly wash 2 cups barberries. Combine with 4 cups water and boil for 15 minutes over high heat. Allow to cool and pass the juice through 2 layers of cheesecloth or a fine-meshed sieve into a pitcher.)

Almond Syrup—Replace water and lime juice with almond milk. (To make almond milk puree 3 cups blanched almonds with 5 cups boiling water in a food processor for 5 minutes until creamy. Strain the mixture through 2 layers of cheesecloth into a bowl. Reserve the almond milk and discard the solids. You can also use ready-made almond milk).

Persian Musk Rose Syrup—Replace rose water with musk rose water.

Basil Seed Syrup—Soak 1 cup of basil seeds *(tokhm-e sharbati)* in 2 cups water for a few hours, then add soaking seeds to the syrup in step 1 with the rose water. This is an excellent syrup, often served to the mother of a newborn baby.

Mint Leaf Syrup—Replace rose water with mint water.

Orange Blossom Syrup—Replace rose water with orange blossom water.

Licorice Syrup—Replace rose water with licorice water.

Palm Syrup—Replace rose water with palm water.

Willow Syrup—Replace rose water with willow water.

Vinegar and Mint Sherbet

SYRUP
6 cups sugar
2 cups water
1½ cups wine vinegar
4 sprigs fresh mint

GARNISH
1 cucumber, peeled and thinly sliced
3 limes, sliced
2 cups fresh mint leaves
1 cup fresh cilantro
2 tablespoons dried rose petals

Makes 1 pint
Preparation time: 10 minutes
Cooking time: 35 minutes

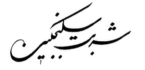

Sharbat-e sekanjebin

1. To make the syrup: Bring the sugar and water to a boil in a medium-sized laminated pot. Simmer for 10 minutes over medium heat, stirring occasionally, until the sugar has thoroughly dissolved.

2. Add the vinegar and boil for 15 to 20 minutes over medium heat until a thick syrup forms. Remove the pot from heat.

3. Wash the mint sprigs and pat dry. Add them to the syrup. Allow to cool. Remove the mint and pour the syrup into a clean, dry bottle. Cork tightly.

4. To make the sherbet: In a pitcher, mix 1 part syrup with 3 parts chilled water and stir well. Keep cool.

5. Fill ½ a glass with crushed ice, slices of cucumber, a slice of lime, a few mint and cilantro leaves, and 1 rose petal. Top up the glass with the sherbet. Serve well chilled. *Nush-e-Jan!*

Bitter Orange Syrup

Makes 2 pints
Preparation time: 5 minutes
Cooking time: 20 minutes

شربت نارنج

Sharbat-e narenj

5–6 pounds bitter oranges
  (2 cups bitter orange juice)
4 cups sugar
2 cups water

Narenj *(wild orange) is known as the bitter orange in English, and* orange amere *in French. The* narenj *tree and fruit existed in the Caspian region 2,000 years ago. The orange graft was brought to Persia by the Portuguese from China; hence the name for the sweet orange in Persian,* porteghal.

1. To make juice use 5 to 6 pounds bitter oranges. First wash and remove a ring of orange peel from around the middle of the bitter oranges. Cut in half. Remove the seeds and press the oranges in a juicer.

2. In a pot, bring the sugar and water to a boil over high heat. Pour in the bitter orange juice and simmer over medium heat for 20 minutes, stirring occasionally. Remove from the heat, cool, pour into a clean, dry bottle, and cork it tightly.

3. In a pitcher, mix 1 part syrup, 3 parts water, and 2 ice cubes per person. Stir with a spoon and serve well chilled. Decorate with orange leaves or orange blossoms. *Nush-e-Jan!*

Lime Syrup

Makes 2 pints
Preparation time: 5 minutes
Cooking time: 25 minutes

شربت آبلیمو

Sharbat-e ablimu

6 cups sugar
2 cups water
1½ cups fresh lime juice

GARNISH
Sprigs of fresh mint
Lime slices

1. In a pot, bring the sugar and water to a boil. Pour in the lime juice and simmer over medium heat, stirring occasionally, for 15 minutes. Cool, pour into a clean, dry bottle, and cork tightly.

2. In a pitcher, mix 1 part syrup, 3 parts water, and 2 ice cubes per person. Stir with a spoon and serve well chilled. Garnish with sprigs of fresh mint and slices of lime. *Nush-e Jan!*

———
VARIATION

Lime and Saffron Syrup *(Sharbat-e za'feran)*—Add ½ teaspoon ground saffron threads to step 1.

Sour Cherry Syrup

3 pounds sour cherries, pitted or
 unpitted, fresh or frozen
5 cups sugar
3 cups water
4 tablespoons lime juice

Makes 1 pint
Preparation time: 20 minutes
Cooking time: 35 minutes

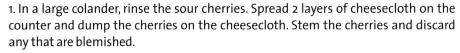

Sharbat-e ab-e albalu

1. In a large colander, rinse the sour cherries. Spread 2 layers of cheesecloth on the counter and dump the cherries on the cheesecloth. Stem the cherries and discard any that are blemished.

2. In a large pot, bring the sugar and water to a boil.

3. Tie up the sour cherries in the cheesecloth and gently lower into the pot. Bring back to a boil, reduce heat, and simmer over medium heat for 25 minutes.

4. Lift the cherries in their cheesecloth and hold above the pot for a minute to let the syrup drain. Place the bundle in a large bowl, transfer the cherries to a jar, and store in the refrigerator. Use the cherries as a preserve, delicious in Persian tea or with yogurt as a dessert.

5. Add the lime juice to the syrup and continue to simmer for 10 to 15 minutes until a syrup forms.

6. Remove the pot from heat and allow to cool. Use a funnel to pour the syrup into a clean, dry bottle and cork tightly. Keep refrigerated and use as needed.

7. In a pitcher, mix 1 part syrup, 3 parts water, and 2 ice cubes per person. Stir with a spoon and serve well chilled. *Nush-e Jan!*

VARIATIONS

Juice the cherries in a juicer. Bring 5 cups sugar, water, and lime juice to a boil in a laminated pan. Add the cherry juice and bring back to a boil. Simmer over medium heat, stirring occasionally, for 10 to 15 minutes until the syrup thicken. Remove the pot from heat and allow to cool. Pour syrup into a clean, dry bottle and cork tightly. Serve as in step 7 above.

Pomegranate Syrup *(Sharbat-e anar)*—Substitute 5 cups fresh pomegranate juice (about 10 pomegranates) for the sour cherry juice.

Beet Syrup *(Sharbat-e choghondar)*—Substitute 4 cups fresh beet juice (about 2 pounds of beets) and 1 cup wine vinegar for the sour cherry juice.

Apricot Syrup *(Sharbat-e zardalu)*—Substitute 6 cups apricot juice and ½ teaspoon ground saffron for the sour cherry juice.

SNACKS & STREET FOOD

غذاهای مُوره‌گران

SNACKS *&* STREET FOOD

One group is in religious convictions devout
Another is full of uncertainty and doubt
Then appeared a messenger from without
"You've both got it wrong; you've both lost out."

Omar Khayyam

قومی متفکرند در مذهب و دین   جمعی متحیّرند در شکّ و یقین

ناگاه برآورد منادی زکمین   کای بیخبران راه نه آنست و نه این

My sisters and I loved the street foods of Iran in our childhood. Our parents forbade us to indulge, saying these snacks were unhygienic and could make us sick. But being forbidden naturally made them even more desirable and tasty. Street foods could be found everywhere, in front of schools, near cinemas, at busy street corners, and in and around the bazaar.

Vendors sold fruit and nut snacks seasonally, starting in the early spring. In early April came baby green unripe almonds *(chaghaleh badum)* with their spring-like nutty flavor. These were sprinkled with coarse salt and eaten with their outer green shells because they were still soft on the outside and jelly-like inside. Another early offering was baby green unripe plums *(gojeh sabz)*. With each bite, a delicious, sour, spring-taste would burst into our mouths. We'd finish a bagful of them on the way home from school.

Summer was a time for berries. A favorite of mine was *shahtut,* known as the "king of berries." They resemble blackberries but grow on trees and are very large, juicy, and lusciously tangy. Even now as I write about them, my mouth is watering. Also irresistible were *tut* (white mulberries)—long, white, and sweet when ripe. Iranians eat the dried version as a replacement for cube sugar. When they are in season, street vendors would mound them on their carts and sell them around the city. For some reason (perhaps my father had once done the local farmer a favor) they would be delivered to our house in wooden crates in the early morning, the sugary berries carefully arranged one beside the other and the top layer covered with mulberry leaves. We loved to eat them before breakfast.

Street vendors were also present in the evenings at popular gathering places such as Sar-e Pol, in the foothills of the mountains, where people would come to enjoy the cooler evening weather. As the season progressed, so would the types of snacks they sold. Among the offerings were fresh, now-mature, shelled almonds and walnuts, usually sold in groups of four *(fal-e gerdu)* in paper cones. Producing this snack is very labor-intensive; vendors pick their nuts in the morning and spend all day shelling them and dropping them in buckets of salt water to keep them fresh for the evening. Another treat was corn on the cob, roasted on all sides on a grill, then dropped into salted water and served hot, with some of the husk left on for handling.

Popular winter street foods were hot roasted beets and steamed fava beans. Iranian beets *(labu)* are much larger and flatter than those found in the U.S. They are also sweeter. Traditionally, they are roasted in bread ovens *(tanur),* then kept on a steamer in the street vendors' carts. The beets are peeled and sliced just before serving. In my childhood, vendors would wrap them in newspapers, but now they use plastic containers. Fava beans are boiled in their pod in salt water and a splash of vinegar, then sprinkled with angelica powder *(gol-par)* and paprika. Winter offerings also include baked potatoes *(sibzamini pokhteh)* served with angelica powder *(gol-par)* and pickles.

There are also more substantial street foods that feed the crowded cities of Iran, such as noodle soup *(osh-e reshteh), and* meat broths *(ab gusht* or *dizzy),* where the meat is removed from the broth, pounded and then served on the side with hot flat bread. Stalls around the bazaar (and at the foot of the mountains to serve climbers) offer a soup made of sheeps' head and feet *(kalleh pacheh).* Tripe soup *(sirab shirdun) is* popular as well. And kababs—especially those made with liver, kidney, or hearts—are also a favorite street food. I have included the recipes for these street-food soups and kababs in the appropriate sections of this book so that you can make them at home in the traditional way they are made in the cook-shops and street stalls of Iran.

با دست با اتّفاق در هم زنیم

پائی نشاط بر سر غم زنیم

پیش از که صبحدم صبوحی زنیم

کین صبح بسی دمد که بادم زنیم

Come, clap our hands in joy, or we won't beat
Grief to the ground beneath our dancing feet;
Let's drink and greet the dawn, since there will be
So many dawns to come that we won't greet.

Omar Khayyam

Dried Fruits and Nuts

آجیل

Ajil

Ajil, the Persian mixture of dried fruits with roasted nuts and seeds, is a wonderful snack for nibbling that appeals both to children and adults and fits in at any time of day. The contents and proportions of this snack depend as much on what is at hand as on the taste of the person who is preparing it. Because it has an infinite number of combinations, there can be no conventional recipe for *ajil*; you have to invent your own. Among the dried fruits to choose from are figs, apricots, peaches, raisins, and mulberries. Dried pears, prunes, and currants can also be used. Nuts and seeds can include roasted hazelnuts, almonds, walnuts, pistachios, cashews, chickpeas, watermelon seeds, and pumpkin seeds. Mix the fruits, nuts, and seeds together and serve in a bowl. People help themselves to what they want, using their fingers.

There are three major *ajil*:

1. *Ajil-e shab-e chahar shanbeh sury* (always served on the eve before the last Wednesday of the year) literally means "red wednesday eve."

2. *Ajil-e shab-e chelleh* or *shab chareh* (night grazing) is associated with winter festivals and always contains watermelon seeds.

3. *Ajil-e moshgel gosha* (unraveling problems): You make a wish and if your wish comes true, you must hand out *ajil* (always made with shelled nuts).

NOTE

For roasting and salting your own raw nuts see the How To section on page 543.

Sweet Chickpea Powder

Makes 3 cups
Preparation time: 5 minutes

Qaoot

2 cups roasted chickpea powder*
1 cup confectioners' sugar

As children we loved qaoot. Today, as adults, we make it for our children and help them eat it, sometimes with our hands and sometimes with spoons. The best way to eat this snack is to take a handful, tilt your head back, and then pour it into your mouth.

1. Mix together the chickpea powder and sugar.

2. Pour into a bowl. *Nush-e Jan!*

Pistachio Qaoot—Combine 2 cups roasted pistachios ground to a powder with ¼ cup roasted chickpea powder, ¼ cup almond powder, 1 cup confectioners' sugar, and ¼ teaspoon cardamom powder.

Sunflower Seed Qaoot—Combine 2 cups sunflower seed powder, 1 cup toasted chickpea powder, 1 cup confectioners' sugar, ½ teaspoon cardamom powder, 1 teaspoon ginger powder, 1 teaspoon coriander seeds powder, and ¼ teaspoon clove powder.

Plum-Paste Rolls (Fruit Roll-Ups)

6 pounds ripe greengage plums
⅓ cup water
½ teaspoon sea salt

Preparation time: 10 minutes
Cooking time: 45 minutes
Drying time: 4–5 days

Lavashak

1. Wash plums and place in a large pot with the water. Cook over medium heat for 30 to 45 minutes or until the flesh falls away from the pit. Stir occasionally to prevent the flesh from sticking to the bottom.

2. Transfer the fruit to a colander placed over a bowl. Press all the juice and flesh through with a masher; only the pits and skin will remain in the colander. The pulp should be smooth. Add salt and stir well.

3. Pour ¼-inch-thick layers into several pan sheets lined with parchment paper. Set out to dry in direct sunlight for 4 to 5 days. (If you use a dehydrator, the process of drying is reduced to a few hours.)

4. Roll up the fruit in the plastic wrap and store in the refrigerator. *Nush-e Jan!*

NOTE

Plum paste rolls, lavashak, the original fruit roll-up, are a special treat that many Iranian children prefer to chocolate. This fruit paste can be prepared with many different fruits, such as apricots, berries, cherries, and any other kind of plum. It is particularly good, however, when made with greengage golden plums.

VARIATION

Puree the pitted fruit in a food processor. Transfer to a large pot, add water, and salt. Bring to a boil. Pass through a meshed colander over a bowl (the pulp should be smooth). Let it cool. Spread the puree as in step 3.

Baked Beets

Labu-ye tanuri

Place 2 pounds beets, unpeeled, in an ovenproof baking dish. Add 2 tablespoons brown sugar (beets in Iran tend to be sweeter and don't need any added sugar, for U.S. beets add 1 tablespoon brown sugar for every pound of beets). Cover the beets with water and bake for 2 to 3 hours at 350°F (180°C), depending on their size. Turn them over occasionally. Add more warm water, if necessary, until tender. Peel and slice the beets. Or, if you prefer, you may steam the beets in a steamer for about 1 hour until tender. *Nush-e Jan!*

Hot Fava Beans in the Pod

Baqala pokhteh

Use 2 pounds fresh fava beans in the pod or 1 pound frozen fava beans. In a large pot, combine 8 cups water and 4 tablespoons salt, and bring to a boil. Add the whole beans in the pod and boil briskly for 10 to 15 minutes (if using frozen fava beans without pods, cook for 5 minutes or until tender). Drain and transfer to a platter, then sprinkle with vinegar and angelica powder *(gol-par)*. I also like to sprinkle with red pepper flakes and paprika. These fava beans make a wonderful winter afternoon snack or appetizer.

Charcoal-Roasted Corn on the Cob

Makes 4 servings
Preparation time: 20 minutes
Cooking time: 10 minutes

Balal

2 tablespoons sea salt
2 quarts warm water
8 ears of corn

1. Prepare a charcoal fire and dissolve the salt in a large container of warm water.

2. When the coals are ready, shuck the corn (keeping the husk for later use) and roast the corn on all sides on the grill, turning the ears frequently.

3. When all sides are well roasted, remove from the grill and immediately plunge them into the salted water. Allow to rest in the salt water for a minute and serve hot on a piece of the husk. *Nush-e Jan!*

Shirazi Lemony Potato Snack

Makes 6 servings
Preparation time: 15 minutes
Cooking time: 15 minutes

2 pounds golden potatoes
¾ cup oil
1 pound yellow onions, peeled and diced into ½-inch cubes
2 Meyer lemons (less acidic and skin is not bitter), seeded and diced into ½-inch cubes, or 2 tablespoons Persian lime powder *(limu-omani)*
2 teaspoons sea salt

1 teaspoon freshly ground black pepper
1 teaspoon turmeric
1 large tomato, peeled and diced

Sangak bread cut into 4-inch pieces, and kept warm
2 bunches tarragon or basil leaves, washed and dried

دوپیازآلو

Dopiazeh alu

NOTE

Use Meyer lemons because their skin is not bitter. If using regular lemon, use the zest, then remove the skin and use the lemon pulp. Or you can replace the fresh lemon with 2 tablespoons Persian lime powder (limu-omani). *

Dopiazeh alu, which means "two onion potatoes," is a popular snack, and vendors selling it are a familiar sight outside cinemas in Shiraz, much like chestnut vendors in winter in New York.

1. Peel and dice the potatoes into ½-inch cubes, and soak in cold water as you are working. Drain the potatoes and dry completely.

2. Heat ½ cup oil in a large skillet over medium heat until hot and add the potatoes. Sauté until golden brown. Remove from heat and set aside.

3. Heat ¼-cup oil in another large skillet until hot. Add the onions, and sauté until golden. Add the lemons and sauté for 2 minutes. Add salt, pepper, and turmeric, and sauté for 1 minute. Add the tomatoes and stir-fry for 2 minutes.

4. Add the potato to the onion mixture and sauté for 2 minutes. Adjust seasoning to taste, and add salt or lemon juice if necessary. Reduce heat and keep warm until ready to serve.

5. Place a tablespoon on a piece of toast or a piece of *sangak* bread (or use any toasted flat bread) and garnish with a handful of fresh herbs. Makes an excellent sandwich. *Nush-e Jan!*

COOKING VARIATION

Use unpeeled potatoes, place in a saucepan, cover with water, and cook for 15 to 20 minutes over medium heat, until tender. Peel and dice and add them to the fried onions in step 3.

Popped Rice

2 cups long-grain Basmati rice
4 cups water or whole milk
2 teaspoons sea salt
4 cups oil for deep-frying

GARNISH
1 teaspoon sea salt or
   confectioners' sugar

Makes 4 cups
Preparation time: 20 minutes
   plus overnight soaking
Cooking time: 11–12 minutes

برنجک

Berenjak

1. Clean and wash rice.

2. Soak the rice in 4 cups water and 1 teaspoon salt for 3 hours, or bring the water and 1 teaspoon salt to a boil, add the rice, and boil for 10 minutes.

3. Drain the rice and pat dry by spreading over paper towels. Set aside overnight.

4. In a deep frying pan, heat the oil over high heat of 375°F (180°C). Drop in 1 grain of rice. If it rises immediately, the oil is ready. Add 1 teaspoon salt. Reduce heat to medium.

5. Place the rice in a fine-meshed metal sieve with handles and dunk in the oil for 20 to 30 seconds (count up to 30) until individual grains of rice swell and rise up. Immediately remove and set aside to cool. Sprinkle with the rest of the salt or 1 teaspoon confectioners' sugar. *Nush-e Jan!*

Popped Lentils

2 cups lentils
4 cups water or whole milk

2 teaspoons sea salt
4 cups oil for deep-frying

Makes 3 cups
Preparation time: 10 minutes
   plus 3 hours of soaking time
Cooking time: 2 to 3 minutes

عسرک

Adasak

1. Clean and wash the lentils. Soak in 4 cups water and 1 teaspoon salt for 3 hours, or boil for 10 minutes.

2. Drain the lentils and dry **completely** by spreading on paper towels overnight.

3. In a deep frying pan, heat the oil over high heat of 375°F (180°C). Add 1 teaspoon salt.

4. Place the lentils in the frying pan and cook for a few minutes until individual lentils swell and rise (1 to 2 minutes).

5. Remove the lentils from the oil, drain, and leave to cool. *Nush-e Jan!*

VARIATION

Wheat grains, chickpeas, mung beans, and barley can also be prepared using this method. You can also roast in step 3 instead of frying. Heat a large, non-stick skillet until very hot. Add the grains or beans and roast until they pop.

HOW TO
MAKE & STORE KITCHEN INGREDIENTS

Yogurt

2 quarts whole milk (8 cups)
1 cups plain yogurt

Makes 6 servings
Preparation time: 20 minutes
plus 12 hours of setting time

ماست

Mast

1. Bring the milk to a boil over medium heat in a very clean, non-reactive pot. *Dirty or greasy utensils will not produce the desired results.*

2. Remove the milk from heat and let stand until cool but not completely cold. *The temperature of the milk is very important at this stage. It should not be too cold or too hot.* If the milk is too cool, the culture will not grow; if it is too warm the heat will kill the bacteria in the culture. If you are using a thermometer, the temperature should be 115°F or 45°C, or with some experience you can test by hand. Put your little finger in the milk and count to 20. The temperature is correct if you can just tolerate the heat.

3. Pour the milk into a Pyrex dish. Pull out the rack in the center shelf of the oven and place the dish on it.

4. Add the yogurt to the four corners of the Pyrex dish. Gently push the rack back inside the oven, close the oven door, and turn on the inside light. *Do not heat the oven.* Allow to rest undisturbed at least overnight. (Yogurt must be stored in a draft-free, protected spot and must not be moved or touched during this period, and your oven is the ideal place for this. As an alternative, cover and wrap the dish with a large towel or blanket and let it rest undisturbed in a corner of your kitchen for at least 24 hours.)

5. Keep the yogurt in the refrigerator and use as needed. *Nush-e Jan!*

VARIATIONS

Drained or Thick Yogurt *(mast-e kisei or mast-e chekideh)*—Pour the yogurt into 3 layers of cheesecloth or a cotton bag, pull the ends together, and then hang the bag for 15 to 20 minutes over a large pot to catch the yogurt drips. Alternatively use a yogurt funnel. All the liquid will slowly drain out, leaving behind a thick and creamy yogurt.

Creamy Yogurt—Add 1 cup half-and-half milk to the yogurt in step 4.

Sweet Yogurt—Add 1 cup sugar to the milk in step 1.

Draining Store-Bought Yogurt—Ready-made yogurt can be drained and thickened by placing it in a bowl on a tray or cookie pan. Place 3 or 4 layers of paper towel over the top of the yogurt for a few hours. The paper towels absorb the excess liquid, which will drain onto the tray under the bowl. This will thicken the yogurt. Store in the refrigerator.

Persian Cheese

½ gallon whole milk
½ cup fresh lime juice
2 tablespoons sea salt (optional)
1 cup plain yogurt
Cheesecloth for straining
  the mixture

2 teaspoons cumin or nigella seeds,
  or 1 teaspoon dried thyme or mint
½ teaspoon sea salt
1 tablespoon plain yogurt

*Makes 6 servings
Preparation and cooking time:
20 minutes plus 4 hours to
settle and set*

Panir

1. Pour the milk into a large pot and bring to a boil over high heat.

2. Add the lime juice and salt to the boiling milk. Stir once. Add the yogurt and stir again. Boil over high heat for 3 to 5 minutes or until the milk's color turns yellowish and curds appear.

3. Line a strainer with three layers of cheesecloth and place the strainer in a large container. Remove the pot from the heat and immediately pour the milk-yogurt mixture over the cheesecloth. Allow to drain for several minutes. Add the seeds or herbs and save the liquid in the large container for step 5.

4. To remove excess water from the milk-yogurt mixture, bundle the free ends of cheesecloth together over the mixture to enclose it. Place the cheesecloth in the center of the strainer and place a heavy weight on top of the cheesecloth. Allow to stand for about 2 hours, then remove the weight. Place it in a container and refrigerate for 1 hour to set thoroughly.

5. Remove the cheesecloth and place the cheese in a sterilized jar. Fill the jar with the strained liquid from step 3 and add ½ teaspoon salt and 1 tablespoon yogurt. Refrigerate until ready to serve.

6. Serve the cheese with bread and a fresh herb platter. *Nush-e Jan!*

Kashk (Sun-Dried Yogurt)

Makes ½ pint
Preparation time: 2 days
Cooking time: 4 days in a warm oven

8 cups plain yogurt	1 tablespoon sea salt

Traditionally *kashk* is sold as a solid and dissolved in water to use in cooking. These days it is also available in jars as a liquid. Or you can make your own. There are many ways to make *kashk*. Here, I am giving both a simple and a more complex method.

SIMPLE METHOD

Make sour yogurt as for the yogurt recipe (page 530) or use commercial plain yogurt. Store yogurt for 2 days at room temperature for it to become sour. Place the soured yogurt in a blender with ½ cup water and 1 tablespoon salt and mix for 5 minutes until smooth. Boil the yogurt until thick, then drain through two layers of cheesecloth. Tie up the corners and allow the liquid to drain from the yogurt (reserve the drained liquid for making black sun-dried yogurt, below). What remains in the cheesecloth is sun-dried yogurt (*kashk*). Roll the drained yogurt into walnut-sized balls and place them on a cookie sheet to dry.

MR. PARSA'S MORE COMPLEX METHOD

Though it is more complex, the result is very tasty.

1. Make sour yogurt per the method above. Transfer the sour yogurt to a Pyrex dish. Cover it with another glass and place it in a warm oven at 140°F to 150°F (60°C to 65°C). After a few hours check the amount of condensation on the lid. No condensation indicates that the temperature is too high. Slight condensation means the temperature is correct. Adjust the oven setting as needed.

2. Leave the glass dish covered in the warm oven for 3 to 4 days; do not disturb.

3. Remove the dish from the oven and uncover it. Observe the color and scent: The contents should be yellowish and have a distinctive smell.

4. Line a strainer with 2 layers of cheesecloth and place it over a large pot. Pour the contents of the container over the cheesecloth. Tie the ends shut and allow to drain for several hours so that the excess water drains away. Catch drips in the pot.

5. Remove the contents from the cheesecloth and place in a food processor. Add 1 tablespoon salt and mix in food processor for 3 minutes.

6. Place *kashk* in an airtight jar and keep in the refrigerator for 2 weeks, or store in separate small plastic bags in the freezer and use as needed.

VARIATIONS

Black Sun-Dried Yogurt *(Qaraqorut)*—Cook the reserved drained liquid from making sour yogurt above (about 4 cups) with 1 cup all-purpose flour over medium heat, stirring constantly until you have a thick black paste, which is extremely sour. Black sun-dried yogurt is eaten with soup and fish, and is sometimes included in sauces.

Sun-Dried Yogurt with Walnuts *(Kashk-e khakestari)*—Add 2 cups ground walnuts and 1 tablespoon mint to the drained yogurt. Mix well and shape into balls.

NOTES

Another method, sometimes used by nomads, is to add water to diluted whole yogurt. Then pour yogurt into a goatskin canteen. Shake for a long time to separate the fat from the yogurt solids. Boil the yogurt solids, drain, and then dry in the sun to create kashk.

In southern Iran, they eat unsalted kashk (loor), *like cream, with dates.*

Cooking Yogurt without Curdling

2 egg whites
1 tablespoon cornstarch

1½ teaspoons sea salt
4 cups plain yogurt

Preparation time: 5 minutes
Cooking time: 15–20 minutes

1. In a mixing bowl, beat the egg whites until frothy. Add the cornstarch, salt, and yogurt, and mix until smooth.

2. Transfer the mixture to a heavy saucepan and, while continually stirring clockwise, heat over medium heat until it comes to a boil.

3. Stop stirring, reduce heat and simmer for 6 minutes until it thickens. Remove from heat and use as needed.

Bulgur and Yogurt Patties

Tarkhineh

Makes 12 patties
Preparation time: 5 minutes
Cooking time: 35 minutes plus
  3 hours of drying time

Tarkhineh *patties are made by Iranian nomads and used as a cooked cereal for breakfast or dissolved in water to make soup. They can also be flavored with various herbs and spices.*

Ready-made *tarkhineh* can be found in Afghan and Middle Eastern groceries, but you can also make it at home. Place 1 cup warm water in a mixing bowl and sprinkle with 1 tablespoon yeast. Allow to stand for 10 minutes, undisturbed. Gradually add 1 cup all-purpose unbleached flour sifted with ½ teaspoon salt, 2 cups bulgur, and 1 cup yogurt. Stir well until you have a sticky dough. Transfer to a bowl. Cover and allow to ferment, at room temperature, for 8 hours (traditionally this was made without yeast and was left for a week or so to ferment). Add more flour if the dough is too sticky. Form the dough into walnut-sized balls and place on a baking sheet lined with parchment paper. Dry in the sun or overnight in a 140°F (60°C) convection oven. Keep in plastic wrap and use as needed.

Clarified Butter (Ghee)

Roghan-e kareh,
  Roghan-e khub

Makes 1 jar (½ pint)
Cooking time: 30 minutes

1 pound butter, cut into small pieces

Clarified butter, also called ghee, gives a delicious nutty taste to rice and pastries and has a higher scorching point than regular butter. It is sold in specialty-food stores, but it is easy to make at home.

1. In a medium saucepan over low heat, melt the butter. When the butter is melted completely and bubbles form on top, raise heat to medium-low. Simmer for 15 to 20 minutes, skimming off the foam occasionally.

2. Begin to stir with a wooden spoon until the majority of the solids are brown (about 15 minutes). Remove from heat and allow solids to settle to the bottom.

3. When cool enough to handle, strain the clear liquid through three layers of cheesecloth to separate the clear butter fat from the milk solids. Discard the solids. Store in a tightly closed jar in your refrigerator for up to 3 months.

Peeling and Seeding a Tomato

There is little to equal the taste of fresh, ripe tomatoes in season; out of season, peeled, canned tomatoes make a good substitute. Most recipes require that fresh tomatoes be peeled. To do so, mark an X on the bottom of each tomato with a sharp knife. Plunge tomatoes into boiling water and blanch for 20 seconds, removing with a slotted spoon. Rinse with cold water. Drain and slip off the skin. To seed, cut them open around the middle, and squeeze out and discard the seeds.

Tomato Paste

Rob-e gojehfarangi

Makes ½ pint
Preparation time: 20 minutes
Cooking time: 1 hour

12 pounds large red tomatoes   2 tablespoons sea salt

1. Wash the tomatoes and peel them. Using a food processor or juicer, extract the tomato juice.

2. Pour the tomato juice into a large laminated pot, add 1 tablespoon salt, and bring to a boil. Reduce the heat and cook for about 1 hour, stirring occasionally with a wooden spoon.

3. Add another tablespoon salt and continue cooking over medium heat until the water evaporates, leaving the paste behind.

4. Fill sterilized jars with the paste, seal them tightly, and store them in a cool, dark place.

Grape Leaves for Dolmeh

50 tender grape leaves
½ cup salt
12 cups water

Snip off the ends of the leaves and wash thoroughly. Stack the leaves in bundles of 25, veins facing up, and tie them with a string. Blanch each stack in boiling salted water for 2 minutes (allowing ½ cup salt for 12 cups water). Drain the leaves in a colander, rinse with cold water, remove the strings, and pat the leaves dry. To use canned grape leaves, simply drain the brine, unroll, rinse in cold water, and pat dry.

NOTE

In America, fresh grape leaves are a rarity. Most of the commercial crop is canned. If you should find fresh leaves, choose the smallest and tenderest ones.

Pomegranate Molasses

Rob-e anar

Makes ½ pint
Preparation time: 20 minutes
Cooking time: 1 hour

8 cups fresh pomegranate juice (if the pomegranate juice is sweet rather than sour, add the juice of 2 limes to make it sour)

1 tablespoon sea salt

1. In a large and heavy laminated pan, pour in the pomegranate juice.

2. Bring to a boil over high heat. Reduce the heat, add 1 tablespoon salt, and let simmer uncovered for about 1 hour or more over medium heat.

3. Gently stir occasionally until the syrup has thickened, then remove the pan from the heat.

4. Sterilize jars in boiling water. Drain and dry thoroughly. Fill the jars with pomegranate molasses. Seal them and keep in a cool, dark place.

Bitter Orange Molasses

Rob-e narenj

Makes ½ pint
Preparation time: 20 minutes
Cooking time: 1 hour

1. Wash and remove a ring of orange peel from around the middle of each orange. Cut each orange in half and remove the seeds. Process the juice in a juicer to make 5 to 6 cups of juice, or use commercial bitter orange juice.

2. Pour the juice into a laminated container. Bring to a boil, reduce the heat, and simmer over medium heat for about 1 hour 30 minutes or until the juice has thickened. Be sure not to overcook. Remove from the heat.

3. Put the bitter orange paste in a sterilized jar, seal it tightly, and store in a cool, dark place.

Dried Tamarind Liquid

Ab-e tamr-e hendi

Makes ½ pint
Preparation time: 10 minutes
Cooking time: 40 minutes

1 pound dried tamarind pods

8 cups water

1. Place the tamarind pods in a large saucepan and cover with the water.

2. Bring to a boil, reduce the heat, and simmer for 30 minutes over medium heat until soft. Add more water if necessary.

3. Place a colander over a bowl, drain the softened tamarind through the colander, and with a masher push through and crush the pods to extract as much liquid as possible.

4. Pour more boiling water over the pods if necessary to extract more liquid.

5. Transfer the liquid into a clean, dry jar, seal, and store it in a cool, dark place.

NOTE

Dried tamarind and liquid tamarind are available at Iranian specialty stores.

Grape Syrup

Dushab-e angur

Makes ½ pint
Preparation time: 40 minutes
Cooking time: 3 hours

20 pounds grapes

1. Wash and separate the grapes from the stems, then place them in a laminated pot. Bring to a boil and simmer over low heat for 45 minutes, stirring frequently, until the grapes are tender.

2. Pass through a fine-mesh colander, press with a masher and squeeze out all the juice. Discard the skins and seeds.

3. Return the juice back to the pot and bring to a boil. Reduce heat and simmer over low heat for a few hours, stirring occasionally with a wooden spoon, until all the juice has evaporated and you have a syrup the consistency of maple syrup.

4. Pour into sterilized jars, seal tightly, and store in a cool, dark place.

Cooking with Saffron

Ashapzi ba za'feran

When buying saffron, choose threads rather than powder (which is too often adulterated with turmeric). Threads should be ground with a cube of sugar, then dissolved in hot water, rose water, or orange blossom water. The saffron-water solution can then be stored in a small glass container in the refrigerator and used as needed. Do not use the unground threads in cooking.

1. In a mortar or spice grinder, grind saffron threads with 1 cube sugar until transformed into a powder (the sugar helps the grinding process).

2. In a glass container dissolve 1 teaspoon saffron powder in ¼ cup hot water. For even more flavor, you can use rose water or orange blossom water instead of hot water. Store in an airtight glass bottle in the refrigerator for up to 3 weeks and use as needed (saffron water molds easily and should be kept in the refrigerator at all times.

Dried Persian Lime Powder

Limu-omani

The lime variety known as Persian lime has been grown in Iran for many centuries. These limes are widely available fresh. Persian groceries stock dried limes (limu-omani, which actually means "lime from Oman"). Dried lime powder (gard-e limu-omani) made from California grown limes is apt to be bitter because it contains ground seeds, but it is easy to make your own from dried Persian limes.

With a knife, crack open the limes, halve them, and remove any seeds. Then grind the dried limes to powder in a food processor and store in an airtight jar.

For *khoreshes,* whole dried limes are often used. They add a distinctive, tangy taste, especially if you squeeze out the juice on your plate when served after cooking.

Verjuice

Ab ghureh

Makes ½ pint
Preparation time: 40 minutes
Cooking time: 15 minutes plus
   time to cool

12 pounds unripe grapes *(ghureh)*
1 tablespoon sea salt

1. Wash the grapes and remove the stems. Drain and pat dry.

2. Using a food processor or juicer, extract the grape juice.

3. Pour the grape juice into a large laminated pot, add 1 tablespoon salt, and bring to a boil. Remove from heat and allow to cool.

4. Fill sterilized bottles with the juice, seal them tightly, and store them in a cool, dark place.

Removing Bitterness from Eggplants

Talkhi gereftan-e bademjan

METHOD #1

Peel and cut the eggplants into slices of desired thickness and length. Place the eggplant slices in a colander and place the colander in the sink. Sprinkle the eggplant slices with water and then with 2 tablespoons salt. Let stand for 20 minutes. The salt will draw out bitter, black juices from the eggplant. Rinse the eggplant with cold water and blot dry.

METHOD #2

Soak the eggplant slices in a large container full of cold water with 2 tablespoons salt for 20 minutes. Drain, rinse with cold water, and blot dry.

Persian Spice Mix for Rice

Advieh-ye polow

Makes about ¼ pint
Preparation time: 40 minutes

2 tablespoons ground dried rose petals
2 tablespoons ground cinnamon

2 tablespoons ground cardamom
1 tablespoon ground cumin

Mix all the ground spices together in a bowl. Store in an airtight container to preserve freshness.

Persian Spice Mix for Khoresh

Advieh-ye khoresh

Makes about ¼ pint
Preparation time: 40 minutes

2 tablespoons ground dried
  rose petals
2 tablespoons cinnamon
1 teaspoon ground cardamom
½ teaspoon freshly ground
  black pepper

1 teaspoon ground angelica *(gol-par)*
1 teaspoon ground nutmeg
1 teaspoon ground cumin
½ teaspoon ground coriander seeds
1 teaspoon *limu-omani*
  (Persian lime powder)*

Grind all the spices and mix. Store in an airtight container to preserve freshness.

Persian Spice Mix for Pickle

Advieh-ye torshi

Makes about ½ pint
Preparation time: 1 hour

2 tablespoons ground green
  cumin seed
2 tablespoons ground black cumin seeds
3 tablespoons ground angelica
  (gol-par)
½ teaspoon freshly ground
  black pepper
1 teaspoon parsley seeds
1 teaspoon turnip seeds

1 teaspoon beet seeds
1 teaspoon star anis seeds
1 tablespoon ground saffron
½ teaspoon ground turmeric
3 tablespoons ground coriander
2 tablespoons ground cinnamon
3 tablespoons ground ginger
1 tablespoon ground cardamom

Mix all the ground spices together. Store in an airtight container to preserve their aroma.

Cleaning Dried Barberries

Tamiz kardan-e zereshk

Fruit of the barberry bush has been popular since ancient times in Iran. Small, red, sour, and tiny (for fresh barberries during harvesting see photo on page 267), barberries are too sour to eat raw and are a valuable source of malic acid. In Iran, barberries (zereshk) are dried and stored. Be sure to use red-colored dried barberries and not dark ones, which may be old and from a previous season. The color and taste of the barberries depend on the quality of the berry. Dried barberries contain a lot of sand. When washed properly, they have a beautiful red color.

Clean barberries by removing their stems and placing them in a colander. Place the colander in a large container full of cold water and allow the barberries to soak for 15 minutes. The sand will settle to the bottom of the container. Take the colander out of the container and run cold water over the barberries. Drain and set aside. Pat dry and use right away or store for later use in a zip-lock bag in the freezer (this helps them retain their fresh color).

Removing Bitterness from Orange Peel

Talkhi gereftan-e pust-e porteqal

Makes 2 jars (½ pint each)
Preparation time: 1 hour
Cooking time: 10 minutes

10 firm, large oranges

1. Wash the oranges. Peel thin layers with a peeler and leave the pith on the orange. Save the oranges for a fruit salad.

2. Cut the orange peel into slivers of desired length.

3. Place the slivers in a large saucepan and cover with water. Bring to a boil, reduce heat, and cook for 10 minutes over medium heat. Drain in a colander and rinse with cold water. Store the orange peel slivers in a plastic bag in the freezer and use as needed.

NOTE

For bitter oranges (narenj), *repeat the boiling, cooking, draining, and rinsing in step 3 several times until the peels are no longer bitter.*

Candied Orange Peel

Pust-e porteqal-e shirin

Makes 3 jars (½ pint each)
Preparation time: 40 minutes
Cooking time: 1 hour

4 large oranges (2 cups orange peel)
2 cups sugar

2 cups water
4 tablespoons lime juice

1. Line a sheet pan with parchment paper. Scrub and wash the oranges. Peel the oranges, leaving the pith on them. Save the fruit for a fruit salad. Cut the orange peels into thin (¼-inch) slivers.

2. To remove the bitterness from the orange peel slivers, place them in a large saucepan and cover with water. Bring to a boil, reduce heat, cook for 10 minutes over medium heat, then drain in a colander, and rinse with cold water (if you use bitter orange, *narenj,* repeat this step 3 times).

3. Place the orange peels back in the saucepan and add 2 cups sugar and 2 cups water. Bring to a boil, reduce heat to medium, and simmer uncovered for 40 minutes. Add lime juice and continue to cook for 5 minutes longer.

4. Drain orange peel and discard syrup. Spread the orange peels on the parchment paper. Allow to dry for a few hours. Store, tightly covered, in a glass container in the refrigerator. Use as needed.

VARIATION

Candied Grapefruit Peel—Grapefruits can be substituted for the oranges. To remove the bitterness from the grapefruits, boil peels for 10 minutes, drain, and rinse with cold water. Repeat this process a second time.

Segmenting an Orange

To peel oranges neatly for salads or desserts, follow the simple procedure shown from left to right. First slice off the skin and bitter pith, cutting straight down (1). You should be able to do this in about 4 slices to make a pentagon (2). Holding the orange over a plate or bowl to catch the juice, slice the knife down one side of a segment, inside the papery membrane, to loosen it (3). Then slice down the other side of the segment (4) to lift it neatly from the membrane. Repeat for each segment.

Seeding a Pomegranate

To seed a pomegranate easily, use a sharp knife to cut the pomegranate in half (1). Hold each half, 1 at a time, seed side down over a bowl and tap the skin with a heavy wooden spoon (2) to dislodge the arils from the membrane that holds them (3). The arils will fall through your fingers into the bowl. A bowl of pomegranate arils (4) makes a wonderful dessert on its own, or with cream, ice cream, or yogurt. The arils are also essential for garnishing Pomegranate Khoresh, *Fesenjun*.

Juicing a Pomegranate in Its Skin

Iranians call juicing a pomegranate in its skin *ablambu*. It allows one to drink the juice of a pomegranate without fuss or mess. Choose a good-looking pomegranate with no blemishes or holes in the skin. Then, holding it in both hands with one thumb over the other, start by gently squeezing one of the raised parts of the fruit (there are usually 4 or 5 hills and valleys). The idea is to squeeze the seeds inside the skin without bursting the skin. This needs to be done gently and systematically, going around the pomegranate until the whole fruit is soft and squishy. Then press it to your mouth, bite into the skin, making a small hole in it with your teeth, while you suck with your mouth and squeeze gently with your hands. You will get a very refreshing burst of juice in your mouth that is both delicious and sensual. Continue working around the fruit, squeezing and sucking, until you have drunk all the juice. It is an art that you will perfect with practice, and once you know how, you will never again see a good-looking pomegranate without wanting to *ablambu* it.

Cutting Butternut Squash

Pumpkins, and acorn squashes are prepared the same way as butternut squashes (shown below). With a heavy cleaver, slice the squash crosswise into 2-inch rings. Remove the seeds with a spoon and use the cleaver to peel the squash. Cut each squash into 1-inch cubes, rinse and drain the cubes, and pat them dry.

How to Make Persian Noodles

2 cups unbleached all-purpose flour
1 teaspoon salt
⅔ cup water

1. In a wide mixing bowl, combine the flour and salt. Create a well in the flour and add the water, gently stirring with your index and middle fingers, clockwise, until you have a dough.

2. Transfer to a lightly floured surface, knead, and roll out to a thin rectangle. Dust with flour, fold, and dust twice more.

3. Use a sharp knife to cut the dough on a floured surface into strips.

4. Spread on a floured pan sheet to dry.

Peeling Fresh Green Walnuts

Fresh green walnuts are hard to find but are available nowadays on the Internet from farmers in California (end of June, much earlier than what is considered a ripe walnut in the U.S.). Wear gloves to prevent blackening your hands and use a knife to make multiple hits on the outer green shell as you turn the nut. It takes a little practice but this method enables you remove the walnut kernels intact from their outer and inner shell. Drop the nuts (kernels) in a large bowl of salted cold water until ready to eat. When ready to serve, drain nuts, peel, and sprinkle with salt.

Soaking Dried Walnuts and Almonds

Place 2 cups dried walnuts (halves or whole) or almonds in a colander and rinse. Transfer to a glass container and cover with boiling water. Allow to cool, cover, and refrigerate overnight. Drain the nuts, peel and sprinkle with salt to taste. Serve as a snack or as a side dish with cheese and bread. *Nush-e Jan!*

Roasting and Salting Raw Pistachios

½ cup lime juice
2 tablespoons sea salt

4 cups raw pistachios, rinsed thoroughly in a colander

In a mixing bowl, combine lime juice (or use water if you don't want the slight tang of lime) and sea salt, and mix well. Add the nuts to the bowl and mix well so that the nuts are evenly seasoned. Allow to soak for 30 minutes. Preheat the oven to 250°F (120°C). Pour out the nuts into a rimmed baking sheet and shake to even out. Bake in the oven for about 1½ hours (shake the baking sheet once every 20 minutes to ensure even drying) until the nuts are dry. Remove from the oven and allow to cool in front of a fan (the fan helps to make the nuts more crunchy). Place in a sieve and shake to remove any excess salt.

Dry Toasting Nuts

Heat a large skillet over medium heat and add nuts, but no oil. Cook over medium heat, shaking the pan occasionally, until the nuts are golden brown—5 to 10 minutes. Store in an airtight jar.

Dry Toasting Walnuts in the Oven

Place oven rack in the center and preheat oven to 350°F (180°C). Spread the walnuts in a rimmed baking sheet and bake for 10 minutes. Beware, walnuts burn easily.

Caramelizing Raw Nuts

Makes: 2 cups
Preparation time: 5 minutes
Cooking time: 15 minutes

2 cups shelled walnuts or any other nuts   ¼ cup grape molasses

Heat the walnuts in a wide skillet over medium heat, shaking the skillet frequently, for 5 to 15 minutes until they are toasted. Do not walk away; the walnuts will burn easily. Line a baking sheet with parchment paper. Reduce heat to very low and add the molasses, shaking and swirling the skillet for 2 to 3 minutes until the syrup covers all the nuts. Remove from heat and spread over the parchment paper. Allow to cool thoroughly. Store in a jar and use as needed.

Perfume Nuts with Jasmine

Place 2 pounds blanched nuts (almonds, pistachios, walnuts, hazelnuts) in a large bowl and sprinkle with 1 cup fresh jasmine flowers. Cover tightly and place in a cool room for 2 days. Replace the wilted flowers with fresh jasmine flowers. Cover and allow to rest for another 2 days. Discard the flowers and store the perfumed nuts in an airtight jar. These perfumed nuts are ground and used in making puddings and pastries such as baklavas.

New Year Wheat-Sprout Pudding

Samanu

1 pound whole wheat grain with skin or 2 cups ready-made sprout flour, *sahan* (wheat malt)* mixed with 4 cups boiling water.
8 cups boiling water
5 cups (2 pounds) sifted all-purpose unbleached flour

2 tablespoons whole unsalted pistachios
2 tablespoons whole almonds
2 tablespoons whole hazelnuts
1 tablespoon rose water

Makes 2 pints
Preparation time: 5 days to make sprouts
Cooking time: 8 hours

In Iran samanu is considered sacred because the wheat sprouts contain an enzyme that sweetens the pudding without adding any sugar. It is sometimes called a miracle pudding because of this.

TRADITIONAL METHOD

1. Place the grain on a cookie sheet and cover with 4 cups cold water. Allow to soak for 2 days, changing the water every day.

2. Drain into a drainer and cover with a cotton cloth or dishtowel.

3. Place the covered drainer of grains in a warm, dark place for a few days. (I found an oven that is not used to be the best place. Sprinkle the grains with cold water twice a day. After a few days the wheat grains should have developed roots and germinated; if not, leave until they have.)

4. Place the sprouts (roots and all) in a food processor, add 4 cups boiling water, and puree until creamy. Pass through a fine mesh sieve or 2 layers of cheesecloth, squeezing out the liquid into a wide pot (discard the pulp remaining in the cheese cloth.) Gradually add the flour to the pot.

5. Fry for 30 minutes, stirring constantly with a wooden spoon. Add 4 cups water and bring to a boil. Cook over medium heat for 30 minutes, stirring constantly with a wooden spoon to prevent lumps. Cover and steep over low heat for 8 hours, stirring occasionally or until the mixture becomes sweet and creamy and the color of peanut butter. (You may steep in a 140°F (60°C) oven overnight instead of steeping over heat.) Add the nuts and rose water and cook for 15 minutes longer. Transfer to a laminated bowl, cover, and place in the refrigerator.

NOTE

In pre-Islamic Iran, a pudding called " sen or sahan" was made from wheat sprouts by Zoroastrians as a celebratory dish. It was made on the last day of the year to sustain the ancestors on their heavenward journey following their annual New Year visit to earth. Halva, which means "sweet" in Arabic, may have come from this pudding, because it is still made for special occasions such as births and funerals.

VARIATION

You can also make *samanu* by using wheat malt flour (called *sahan* in Persian), which is available at Korean or Iranian stores. Soak 2 cups of the wheat malt in 4 cups boiling water, allow to cool, and leave in the refrigerator overnight. Puree in a food processor, transfer to the pot, and continue from step 5 above.

Platter of Sprouts

Sabzeh-na

Time: 10–12 days
Ingredients: 1 cup dry lentils,
Equipment: 1 serving platter,
   cotton dishtowel

1. Place 1 cup dry lentil grains in a bowl, cover with cold water, and allow to soak for 2 days. Change the water once a day.

2. Drain and spread the grains over a cotton napkin and loosely bundle the free ends of the napkin together.

3. Place the napkin with the soaked lentils in the bowl for 2 more days. Sprinkle with water several times a day keeping the napkin moist. The lentils with start to germinate and white roots will start to grow.

4. Remove the napkin bundle from the bowl and spread the lentils over a flat platter. Cover with the same damp cloth and place the platter in a sunny spot for about 2 to 3 days.

5. Check to see if the lentils have sprouted green. Once they have, remove the cloth and sprinkle with cold water twice a day. *It is important that neither too much nor too little water is used*. In several days you will have wonderful sprouts.

VARIATION

Sprouts in a Jar—Place 1 cup lentils in a 2 pint jar and fill with water (use a Mason jar with a screw top lid that has holes). Allow to soak for a few days, changing the water each day by turning the jar upside down over the sink to allow the water to drip out. Refill the jar with water. After 3 to 5 days (depending on the type of lentils used) the lentils will start to germinate. Drain. Keep out of the sun and moisten every day until the sprouts have grown long enough to use.

Sprouting Pot

Sabzeh-na

Time: 15–18 days
Ingredients: 4 teaspoons cress
   seeds, ½ cup water
Equipment: 1 unglazed clay jar
   (4" x 8"), cheesecloth, clear
   plastic bag, small water
   sprayer

1. Submerge the unglazed jar (filled with water) in a container of cold water for 24 hours. Unglazed jars are available at home furnishing stores like Pier 1.

2. At the same time, mix 4 teaspoons of cress seeds (*esparzeh*) in ½ cup water. Stir well and leave to soak uncovered for about 24 hours or until the mixture becomes a gel or paste.

3. Remove the submerged jar from the container, refill the jar with water, place it on a tray and wrap it with one layer of cheesecloth. Spread the seed-gel evenly all over the jar. Moisten the jar and cover it with a clear plastic bag to achieve a moist environment to help the seeds sprout. Leave in a sunny, draft-free spot for 2 days (keep moist by spraying it from time to time). Check the level of water in the jar and refill if needed.

4. Once the seeds have started to sprout, remove the plastic. Moisten twice a day. In 2 to 3 weeks you should have a sprouting jar. You can then place flowers in the jar. I usually use cherry blossoms, hyacinth, or tulips. See Photo on page 570.

CEREMONIES

آداب و رسوم ایرانی

CEREMONIES

CEREMONIAL SETTINGS

SOFREH-YE NAZRI

Sofreh is a cotton cloth, often embroidered with prayers and poems that is spread over a Persian carpet or a table, and on which dishes of food are placed for a meal. *Sofreh* can also refers to the ceremony for which a *sofreh* is prepared. It serves as a ceremonial or religious setting on which various symbolic elements are displayed and from which food is served.

Sofrehs are divided into three kinds: the "presentational *sofreh*," such as the Nowruz setting, *Sofreh-ye haft seen;* the "votive *sofreh*," *nazr,* where a promise is made to God to organize a *sofreh* in return for fulfilling a request; and the "*sofreh* of thanks," when the supplicant's request has been fulfilled.

Sofrehs are usually organized, hosted, and prepared by women for women. The holy figures in whose names the *sofrehs* are set, with a few exceptions, are also usually women. Men can pay for the cost of a *sofreh*, but they cannot participate in it. They can only eat the food if brought to them by a woman at the end of the ceremony.

The ceremony for setting the *sofreh* is carried out by volunteers, all women, who are often family, friends, and neighbors. The food is prepared and prayed over collectively to bless it. After the *sofreh* has been set, the food laid out, the candles lit, and everyone is seated around it, prayers associated with that particular *sofreh* are recited collectively to further bless the food. Iranians have strong beliefs in the power of prayer and the special healing quality of food. The food is then distributed among the participants and neighbors. Some of it is also taken home to family and friends who could not be present. In some contemporary *sofrehs* blessed goodie bags of dried fruit and roasted nuts are also given to participants to take with them.

The dishes prepared and the food provided for a *sofreh* are usually rich and high in calories because they are intended for less fortunate people in the neighborhood. On every *sofreh*, dates, bread, water, and candles are present; dates were Prophet Mohammad's favorite food, bread and water represent blessings from God, and candles represent God (light). Other dishes vary, depending on the *sofreh,* and can include *halva*, a sweet pudding made of wheat flour, and *sholeh zard,* made from rice; and various thick hearty soups *(oshes)* such as noodle soup, *osh-e reshteh*. The rice dishes associated with *sofrehs* are Rice with Dates and Lentils; and Rice with Yellow Split Peas.

Charity is one of the pillars of Islam. However, the concept of religious offerings and *sofreh* go back to pre-Islamic times and are also practiced by Iranian Jews and Zoroastrians.

Charity and taxation, *khoms* and *zakat,* and their offshoots *nazr* and *sofreh* play important roles in taking care of the less fortunate. They bring people together, making them active within the community. The blessing of the food also symbolically shows respect and appreciation for the food of the earth.

Each type of *sofreh* is associated with a particular story or poem, and these are often told or performed during the ceremony. A unique and ancient *sofreh* is know as the "Green Sofreh," *Sofreh-ye sabz,* and is associated with Prophet Khezr (also known as Elias and translated as Elijah in the Bible). This *sofreh* is usually offered at the end of the solar year. Its symbolic association with the color green, which represents rebirth, are very similar to the symbolism of the Nowruz celebration and the *Haft Seen* Setting, which is a celebration of the new year. Interestingly enough, the Zoroastrians believe that the end is also the beginning. This *sofreh,* which is carried out in various forms by Iranian Jews, Zoroastrians, and Muslims, demonstrates the mutual cultural influences and contacts that have existed among Iranians of various religions from ancient times. For me, the symbolism of this ancient Iranian ceremony—the celebration of the earth, the color green, and green food, all are reminders of St. Patrick's day in America. So, perhaps, all is, indeed, one.

Below are some *sofreh*s and the dishes associated with them:

SOFREH-YE HAZRAT-E ROQHIEH: This *sofreh* is the least elaborate, consisting of water, dates, bread, candles, and a brick.

SIBI SESHANBEH: This *sofreh* honors the Tuesday Lady, (also sometimes called *sofreh-ye bibi Hour* and *bibi Nour,* two daughters of the Prophet Mohammad), who was born, married, and died on a Tuesday. The elements of this *sofreh,* flour, vegetables, and legumes, necessary for preparing *osh-e omaj,* are displayed on a Monday night. The hostess, after ablutions, performs the prayer of supplication *(namaz-e hajat),* then leaves the room locking the door. She returns on Tuesday morning, and if there is a palm print on the flour or the salt, her supplication has been accepted, and the *osh-e omaj* is prepared.

SOFREH-YE BIBI ZAYNAB: The special food on this *sofreh* is noodle soup.

SOFREH-YE FATEMEH ZAHRA: The special food for this *sofreh* is *halva.* It is prepared in the name of Fatemeh, the daughter of Prophet Mohammad, the first wife of Ali, and is called *halva-ye Fatemeh Zahra.*

SOFREH-YE HAZRAT-E ABBAS (also known as Abul Fazl, and *Qamar-e Bani Hashem,* "the moon of the Hashemites"): He is a revered Shiite warrior, protector of the martyred Imam Husayn (his half-brother), and. He was the son of Hazrat-e Ali and Fatemeh (Ali's second wife, not the Fatemeh-ye Zahra who was Ali's first wife and the daughter of Prophet Mohammad). This is the most elaborate of the charity *sofrehs.* The special dishes are mixed dried fruit and nuts, *halva, sholeh zard,* varieties of sweets, fresh fruits, a variety of rice dishes, hearty soups, and porridges.

In the pages that follow, I give some details of pre-Islamic ceremonial *sofrehs* and rituals still practiced by Iranians, both inside and outside the country, to celebrate marriage, the new year, and the earth and its seasonal transitions. They all serve to bring people closer to nature.

WEDDING CEREMONY

JASHN-E ARUSI

Turned toward Kaaba, or the Sacred House of God (*ru be Qebleh*), and dressed in white satin or silk with gold embroidery, the bride sits facing a mirror, *ayeneh-ye bakht,* or the mirror of fate. It is usually lit by two candelabra, one on either side, representing the bride and groom. According to tradition the mirror and candlesticks, symbolizing purity and love, should be gifts from the groom. Just before sunset, when he enters the room in the bride's home where the ceremony will be held, what he sees first should be the face of his wife-to-be, reflected in the mirror.

The *sofreh-ye aqd,* a fine hand-sewn wedding cloth glittering with gold and silver threads, is spread out before the mirror. Food and objects traditionally associated with marriage are arranged on the *sofreh,* including:

• A tray of *atel-o-batel* (multicolored herbs and spices to guard against witchcraft and to drive the evil spirits away). This tray consists of seven elements in seven colors: poppy seeds (to break spells and witchcraft), wild rice, angelica, salt and green leaves (to remove the evil eye), nigella seeds, gunpowder, and frankincense (*kondor)* for burning to ward off the evil spirits.

• An assortment of sweets and pastries prepared in the bride's home but paid for by the groom—among them are *noghl,* sugar-coated almonds; *nabat,* sugar crystals; baklava, a sweet, flaky pastry; *tut,* mulberry-almond paste; *nan-e berenji,* rice cookies; *nan-e nokhodchi,* chickpea cookies; *nan-e badami,* almond cookies; and *sohan asali,* honey almonds.

• A large flat *sangak* bread with a blessing (*mobarak-bad*) written in calligraphy with saffron or cinnamon, nigella seeds, or gold.

• A platter of feta cheese, fresh herbs, and bread to be shared with the guests immediately after the ceremony, to bring the new couple happiness and prosperity; a basket of eggs and a basket of almonds and walnuts in the shell to symbolize fertility; a bowl of honey to make the future sweet.

• Two large loaves of sugar, *kallehqand,* to be used in the ceremony; fresh flowers, such as roses, tuberose, gardenia, jasmine, and baby's breath, to express the hope that beauty will adorn the couple's life together.

• An open flask of rose water to perfume and purify the air.

• A needle and seven strands of seven colored threads to sew up the mother-in-law's mouth—only figuratively, of course.

• A small brazier burning wild rue, the fumes of which are said to drive away evil spirits.

• An open Koran or *divan* of Hafez.

The wedding has two phases: the *aqd*, which is the legal ceremony where the contract, *aqd nameh* or *qabaleh*, is agreed upon and signed; and the *arusi*, the reception after the *aqd*, a splendid affair often held in the home of the groom. As the *aqd* ceremony begins, women who are happily married, friends, or relatives of the bride and groom are invited by the bride's mother to gather in the ceremony room. Two of them hold a square of white silk or cotton over the bride's head while another sews a piece of tissue using the seven colored threads; yet another rubs two sugar loaves together to symbolize the raining of sweet joy and happiness down upon the bride and groom. With each stitch, the seamstress chants, "I am sewing the mother-in-law's tongue, now I am sewing the sister-in-law's tongue, now I am sewing up all the other family members' tongues." Others chant, *aziz-ash kon, aziz-ash kon,* "endear her, endear her."

A holy man chosen by the couple reads the marriage contract and recites the traditional prayers. (During the reading of the marriage contract, all the unmarried women are asked to leave the room, the belief being that their chances for marriage might be jinxed.) The holy man then asks the bride, "Young and noble woman, do you realize you are marrying an honorable man for this *mahr*" (security-money or property that the groom agrees to give the bride upon demand)? But the bride remains silent and those in attendance pretend the bride is absent, saying such things as, "She is not here. She went out to gather rosebuds." Again he asks the question. This time the guests might answer, "The bride has gone to the library." The holy man repeats the question three times and the bride finally answers with a shy, barely audible, "Yes." He then declares the couple husband and wife. The groom kisses the bride, although the groom cannot join the bride until the *arusi*, the reception celebration. Traditionally, the *arusi* follows the *aqd* on the same night, or it may be held on a later day.

The bride and groom moisten their little fingers with some honey and place it in each other's mouths, then they each place a *noghl* (page 389) in the other's mouth. Friends and relatives shower them with more *noghls* and coins or rice before offering them their wedding gifts. At this moment the mother of the bride takes off the bride's right shoe and puts out the candles with it. The shoe symbolizes control of her fate, or *bakht*.

To bring sweetness and energy for the wedding night, sometimes an egg omelet, *Khagineh* (page 138), is cooked and sprinkled with the same sugar that the bride and groom were showered with; this is then served to the bride and groom.

The *arusi* is a lavish meal, sometimes with a whole roast lamb as the centerpiece. Jeweled rice (*javaher polow*, page 268), or sweet rice (*shirin polow*, page 262), is always served, along with many other dishes and an elaborate wedding cake. The celebration, with so much feasting, singing, and dancing, is a day for all to remember. After the guests have gone home, it is customary to give the remaining pastries to those who were unable to come and to those who helped make the day a success. The sugarloaf is kept by the bride.

Before they enter their home, the bride kicks over a bowl of water placed in the doorway. The water spilled on the threshold represents enlightenment, happiness, and purification for her new house. A friendly competition starts with the bride and groom as the bride tries to enter her house while stepping on her husband's feet. This act makes the bride the boss in the household.

In recent years, the Persian communities abroad have changed and adopted the lifestyles of their host countries. The Persian marriage ceremony, however, is so old and can be such a beautiful ceremony that it would be a shame not to enact it.

For all the guests to be able to participate, you may choose to have your wedding ceremony setting over a table rather than on the floor. Meet with your holy man and mention the length of the ceremony and perhaps go through a rehearsal (five to ten minutes should be the maximum length of this speech). The bride and groom may wish to recite a favorite poem that applies to the occasion. Remember, every symbol and superstition in the ceremony is intended to create a positive air and energy to bless the marriage with sweetness, fertility, and tranquility. Preparing for the way you will conduct the ceremony is as important as the beauty of the setting. *Mobarak!*

Note: The section read from the Koran during the ceremony is frequently Sura Al-Rum XXX, verses 20–21.

A double-page spread from a mid-nineteenth-century Persian marriage certificate booklet.
The bride's dowry was 30 tomans, a valuable Koran, and a bolt of silk.

THE PROCEDURE FOR A PERSIAN MARRIAGE

Step #1. The suitor, or *khastegar,* with his parents or close elder relatives, pays a visit to the parents and close relatives of his future wife and asks for her hand in marriage.

Step #2. Engagement ceremony, *shirni-khory,* and exchanging of rings and eating of sweets. Both sets of parents give formal permission for the future bride and groom to get better acquainted.

Step #3. *Ba'leh borun,* a ceremony that is attended by the close elder families of both the bride and the groom to discuss financial matters, rules, and conditions of marriage, such as *mahr* and *jahaz,* and items of the dowry listed in the marriage contract. The *mahr* is a sum of money, an object of value, or a piece of property that the groom agrees to give to the bride. It is her financial security in case of marital discord. The bride brings her dowry, or *jahaz,* to her new home. The details of the *mahr* and *jahaz* are spelled out in the *qabaleh,* or marriage contract. The dowry can be silver, gold, carpets, household equipment, sometimes even land and real estate.

Step #4. *Aqd,* or marriage-contract ceremony, the betrothal ceremony where the legal contract, *aqdnameh* or *qabaleh,* is read, agreed upon, and signed. *Aqd* is the legal and religious union of the marriage, while the true ceremony establishes the spiritual union of the bride and groom.

Step #5. *Arusi,* a lavish reception and celebration held after the *aqd.* As the bride and groom walk into the reception, the guests collectively sing a wedding song, which I have included here. Through this reception, the social recognition and union of the bride and groom are established, and this marks the beginning of their married life.

Step #6. *Pa-takhty* (literally, "by the bed"), the last phase of the wedding. Friends and family who were invited for the *aqd* and the *arusi* pay a visit to the newlywed couple the day after the wedding to offer their blessings and more gifts. At the close of *pa-takhty* the couple is considered truly married.

An important point for the mothers of the bride and groom to keep in mind before the ceremony: Remember that this is meant to be a joyful event and a spiritual ceremony and not a performance or competition with another family. Good luck and *mobarak-bad*!

STEPS FOR PLANNING A PERSIAN MARRIAGE

1. Set the wedding date together with both families.
2. Choose a theme, a color, and a flower, and use them throughout the ceremony.
3. Set a budget and choose a bridal gown.
4. Get in touch with the holy man who will perform the ceremony (it could also be performed by any respected member of the family).
5. Get information about the state's marriage laws.
6. Get medical examinations.
7. Make a guest list including addresses. Usually older people are invited for *aqd* (marriage-contract ceremony), and younger people are invited to the reception *(arusi)*.
8. Reserve a place for the reception. Keep in mind that *aqd* is always in the home of the bride's parents or that of her close relatives. *Arusi* is hosted by the parents or relatives of the groom.
9. Print and mail invitation cards. Hand out an explanation of the traditions of a Persian wedding to American friends (available for print out at, http://www.mage.com/cooking/pwc.html).
10. Arrange food catering. You may photocopy the jeweled rice *(javaher polow),* or sweet rice *(shirin polow)* recipes in this book to give to your caterer. If your caterer has any questions on preparing the rice, you may have them contact me.
11. Arrange pastry and flower catering and photography or video.
12. Get in touch with musicians.
13. Make an appointment with your hairdresser and your makeup artist.
14. Make arrangements for the transportation of gifts.
15. Choose and buy a gift for the bride/groom. If you are a member of the groom's close family, you must give a gift to the bride (traditionally jewelry or family jewelry) and vice versa.
16. Arrange a wedding shower (usually arranged by close family or friends of the bride).
17. Prepare a bridal registry. Check with major department stores and specialty shops. Don't feel bad about registering with a department store—the wedding shower is an old Persian custom still practiced in the villages of Iran. A few days before the marriage, an old wise woman of the community goes around with a large bag and collects gifts and household items for the newlywed couple-to-be to alleviate financial difficulties they will face starting their new life. However, it is quite all right to arrange a wedding shower by close friends or relatives.
18. Send out thank-you notes (after you return from your honeymoon).

WEDDING SONG

What a night it will be tonight, it's a lucky night tonight   This house is full of candles and light tonight
Baad-a, baad-a bless it tonight, God willing it's blessed tonight

Emshab che shabist, shab-e morad ast emshab   In khaneh por az sham'-o cheragh ast emshab
Baad-a baad-a mobarak baad, inshallah mobarak bad

امشب چه شبی است، شب مُراد است امشب   این خانه پُر از شمع و چراغ است امشب

بادا بادا مبارک بادا ، انشاالله مبارک بادا

ای شمع تو سوز که شب دراز است امشب   ای صبح تو دم که وقت ناز است امشب

بادا بادا مبارک بادا ، انشاالله مبارک بادا

عروس شاهانه ، ایشالا مبارک باد   جشن بزرگانه ، ایشالا مبارک باد
آیینه را منت که می رود سر بالا   دستمال به دست او می زند نگارا
محمد زبیر سلام کنید صحرا را   آفتاب نزنه شاخ گل رعنا را

بادا بادا مبارک بادا ، انشاالله مبارک بادا

امشب امید که در خواب رود چشم نزنم   خواب در روضه رضوان نکنم خنده به نیم
جای آن منت که خاموش نشیند مطرب   جای آن منت که باشند حریفان تسلیم

مبارک و مبارک ، ایشالا مبارک باد

عروس چه قدر قشنگه ، ایشالا مبارک باد   لعبت مستانه انشالا مبارک باد
سر و فرزانه ، ایشالا مبارک باد   بادا بادا مبارک بادا ، انشاالله مبارک بادا

PERSIAN NEW YEAR CELEBRATION AND FESTIVAL

NOWRUZ

The spring has come, and flower-strewn pastures shine
With buds, all opening now, except for mine.

Nowruz is here; I heard the lilies say,
It would be wrong to grieve on such a day;

Dismiss discord, dissension and distress,
Disdain, disruption, dread, deceitfulness.

But take sweet apples, senjed, samanu,
Take celebration, song, spring's green shoots too,

And scented hyacinths, and kindly send
These "S"s for the table of a friend

(And as for all those dread, repellent "D"s,
Leave them before the doors of enemies).

Nowruz is coming, so dispel the night
From your dark heart; Nowruz will give it light.

Keep her traditions, so that God may bring
Blissful renewal to us with the spring.

نوبهاراست و بود دگل و شاداب چمن   همه گل ها بشکفته بغیر از گل من

حیف باشد دل آزاده بنوروزین   این من هر روز نشینم ز ربان سوسن

هفت شین ساز کن جان من اندر شب عید   شکوه و شین و شغب شته و شور و شیون

هفت سین پاک کن از سبز و ارسنبل سیب   سنجد و سار و سمر و د و سمنو سلوی من

هفت سین را یکی سفره بخواه بنه   هفت شین را بدر خانه بدخواه فکن

صبح عید است برون کن دل این تار   کآخر این شام سیه خانه نماید روشن

رسم نوروز بجا ی آور و ارزید ان خواه   کآور د خالت ما باز به حالی حسن

Malek-o Sho'ara Bahar, written in prison in the 1930s

According to the *Shahnameh* of Ferdowsi, King Jamshid became skilled in all arts and crafts and considered himself to be unique throughout the world. Then even loftier and grander ambitions swelled in his heart, and he began to think of how he could journey through the skies. He ordered that a costly throne studded with jewels be built for him. He sat upon the throne and then commanded the demons who were his slaves to lift the throne from the ground and raise it up toward the heavens. Jamshid sat there splendid as the shining sun, and thus he traveled through the skies. He did all this through the strength of the divine *farr* (a certain power and dignity that great kings are born with). The world's inhabitants were astonished by his glory and power. They gathered together and praised his *farr* and good fortune, and rained jewels upon him; they called this day, which was the first day of the month of *Farvardin, Now Ruz,* or the New Day, and they called for goblets and wine and sat together feasting and rejoicing. From then on, this day was celebrated with rejoicing and pleasure every year. This was the origin of the festival of *Nowruz.*

نشسته بر و شاه فرمان رو

جشن نوروز و یا عید دهقانی

جهان انجمن شد بر تخت او
شگفت فرو ماند از بخت او

به جمشید بر گوهر افشاندند
مر آن روز را روز نو خواندند

سر سال نو هرمز فرودین
بر آسوده از رنج روی زمین

چنین جشن فرخ از آن روزگار
بجا ماند از آن خسروان یادگار

فردوسی

In harmony with the rebirth of nature, the two-week Persian New Year celebration, or *Nowruz,* always begins on the first day of spring (the first day of the month of *Farvardin,* which refers to "the spirits") marked by the vernal equinox, or *Tahvil.* On that day—which may occur on March 20, 21, or 22—the sun crosses the celestial equator. *Nowruz* ceremonies consist of a series of symbolic rituals dating back to ancient times, including:

- Cleaning of the environment, cleansing of the self, confession of sins, and the exorcising of devils, or *divs,* from the house and the community.
- Forgiving yourself and others, and reconciling friendships.
- Dowsing and re-lighting the fires.
- Going in processions to borders, seas, and rivers.
- Disrupting of the normal order of things with boisterous parties.

A few weeks before the New Year, Iranians thoroughly clean and rearrange their homes. They make or buy new clothes, bake pastries, and germinate seeds as signs of renewal. Troubadours, called *Haji Firuz* or "heralds of rebirth," disguised with makeup and wearing red satin outfits, sing and dance through the streets with tambourines, kettle drums, and trumpets to spread good cheer and the news of the coming new year. They sing:

haji firuz-e
sal-i ye ruz-e, sal-i ye ruz-e
ham-e midunan, man-am midunam
eyd-e nowruz-e, sal-i ye ruz-e

Haji firuz is here
It's once a year, it's once a year
Everyone knows it's here, I know it's here
Nowruz is here, it comes but once a year.

The celebration of renewal is attributed to the Sumerian god of sacrifice, Domuzi, who was killed at the end of each year and reborn at the beginning of the new year. The *Haji Firuz*'s disguised face represents his return from the world of the dead, his red costume symbolizes the blood and tragic fate of the legendary Prince Seyavash and the rebirth of the god of sacrifice, while his happiness and singing represent his joy at being reborn.

THE SEVEN "S" SETTING

SOFREH-YE HAFT SINN

In every Persian household a special cover is spread on a carpet or on a table. This ceremonial setting is called *sofreh-ye haft-sinn* (literally "seven dishes' setting," each one beginning with the Persian letter *sinn*). The number seven has been sacred in Iran since antiquity, and the seven dishes stand for the seven angelic heralds of life—rebirth, health, happiness, prosperity, joy, patience, and beauty. The symbolic dishes consist of *sabzeh,* or sprouts, usually wheat or lentil, representing rebirth. *Samanu* is a pudding in which common wheat sprouts are transformed and given new life as a sweet, creamy pudding. It represents the ultimate sophistication of Persian cooking. *Sib* means "apple" and represents health and beauty. *Senjed,* the sweet, dry fruit of the wild olive, represents love. It has been said that when the wild olive is in full bloom, its fragrance and its fruit make people fall in love and become oblivious to all else. *Sir,* which is "garlic" in Persian, represents medicine. *Somaq,* "sumac berries," represent fertility. *Serkeh,* or "vinegar," represents age and patience.

To reconfirm the hopes and wishes expressed by the traditional foods, other elements and symbols are also placed on the *sofreh.* Books of tradition and wisdom are laid out: usually a copy of the holy Koran and/or a *divan* of the poems of Hafez. A few coins, representing wealth, and a basket of painted eggs, representing fertility, are also placed on the *sofreh.* A bitter orange floating in a bowl of water represents the earth floating in space, and the fish in a bowl of water represents Anahita, one of the angels of water and fertility, which is the main purpose of the *Nowruz* celebration. The fish also represents life and the end of the astral year associated with the constellation Pisces. A flask of rose water, known for its magical cleansing power, is also included on the *sofreh.* Sometimes there is also a bowl of fresh milk, representing nourishment for the children of the world, as well as pussy willow branches, pomegranates, figs, and olives, representing time. Nearby is a brazier for burning wild rue, a sacred herb whose smoldering fumes are said to ward off evil spirits. A pot of flowering hyacinth or narcissus is also set on the *sofreh.* On either side of a mirror are two candelabra holding a flickering candle for each child in the family. The candles represent enlightenment and happiness. The mirror represents the images and reflections of creation as we celebrate anew the ancient Persian traditions and beliefs that creation took place on the first day of spring, or *Nowruz.*

On the same table many people place seven special sweets, because, according to a three-thousand-year-old legend, King Jamshid discovered sugar on *Nowruz* (the word candy comes from the Persian word for sugar, *qand*). These seven sweets are *noghls*

I saw a woman pounding light with a mortar and pestle;
There was bread on their spread at noon,
There were greens, a plate of dew, and a
piping hot bowl of affection.

Sohrab Sepehri

من زنی را دیدم ، نور در هاون می کوبید .

ظهر در سفرهٔ آنان نان بود ، سبزی بود ، دوری شبنم بود

کاسهٔ داغ محبت بود .

(sugar-coated almonds); Persian baklava, a sweet, flaky pastry filled with ground almonds and pistachios soaked in honey-flavored rose water; *nan-e berenji* (rice cookies), made of rice flour flavored with cardamom and garnished with poppy seeds; *nan-e badami* (almond cookies), made of almond flour flavored with cardamom and rose water; *nan-e nokhodchi* (chickpea cookies), made of chickpea flour flavored with cardamom and garnished with pistachios; *sohan asali* (honey almonds), cooked with honey and saffron and garnished with pistachios; and *nan-e gerdui* (walnut cookies), made of walnut flour flavored with cardamom and garnished with pistachio slivers.

On the eve of the last Wednesday of the year, *Shab-e chahar shanbeh sury* (literally "the eve of Red Wednesday" or "the eve of celebration"), bonfires are lit in public places and people leap over the flames, shouting, "*Sorkhi-e to az man o zardi-e man az to!*" (Give me your beautiful red color and take back my sickly pallor!). With the help of fire and light, symbols of good, celebrants pass through this unlucky night—the End of the Year— and into the arrival of spring's longer days. Tradition holds that the living are visited by the spirits of their ancestors on the last days of the year. Many people, especially children, wrap themselves in shrouds to symbolically reenact the visits. By the light of the bonfire, they run through the streets, banging on pots and pans with spoons and knocking on doors to ask for treats. This ritual is called *qashogh-zany* and reenacts the beating out, the night before, the last unlucky Wednesday of the year. In order to make wishes come true, it is customary to prepare special foods and distribute them on this night: *Osh-e reshteh-ye nazri* (noodle soup); *Baslogh,* a filled Persian delight; and special snacks called *ajil-e chahar shanbeh suri* and *ajil-e moshkel gosha.* The last, literally meaning "unraveler of difficulties," is made by mixing seven dried nuts and fruits—pistachios, roasted chickpeas, almonds, hazelnuts, peaches, apricots, and raisins.

A few hours prior to the transition to the new year, family and friends sit around the *sofreh-ye haft-sinn.* Everyone sings traditional songs and some recite poems of Hafez and verses from the Koran. I remember an amusing story about my aunt. She would always carry a tattered *divan* of the poems of Hafez and, just prior to the *Tahvil,* while we were all sitting around the *sofreh,* she would ask each of us to make a wish so that she could ask Hafez about our fortune. Then she would lay the closed book, spine down, on the palm of her left hand while she passed her right index finger several times up and down the page edges. With her eyes closed she would begin out loud:

Ay Hafez-e Shirazi to ke mahram-e har razy! To ra be Shakh-e Nabatat qassam. . .
O Hafez of Shiraz, knower of all secrets, by the love of your sweetheart, Shakh-e Nabat...

She would then be silent for a moment (as if allowing the question to be asked) and finally she would open the book by placing her fingernail randomly into the pages. With the first glance at the verses on the page, she would cry out, *"bah- bah!"* (wonderful,

wonderful). She would go on like this for a good minute or two while we sat round-eyed and impatient, waiting to know our fortunes. At last she would begin the first verse of the poem:

Nafas-e Bad-e Saba...   نَفَسِ باد صبا مشک فشان خواهد

The gentle breeze will blow a new vitality to the barren earth
The old will become young...

Exactly at the moment of the equinox, Aqa-jan (our name for our father) would recite the prayer for the transition, wishing for a good life, and we would all repeat after him out loud.

NOWRUZ GREEN MENU

The traditional menu for the *Nowruz* gathering on the day of the equinox usually includes fish and noodles. It is believed they bring good luck, fertility, and prosperity in the year that lies ahead.

• Noodle Soup *(Osh-e reshteh)*—Noodles represent the Gordian knots of life. Eating them symbolically unravels life's knotty problems in the coming year.

• Rice with Fresh Herbs and Fish *(Sabzi polow ba mahi)*—Fresh herb rice represents rebirth, fish represent Anahita, one of the angels of water and fertility.

• Herb Kuku *(Kuku-ye sabzi)*—The eggs and herbs represent fertility and rebirth.

• Bread, Cheese, and Fresh Herbs *(Nan-o panir-o sabzi khordan)*— Represents prosperity.

• Wheat Sprout Pudding *(Samanu)*—Represents fertility and rebirth.

• Sprout Cookies *(Kolucheh-ye javaneh-ye gandom)*—Represents prosperity and fertility.

• Ice in Paradise *(Yakh dar behesht)*—Represent nourishment.

• Saffron Sherbet, and Saffron Tea with Rock Candy *(Sharbat-e Zaferan, Chai-e zafaran ba nabat)*—Represent light and love.

•Baklava *(Baqlava)*; Chickpea Cookies *(Nan-e Nokhodchi)*; Rice Cookies *(Nan-e berenji)*; and Sugar Coated Almonds *(Noghl)*—Represent sweetness and prosperity.

دعای سر سفره هفت سین

O Swayer of our hearts and sight

O Governor of days and nights

O Swayer of feelings and thoughts

Turn our feelings to the best possible

After the *tahvil*, traditionally, the oldest person present begins the well-wishing by standing up and giving out sweets, pastries, coins, and hugs. Calm, happiness, sweetness, and perfumed odors are very important on this day of rebirth, since the mood on this day is said to continue throughout the year. An old saying goes, "Good thought, good word, good deed—to the year end, happy indeed."

The new year celebration continues for twelve days after the equinox occurs. Traditionally, during the first few days, it is the younger members of the family who visit their older relatives and friends, often bringing flowers, in order to show their respect. Sweet pastries and delicious sherbets are served to visitors, and there is a general air of festivity all around. The children receive gifts, usually crisp new notes of money; in America, dollar bills. In the remaining days, the elders return the visits of the younger members of the family.

According to the ancients, each of the twelve constellations in the zodiac governed one of the months of the year, and each would rule the earth for a thousand years, after which the sky and the earth would collapse into each other. The *Nowruz* celebrations, therefore, lasted twelve days, plus a thirteenth day (representing the time of chaos) celebrated by going outdoors, putting order aside, and having parties. On this thirteenth day, called *Sizdah bedar* or "outdoor thirteen picnic," entire families leave their homes to carry trays of sprouted seeds in a procession to go picnic in a cool, grassy place. Far from home, they throw the sprouts into the water, which is thought to exorcise the *divs* and evil eyes from the house and the household. Wishing to get married by the next year, unmarried girls tie blades of grass together. There is much singing, dancing, eating, and drinking. With this, the *Nowruz* celebrations are completed.

NOTE

Nowruz is pronounced "no•ruz" in Tehran, "now•ruz" in eastern Iran and in Afghanistan, and "nav•ruz" in parts of Kurdistan. The English word "new" comes from the Persian "now" and "ruz" is the root of the word rouge in English, as in the color of the sun and thus "day." In parts of Iran "ruz" is still pronounced as rouge.

WATER FESTIVAL

JASHN-E TIRGAN

Jashn-e Tirgan is a summer water festival celebrated in July, on the thirteenth day of the fourth month of the year on the Iranian calendar, called *Tir*. *Tir* refers to the archangel Tir, or Tishtar, "lightning bolt," who appeared in the sky to create thunder and lightning, which announced the much-needed rain.

According to Iranian mythology, in legendary times, by mutual consent between Turan and Iran, Arash-e Kamangir shot his arrow over disputed land on the thirteenth day of the month of Tir to delineate their mutual border. The path of the arrow's flight thus established peace between the two countries. Commemoration of rain falling over peaceful lands may be one of the most ancient origins of summer water festivals. In these festivals, people shower each other with water to symbolize rain and its purity and magical cleansing powers. This festival is still celebrated in some parts of Iran among Armenians and Zoroastrians, and there is much dancing, singing, eating, drinking, playing the tambourine, and reciting poetry. Spinach soup and beet *shuly* are associated with this day.

AUTUMN FESTIVAL

JASHN-E MEHREGAN

Jashn-e Mehregan is an autumn festival celebrated for six days starting on the sixteenth of *Mehr* (ninth or tenth day of October). Its origins lie in an ancient ritual dedicated to Mehr or Mitra, God of Light. *Mehregan* may also be one of the most ancient origins of the thanksgiving harvest ceremonies celebrated in the West. According to Ferdowsi's *Shahnameh* (the Persian calligraphy here), "Feraydun was enthroned and placed the Kayanid crown upon his head, on the first day of the month of *Mehr*, which falls at the autumnal equinox. The Iranian people rejoiced to see his reign; they lit fires and drank wine and inaugurated a great celebration, and they designated the day as a festival." This festival has been passed down through the years to the present.

In Iran, family and friends gather on *Mehregan* to reaffirm friendships and to make loaves of bread such as *surog*, a round, sweet, fried bread, and *kolucheh*. A popular snack to prepare is a roasted nut mixture, *ajil*, to present to the less fortunate encountered on the streets. This celebration ends with bonfires, and fireworks light the way to the promise of a new dawn.

A Sasanian plate depicting a royal ceremony under a vine.

WINTER FESTIVAL

SHAB-E YALDA

Sight of you each morning is a new year
Any night of your departure is the night of yalda.

Sa'di

نظر بر روی تو هر بامداد نوروزی است

شب فراق تو هر شب که هست یلدائی است

In the East more than in the West, lifestyles have often remained more in tune with nature. Therefore, natural rhythms change from morning to evening, from month to month, and finally from season to season. This integration of nature into life cycles is especially true in Iran. The winter solstice, December 21 or 22, is the longest night of the year. In Iran this night is called *Shab-e yalda,* which refers to the birthday or rebirth of the sun. The ceremony is traced to the primal concept of Light and Good against Darkness and Evil in the ancient Iranian religion. This night with Evil at its zenith is considered unlucky. From this day forward, Light triumphs as the days grow longer and give more light. *Shab-e yalda* is in the Persian month of *Day,* which was also the name of the pre-Zoroastrian creator god (deity). Later he became known as the God of Creation and Light, from which we have the English word day (the period of light in twenty-four hours).

In the evening of *Shab-e yalda* bonfires are lit outside, while inside family and friends gather in a night-long vigil around the *korsi,* a low, square table covered with a thick cloth overhanging on all sides. A brazier with hot coals (or an electric one these days) is placed under the table. All night family and friends sit on large cushions (futons) around the *korsi* with the cloth over their laps. Formerly fruit and vegetables were only available in season and the host, usually the oldest in the family, would carefully save grapes, honeydew melons, watermelons, pears, oranges, tangerines, apples, and cucumbers. These were then enjoyed by everyone gathered around the *korsi,* or a fireplace.

On this winter night, in our family my Aqa-jan (how we called our father) would ask us to hold hands around the *korsi* and say the following prayer of thanks to God for the previous year's bounty, and for the prosperity of the coming year.

خدایا به شهر و وطن ما را برکت عطا فرما، به هر کاری که در پیش داریم به یاران و زرع ما را پر برکت، درختان ما را بار بر و بهتر و وطن ما را آباد کن

مملکت ما را از بدی ها محفوظ بدار، به یاران ما را از شغل بد، و ما را تا سال آینده از بدی های زمین و آسمان محفوظ بدار.

Then with a sharp knife, he would cut the thick yogurt, the melon, and the watermelon and give everyone a share. On *Shab-e yalda* the cutting symbolizes the removal of sickness and pain from the family. Snacks are passed around throughout the night: pomegranates with angelica powder *(golpar)* and *Ajil-e shabchareh* or *Ajil-e shab-e yalda,* a combination of nuts and dried fruits, particularly pumpkin and watermelon seeds and raisins. The name of this mixture of nuts literally means "night-grazing," and eating nuts is said to lead to prosperity in days to come. More substantial fare for the night's feast includes eggplant *khoresh* with saffron-flavored rice, rice with chicken, thick yogurt, and saffron and carrot brownies. The foods themselves symbolize the balance of the seasons: watermelons and yogurt are eaten as a remedy for the heat of the summer, since these fruits are considered cold, or *sardi*; and *halva,* the saffron and carrot brownies, is eaten to overcome the cold temperatures of winter, since they are considered hot, or *garmi*. On into the night of festivities the family keeps the fires burning and the lights glowing to help the sun in its battle against darkness. They recite poetry and play music, tell jokes and stories, talk and eat and eat and talk until the sun, triumphantly, reappears in the morning.

Early Christians took this very ancient Persian celebration of Mitra, God of Light, and linked it to Christ's birthday. Today the dates for Christmas are slightly changed, but there are many similarities: lighting candles, decorating trees with lights, staying up all night, singing and dancing, eating special foods, paying visits, and, finally, celebrating this longest night of the year with family and friends.

FIRE FESTIVAL

JASHN-E SADEH

Jashn-e sadeh is the ancient festival of the discovery of fire, which is still celebrated on the tenth of *Bahman* (January 30 or 31) in Iran. According to Ferdowsi's *Shahnameh,* "One day Hushang and a group of his companions were on their way to the mountains when suddenly in the distance a terrifying, black serpent appeared, coming swiftly toward them. Two red eyes glowed on its head and smoke billowed from its mouth. Bravely, nimbly, Hushang seized a rock, dashed forward, and flung it at the serpent with all his strength. Before the rock reached him, the serpent writhed to one side, and the rock struck against another rock. As the two smashed against one another, sparks spurted forth in every direction, so that the landscape was lit up in brilliant splendor. Although the serpent escaped, the secret of fire had been revealed. Hushang gave thanks to the world's Creator, saying, 'This splendor is a divine splendor; we must revere it and rejoice in its presence.' When night fell he gave orders that his men produce sparks from rock in the same manner. They lit a huge fire, and in honor of the divine splendor that had been revealed to Hushang, they instituted a festival of rejoicing. This is called the Sadeh festival, and it was celebrated with great reverence by the ancient Iranians, and the custom is still observed as a memorial of that night."

Throughout the preceding day, the people gather firewood and kindling to build a huge bonfire. After sunset, seven magi clad in white robes arrive with torches to light the fire. The celebration begins. Holding hands and wearing colorful masks, people dance and sing around the fire. There are offerings of sandalwood, frankincense *(kondor),* and aromatic leaves to the fire. Jugglers and dancers perform by firelight, much to the delight of the excited children.

Potatoes and chestnuts, roasted in the ashes of the fire, are associated with this festival, as is barberry soup and mung bean soup. Traditional sweets and drinks are the specialty of this day.

RAMADAN, THE MONTH OF FASTING
RAMAZAN

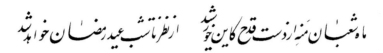

Drink before fasting, drink, don't put your glass down yet,
Since Ramazan draws near, and pleasure's sun must set;
How sweet the roses are! Enjoy them now, for they
As quickly as they bloomed will fall and fade away.

HAFEZ

Ramazan, the Muslim equivalent of Lent, is the ninth month of the lunar calendar, and fasting during *Ramazan* is one of the basic tenets of Islam. For thirty days Muslims must fast from dawn to dusk. Besides total abstinence from food and water, they must also refrain from such things as cigarettes, sex, evil thoughts, and lying. Fasting is a cleansing process for the body and the soul. By fasting, one concentrates less on food and materialism and gives the body a month's rest to detoxify. This cleansing has recently become fashionable in the West by going to health spas.

During this period, fasting is observed from dawn to dusk, so that it is permissible to eat at two times of the day; *sahari* (before dawn) and *eftari* (after sunset). These times used to be announced by a cannon shot across the town, but nowadays by radio, television, and the Internet.

In our house, a few hours before dawn, Aqa-jan (this was what we called our father) was the first to wake up. It was the sound of Aqa-jan's *monajat,* a combination of poetry and improvisational prayers, that pulled us out of bed. I still remember his lyrical voice pouring out devotional prayers before dawn. These magical supplications addressed to God were very soothing and gave me strength and a sense of security, and they sometimes even made me cry.

Soon after Aqajan's prayers, a large embroidered cloth *(sofreh)* was spread on our colorful Persian carpet and covered with an array of warm aromatic and appetizing foods such as saffron-flavored rice, *khoresh,* breads, cheese, fresh herbs, *mast-o khiar* (yogurt and cucumber), and *tah-chin-e morgh* (baked rice with chicken). The *sahari* was a substantial meal since it had to sustain us throughout the day. I remember the radio announcers who reminded us that there was little time left before the last sip of water, the last bite of food, the last cigarette before dawn. After the *sahari,* everyone prayed and then most of us eagerly returned to bed.

The hardest part of the day was the last couple of hours before sunset. I remember Aqajan sitting in a corner over a *sajadeh* (prayer rug) where he meditated, murmuring prayers and waiting for the *Azan-e eftar,* or call for prayer, from the minaret. The kitchen was buzzing with activity at this point. Our housekeeper, my mother, and other members of our family were busily preparing the meals of *eftari* and *sahari.* The smells of the fried onion, garlic and mint, the cutlets, eggplants, and the *kuku* and the kababs were floating throughout the house, driving us all crazy.

Finally, the cry of the muezzin from the local mosque, radio, or television announced the *eftar.* We would all gather around the *sofreh* and samovar. Aqa-jan would always break his fast with a glass of sweet warm water, a soft-boiled egg, and a date. Nonetheless, a sumptuous feast was set on the *sofreh,* including different breads (*sangak, lavash, roghani,* and *shirmal*), cheeses, fresh herbs, butter, marmalade, cutlets, *kuku, mast-o khiar,* sometimes *sholeh zard,* and especially *osh* and soup and different kinds of rice and *khoreshes.* Most important were the sweet fritters (*zulbia va bamieh*), a dessert always associated with *Ramazan.*

In our house, we celebrated practically every night of the month of Ramazan except the night of *Ahyaz* (Ali, the Prophet's son-in-law, was stabbed by an assassin's dagger on the nineteenth and died on the twenty-first); we spent this night in observance of that tragedy. On other evenings we had parties or gatherings of friends and family, as well as open houses. Many would join us for *eftari,* and others would arrive afterward. There was always plenty of food, along with poetry recitations, interesting discussions, raconteurs, music, and games (particularly backgammon and chess). In my mind, I always thought of *Ramazan* as a time of festivity, which reminds me of Hafez's stanza quoted above and of *zulbia bamiyeh* (page 415).

After thirty days, the sighting of the new moon marks the end of *Ramazan,* which is announced on the radio and television. This occasion, *Ayd-e Fetr,* is a popular festival on the Islamic calender. On this day, every good Muslim must break his fast by eating at least a date, and he must give alms both for his own sake and for the sake of all those for whom he is responsible, including the guest who may have spent the previous night under his roof. This type of legal alms consists of a sum of money *(fetriyeh)* corresponding to the price of a maund (about six pounds weight) of wheat. There is also another donation usually passed on to the poorer sections of the community called *kafareh.* This sum is the cash equivalent of an individual's daily food expenses, to cover those who, for some reason or another, were not able to fast during *Ramazan.*

HAJJ *&* THE DAY OF SACRIFICE

AYD-E QORBAN

The *Hajj,* or annual pilgrimage, is one of the pillars of Islam. Every year from the seventh to tenth day of *Ze-l'hajja,* the last month of the Islamic calendar, pilgrims don the *Ihram* (refers to both the sacred state of mind and the seamless white garments worn for the pilgrimage) and visit the Kaaba sanctuary, or the sacred House of God. They kiss the black stone, *Hajar al-Aswad;* perform seven circumambulations of the Kaaba; and ascend, descend, and run between Mt. Safa and Mt. Marwah seven times. For the second stage of the ritual, pilgrims proceed from Mecca to Mina, a few miles away; from there they goes to Arafat, where it is essential to hear a sermon and to spend the afternoon. The last rite consists of spending the night at Muzdalifah, between Arafat and Mina, the following day proceeding to Mina, collecting pebbles on the way with which to stone the devil, represented by pillars, and offering animal sacrifice on the last day of the *Ihram,* which is the *Ayd-e Qorban,* or Festival of Sacrifice. Symbolically reliving the time Abraham was asked to sacrifice his son as proof of his devotion to him (Sura XXXVII (Saffat): 100–111), each pilgrim offers a lamb in sacrifice to God. The sheep must be purchased the day before the holiday. In some parts of Iran, on the day of the festival, henna is applied to the lamb's head and back. The edges of its eyelids must be rubbed with kohl, and sugar is put into its mouth before it is sacrificed. When the sheep is slaughtered, it must be facing Mecca, the Sacred House of God, and it must be killed with a single gash in the neck *(zebh),* but without severing the head *(halal).* The meat is divided into three parts: One portion goes to the family, the second portion goes to friends, the third portion goes to the poor. The skin is usually kept as a rug and sometimes the intestines and the right eye are dried and preserved since they have the power to ward off evil.

During this festival, like any other, friends and family get together and cook a variety of foods associated with this celebration: big pots of meat soup *(ab-gusht),* sheep's head and feet soup *(kalleh-pacheh),* and tripe soup *(sirab-shirdun).* They make many kinds of kababs from the sheep's body parts, including the liver, heart, and kidneys.

PERSIAN PUBLIC BATHS

HAMMAM-E UMUMI

Persian public baths are usually dome-shaped, skylit, and built next to a mosque. The public bath was one of the centers of community life and a source of information, particularly about suitors and marriage possibilities, as well as a place for discussions, singing, dancing, tambourine playing, jokes, gossip, hair coloring, and even doing laundry. From a sociological point of view, therefore, the public bath was of special importance. Women spent the whole day there, socializing and taking steam baths. Before going to the public bath they often prepared snacks and lunch, such as fruits, meatballs, chickpea patties, meat paste, Persian pickles, flat *sangak* bread, romaine lettuce to be eaten with vinegar

syrup *(sekanjebin),* pomegranate seeds with angelica powder and salt, white cheese and fresh herbs, and sometimes even noodle soup.

Generally the public bath has two sections: the *sarbineh,* or dressing room, and the indoor bath, or steam room. In the steam room one can stretch out, have a massage, be scrubbed with a wool bath mitt *(kiseh),* and a white abrasive cream *(sefidab)* that helps the peeling and scrubbing process. The scrubbing and massage are given by a masseur, or *dallak.* All the washing with soap, scrubbing of feet with pumice stone *(sang-e pa),* dyeing of hair with henna, and conditioning take place in the steam room. The final step is a rinse in the large pool *(khazineh),* which is now frequently replaced by showers.

After dressing, one is offered tea, cigarettes, or the hookah. Even today, going to the public bath is an enjoyable ritual for many women, whether they have baths in their own house or not.

For a new mother, going to the bath ten days after her baby's birth is an important ritual and has a special ceremony. The night before this ceremony, women friends and close family wrap the mother's waist with an egg yolk and chickpea powder paste. In the bath they rub this mixture and a special oil *(roghan-e momyai)* all over her body for hours, and celebrate the joy of a healthy birth by passing around drinks made with rose water and basil *(tokhm-e sharbaty),* and sharing pastries and fruits.

MEMORIAL SERVICE

MARASEM-E MAJLES-E KHATM

If wheat springs from my dust when I am dead
And from the grain that grows there you bake bread,
What drunkenness will rise and overthrow
With frenzied love the baker and his dough—
It is a tipsy song his ovens sing!
And, brother, if you seek my grave out, bring
A drum to keep time in the dance—since where
Our sovereign feasts there's no place for despair.

Rumi

When my brother died, I realized that I had no notion of what we Iranians living in exile should and should not do for a funeral. So, I decided to look into our traditions both ancient and modern. When I asked around, I noticed that very few people knew what was to be done; in fact, many relied on what the funeral home told them. For example, at a recent Iranian funeral on Madison Avenue in New York the women were excluded from the prayers. I had not remembered this being the case in Iran. I discovered that the Koran was silent on the subject of funeral rites and that keeping women out of the prayer ceremony and the procession was a Sunni Islamic tradition that Shia Iranians had shunned early on.

Early pre-Islamic and pre-Zoroastrian Iranians buried their dead; the Old Iranian word *dakhmeh* meant grave. When prehistoric Iranians began to settle into agricultural communities, they initially buried their dead under the floors of their houses. Much later burial sites were moved outside the home, and later still, as Iranians came to believe in an afterlife, they started to include certain objects with their buried dead. The graves in northwest Iran's Marlik site from around 11,000 BCE, are a good example.

In later Zoroastrian Iran, burial was strictly prohibited, though there seems to have been some resistance to this by the general population. The Zoroastrian religion prescribed that the dead be exposed to flesh-eating animals and Zoroastrians used (and continue to use) the old Persian word for a grave, *dakhmeh,* to refer to funerary towers on which the dead are placed for birds to eat their flesh. For Zoroastrians, earth and fire were sacred, and therefore burial in the earth and cremation were strictly prohibited because they would defile the sacred earth and flame's purity. The dried bones were then interred in ossuaries. Today, Zoroastrians no longer follow this practice and use crystal glass, stone, or a hardwood coffin. They continue, however, to have Zoroastrian priests, *mobads*, perform the funeral ceremony in Zoroastrian temples, *mab'ad*.

The Koran is silent about funerals, though it says a great deal about death and its significance. The books of prophetic Hadiths only mention that the dead should be buried quickly, handled gently and with respect, and that there should not be any excessive lamentation such as wailing and cutting of the body (Zoroastrians don't believe in any form of loud grieving). In the Islamic tradition detailed funeral instructions are found in the handbooks of *feq* and *taharat* (ritual purity).

Once a person is dead, he should be laid out so that the soles of his feet point to the *qebleh* (Mecca). His eyes and mouth should be closed, his limbs should be straightened out, and his body should be covered. In Iran, a Koran is sometimes placed on the breast immediately upon death or placed upon the body in the grave. The body should be washed and prepared for burial as soon as it is cold (men wash men and women wash women, although spouses may wash each other). There are slight differences among the various traditions about how many times to wash the body, whether cold or hot water should be used, and when soap and perfumes may be used. After cleansing, the body should be anointed with camphor at the points where it touches the ground during prostration: tips of the big toes, forehead, palms of the hands, kneecaps, and tip of the nose. In Iran, a glass of sherbet is also placed next to the deceased so that he can drink from the fountain of *Kowsar* in paradise. Traditionally, buying or making a shroud (*kafan*) before one's death is considered unacceptable. The shroud should be bought by the heirs with money left by the deceased. It should be simple: white cotton (silk is forbidden) and without embroidery or inscriptions. Finally, a fresh cut branch (preferably a date palm) should be placed under each armpit.

When the body is ready, the prayer for the dead (*namaz-e meyyet),* which consists of five *takbirs* without bending or prostration, is performed. The one who leads the prayer should be close to the body with the deceased's head to the right.

Once at the cemetery, the body should be carried to the gravesite in a casket (*tabut*) on the shoulders of the mourners. It is good to assist in the carrying of the casket (usually carried by close male family and friends), even if it is for only a few steps. A pillow of earth should be made for the head, which should be protected by a wooden or brick structure. Traditionally, the body is taken out of the casket and placed in the grave, head first, and on its side facing the *qebleh* (Mecca). Islamic prayers are recited in the ear of the deceased to prepare him for the interrogation by Nakir and Monker. After the grave has been covered with soil, it is sprinkled with water, and mourners plunge their fingers in the earth and recite prayers.

Today, for most of us in exile, performing many of these rituals is not practical. It is more useful to know today that even if a person should die in his bed, the first thing to do is to call 911 and the deceased's physician. There are many laws governing an official death certificate, which are best left to the authorities by calling 911. They will tell you what to do from there on. The next important step is to call a funeral home. Luckily, funeral rituals are similar in many ways for Muslims, Baha'is, and Jews, and the funeral homes and cemeteries in major U.S. cities are equipped to accommodate them. In the Washington area we are lucky to have Mehdi Hatim who is a family counselor at the National Memorial Park Cemetery in Falls Church, Virginia (703 560 4400), and Mr. Saeed Moosavi who performs all Islamic ceremonies (703 938 5777). They can guide you through the whole procedure of washing, anointing, announcements, and burial. Many funeral homes and cemeteries also have a family handbook that can be filled in giving detailed instructions to the funeral home and the family prior to one's death. When I spoke with Mr. Hatim, he mentioned that although it is customary for Americans to start preparing for their death when they reach their fifties, Iranians tend not to do this. He said, "When we want to travel, even for a few days, we make lots of arrangements, but for leaving this earth we Iranians make no prearrangements. As a result there is much confusion and often a great burden on our loved ones." He encourages Iranians to consult him and inform themselves of the possibilities for arranging a funeral.

In the Zoroastrian ceremony, *porseh,* a *sofreh* is spread with the following foods that are blessed by the *mobad* with prayers: a bowl of water, a jar of wine, seven dried nuts and fruits, white *halva,* saffron *halva,* round, fried sweet bread called *surog,* candles, white flowers, sweet and sour garlic and herb croutons, and incense.

Traditionally, there have always been considerable variations in funeral rites in Iran, from region to region, at various times, and based on personal preferences. Most importantly, we should always be respectful of fulfilling the wishes of the deceased. During the ceremony, men and women should wear black (or dark suits). Zoroastrians wear white. A receiving line should be established and seating should be in order of seniority. Senior close members of the family then thank mourners who have come to pay their respects. Only close friends and relatives should then move on to the gravesite. (Arrangements for moving the coffin from the chapel to the burial site can be worked out with the funeral home.) Today it is not possible to bury the dead without a wooden casket (in the past the tradition of burial without a casket was probably for economic reasons and a wooden casket ensures that the body goes "from dust to dust," *as khak be khak*). The coffin is followed in a procession of mourners carrying flowers. At the graveside, a religious man recites prayers (*namaz-e meyyet*) and perhaps reads from the Koran. Then the coffin is lowered into the grave and close family and friends drop in some flowers or a handful of earth.

After the burial it is customary for friends and family to go to a home, restaurant, party room, or hotel to be served an elaborate meal and often some of the deceased's favorite dishes and desserts. Most funeral homes have a viewing room next to the chapel. This is also a good place to hold the initial gathering for the mourners because it is possible also to serve food and drinks there. Some of the foods that might be included are dates (a sacred food), bread cheese and herbs (*sabzi khordan*)), saffron brownies *(halva)*, saffron custard *(sholeh zard)*, rice with yellow split peas *(qeymeh polow)* and potato *khoresh (khoresh-e qeymeh)*, rice with lentils *(adas polow)*, and finally fruit and soft drinks. Turkish-style coffee is also traditionally served at Muslim Iranian funerals.

I like to see plenty of candles, incense burning, and pots of flowers (rather than cut flowers), which should be sent to the chapel, so that they can later be planted at the gravesite. In Qajar Iran it was common to play mournful music on trumpets and drums. Today we might select an appropriate piece of music and a poem or two to be recited. It is also customary for close family and friends to revisit the grave on the third, seventh, and fortieth day, offering more prayers, food, and drink. After the Fortieth Day Ceremony, the oldest member of the deceased's family offers a colorful article of clothing to a younger member, thereby ending the mourning period and indicating that life must go on.

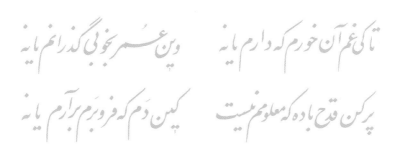

تا کی غم آن خورم که دارم یا نه		وین عمر بخوشی گذرانم یا نه

پر کن قدح باده که معلومم نیست		کین دَم که فرو برم برآرم یا نه

Have I enough? Am I secure or not?
Will blessings and my joys endure or not?
Ah, fill my cup with wine—who knows, the breath
Inhaled, I may exhale for sure or not?

Omar Khayyam

APPENDICES *&* GLOSSARIES

A FEW THOUSAND YEARS OF PERSIAN COOKING AT A GLANCE

You know more about Persian food than you might think. When you ask for oranges, pistachios, spinach, or saffron, you are using words derived from the Persian that refer to foods either originating in the region or introduced from there, for Persia was a great entrepôt of the ancient and medieval worlds. The land was the first home of many common herbs, from basil to cilantro, and to scores of familiar preparations, including sweet and sour sauces, kababs, and almond pastries.

Such preparations are most delicious in their original forms, which you will find in the recipes in this book. All the recipes come from the land Europeans have long called Persia. That name is the Hellenized form of Pars, the southwestern province that was the homeland of the rulers of the first Persian empire. They, however, called themselves Iranians and their country Iran, words derived from Aryan, the name of their ancestral tribes. Nowadays the words are used interchangeably. They describe a people whose civilization and cuisine are ancient indeed.

By 1000 BCE, when the Indo-Aryan tribes called the Medes and the Persians first settled the highlands of the Iranian plateau, the region had been home to great civilizations for thousands of years. In Iran itself, kingdoms had risen and fallen. Among them was the mysterious and widespread civilization whose kings were buried in elaborate tombs at Marlik, near the Caspian Sea, in the second millennium BCE. The people of Marlik produced splendid jewelry, armor, and tools; their gold and silver eating and drinking vessels often displayed the animal motif that remained part of the Iranian tradition. And the styles of their everyday kitchen equipment—some of which is shown on these pages—are echoed in the region today.

We know much more about ancient Elam (present-day Khuzistan, known as "the land of sugar cane"), and area rich in trade. Elam's famed cities were Susa in the lowlands close to Mesopotamia; and Anshan in the Zagros Mountains, set among vineyards, stands of almond and pistachio, and fields of wheat, barley, and lentils. To the northwest was the fertile flood plain of

By 1000 BCE, such utensils as this bronze pot and hanging ladle were in common use at Marlik and other kingdoms in what is now Iran.

Mesopotamia, where power surged back and forth between the empires of Babylonia and Assyria.

Archeology and the cuneiform inscriptions left for posterity tell us much about life in these royal cities. From Assyrian Nimrud for instance, come in ninth century BCE the records of Ashurnasirpal II. In between unnervingly vivid accounts of the lands he had destroyed and the people he had savaged, Ashurnasirpal took care to describe a ten-day feast he had staged at Nimrud. Always grandiose, he claimed it was for "47,074 persons, men and women, who were bid to come from across my entire country," plus thousands more foreign and local guests. The menu included thousands of cattle, calves, sheep, lambs, ducks, geese, doves, stags, and gazelles. There were also items familiar today: bread, onions, greens, cheese, nuts, fresh fruits including pomegranates and grapes, pickled and spiced fruits, and oceans of beer and wine.

Designed so efficiently that the same style is still in use 3,000 years later, this stone pestle from Marlik has a spout for pouring off such local delicacies as pomegranate juice and olive oil.

This king's descendant, Ashurbanipal, would announce his destruction of the Elamite capital two hundred years later ("Susa, the great holy city...I conquered. I entered its palaces, I dwelt there rejoicing; I opened the treasuries...I destroyed the ziggurat...I devastated the provinces, and their lands I sowed with salt."). By then, however, the tide of history was turning, and the ever-warring Mesopotamian kings were soon to meet their Mede and Persian masters.

Conquests began in the seventh and sixth centuries BCE, when the Medes joined Babylon to subdue the Assyrians; the Medes' cousins, the Persians, then overcame Babylonia and went on to conquer Croesus, the famously rich king of Lydia in today's Turkey. The Persian king Cyrus the Achaemenid and his successors expanded the empire until, by the time of Darius, it was the largest the world had yet known. In 522 BCE, Darius' territory, centered on the Persian heartland of Fars, covered two million square miles from the Black Sea to the Persian Gulf, from the Nile in Egypt to the Indus in India. It was the richest of empires: The Greek historian Herodotus, writing in the fifth century BCE, estimated that annual tribute of slaves, animals, foodstuffs, textiles, spices, metals, and gems amounted to a million pounds of silver. And it was ably governed from such cities as Susa (splendidly rebuilt), Babylon, Ecbatana (modern-day Hamadan), and Persepolis on the Persian plateau. A Pax Persica lay over most of the known world.

Persia also inherited the civilizations of the past; they absorbed and transformed the arts of Mesopotamia, Egypt, Lydia, and the Greek colonies of Ionia on the Turkish coast. The Persian Empire's rulers were true cosmopolitans, as Herodotus' contemporary Xenophon noted in describing their cookery. The Persians, he wrote, "have given up none of the cooked dishes invented in former days; on the contrary, they are always devising new ones, and condiments as well." He added, apparently with surprise, that they kept cooks just to invent dishes, along with butlers, confectioners, and cupbearers to serve at table.

For the renown of their cookery, the Persians had Darius and his successors to thank. What we know of Achaemenid cuisine is rather sketchy—we hear of vast banquets at Persepolis where roast camel and ostrich breast were served—but it is clear that the ancient Persians cherished food. Darius paid attention to agriculture. His engineers renewed the irrigation canals that watered his provinces; he expanded the age-old system of underground aqueducts called *qanats* that brought mountain water to the dry Iranian plateau; and he urged experimentation and the transport of seeds and plants. To feed the famed Persian horses, alfalfa seeds were exported to Greece and China; indeed, it is said that the Persian empire could expand because its rulers carried with them the alfalfa seeds to sow for their mounts. To feed humans and for pleasure, plants were transported from province to province: Rice was imported from China and India to Mesopotamia, sesame from Babylon to Egypt, fruit trees from the Zagros Mountains to Anatolia, pistachios from Fars to Syria.

There was also commerce far beyond the borders of empire, for the great trade routes that linked Mesopotamia to China in the east and India in the southeast all met in Persia. This trade continued—it even expanded—through Persia's decline and fall to Alexander in 331 BCE, through the rule of Alexander's Hellenistic successors, the Seleucids, and their successors, the Parthians who came from Khorasan in eastern Iran. It flourished during the restoration of the Persian Empire achieved by the Sasanian dynasty in the third century CE. From India, for instance, came rice and sugar cane, peacocks, and the wild jungle fowl that became the domestic chicken. There was a healthy caravan trade with China. Persian horses (and the alfalfa to feed them) and Persian grapevines appeared there in the second century BCE; in the centuries that followed, Parthian and Sasanian traders introduced the walnut, pistachio, pomegranate, cucumber, broad bean, and pea (known in China as the "Iranian bean"), as well as basil, cilantro, and sesame. Among the plants and fruits that came from China in return, to be disseminated westward to Greece, Rome, and Byzantium by the Persians, were peaches, apricots, tea, and rhubarb.

Such delicious importations marked the luxurious civilization of the Sasanian era. The dynasty built magnificent palace-cities in its homeland of Fars. Their imperial court, however, was at the

A procession of tribute bearers from the far reaches of his vast empire is carved on the staircase of the reception hall of Darius the Great (reigned 522–486 BCE) at Persepolis. This man with his mysterious container—perhaps for precious spices—is a Mede.

A Sasanian gazelle takuk *(rhyton) circa 350* CE.

palace of Ctesiphon not far from what became Baghdad. It was a byword for splendor. Its marble-floored throne room was covered by a 110-foot-high vault, the tallest ever built; the winter carpet was designed in the form of a garden with gems for flowers. The king's throne was set on the backs of carved winged horses and cushioned in gold brocade. His crown of gold and silver, too heavy to wear, was suspended above his head on fine golden chains. The food for his court was served on silver and gilt plates, exquisitely carved and chased, the wine from golden ewers, or from gold and silver rhytons *(takuk)*— drinking horns in the animal-headed style still characteristic of the country.

One might expect attention to pleasure in such a setting, and indeed, it is found in a fourth-century Middle Persian text called *King Khosrow and His Knight*. In this tale, a youth named Vashpur presents himself to the greatest of Sasanian kings. Vashpur is well born, well schooled, skilled in the arts of war and peace alike, but his family has been ruined; he therefore asks King Khosrow to admit him to the royal court and volunteers for any test to prove his worth. King Khosrow chooses to test the youth on his knowledge of cuisine (see page 450).

It might be thought that the conquest of Sasanian Persia by the Arab armies of Islam in 637 would end the rich civilization and the trade, for the desert warriors were rough men, who—according to the Persian poet Ferdowsi—fed on camel's milk and lizards. The Arabs reduced the palace of the Sasanian kings at Ctesiphon to rubble. They tore down the marble-floored throne room; they cut up the famous garden rug and sold the gems that had been attached to it. They melted down the treasures, including the golden ewers and rhytons and dishes, the silver forks and spoons; they scattered the vast libraries and burned the Persian texts. Then they moved on, hacking and burning their way through the cities of the Persian plateau and mountains.

The Sasanians of the sixth and seventh centuries dined in splendid style with the silver spoons and forks (which later went out of fashion) shown here. The handle ends are ornamented with animal heads, an ancient Iranian motif.

What eventually happened, however, was that Persia civilized the Arabs. Within a few generations, the conquerors were building new cities in the circular style of the Sasanian Firuzabad; constructing buildings with the Sasanian vault dome and courtyard; absorbing and extending Persian scholarship; writing poetry in a Persian language reborn and woven with Arabic; wearing Persian clothes; drinking Persian wine; and eating Persian food and writing Persian cookbooks in Arabic. Persia provided the model for the splendid centuries known as the Golden Age of Islam. In return the Arabs introduced Persian cooking ingredients and techniques to north Africa and Europe.

THE PLEASURES OF THE PALACE

The food of medieval Persia—descended from ancient styles, enriched and diversified by trade—was the parent of Persian cookery today. We know something about it from literature and something from a few rare early cookbooks.

One such cookbook was written in Baghdad in 1226 by Mohammad ibn al-Hasan ibn Mohammad al-Karim al-Katib al Baghdadi, a man devoted to his craft, as his preface announces: "Pleasures may be divided into six classes, to wit, food, drink, clothes, sex, scent, and sound. Of these, the noblest and most consequential is food, for food is the body's stay and the means of preserving life." While his book mentions kababs, his recipes focus on meat braises (khoreshes). The herbs and spices are many of those we use today: coriander, cinnamon, ginger, cloves, mint, cumin, caraway, saffron. The sweet and sour and sweet and savory combinations, favored in Iran from ancient times, are the ancestors of those you will find in this book: Iranian cuisine emphasizes fruits, and many dishes combine fruits with meat. Sourness may come from pomegranates, limes, bitter orange (najrenj), vinegar; sweetness comes from sweet fruits or juices, sugar, honey, and date and grape molasses. This cook, as many before him, thickened his sauces with ground almonds, pistachios, and walnuts. Rice, although mentioned in some recipes, is given no special treatment in this early cookbook. The distinctive rice cookery of Iran was invented several hundred years later (see the section on rice).

In the interval, Iran suffered, along with half the world, the onslaughts of the Mongols—Chingis Khan, who liked to call himself "the flail of God," his grandson Hulagu, and a century later, Tamerlane. One would think that nothing could have survived them. So vast was the slaughter that it took more than two hundred years for the Iranian population to reach pre-Mongol levels.

But Iran survived. Indeed, some of her arts thrived under Tamerlane's Persianized successors. It was during the thirteenth, fourteenth, and fifteenth centuries that faience mosaic and miniature painting reached their peaks; it was then the great poets Rumi, Sa'di, and Hafez worked.

And slowly out of the ruins rose the Safavid dynasty. Under them all the arts were reborn. The Safavids built Isfahan, "out of light itself," Victoria Sackville-West would write, "taking the turquoise of their sky, the green of spring trees, the yellow of the sun, the brown of the earth, the black of their sheep and turning these into solid light." This city of gardens, pavilions, palaces, and mosques glowed with the cosmopolitan spirit peculiar to Iran. Its greatest king, Shah Abbas, encouraged trade—including trade with the West—and cherished the civilized arts. He even brought in experts to improve Isfahan's reputedly inferior wine.

The sixteenth and seventeenth-century cuisine of the Safavids, in fact, was close to modern Iranian cookery, although the scale was unique. It was described by a visiting French Huguenot jeweler, Jean Chardin. Chardin reported carefully on all the customs of Iran: His account of a feast at Isfahan gives an idea of his style (see pages 236–237). This was also the period when Persian cooking greatly influenced the cuisines of Mughal India and Ottoman Turkey.

A LITTLE PHILOSOPHY

Most of the recipes in this book would have been at home in Safavid Isfahan, although Iranian cookery has developed since then, of course, and added ingredients, such as tomatoes, potatoes, and green beans from the New World. There are regional variations as well: People around the Caspian and on the Persian Gulf have their own styles of fish cookery, for instance. But certain basic themes remain. There are many yogurt-based dishes, called *borani* after a Sasanian queen who enjoyed them; these are a heritage, perhaps, of the centuries Iran shared a culture with western Asia. There is an emphasis on fruit, as might be expected from a country so rich in it. Fruit is often combined with meat, to make sweet and savory dishes or sweet and sour ones. Iranians love their distinctive rice dishes, their *chelows* and *polows;* in fact, we judge a cook's ability by them.

Besides that, Iranians share attitudes toward food. First, it is part of hospitality, which is central to Persian life. Hospitality must be generous: In traditional Persia, a host would remain standing, serving his guests and eating nothing himself. Customs change, but the attitude remains. Hospitality is like gift giving, the saying goes: One should do it handsomely or not at all.

Next, one should cook according to what is best in season, so that food is as fresh and of as good quality as may be. Fragrance, both during cooking and at the table, is almost as important as taste. And food should be presented handsomely, garnished so that it pleases the eye.

A GLOSSARY OF INGREDIENTS, TERMS AND PERSIAN COOKING TECHNIQUES

A

AFSHOREH

A non-alcoholic beverage made from the juice of fresh fruits such as watermelon, pomegranates, or oranges, and squeezed or processed in a juicer and served over ice.

ALMOND, SWEET (*badam*)

Iran is the center from which almonds spread, on the one hand to Europe and on the other to Tibet and China. Almonds have long been favored by Persian cooks: Fresh baby green almonds in their soft shells, sprinkled with salt, make popular snacks; later in the season, fresh mature almonds are popular; the ripe, dried nuts also provide a delicate flavoring for pastries and act as a thickener for *khoreshes*.

For freshness, buy shelled, unblanched nuts. To blanch, drop the almonds into boiling water, boil for 1 minute, drain, drop into ice water, and slip off the loosened skins. Then spread the nuts on a baking sheet and dry them for 5 minutes in a 350°F (180°C) oven. Blanched almonds may be slivered or ground to powder in a food processor. Store whole or ground blanched almonds in airtight containers in the freezer. To roast, see Nuts, Roasting; to toast, see Nuts, Toasting.

ANGELICA (*gol-par*)

This giant member of the parsley family is named after angels both in English and Persian: The Persian word is a compound of *gol*, or "flower," and *pari*, or "angel." According to folklore, the English name derives from the fact that angelica is best harvested around September 29, the Feast of St. Michael and All Angels. The Persian term honors the herb as a panacea. Its seeds, alone or burned with wild rue, defend against the evil eye; powdered seeds aid digestion; and the pungent roots and leaves are brewed for tea.

Western cooks know angelica in the form of decorative candied leaves. Persian cooks use the seeds and powder as souring agents for dishes containing pomegranates, and in soups and *khoresh*es. Both seeds and powder are sold at Persian groceries.

AQD

Marriage ceremony where vows are exchanged, attended by closest members of both families.

ARUSI

Wedding reception after the *aqd*.

ATEL-O-BATEL

Mutlicolored herbs and spices that guard against witchcraft and evil spirits; consists of seven elements: poppy, wild rice, angelica, salt and green leaves, nigella seeds, gunpowder, and kondor (frankincense).

AYD-E QORBAN

Festival of Sacrifice that recalls the request of Abraham to sacrifice his son.

B

BARBERRIES (*zereshk*)

These are the tart red fruit, high in malic and citric acids, of a bush now only used for ornamental hedges in the West. In Iranian folklore, the thorny wild bushes are said to be the refuge of a gray partridge (white during a certain part of the season), whose wings are stained red by the fruit.

Barberries, usually too sour to be eaten raw (though as children we often enjoyed them as a tart snack), are little appreciated in the West: In Europe, they were once pickled or made into syrups, jam, or wine, and medieval Western recipes mention barberries. However, since the discovery that the barberry bush harbored the spores of a wheat blight, their planting has been prohibited in the West. In Iran, on the other hand, the berries' tart taste and bright, jewel-like color make the fruit a favorite for flavoring and seasoning. Fresh barberry juice (often sold by street vendors in Iran) is said to lower blood pressure and cleanse the system.

The berries usually are dried and stored, and you will find them at

Persian groceries. Be sure to choose red ones: Dark berries may be elderly leftovers from earlier seasons.

For washing see How To section, page 539.

BREADS, PERSIAN (nan)

Among various Persian breads available in this country is *nan-e sangak*, or stone bread, a flat, rectangular loaf 3 feet long, 18 inches wide, and 1 inch thick. It is baked over hot stones—hence the name—and served warm. *Nan-e barbari*, a flat, oval loaf about 2 inches thick, is eaten very fresh and warm, usually for breakfast. *Nan-e lavash*, the oldest known Middle Eastern bread, is a light, crusty oval or disk about 2 feet wide. In Iranian villages it once was baked every few months in a *tanour*, or bread oven, then wrapped in a clean cloth and used as needed, for it keeps very well. Nowadays it is baked fresh every afternoon. *Nan-e sangak* is sold at Persian groceries; *nan-e barbari* and *nan-e lavash* are sold at both Persian groceries and supermarkets. *Nan-e sangak* and *nan-e barbari* should be warmed for 2 minutes on the center rack of a preheated 400°F (200°C) oven. *Nan-e lavash* needs only a minute for perfect consistency.

BUTTER, CLARIFIED / GHEE (roghan-e kareh, roghan-e khub)

A staple in Persian kitchens, ghee is clarified butter, which gives a delicious nutty taste to rice and pastries and has a higher scorching point than regular butter. It is sold in health-food stores and Persian groceries, but it is easy to make at home. See How To section, page 533.

C

CARDAMOM (hel)

This widely available, highly flavored spice, a member of the ginger family, is native to India; traveling via caravan routes, it became a favorite in Iran, Greece, and Rome by classical times.

Cardamom is sold as green, white, or black pods. For Persian cookery, green pods are the first choice because they are unbleached. Black pods have a distinctive smoky flavor best avoided. Within the pods are tiny, black, fragrant seeds, known in Iran as "seeds of paradise." Iranians sometimes suck on the whole pods to sweeten the breath, especially after eating garlic.

In cookery, whole pods serve as decoration for some dishes, and the seeds, extracted with the tip of a knife, flavor rice and sweets. For recipes specifying ground cardamom, Iranians grind the whole spice, pod and all. Commercial ground cardamom is an acceptable substitute.

CAVIAR (khaviar)

The unfertilized, processed roe of the sturgeon, this most exotic of appetizers probably takes its name from the Persian term *mahi-ye Khayedar*, which means literally "egg-bearing fish." The best caviar comes from the Caspian Sea.

CHEESE, PERSIAN (panir)

A soft, white cheese similar to feta, *panir* is made from cow's or goat's milk. Any soft, white cheese is a suitable substitute, or you can make your own. See How To section, page 531.

CHELOW

Cooked plain rice.

CHERRIES, TART OR SOUR (albalu)

Tart cherries are available fresh in the summer and dried, in jars, or frozen all year round in supermarkets or Persian groceries. The following are the ways each type can be prepared for inclusion in Rice with Tart Cherries (page 288). These recipes require 5 minutes of preparation and up to 35 minutes of cooking, and produce enough cherries and syrup for a recipe serving 6 people.

For fresh tart cherries: Use 4 pounds of fresh tart cherries. Rinse them in cold water, remove the stems, and pit the cherries over a stainless steel pot (you don't want to lose any of the juice). Add 1½ cups sugar and cook over high heat for 10 minutes. Drain, saving the cherries and the syrup separately for later use as instructed in the recipe.

For frozen pitted sour cherries: Combine 2 pounds frozen pitted sour cherries with 1 cup sugar, bring to a boil over medium heat, and cook for 35 minutes. Drain, saving the cherries and the syrup separately for later use as instructed in the recipe.

For tart, sour, or morello cherries in light syrup: Use 3 (1½-pound) jars. Drain the cherries, combine them with 1 cup of sugar in a saucepan, and boil over medium heat for 35 minutes. Drain, saving the cherries and the syrup separately for later use as instructed in the recipe.

For dried tart or sour cherries: In a heavy pot, combine 4 cups cherries with 1 cup sugar and 2 cups water. Bring to a boil over medium heat, cook for 35 minutes, and stir in 2 tablespoons of fresh lime juice. Drain, saving the cherries and the syrup separately for later use as instructed in the recipe.

CHICKPEA FLOUR *(ard-e nokhodchi)*

Chickpea flour is made from the chickpea (garbanzo bean). It is sold at specialty and Iranian groceries. Use roasted chickpea flour for cookies and unroasted flour for meatballs and patties.

CILANTRO/CORIANDER *(gishniz)*

Cilantro is native to Iran. It is sold in two quite different forms, both easy to find. Fresh leaves are known in America as cilantro, Chinese parsley, or Mexican parsley and have an intense, musky taste. They need only be rinsed and stemmed before use. The seeds are known as coriander and look like pale peppercorns. They have a concentrated, fiery flavor. They are sold ground for use in cooking, but whole seeds can also be ground in a spice mill or small coffee grinder used exclusively for spices.

CINNAMON *(darchin)*

This spice, made from the bark of various Asian evergreen trees, is one of the oldest: It was first recorded in China in 2500 BCE. It is widely available as sticks (curled pieces of branch bark), chunks (pieces from more intense-tasting bark low on the tree), and ground spice (the kind used in Iranian cookery, Chinese and Vietnamese) cassia cinnamon are familiar varieties, sweet and aromatic. "True" cinnamon, from cinnamon trees in Ceylon, is milder, with more of a citrus scent. Either may be used in Iranian cookery. Just be sure the spice is fresh: Even stored in tightly sealed jars, cinnamon deteriorates after a few months.

CUMIN *(zireh)*

Cumin is the dried seed of a plant in the parsley family. It is native to Iran, from where it was introduced to China in the second century. Pungent, hot, and rather bitter, a little adds complexity to many dishes. Iranian cumin, highest in essential oils and therefore in flavor, is not currently available in the West, but Indian cumin is an acceptable substitute.

CURRY POWDER *(kari)*

Commercial curry powder comes in a range of flavors and intensities from sweet to hot. All are mixtures of roasted, ground spices, generally including turmeric (the source of the yellow color), coriander, cumin, fenugreek, ginger, nutmeg, fennel, cinnamon, cardamom, and various peppers. Sweeter—i.e., milder—curry powder is best for Iranian dishes.

D

DAMI

Rice cooked simply like the Caspian-style *kateh* but combined with herbs and/or vegetables.

DATES *(khorma)*

The date palm has been cherished for millennia in Iran and western Asia for its succulent fruit, which is said to have 360 uses: Among the products made from it have been flour, wine, soft drinks, syrup (dates are 50 percent sugar), and medicine for chest and other ailments. In addition, the pits can be ground to make a coffee substitute, and the sap fermented to make a toddy.

For eating and cooking, you will find three kinds of dates. Soft dates, harvested when unripe, are a delicious fruit just for eating; you will find them in specialty groceries. Semi-dry dates, from firmer varieties, are more syrupy and intense in flavor; the most widely sold U.S. variety is Deglet Noor. Dry dates are sun-dried on the trees, and are very firm and sugary. These hold their shape best in cooked dishes. All three are sold in supermarkets.

DOLMEH

Cooked vegetables or vine leaves stuffed with any mixture of meat, rice, and herbs.

DONBALAN

Lamb fries.

E

EFTARI

During *Ramazan,* the meal breaking the fast just after sunset.

EGGPLANT *(bademjan)*

As many as 40 varieties of eggplant are sold in supermarkets. They range from the familiar long purple eggplant to Japanese and pale lavender Chinese species, narrow and as long as 10 inches. Whichever you choose, make sure the vegetable is firm and the skin smooth and shiny.

Chinese and Japanese eggplants require no particular preparation before cooking. The flesh of the long purple, however, should be steeped before stewing, baking, or frying to draw out its excess, sometimes bitter, juices. To remove bitterness from eggplants, see How To section, page 537.

EYD-E FETRE

Festival celebrating the end of *Ramazan*.

F

FARVARDIN

The first month of the Iranian year.

FAVA BEANS *(baqali)*

Also known as broad beans, fava beans are sold in the pod during the summer at specialty groceries and some supermarkets. Shelled beans are also available frozen. When shopping for fresh beans, choose those with tightly closed, bulging, dark-green pods. If stored in perforated plastic bags, they will keep for 1 or 2 days in the refrigerator.

To shell a bean, press down on the seam near the stem and split the seam with your thumbnail to pop out the beans. Each bean is covered with a protective membrane; split it with your nail and pull it off in 1 piece. Parboiling will simplify this process.

FENUGREEK *(shanbalileh)*

Although its English name—from the Latin *fenum graecum*, or "Greek hay"—refers to a Mediterranean origin, this herb actually is native to Iran, from where it was introduced to the classical world in antiquity and to China in the second century.

Fenugreek seeds are very hard and therefore difficult to pulverize, so this is one herb that is generally sold ground. Some nomadic tribes in Iran soak the seeds to make a jelly, which is said to be good for the digestion. The rather bitter fresh leaves are sometimes baked whole in bread and are an indispensable ingredient in Fresh Herb Khoresh (page 338).

G

GARLIC, SWEET FRESH *(seer-e tazeh)*

This vegetable, which looks like large spring onions and has only the mildest garlic taste, is sold in specialty groceries and farmers' markets in the spring. If it is not available, use regular garlic.

GARMI

"Hot" nature or metabolism, as opposed to *sardi*, or cold nature.

GHEE *(roghan-e kareh)*

See clarified butter, How To section, page 533.

GRAPE LEAVES *(barg-e mo)*

See How To, page 534.

GRAPE SYRUP, MOLASSES, OR PASTE *(dushab-e angur)*

This sweet, syrup is available at Persian, Afghan, and Armenian groceries. You can also make your own. See How To, page 536.

GRAPES, UNRIPE *(ghureh)*

These grapes, used as a souring agent in many Iranian dishes, are sold at Persian groceries in various forms: fresh in season, whole frozen, and canned; as unripe grape juice *(ab-ghureh),* also known as verjuice; and as powdered unripe grapes *(gard-e ghureh)*. Although the taste will not be quite the same, you can substitute fresh lime juice for them in recipes: Allow 4 tablespoons lime juice per 1½ cups unripe grapes, 1 cup juice, or 1 tablespoon powder. See How To section, page 537.

GUSHT-E KUBIDEH

A meat paste made by mashing the meat after cooking it with vegetables.

H

HAFT SINN

The seven items beginning with the Persian letter "sinn" or "s" that are set out for the new year celebration setting, *sofreh-ye haft sinn*.

HAJI FIRUZ

Town troubadours who appear a few weeks prior to the Persian new year to herald the new year.

HAJJ

Annual pilgrimage to the Kaaba at Mecca.

HALVA

In pre-Islamic Iran, a pudding called "*sen or sahan*" was made from wheat sprouts by Zoroastrians as a celebratory dish on the last day of the year to sustain the ancestors on their heavenward journey following their annual new year visit to earth. *Halva,* which means "sweet" in Arabic, may have come from this pudding, because it is still made for special occasions such as births and funerals. I have called the Persian *halva* a saffron brownie.

HAMMAM-E UMUMY

Persian public baths.

HERBS, DRIED *(sabzi-e khoshk)*

If you must use dried herbs, use only ¼ of the fresh herbs called for, to allow for the greater intensity of the dried product. For the best flavor, soak the dried herbs in a sieve set in a bowl of lukewarm water for 15 minutes, then drain them and proceed with the recipe.

I

IBRIQ
A long-handled ewer.

J

JAHAZ
A bride's dowry.

JASHN-E MEHREGAN
Autumn festival celebrated on the ninth or tenth of October, dedicated to Mehr or Mitra, goddess of light.

JASHN-E SADEH
Fire Festival, celebrated on January 31, the hundredth day of winter, by burning a large bonfire.

JASHN-E TIRGAN
Summer water festival, celebrated in July, which honors rainfall.

K

KABAB
Brochette—food grilled or broiled on a skewer or a spit.

KATEH
Smothered Caspian-style cooked rice

KHORESH
A refined braise of meat or poultry with vegetables and/or fruit and nuts.

KHOSHAB
A compote—fruit stewed or cooked in syrup.

KORSI
A low, square table covered with a thick quilt overhanging on all sides, traditionally placed in the family living room. A brazier with hot coals is then placed under the table. In cold winter weather family and friends spend the day and sometimes all night sitting on large cushions (futons) around the *korsi* with their legs underneath the table and the cloth over their laps; hours pass eating, drinking, chatting, reading, reciting poetry, and sometimes playing footsie enjoying the cozy warmth. Today a small electric space heater can be effectively used instead of the brazier and a television often replaces the poetry.

KUKU
An open-faced omelet with other ingredients such as vegetables or meat mixed with the eggs rather than used as a filling. It can be oven-baked in a casserole dish or cooked in a pan on a stovetop, similar to an Italian frittata.

L

LAVASH
A thin flat Persian bread.

LAVASHAK
Fruit paste rolls.

LIMES, PERSIAN *(limu)*
The lime variety known as Persian lime has been grown in Iran for many centuries. These limes are widely available fresh. Persian groceries stock dried limes *(limu-omani)* from California (which sometimes have seeds) and the dried lime powder *(gard-e limu-omani)* made from them. This commercial powder is apt to be bitter because it contains ground seeds, but it is easy to make your own from dried Persian limes: With a knife, crack open the limes, halve them, and remove any seeds. Then grind the dried limes to powder in a food processor and store in an airtight jar.

M

MAHR
A sum of money, piece of property, or object of value a groom agrees to give to his bride as financial security in case of marital discord.

MOKHALAFAT
Appetizers and condiments.

MORABA
Preserves or jams.

MOSAMA
A rich, unctuous braise.

N

NAN
Bread.

NOODLES, PERSIAN *(reshteh)*
Iranian flour noodles are sold dried or toasted at Persian groceries. Lacking Iranian noodles, you may substitute any flat, narrow, dried noodle, such as linguine. See How To section, page 542. To toast noodles yourself, toss them in a hot, ungreased skillet for a few minutes until they are golden brown, or spread them on a baking sheet and broil them under high heat for 30 seconds.

NOWRUZ
The Persian New Year's Day; falls on March 20, 21, or 22, the first day of spring, known as the vernal equinox.

NUTS, ROASTING
See How To section, page 543

NUTS, TOASTING
See How To section, page 543.

O

ORANGE *(porteqal / narenj)*

Oranges come in two main varieties: Sweet or eating oranges, including the California and navel oranges found in every supermarket; and the less often available slightly bitter type, known as the Seville, bitter, wild, or bigerade orange *(narenj)*. The blossoms of the bitter orange are used in Iran for their perfume and for a wonderful jam, called *moraba-ye bahar narenj*. In cookery bitter orange juice and paste impart a fine, astringent taste to many fish dishes.

Bitter or Seville oranges grew wild along the Caspian thousands of years ago. They were taken to China via the Silk Road, and centuries later, a hybridized sweet orange was returned to Iran by Portuguese merchants. The sweet orange reached Europe in the first, tenth, or fifteenth century, according to various sources and ironically, took its Western name from the Persian *narenj*, or bitter orange, while in Iran, the sweet orange is called *porteqal*, after the Portuguese merchants who imported it.

The flesh of the bitter orange is sour, but its juice is much used in Iranian cookery, and some recipes call for the intensity of bitter orange paste, made from the juice. Lacking bitter orange juice, you may substitute ¼ cup fresh sweet orange juice plus 2 tablespoons fresh lime juice for every ½ cup bitter orange juice called for in a recipe. For treatments of orange peel and paste, see below.

ORANGE, BITTER, MOLASSES *(rob-e narenj)*

Bitter orange molasses (also called paste) is sold in Persian groceries. You can also make it at home. See the recipe in the How To section on page 534.

ORANGE PEEL, BLANCHED *(pust-e porteqal)*

You may use either orange peel or tangerine peel for recipes. In either case, the peel should be blanched to remove the bitterness. See How To section, page 540

ORANGE PEEL, CANDIED *(pust-e porteqal-e shirin)*

See How To section, page 540

P

PA-TAKHTY

Literally "by the bed"; friends and family visit a newly married couple in their bed the day after their wedding.

PEAS, SPLIT *(lapeh)*

Yellow split peas, the kind specified in recipes in this book, come in two main varieties, which are interchangeable. Those sold in supermarkets take 20 minutes to cook; however those sold in Persian groceries take at least 40 minutes, and you should adjust recipe cooking times accordingly.

PERSIAN SPICE MIX *(advieh)*

The spice mix called for in Persian recipes is sold at Persian groceries, but it is easy to make at home. Families have their own various spice mixtures. You can make mine; see page 538.

PICKLES, PERSIAN *(torshis)*

Whenever the *sofreh* or tablecloth is spread for a Persian meal, you will find a variety of pickles and relishes that, like chutneys in India, lend piquancy to the main courses. Most *torshis* are made from vegetables or fruits, spices, and good vinegar. Persian groceries usually stock a variety of them.

PISTACHIO *(pesteh)*

These delicious nuts with their beautiful green color are native to Iran: Nicolaus of Damascus wrote in the first century BCE: "The youths of the Persians were taught to endure heat, cold, and rain; to cross torrents and to keep their armor and clothes dry; to pasture animals, to watch all night in the open air, and to subsist on wild fruit, such as pistachios, acorns, and wild pears." In Iran, pistachios are used for dishes ranging from soup to desserts. The English term, among others, derives from the Persian.

Buy fresh pistachios unsalted in undyed shells. (Shells are sometimes dyed red to conceal imperfections.) See How To section for roasting and salting pistachios, page 543.

PLUM *(gojeh)*

Fresh plums, in varieties ranging from purple to gold, are best bought during the summer months from local growers. In Iran, the small, round, green unripe or baby green variety known as *gojeh*—available in the U.S. in Persian groceries in the spring—are a favorite snack. They are also used as a souring agent in *khoreshes* and *oshes* and as a compote. For use throughout the year, different varieties of dried plums are sold at health food stores and Iranian groceries. They require only rinsing before use in a recipe.

POLOW

Cooked rice (usually mixed with fruit or vegetables).

POMEGRANATE *(anar)*

The red pomegranate, native to Iran and cultivated there for at least 4,000 years, is considered the fruit of heaven; in fact, it was probably the real "apple" in the Garden of Eden. The ancients commended it. Among them were King Solomon, who had a pomegranate orchard. And Prophet Mohammad said, "Eat the pomegranate, for it purges the system of envy and hatred."

The fruit grows on large bushes or small trees, whose masses of crimson flowers brighten the pale mud walls of villages in Iran, Spain, and Italy. In Persian folk medicine, every part of the plant is believed to have virtue. The dried and powdered skin of the roots and fruit make a tea drunk to sweeten the breath, correct menstrual irregularity, kill parasites, and relieve nausea. Another tea, made from young shoots and leaves, fresh or dried, is a good remedy for nausea, lack of appetite, anemia, and headaches. The flowers repel insect pests—even honeybees avoid them—and provide yet a third tea, good for soothing uneasy stomachs.

Pomegranates, ranging in taste from sweet to sour-sweet, have a special place in Iranian cookery. The fresh seeds, or arils (the edible part of the fruit), sprinkled with a little salt and angelica powder, make a tart appetizer, and they add a bright note to green salads. Pureed and strained,

the seeds produce a refreshing juice for drinking or for flavoring soups and *khoreshes*. Or the juice may be reduced to a paste, a favorite souring agent, particularly in central and southern Iran. Most recipes that include pomegranate, which is classified as a cold food, also include hot foods like walnuts or ginger for balance.

Pomegranates are available in supermarkets in the fall and winter. Choose deep red fruits without blemishes. They will keep at home for about a week at room temperature. I have been able to keep them fresh at the end of the season for 3 weeks or more by wrapping them in newspaper and keeping them in the refrigerator drawer.

For seeding a pomegranate, and for juicing it in its own skin *(ablambu)*, See How To section, page 541.

POMEGRANATE JUICE *(ab-e anar)*

See How To section, page 541.

POMEGRANATE MOLASSES *(rob-e anar)*

Pomegranate molasses are available in specialty stores and Persian groceries. To make your own, See How To section, page 535.

Q

QABALEH

Marriage contract, determined at the *ba'leh borun* ceremony, which states the terms of the *jahaz* and *mahr*.

QAOOT

Sweetened roasted chickpea or nut powder.

QEYMEH

Small ½-inch cubes of meat sautéed and seasoned in oil.

QORMEH

One-inch pieces of meat sautéed in oil with seasoning, to keep on hand in the refrigerator.

QUINCE *(beh)*

This big tree, a relative of the rose, is native to Iran, and cultivation probably started there, where the fruit's hard, astringent flesh, somewhere between an apple and a pear but with a special aromatic perfume, lends tartness to *khoreshes*, jams, custards, and sherbet drinks. Its blossoms are also used to make a popular jam. Although quinces are available in supermarkets during the late autumn and winter, the biggest and best ones are sold in Persian groceries. When shopping, choose firm, unblemished fruit. At the end of the season you can wrap individual quinces in newspaper and store them in the refrigerator drawer for 2 to 3 weeks.

Some varieties of Persian quinces can be eaten raw. The U.S. quince generally cannot. To prepare it for cooking, simply rub off the fuzz.

R

RHUBARB SYRUP

See recipe, page 499.

RICE FLOUR *(ard-e berenj)*

This delicate flour made from rice grains contains no gluten, so it cannot be used in bread making, but it is a fine thickener for *oshes*, *khoreshes*, puddings, and sweets, such as delicate rice cookies, a favorite in Iran. The flour is sold in supermarkets.

RICE STARCH *(neshasteh-ye berenj)*
This is a fine powder thickener, much like cornstarch, which may be substituted for it.

ROSE PETALS *(gol-e sorkh)*
The blossoms of scented roses have lent flavor and color to food and drink since ancient times. In Persia there was a rose petal wine; there is also rose petal jam and rose-flavored honey; and rose petals flavor many sweet and savory dishes. Any scented rose petals may be used in cookery, provided they are free of pesticides, but dried ones are intense in flavor and convenient to use. They are sold in Persian groceries and health food stores.

ROSE WATER *(golab)*
Few scents are more characteristic of Iran than that of rose water: It freshens the air in mosques and other public places; it is a part of every woman's makeup; and men use it as a cleanser for their mustaches and beards. Along with rose petals, it is a frequent ingredient in savory dishes and especially in pastries.

Rose water is sold at Persian groceries. If it is kept cool, its aroma lasts for years. See Rose section, page 379.

S

SABZI-KHORDAN
Fresh herbs served at table.

SAFFRON *(za'feran)*
See Saffron section, page 222. For use in cooking, see How To section, page 536.

SAMOVAR
A metal urn with a device for heating water for tea. A teapot kept on top brews tea throughout the day.

SARDI
"Cold" nature or metabolism; see *garmi.*

SHAB-CHAREH OR AJIL
A mixture of nuts, dried fruits, and seeds, which literally means "night-grazing."

SHAB-E YALDA
The longest night of the year; the winter solstice; celebration of the rebirth of the sun, spent as a night-long vigil around the *korsi.*

SHARBAT
Syrup made of fruit juice cooked with sugar or honey and stored in bottles to use as needed for making sherbets.

SIZDAH BEDAR
The thirteenth day after Nowruz, typically celebrated with outdoor picnics.

SOBHANEH
Breakfast.

SOFREH
A cotton cloth embroidered with prayers and poems that serves as a tablecloth on a table or is spread on a Persian carpet.

SOFREH-YE HAFT SINN
The setting on a handmade cloth for the Persian New Year.

SUMAC *(somaq)*
The red-berried sumac bush—*Rhus coriaria,* not to be confused with the poisonous white-berried species—provides one of the favorite flavorings for Persian cooking. To make it, the berries, along with leaves and branches, are boiled in water, then sieved to make sumac juice; or the berries alone are dried and crushed to a powder. The latter, sold in Persian groceries, is the more usual form of the spice; it is kept in the kitchen and on the table, along with salt and pepper.

Sumac is prized as a digestive, and even more prized as a pleasantly astringent souring agent: Iranians prefer its taste to that of lemon. It adds distinction to breads, marinades, soups, and *khoreshes,* among other dishes. It is also delicious when sprinkled on kababs or onion salads, or mixed with yogurt.

T

TAH-CHIN
Lamb or chicken, marinated in egg, yogurt, and saffron, mixed and arranged in the bottom of a pot or baking dish and cooked for a long time, until a golden crust forms *(tah-dig).*

TAH-DIG
A layer of golden rice that sticks to the bottom of the pan when rice is cooked.

TAMARIND *(tamr-e hendi)*
A native of tropical East Africa or perhaps India (which is where the Persian name comes from), now widely grown, the tamarind tree bears pods that are used to make a souring agent indispensable not only in curries but in many Southern Iranian dishes. The partly dried, seeded pods are sold in Indian and Persian groceries, as are the liquid flavoring and the paste made from them. To make your own liquid or paste, see below.

TAMARIND LIQUID
(ab-e tamr-e hendi)
See How To section, page 535.

TANUR
Bread oven.

TOMATO *(gojehfarangi)*
There is little to equal the taste of fresh ripe tomatoes in season; out of season, peeled, canned tomatoes make a good substitute. Most recipes require that fresh tomatoes be peeled. See How To section, page 534.

TURMERIC *(zardchubeh)*
Turmeric, a native of southeast Asia that is now grown in tropical climates throughout the world, comes from the rhizomes of a plant in the ginger family. Although the dried rhizomes are available, they are hard and difficult to grind. Ground turmeric is perfectly good.

W

WALNUT *(gerdu)*
The walnut is native to Northern Iran and spread to the West and China from there. Walnuts feature in many Persian dishes, especially those containing pomegranates. Peeled and salted, they make a delicious snack. See How To section, page 543.

WHEY
See Yogurt, Sun-Dried *(kashk)*.

Y

YOGURT, SUN-DRIED *(kashk)*
In the West, whey means the thin liquid separated from milk curds during cheesemaking. The term is often used to refer to the Persian *kashk*. In Iran, however, *kashk* refers to drained, salted, sun-dried yogurt, used as a souring agent in many dishes. *Kashk* is sold in both solid and liquid form at Persian groceries. You may substitute sour cream, but if you do, you will not get the distinctive, slightly sour taste of *kashk*.

YOGURT, HOMEMADE *(mast)*
　　YOGURT, DRAINED *(mast-e kisei)*
See How To section, page 530.

USEFUL KITCHEN INGREDIENTS

Whenever possible, use fresh herbs, beans, fruit, and nuts, which are more and more commonly available in most supermarkets. Below is a list of some essential ingredients that should be kept in your pantry in dried form. Make the syrups, jams, and pickles from time to time, store them in jars, and use as needed.

DRIED HERBS	
Angelica	Gol-par
Basil	Reyhan
Bay leaf	Barg-e bu
Chives	Tareh
Cilantro	Gishniz
Dill weed	Shivid
Fenugreek	Shanbalileh
Mint	Na'na
Persian lime powder	Gard-e limu-Omani
Persian limes, whole dried	Limu-Omani
Summer savory	Marzeh
Tarragon	Tarkhun

DRIED BEANS	
Barley	Jow
Chickpeas	Nokhod
Green fava beans or lima beans	Baqali
Kidney beans	Lubia qermez
Lentils	Adas
Pinto beans	Lubia chiti
Yellow fava beans	Baqali-e zard
Yellow split peas	Lapeh

SPICES	
Cardamom	Hel
Cinnamon	Darchin
Cloves	Mikhak
Cumin seed	Zireh
Curry powder	Kari
Ginger	Zanjebil
Nigella seeds (black caraway seeds)	Siah daneh
Nutmeg	Jowz-e hendi
Persian spice mixture	Advieh
Saffron	Za'feran
Sumac	Somaq
Turmeric	Zardchubeh
Vanilla	Vanil

MOLASSES & PASTES	
Bitter orange molasses	Rob-e narenj
Grape molasses	Shireh-e angur
Pomegranate molasses	Rob-e anar
Tomato paste	Rob-e gojeh farangi

SYRUPS & JAMS	
Orange peel	Pust-e porteqal
Sour cherry preserve	Moraba-ye albalu
Vinegar syrup	Sekanjebin

DRIED FRUITS, FLOWERS & NUTS	
Almond slivers	Khalal-e-badam
Barberries	Zereshk
Bitter orange	Narenj
Dates	Khorma
Dried apricots	Qeysi
Orange blossom	Bahar narenj
Pistachio slivers	Khalal-e-pesteh
Pistachios	Pesteh
Prunes	Alu
Quince blossom	Gol-e beh
Raisins	Keshmesh
Rose petals	Gole-e sorkh
Tamarind	Tamr-e hendi
Walnuts	Gerdu

OTHER	
Bitter orange	Narenj
Chinese or wild olives	Senjed
Garlic	Sir
Jujube	Annab
Lemon juice	Ablimu
Olive oil	Roghan zeytun
Onions	Piaz
Quince	Beh
Rice, long grain (Basmati)	Berenj-e dom siah
Rose water	Golab
Sundried yogurt	Kashk
Verjuice (unripe grape juice)	Ab-ghureh
Vinegar	Serkeh

MY MOTHER'S CLASSIFICATION OF "HOT" AND "COLD" FOODS

People are considered to have "hot" and "cold" natures, as does each type of food. This concept has nothing to do with the temperature or the spice and pepper content of the food; it is a system particular unto itself. For Persians, it is essential for persons with "hot" natures to eat "cold" foods and vice versa, in order to create a balanced diet. Recipes in this book present a balanced diet by combining the opposing elements of "hot" and "cold." Please note that, according to my mother, both the pharmacological and culinary qualities of the spices are considered when used in a recipe.

Meat

Beef, veal	cold
Duck	hot
Hen	hot
Lamb	hot
Red snapper	hot
All other fish	cold
Rooster	cold
Turkey	cold

Vegetables

Beets	cold
Cabbage	cold
Cardoons	cold
Carrots	hot
Cauliflower	cold
Celery	cold
Corn	hot
Cucumber	cold
Eggplants	cold
Garlic	hot
Grape leaves	cold
Green beans	cold
Green peas	cold
Green peppers	hot
Lettuce	cold
Mushrooms	hot
Okra	hot
Onions	hot
Potatoes	cold
Pumpkins	cold
Rhubarb	cold
Shallots	hot
Spinach	cold
Tomatoes	cold
Turnips	cold

Cereals & Beans

Barley	cold
Barley flour	cold
Chickpeas	hot
Cornstarch	hot
Kidney beans	cold
Lentils	cold
Mung beans	hot
Pinto beans	cold
Rice	cold
Wheat flour	hot
Yellow fava beans	cold
Yellow split peas	hot

Fruits & Nuts

Almonds	hot
Apples	hot
Apricots	cold
Barberries	cold
Dates	hot
Figs	hot
Grapefruit	cold
Mangoes	hot
Nectarines	cold
Oranges	cold
Peaches	cold
Pears	neutral
Pistachios	hot
Prunes	cold
Quinces	hot
Raisins and grapes	hot
Sweet melon	hot
Tart cherries	cold
Walnuts	hot
Watermelon	cold
Persian limes	cold

Spices

Cardamom	hot
Cinnamon	hot
Cloves	hot
Cumin seed	hot
Curry powder	hot
Ginger	hot
Nigella seed	hot
Nutmeg	hot
Pepper	hot
Saffron	hot
Salt	hot
Sumac	cold
Turmeric	hot
Vanilla	hot

Herbs

Bay leaf	hot
Chives	hot
Coriander	cold
Dill weed	hot
Fenugreek	hot
Garden angelica	hot
Marjoram	hot
Mint	hot
Parsley	hot
Tarragon	hot

Dairy

Eggs	hot
Feta cheese	neutral
Milk	cold
Sun-dried yogurt	hot
Yogurt	cold

Other

Coffee	cold
Honey	hot
Lemon juice	cold
Persian pickles	hot
Pomegranate molasses	cold
Rose water	hot
Sour grape juice	cold
Sugar	cold
Tamarind	cold
Tea	neutral
Tomato paste	cold
Vinegar	hot

PERSIAN—ENGLISH LIST OF INGREDIENTS

Ab-ghureh	Verjuice (unripe grape juice)	Baqali-e zard	Yellow fava bean	Kakuti	Wild thyme
Ablimu	Lime or lemon juice	Barg-e bu	Bay leaf	Kalam	Cabbage
Adas	Lentil	Barhang	Allium	Kangar	Cardoon
Advieh	Persian mixture of ground spices	Beh	Quince	Karafs	Celery
		Beh-e japoni	Japanese quince	Karafs-e kuhi	Wild celery
Aeklil-e kuhi	Rosemary	Behlimu	Lemon verbena	Kari	Curry powder
Ajil	A mixture of nuts, dried fruits, and seeds	Berenj	Rice	Kashk	Sun-dried yogurt
		Bidmeshk	Musk willow	Kasni	Chicory
		Bumadaran	Yarrow	Keshmesh	Raisin
Albalu	Sour cherry	Cha'i	Tea	Khalal-e-badam	Almond slivers
Alu	Prune	Chavdar	Rye	Khalal-e-pesteh	Pistachio slivers
Alu zard	Golden plum	Daneh-ye khashkhash	Poppy seed	Khardal	Mustard
Anar	Pomegranate			Khiar	Cucumber
Anbeh	Mango	Darchin	Cinnamon	Kholfeh	Purslane
Anjir	Fig	Dugh	A yogurt drink with mint	Khorma	Date
Annab	Jujube			Khormalu	Persimmon
Ard-e javaneh-ye gandom (sahan)	Malt wheat or Wheat sprout flour	Fandogh	Hazelnut	Konjed	Sesame
		Felfel-e bahareh	Allspice	Labu	Steamed red beets
Ardeh	Roasted sesame paste	Gard-e nan	Baking powder	Lapeh	Yellow split pea
		Garmak	Cantaloupe	Limu-omani	Dried Persian lime
Arzan	Millet	Gerdu	Walnut	Lubia chiti	Pinto bean
Avishan-e kuhi	Oregano	Ghureh	Unripe grapes	Lubia qermez	Kidney bean
Avishan-e shirazi	Thyme	Gilas	Cherry	Maash	Mung bean
		Gishniz	Cilantro weed, also coriander seeds	Marchoubeh	Asparagus
Azgil	Medlar			Maryam goli	Sage
Badam	Almond	Gojeh sabz	Baby green plum	Marzangush	Marjoram
Baderang	Bergamot	Gol gab zabun	Borage	Marzeh	Summer savory
Badian	Anise	Golab	Rose water	Mey	Wine
Badian-e khatai	Star anise	Golabi	Pear	Meygu	Shrimp
		Gole-e sorkh	Rose petals	Mikhak	Clove
Bahar narenj	Orange blossom	Gol-par	Angelica	Miveh	Fruit
Balaghuti (shahi)	Watercress	Hel	Cardamom	Musir	Persian shallot
		Hulu	Peach	Nabat	Sugar crystals
Bamieh	Okra	Ja'fary	Parsley	Nan	Bread
Baqali	Green fava bean or lima bean	Jow	Barley	Na'na	Mint
		Jow-e dosar	Oat	Nardun	Dried pomegranate arils
Baqali or baqala	Fava bean	Jowz-e hendi	Nutmeg		
		Jush-e shirin	Baking soda		

Narengi	Tangerine
Narenj	Bitter orange
Noghl	Sugar-coated almonds
Nokhod	Chickpea
Osh	Hearty soup
Panir	Persian cheese, like feta
Pesteh	Pistachio
Piaz	Onion
Piazcheh	Spring onion, or scallions
Porteghal	Orange
Pust-e porteqal	Orange peel
Qeymeh	Small, ½-inch cubes of meat, sautéed and seasoned
Qeysi	Dried apricot
Qormeh	1-inch chunks of meat, sautéed and seasoned
Razianeh	Fennel
Reshteh	Noodle
Reyhan	Basil
Rivas	Rhubarb
Rob-e anar	Pomegranate molasses
Rob-e narenj	Bitter orange molasses
Roghan-e karchak	Caster oil
Roghan-e zeytun	Olive oil
Sabzeh	Sprouts
Sahlab	Powdered orchid root
Samanu	Wheat sprout pudding
Sekanjebin	Vinegar syrup
Senjed	Chinese or wild olive
Serkeh	Vinegar
Shabdar	Clover
Shagayegh	Poppy

Shah balut	Chestnut
Shahdaneh	Hemp seed
Shalgham	Turnip
Shamdani-e mo'atar	Rose geranium
Shanbalileh	Fenugreek
Shireh-e angur	Grape molasses
Shirin bayan	Licorice
Shirinak	Le mache (lettuce)
Shivid	Dill
Siah daneh	Nigella seed
Sib	Apple
Sibzamini	Potato
Sir	Garlic
Sirab shirdun	Tripe
Sobus-e gandom	Wheat bran
Somaq	Sumac
Sombolative	Valerian
Sussan anbar	Peppermint
Tamr-e hendi	Tamarind
Tareh	Chives
Tareh farangi	Leek
Tarkhineh	Bulgur and yogurt patties
Tarkhun	Tarragon
Tartizak	Garden cress
Taruneh	Heart of palm
Torobcheh	Radish
Torshak	Sorrel
Torshi	Persian pickles
Tusorkh	Grapefruit
Tut	Mulberry
Valak	Wild leek
Vanil	Vanilla
Yas	Jasmine
Yonjeh	Alfalfa
Zaban	Tongue
Zaban-e madar shohar (mother-in-law's tongue)	Cactus

Za'feran	Saffron
Zanbagh	Iris
Zanjebil	Ginger
Zardchubeh	Turmeric
Zereshk	Barberries
Zireh-ye kuhi	Ajuwan
Zireh-ye sabz	Cumin
Zireh-ye siah	Caraway seeds
Zofa	Hysoppe

ENGLISH–PERSIAN LIST OF INGREDIENTS

Ajuwan	Zireh-ye kuhi	Chives	Tareh	Le mache	Shirinak
Alfalfa	Yonjeh	Cilantro weed, also coriander seeds	Gishniz	Leek	Tareh farangi
Allium	Barhang			Lemon verbena	Behlimu
Allspice	Felfel-e bahareh			Lentil	Adas
Almond	Badam	Cinnamon	Darchin	Licorice	Shirin bayan
Almond slivers	Khalal-e-badam	Clove	Mikhak	Lime or lemon juice	Ablimu
Angelica	Gol-par	Clover	Shabdar		
Anise	Badian	Cucumber	Khiar	Malt wheat or wheat sprout flour	Ard-e javaneh-ye gandom (sahan)
Apple	Sib	Cumin	Zireh-ye sabz		
Asparagus	Marchoubeh	Curry powder	Kari		
Baking powder	Gard-e nan	Date	Khorma	Mango	Anbeh
Baking soda	Jush-e shirin	Dill	Shivid	Marjoram	Marzangush
Barberries	Zereshk	Dried apricot	Qeysi	Meat sauce, 1-inch chunks of meat, sautéed and seasoned	Qormeh
Barley	Jow	Dried Persian lime	Limu-Omani		
Basil	Reyhan				
Bay leaf	Barg-e bu	Dried pomegran-ate arils	Nardun		
Bergamot	Baderang			Medlar	Azgil
Bitter orange	Narenj	Fava bean	Baqali or baqala	Millet	Arzan
Bitter orange molasses	Rob-e narenj	Fennel	Razianeh	Mint	Na'na
		Fenugreek	Shanbalileh	Mulberry	Tut
Borage	Gol gab zabun	Fig	Anjir	Mung bean	Maash
Bread	Nan	Fruit	Miveh	Musk willow	Bidmeshk
Bulgur and yogurt patties	Tarkhineh	Garden cress	Tartizak	Mustard	Khardal
		Garlic	Sir	Nigella seed	Siah-daneh
Cabbage	Kalam	Ginger	Zanjebil	Noodle	Reshteh
Cactus	Zaban-e madar shohar	Golden plum	Alu zard	Nut mix	Ajil
		Grape molasses	Shireh-e angur	Nutmeg	Jowz-e hendi
Cantaloupe	Garmak	Grapefruit	Tusorkh	Oat	Jow-e dosar
Caraway seeds	Zireh-ye siah	Green fava bean or lima bean	Baqali	Okra	Bamieh
Cardamom	Hel			Olive oil	Roghan-e zeytun
Cardoon	Kangar	Hazelnut	Fandogh	Onion	Piaz
Caster oil	Roghan-e karchak	Heart of palm	Taruneh	Orange (bitter or Seville)	Narenj
Celery	Karafs	Hemp seed	Shahdaneh		
Cherry	Gilas	Hysoppe	Zofa	Orange (sweet)	Porteghal
Chestnut	Shah balut	Iris	Zanbagh	Orange blossom	Bahar narenj
Chickpea	Nokhod	Japanese quince	Beh-e japoni	Orange molasses (bitter orange)	Rob-e narenj
Chicory	Kasni	Jasmine	Yas		
Chinese or wild olive	Senjed	Jujube	Annab	Orange peel	Pust-e porteqal
		Kidney bean	Lubia qermez	Oregano	Avishan-e kuhi

Parsley	Ja'fary
Peach	Hulu
Pear	Golabi
Peppermint	Sussan anbar
Persian cheese	Panir
Persian pickles	Torshi
Persian shallot	Musir
Persimmon	Khormalu
Pinto bean	Lubia chiti
Pistachio	Pesteh
Pistachio slivers	Khalal-e-pesteh
Pomegranate molasses	Rob-e anar
Poppy	Shagayegh
Poppy seed	Daneh-ye khash-khash
Potato	Sibzamini
Powdered orchid root	Sahlab
Prune	Alu
Purslane	Kholfeh
Quince	Beh
Radish	Torobcheh
Raisin	Keshmesh
Rhubarb	Rivas
Rice	Berenj
Roasted sesame paste	Ardeh
Rose geranium	Shamdani-e mo'atar
Rose petals	Gole-e sorkh
Rose water	Golab
Rosemary	Aeklil-e kuhi
Rye	Chavdar
Saffron	Za'feran
Sage	Maryam goli
Sesame	Konjed
Shrimp	Meygu
Small, ½-inch cubes of meat, sautéed and seasoned	Qeymeh
Sorrel	Torshak

Soup, hearty	Osh
Sour cherry	Albalu
Spice mix, Persian	Advieh
Spring onion, or scallions	Piazcheh
Sprouts	Sabzeh
Star anise	Badian-e khatai
Steamed red beets	Labu
Sugar crystals	Nabat
Sugar-coated almonds	Noghl
Sumac	Somaq
Summer savory	Marzeh
Sun-dried yogurt	Kashk
Tamarind	Tamr-e hendi
Tangerine	Narengi
Tarragon	Tarkhun
Tea	Cha'i
Thyme	Avishan-e shirazi
Tongue	Zaban
Tripe	Sirab shirdun
Turmeric	Zardchubeh
Turnip	Shalgham
Unripe grapes	Ghureh
Unripe plum or baby green plum	Gojeh sabz
Valerian	Sombolative
Vanilla	Vanil
Verjuice (unripe grape juice)	Ab-ghureh
Vinegar	Serkeh
Vinegar syrup	Sekanjebin
Walnut	Gerdu
Watercress	Balaghuti (shahi)
Wheat bran	Sobus-e gandom
Wheat sprout pudding	Samanu
Wild celery	Karafs-e kuhi
Wild leek	Valak
Wild thyme	Kakuti
Wine	Mey

Yarrow	Bumadaran
Yellow fava bean	Baqali-e zard
Yellow split pea	Lapeh
Yogurt mint drink	Dugh

ENGLISH–PERSIAN GLOSSARY OF COMMON TREES, PLANTS, AND FLOWERS

Acacia	Anbar (aghaghi)
Ash	Zaban-e gol
Ash, European	Zaban gonjeshki
Aster	Gol-e mina
Bay, laurel	Barg-e bu
Beech, Oriental	Rash
Bougainvillea	Gol-e kaghazi
Boxwood	Shemshad
Carnation	Gol-e mikhak
Cedar, blue atlas	Cedre
Cedar, deodar	Cedre deodar
Chamomile	Babuneh
Chestnut, horse	Shah balut
Chestnut, sweet or Spanish	Shah balut
Chrysanthemum	Gol-e davudi
Cypress	Derakht-e zarbin
Cypress, gray or silver	Derakht-e sarv-e noghrei
Cypress, Italian	Derakht-e sarv
Dahlia	Kokab
Damask rose	Gol-e mohammadi
Elm	Narvan-e chatri
Elm, caucus	Narvan-e qaraghaj
Elm, mountain	Narvan-e kuhi
Fir	Senobar (narrad)
Fir, black	Senobar-e siah
Fir, red	Senobar-e ghermez
Fir, silver	Senobar-e noghrei
Fir, white	Senobar-e sefid
Geranium	Shamdani
Hollyhock	Gol-e khatmi
Honeysuckle	Pich-e amindoleh
Iris	Zanbagh
Jasmine	Yas
Juniper	Ardij (hab-al arar)
Lantana	Gol-e shahpasand
Lavender	Austokhodus
Lilac, flower	Gol-e yas-e derakhti
Lilac, tree	Yas-e derakhti
Linden flowers	Zirfun (tilleul)
Magnolia, deciduous	Magnolia bahareh
Magnolia, evergreen	Magnolia
Maple	Afra-ye sefid
Maple, Norway	Afra-ye chenari
Maple, red	Afra-ye ghermez
Maple, Sycamore	Afra-ye bozorg
Marigold (calendula)	Gol-e hamisheh bahar
Mesquite	Ghaf, Jeghjeghei
Musk rose	Nastaran
Myrtle	Turi
Narcissus	Gol-e narges
Nasturtium	Ladan
Oak	Balut
Oak, cork	Balut-e chub panbeh
Oak, green	Balut-e sabz
Oak, red	Balut-e ghermez
Oleander	Kharzahreh
Pansy	Banafsheh
Penny royal	Puneh-ye kuhi
Peony	Gol-e sadtomani
Periwinkle	Gol-e telegraphi
Persian musk rose	Gol-e nastaran
Petunia	Gol-e atlasi
Pine	Derakht-e kaj
Pine, Aleppo	Kaj-e halab
Pine, black	Kaj-e siah
Pine, eastern white	Kaj-e sefid
Pine, Scotch	Kaj-e jangali
Pine, stone	Kaj-e sangi
Plane, Oriental or chennar tree	Chenar
Poplar, Lombardy or black	Tabrizi
Primrose	Pamchal
Quince blossom	Gol-e beh
Rhododendron	Arasteh
Safflower	Golrang
Salvia	Gol-e salvi
Silk tree, hardy	Abrisham
Snapdragon	Gol-e meymuni
Spiraea or bridal wreath	Gol-e morvarid
Spruce, Norway	Senobar
Staghorn sumac	Somagh
Sunflower	Aftab gardun
Tamarisk	Gaz angabin
Tree-of-heaven	Arar
Trumpet vine	Pich-e shaypury
Tuberose	Gol-e maryam
Tulip	Gol-e laleh
Upright fir	Senobar-e arasteh
Verbena	Verven
Water lily	Niloufar-e abi
Willow	Beed-e ma'muly
Willow, golden weeping	Beed-e sefid
Willow, musk	Beed-e moshk
Willow, weeping	Beed-e-majnun
Wintersweet	Gol-e yakh
Wisteria	Glisin
Yellow jasmine	Gol-e zard
Yew	Sorkhdar
Zinnia	Gol-e azar

MENU SUGGESTIONS

Breakfast
Hot bread, usually *barbari*
Hot sweet tea
Feta cheese
Butter
Fig or quince preserve

2. Fried eggs
Hot *barbari* bread
Hot sweet tea or hot milk
 with honey; butter, pre-
 serves

An active day:
Halim or porridge
Hot tea and bread

2. Head and feet soup
Tripe soup
Hot bread
Hot sweet tea

Lunch
Ground meat or chicken
 kabab with grilled tomato
 and sumac
Lavash bread; fresh herbs
Yogurt drink

2. Eggplant *kuku*
Sour cherry rice
Cucumber and tomato salad
Fresh herbs and bread
Sour cherry drink *Sharbat-e
albalu*

Spring
Rice meatballs
Yogurt
Bread
Fresh herbs
Fruit of the season
Hot tea

2. Stuffed vegetables
Yogurt
Baked rice with chicken
Fresh herbs, bread and
 feta cheese
Fruit of the season
Hot tea

3. Fresh herb *kuku*
Drained thick yogurt
Fresh herbs and feta cheese
Hot bread

4. Potato *khoresh*
Fava bean and fresh dill rice
Chicken kabab
Fresh herbs
Bread
Yogurt and cucumber
Melon or grapes
Hot tea

Summer
Yogurt and cucumber
Eggplant *kuku*
Fresh herbs, feta cheese, and
 lavash bread

2. Romaine lettuce with
 vinegar syrup
Chickpea patties with
 lavash bread
Fresh herbs and feta cheese

3. Cold yogurt and
 cucumber soup
Fresh herbs, feta cheese, and
 lavash bread
Meat *kuku*

Winter
Any of the *oshes*
Heart, liver kabab
Fresh herbs, feta cheese, and
 lavash bread
Paradise custard
Hot tea

2. Any of the *oshes*
Meat patties with *lavash*
 bread
Fresh herbs, pickles
Vinegar syrup

3. Baked leg of lamb
Rice with lentils
Pickles
Cucumber and tomato salad
Fresh herbs, feta cheese, and
 lavash bread, hot tea

4. Pomegranate *khoresh*
Jeweled rice
Roasted duck
Cucumber and tomato salad
Melon, hot tea

5. Cream of barley soup
Stuffed chicken
Saffron-flavored steamed
 plain rice
Fresh herbs, feta cheese;
 and bread
Melon, grapes
Hot tea

Sunday Brunch
Rice with meat kabab
Grilled tomato
Yogurt
Cucumber and tomato salad
Fresh herbs and feta cheese
Yogurt drink

Dinner
Pistachio and Pomegranate
 Meatballs
Orange *khoresh* served with
Saffron Flavored Rice
Salad
Hot tea

2. Quince or apple *khoresh*
Baked saffron yogurt rice
Salad
Yogurt and cucumber dip
Quince-lime syrup drink

New Year's Dinner
Noodle soup
Fresh herb *kuku*
Fresh herb rice
Smoked white fish
Cucumber and tomato salad
Bread, fresh herbs, and
 feta cheese
Pickles
Melon
Hot tea

Persian / American
Thanksgiving
Sweet and sour stuffed turkey
Sour cherry rice
Butternut squash or
 pumpkin *khoresh*
Saffron-flavored rice
Cucumber and tomato salad
Fruit pickles
Fresh herbs, cheese, bread
Saffron brownie
Hot tea

Wedding
Sweet rice
Stuffed whole lamb
Chicken kabab
Fresh herbs
Fresh herb kuku
Potato *kuku*
Pomegranate *khoresh*
Tomato and cucumber salad
 Shirazi-Style

Funeral Wake
Rice with lentils
Rice with potato *khoresh*
Saffron brownie
Dates, Turkish coffee

Fruit
To most Iranians, dessert is
fruit. Certain kinds of fruit
are also used as appetiz-
ers, such as watermelons,
pomegranates, grapes, and
white mulberries. Fruit is also
frequently used as a morning
and afternoon snack. Iranians
generally do not mix fruits
together and eat one kind of
fruit at a time.

IRANIAN STORES & RESTAURANTS

INTERNET STORES

D'ARTAGNAN
280 Wilson Ave.
Newark, NJ 07150
(800) 327-8246
www.dartagnan.com
Duck, quail, pheasant and many other specialty products are available here.

THE DATE PEOPLE
P.O. Box 808
Niland, CA 92257
(760) 359-3211
A wonderful source for many varieties of fresh, organic dates.

DEAN AND DELUCA
(800) 221-7714
www.deananddeluca.com
atyourservice@deandeluca.com
Verjuice and many other fine foods.

FARM 2 MARKET
Box 124, Trout Town Rd.
Roscoe, NY 12776
(800) 477-2967
info@farm-2-market.com
www.farm-2-market.com
Suppliers of fresh fish, especially Queens River Sturgeon from the Columbia River Basin near Sacramento, California.

SHAHRZAD INT.
6435 Roswell Rd. N.E.,
Suite A
Atlanta, GA 30328
(404) 257-9045
sales@shahrzad.com
www.shahrzad.com
A wide selection of specialty ingredients can be purchased from their website.

SOOFER CO. / SADAF
2828 S. Alameda St.
Los Angeles, CA 90058
(800) 852-4050
(323) 234-6666
info@sadaf.com
www.sadaf.com
Unripe grapes (ghureh) in brine, liquid kashk and many other Persian specialty products are all available at their website.

VANILLA SAFFRON IMP.
949 Valencia St.
San Francisco, CA 94110
(415) 648-8990
Fax: (415) 648-2240
www.saffron.com
saffron@saffron.com
Order pure sargol Iranian saffron threads, and get detailed information about saffron.

ALABAMA

ALI BABA RESTAURANT
1694 Montgomery Hwy.,
110
Hoover, AL 35216
(205) 823-2222

ARIZONA

HAJI BABA MRKET & REST
1513 E. Apache Blvd.
Tempe, AZ 85281
(480) 894-1905

PERSIAN ROOM
17040 N. Scottsdale Rd.
Scottsdale, AZ 85255
(480) 614-1414
www.thepersianroom.com

ROSE MARKET
2515 N. Scottsdale Rd. #7
Scottsdale, AZ 85257
(480) 945-5577

SHISH KEBAB HOUSE
5158 W Olive Ave.
Glendale, AZ 85302
(623) 937-8757

TASTY KABOB PERSIAN BISTRO
1250 E. Apache Blvd. #116
Tempe, AZ 85281
(480) 966-0260
www.tastykabobaz.com

CALIFORNIA (NORTHERN)

ZAND PASTRIES
1401 Solano Ave.
Albany, CA 94706
(510) 528-7027
www.zandpastry.com

BAHAR MARKET
811 W. Hamilton Ave.
Campbell, CA 95008
(408) 378-7477

TAK FOOD MARKET
9045 Fair Oaks Blvd.
Carmichael, CA 95608
(916) 944-3188

INTERNATIONAL MARKET
1106 Meadow Ln.
Concord, CA 94520
(925) 676-7844

FARM FRESH PRODUCE
10021 S. Blaney Ave.
Cupertino, CA 95014
(408) 257-3746

BIBI BAZAAR
251 Hartz Ave.
Danville, CA 94526
(925) 831-2424

FAZ RESTAURANT
600 Hartz Ave.
Danville, CA 94526
(925) 838-1320
www.fazrestaurants.com

DAMAVAND MARKET
37012 Towers Way
Fremont, CA 94536
(510) 793-2606

ROYAL FOOD MARKET
1602 Washington Blvd.
Fremont, CA 94539
(510) 668-1107

YEKTA MARKET
41035 Fremont Blvd.
Fremont, CA 94538
(510) 440-1111

FRESNO DELI
2450 E. Gettysburg
Fresno, CA 93726
(559) 225-7906

EASTERN MARKET
2400-M Coffee Rd.
Modesto, CA 95355
(209) 575-0344

ROSE INT. MRKT
1060 Castro St.
Mountain View, CA 94040
(650) 960-1900
www.rosemarketcatering.com

FAZ RESTAURANT
5121 Hopyard Rd.
Pleasanton, CA 94588
(925) 460-0444
www.fazrestaurants.com

ARIAN DELI MART
9663-A Folsom Blvd.
Sacramento, CA 95827
(916) 363-6982

MID EAST MARKET
1776 El Camino Real
San Bruno, CA 94066
(650) 875-7100

MAYKADEH RESTAURANT
470 Green St.
San Francisco, CA 94133
(415) 362-8286
www.maykadehrestaurant.com

SAMIRAMI'S IMPORTS
2990 Mission St.
San Francisco, CA 94110
(415) 824-6555

U.N. MARKET
900 Post St.
San Francisco, CA 94109
(415) 563-4726

YAS RESTAURANT
1138 Saratoga Ave.
San Jose, CA 95129
(408) 241-5115
www.yaasrestaurant.com
info@theyasrestaurant.com

ZARE AT FLY TRAP
606 Folsom St (at Second Street)
San Francisco, CA 94107
(415) 243-0580
www.zareflytrap.com

BIJAN BAKERY
441 Saratoga Ave.
San Jose, CA 95122
(408) 247-4888
www.bijanbakery.com

ETMINAN RESTAURANT
5754 Santa Teresa Blvd.
San Jose, CA 95123
(408) 226-5992

ARAM BAKERY
5837-A Camden Ave.
San Jose, CA 95124
(408) 448-3019

INTERNATIONAL FOOD BZR
2052 Curtner Ave.
San Jose, CA 95125
(408) 559-3397

PERSIAN CENTER BAZAAR
398 Saratoga Ave.
San Jose, CA 95129
(408) 241-3700

HATAM RESTAURANT
821 B St.
San Rafael, CA 94901
(415) 454-8888

CHATANOGA RESTAURANT
2725 El Camino Real
Santa Clara, CA 95051
(408) 241-1200
www.chatanogaonline.com

ATTARI DELI
582 S. Murphy Ave.
Sunnyvale, CA 94086
(408) 738-3030

CHELOKABABI
1236 Wolfe Rd.
Sunnyvale, CA 94086
(408) 737-1222
www.chelokababi.com

FAZ RESTAURANT
1108 N. Mathilda Ave.
Sunnyvale, CA 94089
(408) 752-8000
www.fazrestaurants.com

MANDAVI BAZAAR
31804 Alvarado Blvd.
Union City, CA 94587
(510) 475-7856

KASRA MARKET
1270 C Newell Ave.
Walnut Creek, CA 94596
(925) 256-7777

**CALIFORNIA
(SOUTHERN)**

HATAM RESTAURANT
1112 N. Brookhurst St.
Anaheim, CA 92801
(714) 991-6060
www.hatamrestaurant.com

ARAM RESTAURANT
138 S. Beverly Dr.
Beverly Hills, CA 90212
(310) 859-8585

BRISTOL DELI AND MARKET
3033 S. Bristol #G
Costa Mesa, CA 92626
(714) 545-7177

ORCHID RESTAURANT
3033 S. Bristol St.
Costa Mesa, CA 92626
(714) 557-8070
www.orchidrestaurant.us

POURI BAKERY
109 S. Adams Ave.
Glendale, CA 91205
(818) 244-4064

SHAMSHIRI RESTAURANT
122 W. Stocker
Glendale, CA 91202
(818) 246-9541

SHIRAZ RESTAURANT
211 S. Glendale Ave.
Glendale, CA 91205
(818) 500-8661

STOP IN RESTAURANT
452 W. Stocker
Glendale, CA 91205
(818) 241-9960

BEZJIAN GROCERY
4725 Santa Monica Blvd.
Hollywood, CA 90029
(323) 663-1503

SULTANI RESTAURANT
1535 N. LaBrea
Hollywood, CA 90028
(323) 876-3389
www.sultanigoodfood.com

CASPIAN RESTAURANT
Heritage Square
14100 Culver Dr.
Irvine, CA 92714
(949) 651-8454
www.caspianrestaurant.com

SUPER IRVINE
Heritage Square
14120 Culver Dr. Ste. B
Irvine, CA 92604
(949) 552-8844
www.crownvalleysuperirvinepersian
market.com
moariarad@yahoo.com

DARYA RESTAURANT
12130 Santa Monica Blvd.
Los Angeles, CA 90025
(310) 442-9000
www.darya.com

DOWNTOWN KABOB
934 S. Los Angeles St.
Los Angeles, CA 90015
(213) 612-0222

CHARLIE KABOB
10800 W. Pico Blvd.
Ste 302
Los Angeles, CA 90064
(310) 393-5535
www.charliekabob.com

FARID RESTAURANT
635 S. Broadway #835
Los Angeles, CA 90014
(213) 622-0808

JAVAN RESTAURANT
11500 Santa Monica Blvd.
Los Angeles, CA 90025
(310) 207-5555
www.javanrestaurant.com

MASSOUD RESTAURANT
1300 South San Pedro
Unit 201
Los Angeles, CA 90015
(213) 748-1768

SHAHRZAD RESTAURANT
1442 Westwood Blvd.
Los Angeles, CA 90024
(310) 470-3242

SHEKARCHI KABAB
914 S. Hill St.
Los Angeles, CA 90015
(213) 892-8535

HATAM RESTAURANT
25800 Geronimo Rd. #402
Mission Viejo, CA 92691
(949) 768-0122
www.hatamcuisine.com

SHAMSHIRI RESTAURANT
19249 Roscoe Blvd.
Northridge, CA 91234
(818) 885-7846

DARYA RESTAURANT
3800 S. Plaza Dr.
Santa Ana, CA 92704
(714) 557-6600
www.daryasouthcoastplaza.com

BANDAR RESTAURANT
825 4th Ave.
San Diego, CA 92101
(619) 238-0101
www.bandarrestaurant.com

PARSIAN INT. MARKET
4020 Conway St.
San Diego, CA 92111
(858) 277-7277

DARYA RESTAURANT
1998 N. Tustin St.
Orange, CA 92665
(714) 921-2773
www.daryarestaurant.com

TEHRAN MARKET
1417 Wilshire Blvd.
Santa Monica, CA 90403
(310) 393-6719

SHIRAZ RESTAURANT
15472 Ventura Blvd.
Sherman Oaks, CA 91403
(818) 789-7788
www.shirazrestaurant.net

TOCHAL MARKET
15030 Ventura Blvd.
Sherman Oaks, CA 91403
(818) 784-2763

HAWTHORNE MARKET
24202 Hawthorne Blvd.
Torrance, CA 90505
(310) 373-4448

NAAN & KABOB
416 E. 1st St.
Tustin, CA 92780
(714) 665-2262

CONNECTICUT

SAYAD INT. MARKET
95 Fenn Rd.
Newington, CT 06111
(860) 666-7846
www.sayadinternational.com

**DISTRICT OF COLUMBIA
(WASHINGTON)**

MOBY DICK KABOB
1070 31st St. N.W.
Washington, DC 20007
(202) 333-4400

1200 Connecticut Ave. N.W.
Washington, DC 20036
(202) 833-9788
www.mobysonline.com

FLORIDA

DAMASCUS MIDEAST MRKT
5721 Hollywood Blvd.
Hollywood, FL 33021
(954) 962-4552

ALI BABA RESTAURANT
1155 W. State Rd. 434 #105
Longwood, FL 32750
(407) 331-8680
www.alibabaorlando.com

SHIRAZ KABAB CAFE
9630 S.W. 77th Ave.
Miami, FL 33156
(305) 273-8888

BHA! BHA! PERSIAN BISTRO
847 Vanderbuilt Beach Rd.
Naples, Fl 34110
(239) 594-5557
www.bhabhapersianbistro.com

CASPIAN PERSIAN GRILLE
7821 W. Sunrise Blvd.
Plantation, FL 33322
(954) 236-9955

NU TASTE IMPORTED SPEC.
7817 W. Sunrise Blvd.
Plantation, FL 33322
(954) 382-4026

GEORGIA

MIRAGE RESTAURANT
6631 Roswell Rd.
Suites B & C
Atlanta, GA 30328
(404) 843-8300
www.miragepersiancuisine.com

PERSEPOLIS RESTAURANT
6435 Roswell Rd. NE #B
Atlanta, GA 30328
(404) 257-9090
www.persepoliscuisine.com
persepoliscuisine@gmail.com

SHAHRZAD INTERNATIONAL
6435 Roswell Rd. NE Ste. A
Atlanta, GA 30328
(404) 257-9045

ILLINOIS

MIDDLE EASTERN GROCERY
1512 W. Foster Ave.
Chicago, IL 60640
(773) 561-2224
www.eastbakeryandgrocery.com

PARS PERSIAN STORE
5260 N. Clark St.
Chicago, IL 60640
(773) 769-6635
www.parsstore.com

REZA'S RESTAURANT
432 W. Ontario
Chicago, IL 60654
(312) 664-4500
www.rezasrestaurant.com

REZA'S RESTAURANT
5255 N. Clark St.
Chicago, IL 60640
(773) 561-1898
www.rezasrestaurant.com

WORLD HARVEST FOODS
519 E. University Ave.
Champaign, IL 61820
(217) 356-4444
www.worldharvestfoods.com
mohammad@worldharvestfoods.com

KANSAS

KC GRILL N KABOB
8611 Hauser
Lenexa, KS 66215
(913) 541-1900

CASPIAN BISTRO
8973 Metcalf Ave.
Overland Park, KS 66212
(913) 901-9911

TEHRAN MARKET
10412 Mastin Street
Overland Park, KS 66212
(913) 438-3663

MARYLAND

BISMILLAH HALAL MEAT
1401 University Blvd.
Langley Park, MD 20787
(301) 434-2121
www.mytabeer.com
sales@mytabeer.com

**CAEZAR INTERNATIONAL
MARKET AND RESTAURANT**
6801-D Douglas Legum Dr.
Elkridge, MD 21075
(443) 755-9444
www.sizarfood.com

CAPSIAN KABOB
19911-C North Frederick Rd.
Germantown, MD 20876
(301) 353-0000/1
www.caspiankabob.com

JOHNNY'S KABOB
12933 Wisteria Drive
Germantown, MD 20874
(240) 686-4518

MOBY DICK KABOB
7027 Wisconsin Ave.
Bethesda, MD 20815
(301) 654-1838
www.mobysonline.com
mobys@mobysonline.com

MOBY DICK KABOB
105 Market St..
Gaithersburg, MD 20878
(301) 987-7770
www.mobysonline.com
mobys@mobysonline.com

ORCHARD MARKET & CAFE
8815 Orchard Tree Ln.
Towson, MD 21286
(410) 339-7700
www.orchardmarketandcafe.com

**ROCKVILLE GOURMET
HALAL MEAT**
1331-C Rockville Pike
(Sunshine Square)
Rockville, MD 20852
(301) 424-4444

SADAF HALAL RESTAURANT
1327-K Rockville Pike
Rockvill, MD 20852
(301) 424-4040

SAM'S CAFE & MARKET
Ritchie Shopping Center
844 Rockville Pike
Rockville, MD 20852
(301) 424-1600
www.samscafeandmarket.com

**TANOOR BAKERY, GROCERY
& RESTAURANT**
15108 Fredrick Rd
Unit A
Rockville, MD 20850
(301) 545-1911

YAAS CAFE & MARKET
765 F&G Rockville Pike
Rockville, MD 20852
(301) 279-2121

**YEKTA GROCERY &
RESTAURANT**
1488 Rockville Pike #A
Rockville, MD 20852
(301) 984-1190
www.yekta.com

MASSACHUSETTS

KAROUN RESTAURANT
839 Washington St.
Newton, MA 02160
(617) 964-3400

LALA ROKH RESTAURANT
97 Mt. Vernon St.
Boston, MA 02108
(617) 720-5511
www.lalarokh.com

SUPER HERO'S
509 Mt. Auburn St.
Watertown, MA 02472
(617) 924-9507

TABRIZI BAKERY
56-A Mt. Auburn St.
Watertown, MA 02172
(617) 926-0880
www.tabrizibakery.com

MINNESOTA

CASPIAN BISTRO
2418 University Ave. SE
Minneapolis, MN 55414
(612) 623-1113

MISSOURI

KABOB HOUSE
8950 Wornall Rd.
Kansas City, MO 64114
(816) 333-2744

CAFÉ NATASHA
3200 S. Grand Blvd.
St Louis, MO 63118
(314) 771-3411
www.cafenatasha.com

NEVADA

HABIB'S RESTAURANT
2575 S. Decatur Blvd.
Las Vegas, NV 89102
(702) 870-0860
www.habibspersiancuisine.com

**MEDITERRANEAN
GOURMET MARKET**
4147 S. Maryland Pkwy.
Las Vegas, NV 89119
(702) 731-6030
www.paymons.com

NEW JERSEY

SHAHRZAD RESTAURANT
1086 River Rd.
Edgewater, NJ 07020
(201) 886-9100
www.theshahrzad.com

TEHRAN SUPER
288A Main St.
Hackensack, NJ 07601
(201) 489-4990

NEW YORK

COLBEH RESTAURANT
43 West 39th St.
New York, NY 10018
(212) 354-8181
www.colbeh.com

INTERNATIONAL GRC STORE
543 Ninth Ave.
New York, NY 10018
(212) 279-1000

KALUSTYAN'S
123 Lexington Ave.
New York, NY 10016
(212) 685-3451
www.kalustyans.com
sales@kalustyans.com

NADER FOOD MARKET
1 E. 28th St.
New York, NY 10016
(212) 686-5793

PATOUG RESTAURANT
220-06 Harding Expwy.
Bayside, NY 11364
(718) 279-3500

PERSEPOLIS RESTAURANT
1407 Second Ave.
New York, NY 10021
(212) 535-1100
www.persepolisnyc.com
contact@persepolisnyc.com

SULTAN'S DELIGHT
7128 5th Ave.
Brooklyn, NY 11209
(718) 567-2252

A TO Z FOOD MARKET
703 Middleneck Rd
Great Neck, NY 11023
(516) 829-3525

PERSIAN TEA ROOM
249-38 Horace Harding
Expwy.
Little Neck, NY 11362
(718) 631-7676
persiantearoom
info@persiantearoom.net

KABUL KABAB HOUSE
4251 Main St.
Flushing, NY 11355
(718) 461-1919
www.kabulkabab.com
info@ kabulkabab.com

COLBEH RESTAURANT
75 North Station Plaza
Great Neck, NY 11021
(516) 466-8181
www.colbeh.com

SHISH KABAB PALACE
90 Middleneck Rd.
Great Neck, NY 11021
(516) 487-2228

AYHAN'S SHISH KEBAB RESTAURANT
283 Main St.
Port Washington, NY 11050
(516) 883-9309
www.ayhans.myshopify.com

INT. FOOD MARKET
212 Mineola Ave.
Roslyn Heights, NY 11577
(516) 625-5800

NORTH CAROLINA

CAFÉ PARVANEH
400 JS Elliot Rd.
Chapel Hill, NC 27514
(919) 929-2779
www.cafep.com

KABOB HOUSE
6432 E. Independence Blvd.
Charlotte, NC 28212
(704) 531-2500

OHIO

ALADDIN'S BAKING COMPANY
1301 Carnegie Ave.
Cleveland, OH 44115
(216) 861-0317
www.aladdinbaking.com

OKLAHOMA

MEDITERRANEAN GRILL
7868 S. Western Ave.
Oklahoma City, OK 73139
405-601-8959
www.themedgrill.com

ZORBA'S
6014 N. May
Oklahoma City, OK 73112
(405) 947-7788
www.zorbasokc.com

TRAVEL BY TASTE MARKET & RESTAURANT
4818 N. McArthur
Warr Acres, OK 73122
(405) 787-2969
www.travelbytaste.com

OREGON

ROSE INTERNATIONAL FOODS
6153 SW Murray Rd.
Beaverton, OR 97008
(503) 646-7673
www.rosemarket2007.
googlepages.com/rose
rosemarket2007@gmail.com

PERSIAN HOUSE RESTAURANT & LIBRARY
1026 S.W. Morrison St.
Portland, OR 97205
(503) 243-1430
www.persianhouse.ypguides.net
persianhouse@aol.com

BLUE TANGERINE RESTAURANT
7361 S.W. Bridgeport Rd.
Tigard, OR 97224
(503) 620-9631
www.tangerinerestaurant.com
info@etangerinerestaurant.com

PENNSYLVANIA

PERSIAN GRILLE
637 Germantown Rd.
Lafayette Hill, PA 19444
(610) 825-2705
www.persiangrill.net
info@persiangrill.net
bimal@persiangrill.net

TENNESSEE

INT. FOOD MARKET
206 Thompson Ln.
Nashville, TN 37211
(615) 333-9651

TEXAS

ALBORZ PERSIAN CUISINE
3300 W. Anderson Ln. #303
Austin, TX 78757
(512) 420-2222
www.alborzpersiancuisine.com

PARS MEDITERRANEAN SUPERMARKET & DELI
8820 Burnet Rd.
Austin, TX 78757
(512) 452-4888

PHOENICIA BAKERY & DELI
2912 S. Lamar Blvd.
Austin, TX 78704
(512) 447-4444
www.phoeniciabakery.com

PHOENICIA BAKERY & DELI
4701 Burnet Rd.
Austin, TX 78756
(512) 323-6770
www.phoeniciabakery.com

ABDALLAH'S RESTAURANT
3939 Hillcroft #100
Houston, TX 77057
(713) 952-4747

ADAMS SUPERMARKET
12280 Westheimer #5
Houston, TX 77077
(281) 249-0024

CAFE CASPIAN
12126 Westheimer
Houston, TX 77077
(281) 493-4000
www.cafecaspian.com

DARBAND KABAB
5670 Hillcroft
Houston, TX 77036
(713) 975-8350

DIMASSIS MED. BUFFET
5160 Richmond
Houston, TX 77056
(713) 439-7481
www.dimassisbuffet.com

DROUBI'S BAKERY & DELICATESSEN
7333 Hillcroft
Houston, TX 77081
(713) 988-5897

DROUBI'S CAFÉ
2721 Hillcroft
Houston, TX 77057
(713) 334-1829

DROUBI'S MEDITERRANEAN CAFÉ
919 Milam St.
Houston, TX 77002
(713) 571-6800

FADI'S MEDITERRANEAN GRILL
8383 Westheimer Ste. 112
Houston TX, 77063
(713) 532-0666
www.fadiscuisine.com

GARSON
2926 Hillcroft
Houston, TX 77057
(713) 781-0400
www.garsonhouston.com

KASRA PERSIAN GRILL
9741 Westheimer
Houston, TX 77063
(713) 975-1810
www.kasrahouston.com

PHOENICIA SUPERMARKET
12141 Westheimer
Houston, TX 77077
(281) 558-8225
www.phoeniciafoods.com

SHISH KABOB CAFÉ
2472 S. Hwy. 6
Houston, TX 77077
(281) 759-7300

SKEWERS CAFÉ & GRILL
3991 Richmond
Houston, TX 77027
(713) 599-1444

SUPER VANAK
5692 Hillcroft
Houston, TX 77036
(713) 952-7676
vanak@amsn.com

ANDRE IMPORTED FOODS
1478 W. Spring Valley
Richardson, TX 75080
(972) 644-7644
www.andrefood.com

MEDITERRANEAN CAFÉ
100 S. Central Expwy. #49
Richardson, TX 75080
(972) 234-6444
zzozan@yahoo.com

ALI BABA INTERNATIONAL FOOD MARKET
9307 Warzbach Rd.
San Antonio, TX 78240
(210) 691-1111

CARAVAN INT. FOODS
5891 Babcock Rd.
San Antonio, Tx 78240
210-699-9000

VIRGINIA

ASSAL MARKET
112 Glyndon St NE
Vienna, VA 22180
(703) 281-5050

BREAD & KABAB
3407 Payne St.
Falls Church, VA 22041
(703) 845-2900

HALAL MEAT
155 Hillwood Ave.
Falls Church, VA 22046
(703) 532-3202
www.halalco.com
halalco@halalco.com

IRAN SARA
6039 Leesburg Pike
Falls Church, VA 22041
(703) 578-3232

KABOB BAZAAR
3133 Wilson Blvd
Arlington, VA 22201
(703) 522-8999

MAMA LAVASH
2190-A Pimmit Dr.
Falls Church, VA 22043
(703) 827-7788

MASH HASSAN PERSIAN MARKET & BAKERY
46970 Community Plaza #111B
Sterling, VA 20164
(703) 948-9155

MOBY DICK KABOB
6854 Old Dominion Dr.
McLean, VA 22101
(703) 448-8448
www.mobysonline.com

MOBY DICK KABOB
12154 Fairfax Town Ctr.
Fairfax, VA 22033
(703) 352-6226
www.mobysonline.com

SAUSON MARKET
21770 Beaumeade Circle
Unit 120
Ashburn, VA 20147
(703) 288-0019
sauson@gmail.com
www.sauson.com

SHAMSHIRY KABOB
8607 Westwood Center Dr.
Vienna, VA 22182
(703) 448-8883
www.shamshiry.com

SHIRAZ SUPERMARKET
8486-G Tyco Rd.
Vienna, VA 22102
(703)922-9566

YAS BAKERY & SUPER
137 Church St. N.W.
Vienna, VA 22180
(703) 242-4050
www.yasbakery.com

WASHINGTON

PARS MARKET
2331 140th Ave NE
Bellevue, WA 98005
(425) 641-5265
parsmarket@hotmail.com

CASPIAN RESTAURANT & GRILL
5517 University Way N.E.
Seattle, WA 98105
(206) 524-3434
www.caspiangrill.com

KOLBEH RESTAURANT
1956 1st Ave. S.
Seattle, WA 98134
(206) 224-9999
www.kolbehseattle.com

PACIFIC INTERNATIONAL GOURMET FOODS
12332 Lake City Way NE
Seattle, WA 98125
(206) 363-8639

WISCONSIN

SHIRAZ PERSIAN GRILL
2921 N. Oakland Avenue
Milwaukee, WI 53211
(414) 967-1000

www.shirazpersiangrill.com

CANADA

AKHAVAN MARKET
6170 Sherbrooke W.
Montreal, QC H4A 1X1
(514) 485-4887
www.akhavanfood.com
info@akhavanfood.com

BAMDAD SUPERMARKET
20 Graydon Hall Dr.
Don Mills, ON M3A 2Z9
(416) 447-5022

KAROUN RESTAURANT
5 Glen Cameron Rd. #27
Thornhill, ON
L3P 5W2
(905) 886-4443

LADAN PASTRY
2016 Lawrence Ave. E.
Scarborough, ON
M1R 2Z1
(416) 288-0253

THE MEAT SHOP
1346 Lonsdale Ave.
N. Vancouver, BC
V7M 3H2
(604) 983-2020

NADER SUPERMARKET
48 Dundas St. W.
Mississauga, ON
L5B 1M7
(905) 949-6895

NANCY FOOD
1875 Darden Ave
N. Vancouver, BC
V7P 1T8
(604) 987-5544

NASR FOODS
1996 Lawrence Ave. E.
Scarborough, ON
M1R 2Z1
(416) 757-1611
nasr@nasrfoods.com

PARS DELI MARKET
143 Lonsdale Ave.
N. Vancouver, BC
V7M 2J8
(604) 988-3515

SEDAQAT RESTAURANT
3342 Danforth Ave.
Scarborough, ON
M1L 1C7
(416) 699-2099

SHIRINI-SARA PASTRY HOUSE
1875 Leslie St. #6
North York, ON
M3B 2M5
(416) 510-1050
www.shirinisara.com

YAAS BAKERY AND RESTAURANT
1860 Lonsdale Ave.
N. Vancouver, BC
V7M 2J9
(604) 990-9006

NOTE

The specialty groceries listed above all carry various ingredients used in Persian cuisine. If there isn't one in your area, some stores offer mail order service while others, the major ones listed at the beginning, have websites and can take Internet orders.

This list of stores and restaurants is current as of October 2010, but it is by no means comprehensive. We update the list continuously; the most current version may be accessed online at: www.mage.com/cooking.html

EQUIVALENT MEASURES

Note that all spoon and cup measurements used in this book are level. It is not easy to convert with absolute accuracy measurements for the kitchen, but absolute accuracy is usually not required (except for sauces, cakes, and pastries). The tables below give the nearest convenient equivalents in both metric and British imperial measures, while the formulas give a more precise conversion factor. British dry measures for ounces and pounds are the same as American measures. Liquid measures, however, are different.

LIQUID MEASURES

U.S.	METRIC	UK (IMPERIAL)
1 TEASPOON (⅓ TABLESPOON)	5 ML	1 TEASPOON
2 TEASPOONS	10 ML	1 DESSERT SPOON
1 TABLESPOON (3 TEASPOONS)	15 ML	1 TABLESPOON (½ FL. OZ.)
2 TABLESPOONS (⅛ CUP)	30 ML	2 TABLESPOONS
¼ CUP (4 TABLESPOONS)	60 ML	4 TABLESPOONS
⅓ CUP (5⅓ TABLESPOONS)	80 ML	8 DESSERT SPOONS (2½ FL. OZ.)
½ CUP (8 TABLESPOONS)	120 ML	SCANT ¼ PINT (4 FL. OZ.)
⅔ CUP (10⅔ TABLESPOONS)	160 ML	¼ PINT
¾ CUP (12 TABLESPOONS)	180 ML	GENEROUS ¼ PINT (6 FL. OZ.)
1 CUP (16 TABLESPOONS)	240 ML	SCANT ½ PINT (8 FL. OZ.)
2 CUPS (1 PINT, ½ QUART, OR 16 FL. OZ.)	480 ML	GENEROUS ¾ PINT
2½ CUPS	600 ML	1 PINT (20 FL. OZ.)
3 CUPS (1½ PINTS OR ¾ QUART)	720 ML	1¼ PINTS
4 CUPS (2 PINTS OR 1 QUART)	960 ML	1½ PINTS (32 FL. OZ.)
5 CUPS	1.2 LITERS	2 PINTS (1 QUART, 40 FL. OZ.)
CUPS X 0.24 = LITERS	LITERS X 4.23 = CUPS	—

LINEAR MEASURES

U.S. & UK	METRIC
¼ INCH	6 MM
½ INCH	13 MM
1 INCH	2.5 CM
2 INCHES	5 CM
3 INCHES	7.5 CM
6 INCHES	15 CM
1 FOOT	30 CM

SOLID MEASURES

1 POUND = 16 OUNCES	1 KILO = 1000 GRAMS
OUNCES X 28.35 = GRAMS	GRAMS X 0.035 = OUNCES

U.S. & UK	METRIC
1 OZ.	28 GRAMS
3½ OZ.	100 GRAMS
¼ POUND	112 GRAMS
⅓ POUND	150 GRAMS
½ POUND	225 GRAMS
1 POUND	450 GRAMS
2.2 POUNDS	1 KILOGRAM

OVEN TEMPERATURES

$°C = (°F - 32) \div 1.8$	
$°F = (°C \times 1.8) + 32$	
FAHRENHEIT	CENTIGRADE
200°	95°
250°	120°
300°	150°
350°	180°
400°	200°
450°	230°
500°	260°

ACKNOWLEDGMENTS

I would like to thank Dick Davis, who has not only made wonderful translations of many of the poems in this book but also for his superb translation of Ferdowsi's *Shahnameh* from which I have used several sections relating to Persian ceremonies; Djalal Khaleghi Motlagh, who sent me *Khosrow and His Knight*; Abolala Soudavar, who allowed me to use several miniatures from his excellent *Art of the Persian Courts* and who kindly brought me back a copy of *Drakht-e Asurik* from Iran.

My first advisers on traditional Persian food were my mother, aunts, and sisters. I am also indebted to the late Mrs. Nowshiravani and the late Mrs. Ma'sumi for parting with many of their Persian cooking secrets and techniques. I would like to thank Mojdeh Bahar for testing the *tah-digs,* Esmat Akhavan for her pastry recipes, Shohreh Amin for her Kermani recipes, Nasrin Rafi for her Azerbaijani recipes, and Alex Parvini for his Shirazi *do piazeh alu* recipe. I would also like to thank Sheila Saleh for lending me her antique samovars for photography.

I have been lucky over the years to have had many good assistants from Georgetown University. For this edition, I would like to thank Jonathan Gotterer and Michael Quinn for their invaluable help in the kitchen: preparing, testing, tasting, and retesting recipes, which they carried out with aplomb and grace.

I would like to thank Harry Endrulat for his careful reading and copyediting. I am indebted to our friend and neighbor George Constable for his many astute editorial suggestions. I thank and cherish my sons: Zal, for his luminous understanding of the mood of the book and his many profound suggestions, including encouraging me to include vegetarian variations for many of the recipes in the book; and Rostam, for beautifully redesigning the book's jacket and for his insightful suggestions for the interior. Finally I would like to thank my husband Mohammad, who besides being the love of my life is also my editor and publisher.

CREDITS

INDEX

COOKING NOTES